The Complete Live-Aboard Book

The Complete Live-Aboard Book

by **Katy Burke**

Illustrations by
Bruce Bingham

SEVEN SEAS

For Bruce

Without him to share it all, a boat would be just another place to live and this book would never have happened.

Published by Seven Seas Press, 21 Elm Street, Camden, Maine 04843.

3   5   7   9   HL/HL   10   8   6   4

Library of Congress Cataloging in Publication Data

Burke, Katy.
  The complete live-aboard book.

  Includes index.
  1. Boat living. I. Title.
GV777.7.B87   1982   797.1′2   82-16933
ISBN 0-915160-50-1

Manufactured in the United States of America by Halliday Lithograph
Edited by James R. Gilbert
Book design by Irving Perkins Associates

First Printing, 1982
Second Printing, 1984
Third Printing, 1987

Acknowledgments

SPECIAL THANKS MUST go to Murray Davis, publisher and dear friend, who bought my first manuscript and gave me my start as a writer, and whose support and encouragement has been continuous.

Other editors, too, have been of tremendous help along the way, most particularly Patience Wales, Gail Anderson, Jeff Spranger, Jim Brown, Wayne Carpenter and, especially on this book, Jim Gilbert.

I met and talked with hundreds of fellow live-aboards, all of whom shared freely of their time, their experiences and their feelings. While I can't begin to name them all, I am especially grateful to Gainor Roberts and George Cranston on *Endymion II;* Ed LaVigueur and June MacQuarrie aboard *Impulse;* Dick (who took a wealth of pictures), Helen and Valarie Pentoney on *Heron;* Jack and Pat Tyler from *Felicity;* Danny and Susan Wilson aboard the incredible *Sakonnet;* Bill and Laura Free on *Leau Claire;* Dick and Dianne Drysdale from *Brigadoon;* Ruth and Larry Penn aboard *Quick Step;* Fred Bingham on *Outboard Bound;* Betsy Greenacre of *All Hours;* Dave and Dottie Etzel from *Sweetie Face II;* Walter and Marjorie Swanson of *Swan;* Brendan Burrows and Ann Derrick on *Buffalo Blue;* Chuck and Laurie Paul aboard *Daisien;* Ed and Alice Seeley on *Lady Alice;* Tim Coughlin and Shauna Steinburn on *Abumba;* Jim and Kathy Lindner; Ruth and Bob Comstock on *Rhapsody;* and Walter B. and Marianne Stevens on *Merrywing,* who not only shared their experiences but willingly spent countless hours proof-reading the original manuscript.

Manufacturers, builders and designers from throughout the marine field offered advice, opinions and technical expertise. These included Jay and Robin Benford; Steve Seaton; Frit Cherubini; Wynn Durbeck; Henry Mohrschladt; Willie Luther; Will Keene of Edson Int.; J. Patricia Townsend of June Enterprises; Michelle Calligan of Ped-Mo Int.; Jim Andrew from Bumble Bike; Robert Workman of Bickerton Bicycles; Salvatore Corso of Stuyvesant Bicycles; Betsy Annese from Bigelow-Sanford, Inc.; Alice Burke of Richmond Ring Co.; Jaclyn Brown Young from Fatsco; Eric Shepard of Jay Stuart Haft Co.; William Cantor of Allcraft Corp.; Richard Yonwin from Espar Products; H.R. Rogers from Marine Heat Corp.; L. Gale Noel of Marine Development Corp.; Tom Curtin of Sudbury Laboratory, Inc.; Leo vanHemert from W.H. Denouden, Inc.; Elsie Parks of Sailing Specialties, Inc.; Tom Sanders from Pastime Products, Inc.; John Becker of Onan; Marianne Wright of Energy Saving Systems; Judy Talley of Mercantile Mfg. Co.; Jim Russell from Honeywell; David Moldausky of Adler-Barbour Marine Systems; Lois Grunert from The Grunert Co.; Phillip Williams of Crosby Marine Refrigeration Systems; William Rice of Yachting Tableware Co.; J. D. White from ITT Jabsco Products; Lisa Whittemore of Imtra Corp.; Charles Hall from Basic Designs, Inc.; Richard Williams of General Ecology, Inc.; G. Victor Willman of Raritan Engineering Co.; Jim Bridegum of American Appliance Mfg. Corp.; E. Vaughn Deal of Rule Industries, Inc.; Philippe Drapeau of Clone Boats; Dale Denny of Oxford, Maryland; and Bennett Scheuer of Knock on Wood.

This book is dedicated to Bruce, but I have to say thank you to him here, too, for serving as technical editor, illustrator extraordinaire, photographer, advisor and a fantastic sounding-board for every idea and thought entered in these pages.

And last but by no means least, a thank you to Andrew Rock of Seven Seas Press, who had the courage to say, "You just finish writing the book and let *us* do the rest." I did, they did, and here it is.

Contents

Preface

THIS BOOK IS for people who live aboard or would like to live aboard a boat as a permanent home. There's nothing new about the concept; it's just that it used to be limited pretty much to the Chinese and the odd American recluse. Today, houseboat communities are a common sight and virtually every marina has its share of live-aboards—some on powerboats and more on sailboats.

Cruising is often, but not always, a part of living aboard. Certainly anyone who goes cruising is "living aboard." But it may be only for the duration of the cruise—even if the cruise lasts for several years. Here, I believe, lies a subtle dividing line between the "cruiser" and the "live-aboard." The pure cruiser is traveling with a specific destination and generally within a specific time period: "We'll do the Caribbean this winter, then head across to Portugal . . ." His boat is a vehicle to get him there—a vacation cottage at best. *Home* is back ashore; rented out perhaps, but waiting for him to return and resume his normal life.

The true live-aboard *is* living his normal life. A lot of us are vagabonds, to be sure. But we are more apt to be found up a creek somewhere working on our boats or ashore working at jobs to finance the next "cruise" than swinging at anchor in one of the better known watering holes frequented by world cruisers. For us, boats themselves are a wonderful way of life. If we don't get to Pago Pago this year, then maybe next year. And if not next year, so what? We already like where we are and what we're doing, so there's no rush to cram it all into one sabbatical or leave of absence.

While I hope cruising people and part-time live-aboards will find much of value here, the book is really geared towards those who approach boat living as a lifestyle. It is about making a boat into a comfortable *home*. I have tried to stay away from topics that are applicable to boating in general—basic seamanship, navigation and knot-tying, for instance—since they are of concern to everyone in boating. Much reference material is readily available on such subjects.

I have concentrated instead on topics I believe directly affect the comfort and convenience of a boat being used day-in and day-out as a home and only sometimes as a "vehicle."

I would hope, too, that this book will offer encouragement to anyone "on the brink" and about to jump. Come on in, the water's fine! Don't get bogged down in making plans and dreaming about what you're *going* to do. Don't think all these suggestions and improvements must be done *before* you move aboard in order to achieve the perfect live-aboard boat. It'll never happen!

The only really important point if you truly want to live aboard, is make the commitment and follow through with it. This is the hardest part. Once the commitment is made it gets easier and easier, until the only question remaining is: "Why did I wait so long?"

Katy Burke
aboard *Saga*
Key Biscayne, Florida

May, 1982

The Complete Live-Aboard Book

Choosing the Boat

1

"A continuous compromise"

FOR SOME PEOPLE, choosing a boat to live aboard is not an issue. They already own a boat, have presumably spent weekends and vacations on her, and are simply planning on making her their permanent home. But let's assume you're in the market for a boat that will make a comfortable home. What are some of the basic requirements? It's unlikely your first boat will be either your last boat or your ideal home. The only way to know what boat will keep *you* happy and satisfied is to live aboard one for awhile and discover what works best for you. For instance, you may feel you cannot exist without a chart table. But after a few months you may realize you never use it as a chart table, that it's just a catch-all for miscellaneous gear. What you really need is a bank of fiddled shelves.

Requirements are always subject to change, anyway. That's why so many live-aboards (Bruce and I are prime examples) are forever tearing out something and installing something else in its place. So, if you find a boat that meets your *basic* requirements, and you like her, don't be too hasty about rejecting her if she isn't quite perfect on all accounts.

TYPE OF BOAT

Many people never debate the merits of sail versus power. But perhaps they should. Powerboat people simply look at powerboats and sailors look at sailboats. It rarely occurs to a sailor that he might be happier with a powerboat for a *home*.

SAILBOATS

Pound for pound and dollar for dollar you get less livable, usable space in a sailboat than a powerboat. Roughly 35 percent of a cruising sailboat's weight is ballast, dead weight that does not translate into payload. It gives the boat stability under canvas, but provides nothing in terms of livability. Of course, a powerboat has proportionately more space and weight devoted to engine and tankage, but at least they give you something in return—power and crusing range. Finally, the inherent hydrodynamic shape of a sailboat gives you less usable room than a powerboat of equal displacement.

3

So why have a sailboat? If your goal is not simply living aboard, but long-distance cruising under sail, then a sailboat is clearly the only choice. Even if cruising is a goal for the future, there's much to be said in favor of buying her now, thus giving yourself time to pay her off, time to get used to her, time to learn to sail her really well and time to learn what changes you need to make before leaving on a long cruise. But, and here's the emotional part, is your goal of ocean passage-making realistic, or is it just a dream? And how big a price, in terms of cramped living quarters and lack of stowage space, are you willing to pay year-in and year-out to sustain a dream you may never realize.

This is not said to sound negative or even anti-sailboat. But couples who know most of their time will be spent dockside should at least consider that there might be an alternative to a sailboat. Owning a sailing dinghy as the ship's tender may satisfy the occasional urge for a sail. Bruce's brother is an interesting example of the dinghy alternative.

When Fred lived in a house his cruising sailboat was his pastime—a very important part of his life, to be sure, but primarily a source of recreation. Several times a week he would take her out for an evening sail after work and about once a month for a weekend cruise. Now that he lives aboard he admits it's too much trouble getting her ready to take out for a short sail. The cockpit awning must be taken down and stowed, dirty dishes either cleaned up or secured in the sink and everything else loose below stowed away.

It's much easier for him to jump in the dinghy and take a short sail around the harbor.

He finds that more fun, anyway, since he can sail into all sorts of nifty little places where he could never take his big boat. He has no intention of switching to a powerboat, however, since his long-range plans include extensive cruising and much of his spare time is spent getting *Outward Bound* fitted out for passage-making.

For the mechanically inept, a sailboat may be the answer. You could go to the ultimate extreme and have no engine, no refrigeration, Herreshoff's famous wooden bucket for a head, and lighting by kerosene and candles. Some have found happiness that way, but most of us wouldn't put up with it for more than a weekend. The majority of modern sailboats have an inboard auxiliary engine, electric lights, *some* electronics and often *some* type of refrigeration. You rarely achieve utter simplicity on a sailboat, although you generally acquire less of the complicated gear. But I have been aboard sailboats with refrigerator and freezer, electric stove, dishwasher, trash compactor, blender, electric toaster, electric heating and air conditioning, a maze of electronics, electric heads, pressure water system and, of course, a whopping big generator. An engine is an engine and must be attended to—even on a sailboat. Unfortunately, the engine is too often stuck away like an afterthought in a place where even routine maintenance is a job for a contortionist. I'm sure that's partly why so many sailboat auxiliaries are neglected.

There is one big plus from living on a sailboat. If you do any cruising at all, and do it under sail, the saving in fuel costs can be tremendous. In these days of soaring fuel prices, a measure of independence from the fuel dock is an excellent reason for choosing sail over power. When cruising on a shoestring, sailing becomes even more attractive.

It's the shape of sailboats that makes them less spacious than powerboats (See Figure 1). Sailboats are designed to slide through the water with as little resistance as possible. Thus, a sailboat's hull shape is much "finer" than a powerboat, something you pay for in lack of space. This quickly becomes apparent when considering the forward compartment. The

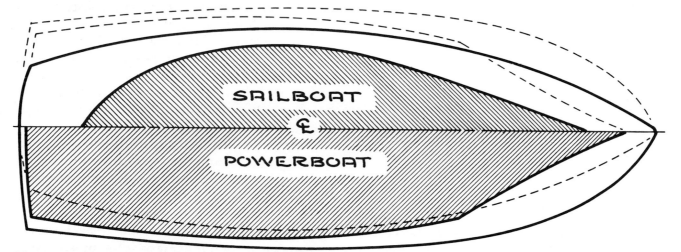

Figure 1 *Comparing the lines (plan view) of a sailboat and a powerboat of the same length on deck reveals why power boats are more spacious below.*

shape of a sailboat's hull narrows rapidly, particularly if the bow has any hollow to it, leaving a very narrow triangle for a cabin sole and a tapered, V-shaped area that usually becomes a forward berth. A powerboat narrows at the bow, too, but more often its bow does not taper as radically as the long gentle sweep of a sailboat bow, so its berths are fuller in the same area.

A sailboat narrows at the aft end as well. Even with a transom stern, the hull lines still converge below the waterline. A transom-sterned powerboat will carry much of its beam *all* the way aft, below the waterline as well as above.

The differences in shape are even more obvious when viewing a boat in section (See Figure 2). A powerboat has sections that appear "squarish." A sailboat's sections are more smoothly curved and have a great deal more taper. This is true even in a hard-chine sailboat. While the sailboat may have deeper draft, much of that draft is a narrow, ballasted keel.

Obviously, a beamy sailboat with full waterlines will give you more living space than a fine, narrow boat of the same length. But she'll also be heavier and slower. It's a compromise only you can resolve—based on how you intend to use the boat.

In every anchorage, in every live-aboard community, you'll find several trimarans and occasionally a catamaran being used as boat

homes. The owners usually insist they wouldn't live on any other type of boat if you *gave* it to them. Their biggest disadvantage is that to perform well multihulls must be kept light and most of them seem to be lightly constructed. When loaded down with live-aboard gear, multihull sailing performance is bound to suffer.

For living aboard *and* cruising, a sailboat cer-

Figure 2 *Looking at the same two boats in section shows an even greater difference in interior volume.*

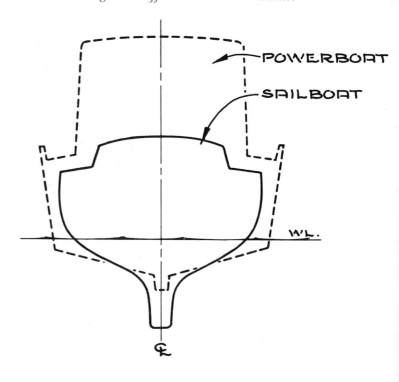

tainly deserves serious consideration. But if comfort and livability are the prime criteria and long-distance cruising a minor consideration, don't ignore the fact that there might be another way.

POWERBOATS

My preference in a powerboat is for a true displacement boat, not a boat with a planing or semi-planing hull. Older wood or steel yachts, such as Trumpy, Consolidated and Burger come to mind. "Yacht" seems more appropriate than "boat" for them. Modern trawler types, such as the Grand Banks and the Krogen trawlers also fit into this category. Semi-displacement boats require an incredible amount of power to get them up on plane and to keep them there, necessitating larger engines and more space devoted to tankage—to say nothing of the large amounts of money required to operate them.

Wide beam and hard-bilged sections do provide tremendous living space inside semi-displacement boats, however. It's their propensity for gobbling fuel that detracts so much from their desirability. Increasingly, powerboat manufacturers are adding displacement boats to their lines.

Sportfishing boats are just that, for sport, not for living aboard. Aside from the hull shape, they have a disproportionate amount of cockpit space—fine for fishing but too much wasted area for efficient living aboard—unless they are very large.

While I've already mentioned that power-

boats have more living space and greater storage capacity, I should add that powerboat storage areas are often more "usable." You're less likely to find odd-shaped little bins where it's difficult to find something that fits into them (See Figure 3). Our schooner had four lockers along each side of the forward bunk that we used for clothes storage.

In the interest of using every inch of available space, we built the lockers to the shape of the hull. This meant they were V-shaped (viewed in cross-section) coming to a point at the bottom. So all our clothes were scrunched up in the V. It was impossible to stack things neatly or prevent them from getting wrinkled. Had we put some kind of flat bottom into the lockers, they would have been so shallow as to be virtually useless.

A powerboat, on the other hand, will maintain its squarish section for a greater depth of its hull, providing more usable space under settees and berths as well as a wider cabin sole. The wider sole contributes greatly to a feeling of spaciousness. Two boats can have an identical layout, a settee on one side and a counter opposite, for example, but if one has a sole width of 3 feet and the other only 2 feet and part of *that* the sloping side of the hull, the boat with the wider sole will feel infinitely larger and roomier than the narrow one.

The shape of the waterline is as important as the sections. Many of the new trawler-type cruising powerboats carry their wide beam a long way forward as well as aft. This gives them very rounded bows ("pumpkin seed" waterlines) and, therefore, large forward compartments. It also makes them harder to push through the water, so they're slower and less economical to run. Watch some of the older, narrow powerboats when they're underway. With their fine waterlines and hollow bows, they seem to glide effortlessly through the water, showing a clean bow wave and a no-fuss wake. But again, those fine lines and narrow ends give you compartments with more taper and, therefore, small storage spaces.

I'll admit to a bias towards those old power yachts. There is a stateliness about them, with their varnished mahogany Dutch paneling, be-

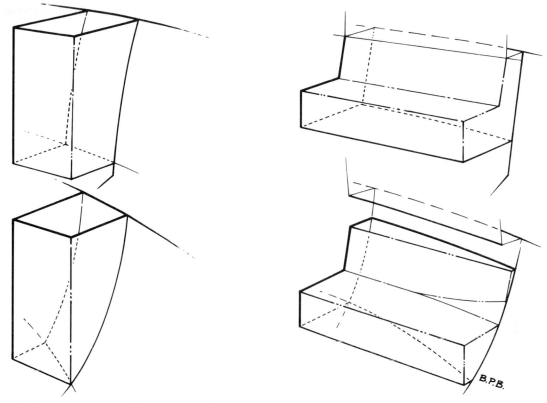

Figure 3 *Hull shape makes a difference in usable storage space. Compare a typical squarish powerboat hanging locker and settee stowage areas (top) with the triangular-shaped compartments of a sailboat (below).*

veled glass window panes and gleaming brass appointments, that bespeaks an elegant style of living difficult to achieve on a newer boat, no matter how posh it might be. I've seen quite a few for sale at astonishingly low prices, not because they were in bad shape, but merely because of their age. Of course, a bargain purchase price can't be considered by itself. You must keep in mind both the maintenance expense and the time required to keep (or restore) her in the style to which she is accustomed. And because of her age, you will most likely be faced with major repair jobs sooner and more often than with a newer boat.

Powerboats have more and larger windows (you really can't call them ports) than most sailboats, which gives them an even greater feeling of space and airiness. You'll especially appreciate this quality on dark and rainy days. Please don't protest about big windows being stove in by heavy seas. We're talking about *livability*, not crossing the Atlantic in a Force 9 gale! Besides,

we are living in an age of Plexiglas and Lexan, plastics that are much more rugged in rough conditions at sea.

More space is devoted to the engine compartment on a powerboat, as it should be. (This is balanced somewhat by the fact that many sailboats must sacrifice forepeak or a quarterberth to bags of sails.) The engine is your only source of power and it should be in an area large enough so that every engine component is accessible and nobody needs to turn into a pretzel to perform maintenance or repairs. I've been in some engine rooms on large powerboats that were a tinkerer's paradise, with work benches, vises, rows of tools neatly hung on pegboard hooks. For the mechanically inclined, a powerboat can be heaven on earth (See Plate 1).

You generally find more amenities on powerboats, although this can have its drawbacks. If many of the goodies require 110-volt power you may find yourself tied to the dock by an

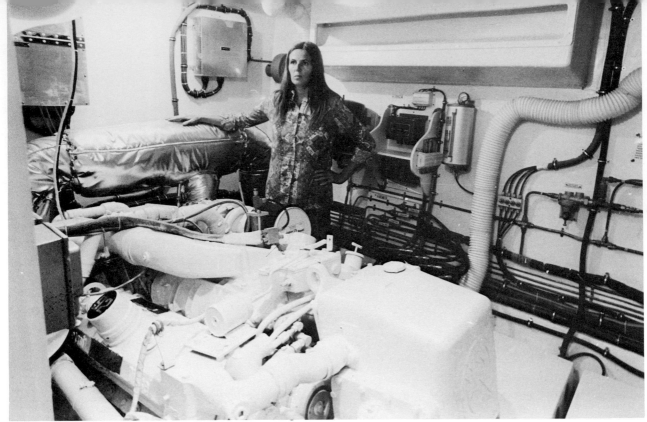

Plate 1 *Large power yachts have big engine rooms, complete with plenty of shelving and work space.*

electric umbilical cord unless you can generate power on board. I used to think the reason anchorages were filled with sailboats and marinas were filled with powerboats was because sailors were basically skinflints. But then I realized many powerboats couldn't be away from a dock for very long or their milk would go sour and they wouldn't be able to use their stoves or plug in their toasters. There are so many pleasant aspects to anchoring out—aside from cost—that it's really a shame to own a boat incapable of being on its own for more than a few hours at a time.

One advantage to a powerboat is that it requires a smaller crew than a sailboat of the same length or, more accurately, displacement. I know several couples with 50-foot and larger powerboats who handle them with ease under any condition, whereas they couldn't begin to cope with a 50-foot sailboat except with additional crew. And the last thing most live-aboards want is needing crew—even temporary crew—to take your boat out for a short evening cruise. That's a fast way to destroy that feeling of freedom and independence you worked so hard to achieve!

MOTORSAILERS

Motorsailers, or "full-powered auxiliaries" as some manufacturers call them, offer an interesting compromise for the sometime sailor. They're roomier and more comfortable below compared to a sailboat of similar size and generally have an enclosed steering station to protect the helmsman in bad weather. Most of the ones I've been aboard seemed to be solidly built and rugged enough to handle offshore work.

Because of their hull shape, motorsailers are not top performers when sailing to weather, but off the wind they do pretty well. The efficiency is obvious—you can sail when wind and weather are favorable, power when they're not. Under power, fuel consumption can be reduced by hoisting some sail—as long as the wind is aft of the beam and blowing harder than the speed of the boat.

While motorsailers have larger engine compartments and more tankage than sailboats, they are less likely to carry a large inventory of sails. If they are equipped with working sails only and the jib is of the roller-furling type, none of the space below will be taken up by bulky sail bags. Since the engine is considered more important on a motorsailer, it's more likely to be well installed, in an easily accessible area.

A motorsailer is not likely to satisfy anyone whose primary concern is fast passage-making under sail. They are slow and cumbersome compared to a pure sailboat and their pilothouses, while cozy and comfortable in nasty weather, prevent you from getting an unobstructed view of the sails. Pilothouses also make it hard to "feel" the wind—another important consideration for performance sailing.

A motorsailer does not, of course, *have* to have a pilothouse. We consider our *Saga* a motorsailer, primarily due to her hull shape and displacement. Yet she does not have a permanent pilothouse, just a dodger. She's also an able sailer and rugged enough for offshore work.

Anyone who wants the creature comforts of a powerboat with the option of sailing whenever the mood strikes, will find a motorsailer an excellent choice. In fact, as the world becomes more energy-conscious, many powerboat folk, who never before thought of sail, are beginning to look at motorsailers.

HOUSEBOATS

Houseboats are in a world all by themselves. While they're not true "cruising" boats, except in protected waters, they certainly must be mentioned in any discussion about living aboard. More and more houseboat communities are springing up along waterfronts everywhere from San Diego to Seattle to Florida. The vast majority of houseboats don't go anywhere—they're used as permanent residences by people getting away from the taxation, hassles and pressures of living on land.

Some houseboats are absolutely gorgeous, elaborate, spacious two-story floating homes, with full-sized rooms and sundecks on top, shingled siding and sliding glass doors—complete with potted plants and hanging flowers everywhere. To get a feeling of what house-

boat living can be like, thumb through Ferenc Matés beautiful book, *Waterhouses.* If you're one of those people who's always sneered at the very word "houseboat," *Waterhouses* may change your thinking.

Waterfront property is desired by many and affordable by only a few. Living on a houseboat is like having your cake and eating it, too. Dockage for even a large houseboat can be much cheaper than the monthly payments on a choice piece of waterfront acreage, especially in resort areas. Taxes on waterfront property are invariably higher than any other location, since it's considered desirable. Yet some states still levy no property taxes against boats. Conversely, those states that allow a "homeowner's exemption" (California is one) on state income tax extend that exemption to trailer homes and boats, as long as it is your one and only residence.

Since the majority of stock houseboats are not built to withstand the rigors of the open sea, their construction is generally lighter and less expensive than sea-going boats. Their "squareness" makes them easier and cheaper to build. You'll find many parallels between trailer home construction and houseboats. All this translates into "waterfront property" at bargain prices.

I've seen a few houseboats that were so "permanent" they had no engine, although I don't think that's a good idea. Mobility is important in an emergency—such as when the boat alongside yours catches on fire. Some marinas in hurricane areas will not permit boats with no means of propulsion to dock.

Many people do use their houseboats for

cruising, of course. There are thousands of miles of protected lakes, rivers and waterways that make superior cruising grounds. With its shallow draft, a houseboat can go places where its seaworthy sister wouldn't dare. But with all that topsides and very little boat in the water, houseboats can be a real handful in a crosswind. The engine should have enough power to keep it maneuverable and move it to safety *fast* if the weather starts to go bad. A good engine or a generator will be needed on a cruising houseboat, so you can run those "household" appliances away from the dock.

For a retirement couple seeking not adventure on the high seas, but a peaceful lifestyle without the headaches of shore living, a houseboat might be ideal. Dollar for dollar, pound for pound, a houseboat gives you more living space than any other type of boat. You get living rooms that rival apartments and galleys that are really kitchens. They can be furnished with comfortable "house-type" furniture if you wish. You can have virtually all the amenities of a house on shore—with no lawn to mow and a spectacular, ever-changing view from the "back porch."

SIZE OF BOAT

How big a boat do you need or want? The two aren't always the same. How small a boat can you get by with? My first advice is, "as big a boat as you can afford to maintain, yet small enough so you can handle her easily." Obviously there's a lot more to it than that, so let's look at some of the pros and cons of large and small boats, sail and power, and try to define *size*.

DISPLACEMENT

Don't get locked into thinking of boat size solely in terms of length. Too many other factors play an important part—length on the waterline, beam, draft, amount of freeboard, shape of the sections and whether the lines are fine or full. The best boat size indicator and one that takes into account *all* these factors, is her displacement or weight.

Displacement is not just the weight of the boat itself. It's what the boat *should* weigh with all normal cruising gear aboard (less than true live-aboard gear, by the way): water and fuel tanks half-full, ice and stores, clothing and a reasonable amount of personal gear—plus the weight of one-half the number of people the boat will sleep. If she has four bunks, for instance, the designer will add the weight of two average-sized adults. If you launch a brand-new boat and she floats right on her lines, you know you're in trouble!

Two boats might be the same length, say 35 feet, but one displaces 12,000 pounds and the other 17,000 pounds. The heavier one may have greater beam and/or draft and, if it's a sailboat, will probably have a proportionally greater amount of ballast. It will also have a bigger payload capacity and be able to swallow up more gear than the lighter one of the same length. Of course, it will need more power to move it along, too.

Since displacement is not as critical (within reason) on a powerboat as on a sailboat, let's concentrate on sail for a moment. A sailboat's displacement can have considerable effect on her performance. A light displacement boat is generally a racing boat or a weekend cruiser. As long as it's kept light it's fast and lively. But once you start to load on live-aboard equipment you'll quickly have a sluggish sailboat, and a crowded interior to boot.

Medium to heavy displacement sailboats are a better choice but they always require making compromises. Overload *any* sailboat and you hamper its performance. Overload a medium displacement boat and you're turning her into a slower, heavy displacement boat. Overload a heavy displacement boat and you're making an already slow boat even slower.

I assume you *will* overload her; it's the rare live-aboard who doesn't. We all start out with good intentions about simplifying our lives, but eventually every nook and cranny is stuffed full. The more nooks and crannies a boat has to begin with, the less we have to leave ashore, right? So, even a lumbering heavy displacement boat gets overloaded to where she can hardly get out of her own way.

If performance ranks high on your list, and it certainly should if your long-term plans include long-range cruising, stay away from the really heavy displacement boat. You may think a knot or less of speed doesn't make that much difference. But over a long haul it can make a difference of a few days, and that may be important when running low on water or if a crew member is ailing. When the time comes to claw off a lee shore in a blow you'd damn well better have a boat that can sail to weather, and sail to weather well!

Some don't want to sail around the world but just want to live on a nice, comfortable boat and muck around under sail sometimes. Others are the laid-back types who say four knots is fast enough as long as the sun is warm and the beer cold. Some of those big heavy boats are absolute palaces inside and they'll absorb scuba gear and the complete Encyclopedia Britannica while still leaving room for the wok and a ham radio. Not bad! Underway, they may be slow but the wake of a passing fishing boat won't spill any drinks, either. We're back to that how-do-I-want-to-use-my-boat question. Only *you* can answer it.

LARGE OR SMALL—MORE COMPROMISES

The advantages of a small boat are numerous. All the gear is proportionately smaller, making it inexpensive to buy and easy to handle. Well, as inexpensive as anything with the word "marine" attached to it can be! As an example, *Sa-*

brina's primary anchor was a 15-pound plow with 35 feet of 5/16-inch chain. Her secondary anchor was a 12-pound Danforth. Compared to our schooner, with her 50-pound cast Danforth and 22-pound Hi-Tensile Danforth—both with 3/8-inch chain—plus a 50-pound yachtsman, *Sabrina's* ground tackle was child's play.

On a small sailboat, hardware, rigging and sails are proportionately smaller and less expensive as well as easier to handle. This is truly appreciated on long passages. The off-watch can sleep soundly, knowing that one person on deck can handle the boat without assistance and without getting in trouble. On the schooner, it seemed the off-watch person was constantly being called topside to lend a hand. A good night's sleep was hard to come by except at anchor.

Dockage is always cheaper, except on those rare occasions when a marina has a minimum-length charge, usually for boats 30 feet and under. We found marinas in congested areas (like southern Florida during the winter) would be full until they realized we were only 20 feet long. Then they'd manage to squeeze us in.

A small boat is easier to keep shipshape than a large one. Not only because pints or quarts of paint are used instead of gallons, but also because less work time is involved. I could sand every bit of *Sabrina's* topside brightwork in a day and get it varnished the next morning. A complete washdown only took a few minutes. We could clean and wax the hull from the dinghy in an hour. We could clean, sand and paint the bottom on one tidal cycle. The schooner took at least two tides to work all the way around her bottom.

Sailing a small boat is less tiring than a large one and that makes it more fun to sail. We would often drop the anchor on *At Last* and collapse in our bunks, exhausted from handling her many sails and heavy gear. With *Sabrina,* we would snug her down and row ashore to explore the town, still fresh and full of energy. We were also more inclined to hoist the sails and go for a little sail just for the fun of it, since she was so easy to get underway. On the schooner, we usually thought twice because of the work involved and, more often than not, we decided *not* to go.

There is, of course, much to be said in favor of a large boat. Its carrying capacity is much greater, so you can cram in a lot more gear. On *Sabrina* we were extremely weight-conscious. Bruce cut "lightening" holes all over her—in berth tops, bulkheads, lockers—he even removed sections of the fiberglass liner that weren't structural. Altogether he removed 260 pounds of excess weight! I was amazed at how it added up. That allowed us to carry an additional 260 pounds of canned goods and other gear. Weight distribution was critical, too. We were constantly watching where we placed heavy items, since it would affect trim and hence performance.

The larger the boat, the less you have to leave on shore—within reason, of course. Besides storage space, a big boat will give you more living space, an enclosed head with a shower, a private stateroom with a door you can close—even separate dining and living areas. Some people need more space than oth-

ers. Bruce and I are lucky we get along so well. We could be together in 20 feet of open space for 24 hours a day without getting on each other's nerves. We've learned to grant each other "privacy" in small ways even when there's really no place to go, except on deck, to be physically alone.

For us, privacy is a state of mind that doesn't require a closed door. I know this isn't true of many people, especially where children are concerned. They need a place to study or play and be out of your hair, or where they can be tucked in bed at night when you're entertaining in the main saloon. A small boat calls for greater compatibility—and a degree of tolerance for one another's shortcomings.

A larger boat will provide a greater carrying capacity for water, fuel and stores, enabling you to remain independent of shore for longer periods of time. You can have more of the "niceties," too, such as a hot water heater, pressure water system, refrigeration, even central heating and air conditioning. Of course, these luxuries are complicated systems and if you can't repair them yourself, you're not as independent as you thought.

Keep in mind that if you increase the size of the boat from 20 feet to 30 feet, for example, which effectively doubles the boat's displacement, you're not necessarily doubling its living space. Only a part of the increase will be useable. The larger the boat the greater the need for more sail stowage and fuel tank space, a larger engine compartment and, if a sailboat, more ballast. Construction will be heavier and take up more space. The companionway ladder will probably be larger and therefore at a greater angle, so it will intrude deeper into the living area.

Going from, say, 30 feet to 35 feet, more often than not each compartment will be slightly larger without adding any new spaces. A typical stock 30-foot sailboat might have the galley aft to one side with a quarterberth and chart table opposite, settees with a table amidships, next the head and hanging locker(s) on opposite sides and then V-berths forward. A typical stock 35-footer will often have an identical layout—the only difference being that the galley, chart table and head compartments are each slightly larger. The amenities—enclosed shower, refrigeration, stove with an oven, pressure water system, electronics gear—would all be basically the same. You may get a little more storage and elbow room, but you pay for it with larger and harder-to-handle gear, heavier and more expensive hardware and higher docking fees.

The larger a boat is, the more complicated her systems become. Between them, a large boat's wiring, plumbing and pump systems, along with its sophisticated electronic gear, can make living aboard a difficult, expensive proposition. Unless you're mechanically inclined and enjoy messing around with motors and electronics—or can afford to have it done—you may find you're far happier in the long run with a smaller and simpler boat. You'll spend less time doing repair jobs and maintenance and more time relaxing, reading, daydreaming or doing whatever you like best.

I've already mentioned that *Sabrina*'s size never bothered me when we were under way. It was only when we stopped to work that the inconveniences started to surface. I think, too, you'll find you're more susceptible to cabin fever on a small boat than on a large one. A big boat with big cabins is less likely to foster that hemmed-in feeling. On small boats it's important to have fewer bulkheads and separate compartments to create open space, light and the feeling of airiness.

While I've tried to show why displacement is a better indicator of a boat's size than just length, most people (including me) still think first, "How long is it?" Then I consider whether she's a "big" 30-footer or a "little" 30-footer. I've met quite a few boat owners who bought a 35-foot boat when a 32-footer would have served just as well, and cost less simply because the boat *was* 35 feet long. It made them feel like they had a bigger boat even though they really didn't.

The difference between length and size will take on more meaning when you decide to sell a small boat. It's hard to sell a 30-foot boat for, let's say, $40,000, when there's a 35-footer in the next slip selling for $36,000. The 30-footer may have a longer waterline, greater displacement, more interior space and, in fact, be a bargain at $40,000, but the initial impression of the buyer will be that you're asking too much money. After all, she's *only* a 30-footer! It'll take some patient explaining to convince most buyers that the "smaller" boat might really be bigger, and the better value.

NEW, USED OR CUSTOM?

More often than not, whether to buy a new boat or a used one is a question of cost. New boats are expensive, for a number of reasons. The base price of a new stock boat is just the beginning and you can start adding on from there. Even a "complete" price with all options included is still only the beginning. Hundreds of items, large and small, inexpensive and costly, will still have to be purchased. This includes everything from docklines to ensign staff, from a flashlight to a marine radio. *Sabrina* was purchased new. I was overwhelmed when I looked at the stockpile of gear that we had to buy for her (See Plate 2).

A used boat, however, is likely to have many of these extras on board. Frequently, electronics and other expensive gear are included in the purchase price.

A new boat is generally covered by some type of warranty for a specified length of time. Added new equipment is also covered by warranty. With a used boat, you buy her "as is," with no warranties and no protection. The head, the navigation lights and other such items on a new boat will conform to existing federal laws. With a used boat you may have to make some expensive modifications to bring her into compliance. Such costs should be considered as part of your purchase price. Also on the plus side for a new boat is that it's easier to get both financing and insurance. Bankers aren't too enthusiastic about lending money for old boats, most particularly old *wood* boats.

Many builders of stock boats offer a choice of interior arrangements, and you get a choice of colors and patterns for both the interior and the hull. Be wary, however, of asking stock builders to make any major structural changes.

Plate 2   *The stockpile of gear for a new boat will increase at an alarming rate.*

If it means they have to pull the boat off the assembly line, make new drawings for the workers to follow and spend time building special components, you can bet it's going to cost you a small fortune. If you feel you must have major changes, you're probably better off looking for another boat.

A used boat will have had many of the "bugs" worked out, little things here and there already taken care of. Of course you're also liable to be getting a few mistakes here and there. A prime example could be the electrical system. Previous owners may have added extra lights and circuits throughout the boat haphazardly, leaving you with a nightmare of wiring to sort through the first time something goes wrong.

I still believe, however, that you get the best value by buying a *good* used boat. Your best insurance for getting a good one is to hire a reliable surveyor. A survey is as important and necessary for a used fiberglass boat as it is for a wood one. A used boat will cost less than a new one initially, but it could wind up costing more in the long run. The expense of refastening a wood boat or replacing a tired engine can quickly eat up anything you've saved by buying used instead of new.

About the only way to have *everything* your way is to have a boat custom designed and built, or to build it yourself. A custom boat is a very expensive proposition. I only recommend it to a person with a great deal of money to spend and enough live-aboard experience to know *exactly* what he wants.

For a custom boat to be successful, a solid understanding and mutual trust must exist between the owner, the designer and the builder. The owner, particularly, must know what he can realistically expect from the other two. It may be his money and his boat, but the end product will always bear their names. No designer or builder worth his salt is going to produce a monstrosity that will damage his reputation for as long as it floats.

Building your own boat from scratch is a solution recommended to only a very select few. It takes a special sort of perseverance to see such a project through to completion. For every one that succeeds, many end in sad failures. To build your own boat successfully, you must have good basic carpentry skills, experience in whatever hull medium you choose, a realistic idea of the time involved and, if you're married, a willing and understanding spouse. I've seen more than one marriage end in divorce because papa poured every spare minute and every dollar he could lay his hands on, year after year, into what finally became known as "that damn boat." Amateur boatbuilding becomes an obsession to those who become involved. The successful projects most often are those in which all family members actively share the obsession.

Some people approach the used-boat market with the idea of buying an inexpensive boat that needs work. Bruce and I did that with *At Last,* and while I don't regret it (it *did* get us on the water and living aboard) I have to say that I don't ever want to do it again! The biggest drawback is that your boat is not your home.

Rather, you are living in your workshop, with no place to go in the evening when the day's work is done. Every night we rinsed the sawdust out of the dishes before we cooked dinner and shook the wood shavings out of the bunk before we went to bed! Like amateur boatbuilders starting from the keel up, some succeed, thus proving that it can be done. But, sadly, too many try it and fail.

BUT DEAR...
THE BABIES
NEED SHOES

B.P. Bingham

Also, as with building a boat from scratch, you must possess really good basic carpentry skills to restore a boat. And completing the job will take longer than you think—I guarantee it. We found that much of the rebuilding—tearing out and replacing a bad piece of joinerwork, for instance—was more difficult and took more time and money than if we had built it from scratch.

The biggest trap of all is what I refer to as the Domino Effect: one "little project" leads to one *more* "little project." Pretty soon it has mushroomed into an overwhelming undertaking. When we bought *At Last*, the first thing we

did was rebuild most of the interior, one section at a time. That enabled us to live aboard and keep cruising at the same time. Then we decided to replace the cabin top and beams, giving the new ones more crown so we could have full standing headroom. So, off came the top.

Now we were living under a plastic dropcloth roof. Luckily, it was summer. Ah, but then the Domino Effect started. As long as the cabin top was off, we thought, why not replace the cabin trunks too? After all, they weren't in top-notch condition.

With the cabin trunks off, it seemed the perfect time to recanvas the decks. So we ripped off all the cracked canvas. Then . . . you guessed it, with the old canvas gone, we figured we might as well replace the deck, since the old one leaked badly in many places.

By this time winter was approaching and we had to move ashore to keep warm. It was a far cry from our original idea of a live-aboard boat.

Buying a boat is always an emotional experience. But it's important to be realistic about your budget, the time available and your own

capabilities as a carpenter and mechanic. You may be better off in the beginning with a small boat you can cope with rather than starting off with a large one that needs so much work done it may be your undoing. You can always "trade up" as you gain experience. But a half-finished project will be difficult, if not impossible, to sell.

To build your own, you must have the skills, the time and the patience to achieve a professional-looking end product or you will never be able to recoup your investment. It may not bother *you* if some of the work looks amateurish, but when it's time to sell your dreamboat, your ego and your pocketbook are liable to be in for a rude awakening.

HULL MATERIAL

FIBERGLASS

The majority of boats built today are of fiberglass. Manufacturers like fiberglass because it is a fast way to turn out a good, strong hull, using primarily semi-skilled labor. Master carpenters are few and far between and a traditionally built wood hull can't be completed in just a few days or months.

With a fiberglass boat you never have to worry about worms or dry rot. There is less chance of fiberglass developing leaks and you get much more usable interior space than in a traditionally built wood boat. Hull maintenance is fairly easy compared to boats of other materials, although fiberglass is certainly not as maintenance-free as some would have you believe. It still must be cleaned and waxed periodically and once a dark-colored gel coat starts to fade, the only solution is to paint it.

At that point, spend the money and have it sprayed with a linear polyurethane paint. You won't have to wax it or worry about it for years to come. We sprayed our fiberglass *Trinka* dinghy five years ago with black linear polyurethane paint. Since then she has been in almost constant daily use. She's been bashed against rocks, thrown up into barnacle-encrusted pilings and scraped across rough cement sea walls. She is just now starting to show wear and tear, but the black is still shiny and there's not the slightest sign of chalking.

We've never waxed it and only hosed it off a few times. If it weren't for the varnished seats, trim and the bottom paint, I could call her maintenance-free! The topsides certainly are.

Many people object to the smell of fiberglass, and I'm one of them. However, *Sabrina* was fiberglass and there was only the slightest hint of "glass" odor when she arrived. And that quickly disappeared. Actually, the prevalent smell was of teak, and I didn't object to that at all! Let me give a word of warning here. If you step aboard a brand-new boat and the smell of fiberglass is overpowering, it's a good indication that the builder is trying to push his boats along the assembly line too fast by over-catalyzing the resin for a quick cure. It's really the chemical reaction, not the resin alone or the cloth that causes the odor.

Over-catalyzing makes the hull brittle, so it's more susceptible to crazing, cracking and chalking. It makes the boat inherently weaker than one that's been allowed to cure slowly. Be wary of any fiberglass boat that *smells* too strongly like "fiberglass." A boat less than four years old that's chalking badly has been over-catalyzed and is already brittle.

While we're talking about checking on construction quality, don't be mesmerized by a lot of teak joinerwork. Crawl around and look at the hull-to-deck joint, always a potential source of leaking. Are the two just glassed together or are they bolted as well? How are the chainplates installed? Are the bulkheads solidly glassed-in or are they stuck in with a few tabs of glass tape? If there is no hull liner, the berths and counter tops are generally considered as longitudinal stiffners—an arrangement that's perfectly acceptable as long as they, too, are solidly bonded to the hull.

Deck hardware that will receive a strain, like cleats and mooring bitts, should be backed up with a metal plate or a piece of plywood glassed in—and they should be through-bolted, not screwed. Stamp around on the deck and see if it feels solid or if it flexes under your weight.

I detest working with fiberglass and I know many who share this dislike. However, I have done some glass work and it is less difficult than I had imagined. Many modifications to a glass boat—installing shelves over the forward bunks, for instance—require some glassing. You'll either have to face up to doing it yourself or pay to have it done. Luckily for me, Bruce

enjoys fiberglass work and is very good at it, so I can usually push that part of the job off on him!

One problem common in fiberglass boats is condensation. Most live-aboards eventually add some type of insulation, such as foam-backed vinyl, on the underside of the decks and cabin top or sometimes glue carpet against the hull. Besides eliminating condensation and keeping the boat cooler in the summer and warmer in cold weather, insulation also helps keep noise levels down—an added bonus in a busy marina or anchorage.

In the early days of fiberglass production, boats were almost *all* glass, invariably white with perhaps a bit of pastel trim. They had all the inviting warmth of a refrigerator. Thus, the term "clorox bottle" was born. Thank heavens builders have gotten away from that (See Plate 3). Recently, I've been aboard quite a number of glass boats where it was impossible to tell when I stepped below whether I was in a glass or wood boat. Even on deck many things are being done to keep a boat from having that cold, all-glass appearance—wood hatches, toe rails and cabin trim, to mention just a few. With the advent of linear polyurethane paints, more unique and different color schemes are starting to appear. Just because you choose a fiberglass boat doesn't mean it has to look like everyone else's.

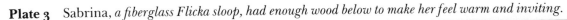

Plate 3   Sabrina, *a fiberglass Flicka sloop, had enough wood below to make her feel warm and inviting.*

Plate 4 *Our lovely wood schooner* At Last *spent a lot of time on the ways and we spent a lot of time working on her.*

WOOD

Wood is by far the easiest material for most people to work with. If you make a mistake with wood, it's fairly easy (though often quite infuriating) to chuck it and start over. Botch up a glassing job, however, and it may take many hours of chiseling and grinding to correct it.

Used wood boats are generally cheaper than used fiberglass boats, but it's getting harder and harder to find a good one. When you do, even if it passes a rigorous survey, it will still be difficult to finance or insure. Keep in mind, too, that the resale value of a wood boat will be lower than a comparable glass boat.

A wood boat may be easier to work on, but it will also require a great deal more work (See Plate 4). Seams will need caulking and paying, she'll need to be sanded and painted and sooner or later you'll probably have to do some refastening or add sister frames. Stay away from any wood boat that's showing signs of "hogging" or sagging, causing the sheerline to hump, or "hog" amidships. It's most prevalent

on boats with long overhangs and is a sign the entire structure is weakening. I've seen it happen to both sailboats *and* powerboats, although more often to sailboats that have been hauled and improperly blocked up when stored for long periods.

With a wood boat, you'll have to maintain a constant vigilance against worms and dry rot. Once either is discovered, steps must be taken *immediately* to remedy the problem. If not, you'll be facing a tremendous repair job—or a total loss if you ignore the problem long enough. Don't be lulled into thinking that worms are only a problem in the tropics. They're as active in Long Island Sound, as they are in Biscayne Bay. Dry rot is also a universal concern, but it's especially bad in the Great Lakes where boats are always in fresh water. Dry rot is actually *wet rot*. It's a fungus that thrives in wood in a condition of moisture, heat and no air. Ventilation is the first and best preventive.

Wood is, in itself, an excellent insulator. It's unlikely that condensation will be the kind of bother it is on boats built of other materials. A wood boat built by traditional methods, with steam-bent or sawn frames, carvel planking, hanging and lodging knees will obviously provide less living space. This is also true of a V-bottom plywood boat, but less so with one that is strip-planked.

With the arrival of a new generation of epoxies on the boatbuilding scene, more boats are being constructed of wood, although not in the traditional fashion. Fiberglassing over planked wood hulls has been tried, but not with great success, primarily because while wood shrinks and swells, polyester resins and fiberglass cloth do not. The fiberglass eventually cracks, separates from the wood and lets water seep in. Or worse, lets water become trapped between glass and wood, and lets rot begin.

Dynel cloth and epoxy resin have greater flexibility than glass cloth and polyester resin, and will "give" somewhat with the wood. New building techniques, most notably the Gougeon brothers' W.E.S.T. System of epoxy saturation, are producing light, strong hulls with the warmth and beauty of wood yet also impervious to teredo worms and dry rot. Many say such a boat gives them the best of both worlds. These methods do not lend themselves to mass production, so if this is what you want, you'll either have to build it yourself or have it built as a custom boat.

METAL

You're not apt to find many boats on the market in steel or aluminum. Only a handful of builders in the United States specialize in either material. You will find a few large power yachts built of steel and aluminum and an occasional sailboat. Most of the steel yachts are built in Europe, primarily in Holland and Germany. Most U.S. steel boatyards are turning out workboats. Steel boat construction is on the increase. But, as steel prices only rise with the "normal" rate of inflation resin, a petroleum derivative, takes quantum leaps.

The best steel for boat construction is Corten. If a steel boat is maintained properly from the very start there shouldn't be much problem with rust. Check a metal boat interior carefully to be sure there are no "pockets" where water can be trapped. Look for extra-large limber holes in the floors. The floors are usually made of thicker metal to allow for some rusting without weakening the hull. Steel and aluminum do require special primers and only certain types of paint are compatible. Many small yards do not understand the importance of surface preparation and using the right finishes, so if you're not going to do the work yourself, be prepared to supervise boatyard employes closely.

While owners of steel and aluminum boats need have no worries about worms and dry rot, they may have big worries about electrolysis. When two dissimilar metals are close to one another under saltwater, the less "noble" one will start to disintegrate. Zinc is the least noble metal in the electrolytic scale, which is why it is used as a sacrificial anode on all types of hulls. But extra care must be taken on metal boats. Trouble can occur even if an owner has taken great pains to check his electrical system, shore outlets and connections, and has made sure that everything is grounded. A neighboring boat with an electrical cord dropped in the water can create enough current to start attacking the welds. Aluminum boats are even more susceptible than steel ones. I've seen aluminum boats at docks with zinc annodes hanging in the water on the end of wires attached to the shrouds and other pieces of bare metal with alligator clips to provide more protection against electrolysis.

My only personal experience with a metal boat was helping deliver a 65-foot steel trawler yacht from San Francisco, California, to Vancouver, B.C., in the early spring. I was so cold for the entire trip that finally I moved my bunk to the cabin sole of a stateroom located directly above the engine room. In fairness I can't say it was only because the boat was steel. She had very little insulation and I was amazed that a yacht of that size, which spent much of her time in northern waters, had no heating system. It did point up the need for plenty of good insulation on a metal boat, particularly if you're going to live on one. Steel is the strongest boat-building material, but it's also the heaviest, which is why it's so seldom used for small boats.

FERROCEMENT

Fifteen years ago, ferrocement was touted as the answer to the amateur boatbuilder's prayer: so simple and so cheap that any fool could build himself a 50-foot brigantine and sail off into the sunset to live happily ever after. It's partly true—the materials that go into a ferrocement hull *are* cheap. But it has to be the slowest, the most tedious method of boat-building ever invented. The hull is only a small percentage of the total cost of a boat. Once it's completed you're less than one-quarter of the way to a finished boat.

I have seen a few (very few) ferrocement boats that were gorgeous, with hulls as smooth and fair as fiberglass. These were built by people with the perseverance, money and skills to see the project through and do it well. They are the exception, not the rule. For every ferrocement boat launched dozens of half-completed hulks lay in boatyards and backyards—concrete monuments to shattered dreams, broken marriages and financial disasters. Many

that do make it to launching day are so poorly executed they're a blight on the waterfront.

I remember one poor man in California who spent nine years building a ferrocement ketch. He had no skills, just a dream—anyone could do it, right? For nine years he poured all his time and money into what had to be the epitome of the wrong way to do everything. The hull was a mass of lumps and humps and the masts were pieces of plywood nailed into a box section. Launching day finally arrived. The boat was swung over a seawall and lowered into the water. We watched in horror as she rolled over on her side and stayed that way, spreaders in the parking lot. Her owner collapsed and an ambulance was called. We learned later he had suffered a complete nervous breakdown. As far as I know the boat, her masts removed, is still floating at a mooring with a permanent list.

You can find some real bargains in ferrocement boats. If you only have a little money to spend it might be tempting. But think twice before you do it. Ferrocement has developed such a bad reputation that even a good boat has a low resale value. The bargain today is most likely to be an even bigger bargain for whoever buys her from *you*. In the long run, it's no bargain.

2

Cabin Plans

"The ultimate jigsaw puzzle"

UNLESS YOU'RE HAVING a custom boat built, you're pretty much stuck with the boat you now own or buy. Changes can be made, even quite extensive ones, depending on your ability as a carpenter and your pocketbook. But I would caution anyone against making major structural changes, like moving bulkheads, without first consulting a naval architect. Such changes can have a tremendous effect on the trim and stability of the boat.

THE PIECES

Before we go into a cabin-by-cabin discussion, consider some general aspects. First is headroom. Virtually all boats being built today large enough to be considered live-aboard boats have standing headroom. But a surprising number of older designs don't. There's an old sailor's adage that goes, "When you're below, you're either sitting down or lying down. If you want to stand up, go topside."

That may be fine for day-sailing or weekend cruising, but for living aboard permanently you must be able to stand up, turn around, pull up your pants, stretch and walk around with-

out feeling cramped or hemmed in. Moving about or standing in a stooped-over position will give you back problems you never knew you had. And cooking with your head wreathed in a cloud of steam is hardly pleasant.

Short people have an easier time of it on most boats. There's nothing worse than being 6 feet, 2 inches tall on a boat with 6-foot, 1-inch headroom. One tall friend of mine, who also happens to be balding, always wears a wool watch cap below to keep his noggin from turning black and blue.

Another point to consider is traffic flow. For instance, if the dining table leaves are up, can you get from the galley to the head without making people at the table get out of the way or having to lower one of the leaves (See Plate 1)? Can the cook work in the galley without being bumped by someone trying to move from one part of the boat to the other?

On some sailboats, for example, the galley counter extends athwartships, becoming part of the companionway steps. In such a layout can you put down a bowl of brownie batter without having it stepped on more than every other time?

On boats with aft cabins, you'll want to be

Plate 1   *On this Cherubini 44, people can move fore and aft even with the table leaves raised.*

able to go aft without going on deck (See Plate 2). The access should be more than a narrow crawl space alongside the engine. I know this design feature is sometimes difficult to achieve, but I would rather *not* have an aft cabin if it meant I had to don foul weather gear and dash through the rain just to get to bed on a stormy night. That would come under the heading of camping out, not living aboard.

Two other musts on a live-aboard boat are good lighting and ventilation. There are many ways of correcting a boat that is lacking in these respects (See lighting, ventilation chapters) so on these accounts alone I wouldn't too hastily reject a boat I really liked.

All shelves, including those inside cabinets, will require high fiddles to keep things in place. This is true for both powerboats and sailboats, even those that never leave the dock. The best fiddles are cut down at the corners to permit cleaning the shelves. For open shelves without doors, I consider 3-inch fiddles to be the minimum. Adding or changing fiddles can be done at a later date if existing ones are inadequate.

Well thought out boats will have handholds on all ladders or steps, along the cabin carlins

Plate 2   *Saga's head is located in the passageway leading to the aft cabin. Engine access is through panel at lower right.*

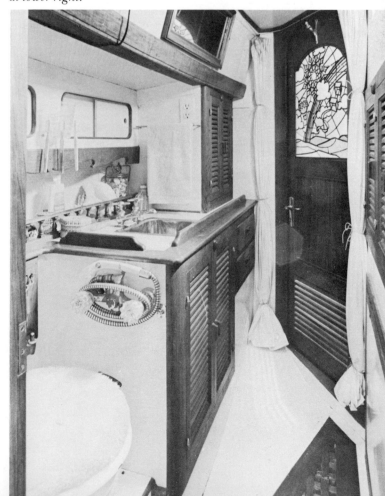

Plate 3   Saga's *workshop is a great place for building and repair projects.*

and/or built into partial bulkheads to permit safe movement below when the boat is heeled or rolling. Powerboats with wide-open saloons often have handholds running down the center of the overhead.

A really comfortable live-aboard boat will be big enough to have separate *private* sleeping compartments and head, as well as enough room to accommodate its owner's special interests. If you read a great deal and want lots of books, look for a boat with plenty of bookshelves (or space to install them), and one that's able to carry the added weight. You'd be amazed at how much a library of hard-cover editions weighs. I try to buy paperbacks whenever possible.

Photographers who need a darkroom will want a boat with a large head or a stateroom that can be converted to a darkroom. Tinkerers and do-it-yourselfers will want a workshop (See Plate 3) or at least space to install a workbench and accessible space to store tools.

Gourmet cooks will want a boat with an oversized galley and plenty of counter space (See Plate 4). I know one couple with a passion for music who installed a small harpsichord in the main saloon. Moving aboard shouldn't mean giving up favorite hobbies or interests (See Plates 5 and 6). If the sacrifices are too great or the existence too Spartan, nobody will be happy for long aboard a boat. Let's take a close look at separate living areas and see what it takes to make each one comfortable and livable.

Plate 4   *This galley on an Endeavour should make any gourmet cook happy.* (PHOTO COURTESY ENDEAVOUR YACHT CORP., PHOTO BY SKIP GANDY)

Plate 5 Saga's *forward stateroom does double-duty as a drawing room/office for Bruce.*

Plate 6 *Betsy has a writing desk tucked into a corner of her stateroom on* All Hours.

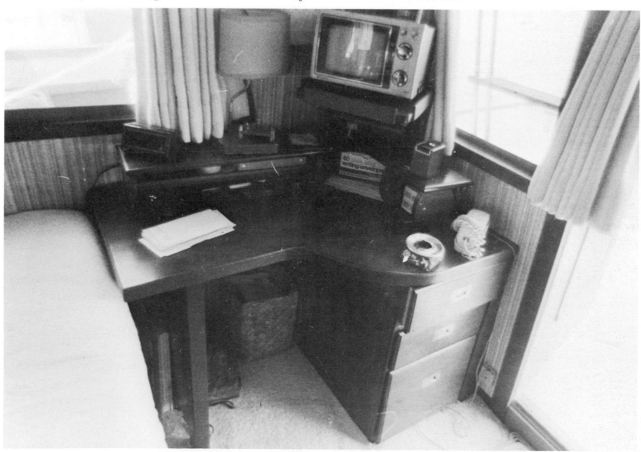

MAIN SALOON

Here is where you spend most of your waking hours. Comfortable seating is of paramount importance (See Plate 7). Normal seating height for a dinette seat is 18 inches. A sofa or easy chair is deeper and therefore lower— about 16 inches above the sole. Since a settee frequently does double duty as a chair for sitting upright at a table and as a sofa for leaning back and relaxing (See Plate 8), if it's totally comfortable for one function it won't be for the other.

My own preference in such cases is to opt for a comfortable sofa and add pillows or cushions, if need be, at mealtimes. Some sailboats have extra-high settees to create space for large water tanks beneath them. The additional tankage may be needed for ocean passages. But it's a terrible sacrifice from a comfort standpoint. You never feel right if your feet barely reach the cabin sole, like a little kid riding on a bus.

The settee back is most comfortable at a slight angle, not straight up and down (See Plate 9). If the settee extends outboard under the deck, you should be able to lean back against the cushion without cracking your head on the cabin trunk. This can sometimes be rectified if the settee is wide enough by installing a cabinet outboard of the settee to fill in the space under the deck. At least 3 feet is the bare minimum from the top of the cushion to the overhead, and 3 feet, 3 inches is much better.

Avoid permanent berths in the main saloon. Often a dinette converts to a double berth or the settee doubles as a bunk (See Plate 10).

Plate 7 *These padded chairs can't be beat for comfortable seating.* (PHOTO COURTESY ENDEAVOUR YACHT CORP., PHOTO BY SKIP GANDY.)

Plate 8 *This Endeavour's settee doubles as a dinette, but chairs are installed opposite.* (PHOTO COURTESY ENDEAVOUR YACHT CORP., PHOTO BY SKIP GANDY.)

Plate 9 *A settee back is most comfortable at a slight angle. An end table could be a hanging locker top or a cabinet with a shelf over.*

Consider these only as temporary sleeping quarters for occasional guests, or as sea berths underway, never for regular use. One of the fastest ways to tire of living on a boat is having to make up a bunk every night and completely disassemble it each morning. Worse yet is using a sleeping bag every night. Assigning a child a pilot berth in the main saloon as a permanent bunk is also unfair to him and to you.

In addition to comfortable seating, try to provide some kind of end table (See Plate 9). That could be a hanging locker or cabinet with a shelf over or a dinette that lowers to coffee table height. You'll want a place to put your coffee mug, ash tray and magazines within easy reach.

If you entertain often, will the main saloon seat as many people as you're likely to invite at one time? Can your guests move around without tripping over each other's feet? Is the saloon spacious enough (See Plate 11) so it doesn't feel like a chicken coop?

On paper, powerboat layouts may look about the same as sailboat interiors. But don't be fooled. Two boats of the same length can have similar arrangements—settee and table to starboard, galley to port, for instance—but the powerboat will have greater cabin sole area, bigger windows or ports, more storage in lockers and under settees (due to hull shape), and an overall greater feeling of light and space. These features are sometimes hard to visualize merely by looking at a scale drawing.

Large powerboats allow the luxury of a sofa and chairs. Small to medium size powerboats frequently use the settee as a dinette (See Plate 12). Usually, the tables are of the hi-lo type that can be raised for eating (about 11 inches above the top of the cushion) and lowered to coffee-table height. Be sure there's enough room for legs and feet with the table lowered. If the table is on a fixed pedestal and lowers to convert to a double bunk, it may be a little snug.

Plate 10   Saga's *dinette once converted to a double berth. Since it was never used as a bunk, we changed to a slim table leg that would give us ample legroom.*

Plate 11 *The saloon on this Vagabond 42 will seat a large number of people and still feel spacious.*

Plate 12 *This roomy medium-sized powerboat has a sofa **and** a settee that can be used as a dinette with the hi-lo table.*

Galley

The galley on most sailboats today is located aft, near the companionway, where there's good light and ventilation, adequate headroom and where the cook presumably can be part of the group on deck. Only in a few old sailboats is the galley tucked into a cramped, stuffy forepeak. Motorsailers and powerboats sometimes are roomy enough for a separate galley and dinette, although the galley is generally part of the saloon or deckhouse (See Plates 13 and 14).

I prefer a galley that is near the saloon but separated by at least a partial bulkhead (See Plate 15), or perhaps by a solid bulkhead with a pass-through cutout (See Plate 16). I enjoy cooking and entertaining but I detest being totally isolated from my guests. I like being able to hide the messy pots and pans yet still remain in the conversation.

Normal counter height in a kitchen is 36 inches. It should be the same in a galley but I'm amazed at how often it isn't. It's imperative to be able to stand comfortably at the counter. Sailboats have such narrow cabin soles that frequently part of the sole is the sloping side of the hull. I've never found this objectionable as long as the angle isn't too great. About the only remedy is to raise the cabin sole or install a step in front of the counter, although the boat has to have plenty of headroom before this is possible.

I've only seen a kick space along the bottom of a galley counter on a few very large, luxurious power yachts. Sometimes the cabin sole isn't wide enough for this space, but mostly it's an expensive feature to build. Consider yourself lucky if you have it on your boat (See Plate 17).

Keep the cook happy and your chances for successful living aboard rise considerably. My biggest beef with production boat builders—

Plate 13   *The dinette on this powerboat is directly across from the galley.*

Plate 14 *This houseboat has room enough for a separate dining room.* (PHOTO COURTESY BLUEWATER YACHTS.)

Plate 15 *A houseboat galley separated from the main saloon by a partial bulkhead.* (PHOTO COURTESY BLUEWATER YACHTS.)

Plate 16 *On this Cherubini the galley is completely separate from the saloon, but with a pass-through cutout in the bulkhead.*

Plate 17 *The galley on this Hatteras motor yacht has a kick space along the counter bottom. Another nice feature is the double sink with one side shallow and one side deep.*

both sail and power—is building a boat they claim sleeps six or eight (implying that many will be aboard for more than just a day) and then allotting a dinky little corner to the galley —where there's barely enough room to prepare a minimal meal for one or two, let alone the army the boat is intended to sleep.

Most people cruising for a few days or a few weeks simply eat more canned food than usual or prepare food at home they can reheat under way. When you live aboard you *are* at home and the galley assumes much greater importance. All food preparation is done on board and, as any good cook knows, what's needed (aside from the sink and the stove) is plenty of counter space (See Plate 18). See the chapter on the galley for several approaches to gaining additional counter space.

Top-loading ice boxes do the best job of keeping cold air from escaping when they're opened. This is a feature rarely found on modern powerboats today. It's not as critical with refrigeration, of course, since you're not carrying ice. But the same principle applies.

A large ice box or refrigerator might seem like a great feature. However, only a relatively few items in reality must be kept cold. It's much

more economical to keep a small, full box cool than trying to cool down a large half-empty one. On the other hand, a large freezer is wonderful, providing you have the electrical capacity to handle it. That's a luxury I have on occasion yearned for, particularly when we're off on long cruises.

Pay particular attention to the location of the ice box or refrigerator. If it's near the engine compartment it will undoubtedly need extra insulation. The better the insulation (closed-cell urethane foam is best), the easier it will be to keep cold.

Make sure the top is insulated as well—a slab of ¾-inch lumber is not enough. Hauling ice to

Plate 18 *The galley on a Vagabond 42 is located in a walk-through. It has plenty of counter space, a double sink over the centerline and plenty of stowage including soffet cabinets.*

the boat every day can become an expensive pain in the neck. On the other hand, refrigeration systems independent of dockside electricity use a lot of power and usually require running the engine or generator daily.

I know there's a school of thought that says doing without refrigeration is the best solution. Personally, I think it's ridiculous to deprive yourself of this so-called luxury when you're living aboard. Bruce and I did without it on our schooner and I assure you we *did* miss it. Lugging ice to *Sabrina* became well worth the effort every time I drank a glass of cold milk or ate a crispy green salad. Bruce's reward was ice-cold Milky Way bars.

A proper galley sink is adequate if a dinner plate will lay flat in it and a large pot will fit under the faucet. Deep sinks are handy—unless they're so deep the bottom is at or below the waterline, requiring a pump to empty it. A pressure water system is a great convenience, provided there's a hand pump as well to draw water if something mechanical goes wrong.

Stoves installed on a boat's fore-and-aft axis should be gimballed, even on powerboats, although they seldom are. A passing wake can roll a powerboat and spill the hot soup as easily as when heeling on a windward beat in a sailboat. Gimballed or not, every stove needs guard rails or metal fiddles—cut down at the corners to make room for pan handles—and adjustable pot clamps (See Chapter 14).

Sometimes stoves are installed so they are partially under a deck, creating a potential fire hazard. If the stove is even close to the deck, be sure a pot can sit on the back burner and still clear the edge of the cabin trunk. Most marine stoves with ovens are insulated so the outside doesn't get too hot. But if the oven is not insulated, the area around the stove must be. The result may be scorched wood, blistered paint, or worse.

I always look for at least a couple of drawers in a galley—the more the better. If there are built-ins, such as dish racks, take out your tape measure to see if a dinner plate (usually 10½ inches in diameter) will actually fit, or if the rack will only take a lunch-size plate. Actually, I prefer a boat with wide-open storage areas so I can divide it up myself, designing each compartment to fit my own pots, pans and other galley gear.

STATEROOMS

Sleeping quarters work best when they're separate, private staterooms with closing doors. This is true for you, your children and anyone else who lives aboard. Guests who play cards all night when you want to sleep should be able to do so. If you don't feel well and need rest or if you just want to be alone for awhile, separate quarters are a necessity. Children need a place to study and their own quarters at bedtime when you're entertaining.

Couples who like to sleep together won't be happy for long unless the boat has a double berth. Temporary sea berths can be set up in the saloon, but for day-to-day living you'll want a permanent double bunk in an enclosed stateroom (See Plate 19).

Ideally, a stateroom should be large enough to include a dresser with drawers, a hanging locker and a place to sit (aside from the berth) (See Plate 20). You're more apt to find this layout on a powerboat than on a sailboat (See Plate 21). On many sailboats, you're lucky just to get a double bunk that can be closed off, usually in the forepeak. As a minimum, look for good reading lamps and enough shelving to hold books, lotion, coffee cups and all the little odds and ends that invariably end up near your bunk (See Plate 22). I do insist on sheets, pillow cases and blankets—no sleeping bags. If you wouldn't consider them in a bedroom on shore, why settle for less in your floating home?

Plate 19 Saga's aft cabin has a large double berth, plenty of drawers and shelves and (not shown) a deep hanging locker.

Plate 20 *This stateroom has a double bunk, drawers and shelving and a dresser with its own seat.* (PHOTO COURTESY ENDEAVOUR YACHT CORP., PHOTO BY SKIP GANDY.)

Plate 21 *A powerboat is more likely than a sailboat to have a stateroom that rivals any bedroom on shore.*

Plate 22 Saga's *forward stateroom, ready for company, with sheets, blankets and pillow cases—no sleeping bags.*

When you're boat-shopping, don't by shy about jumping into a bunk. That's the only way to find out if it's really comfortable. Forepeak V-bunks are narrow at the forward end, so be sure there's room for two pairs of feet to wriggle around. The only way to make certain a berth is long enough is to lie down and stretch out.

When the bunk extends outboard under a shelf, see if there's enough clearance to roll over without bashing your hips or shoulders. You should be able to sit up on at least part of the berth. It's likely your feet *will* extend under a deck or cabinet, but check for sitting headroom—a minimum of 36 inches—on the rest of the bunk.

I've heard it said again and again that forepeak berths are impossible to sleep in at sea. Frankly, I think that's an exaggeration. Even when cruising the majority of time is spent in port or at anchor, not at sea, and the forepeak is usually the best place for a berth (See Plate 23). There's usually a large hatch to provide ventilation and it's probably the easiest section of the boat to close off for privacy.

Underway, the forepeak is the quietest place on the boat when the engine is running or when someone is banging about in the galley. I've spent many hours sleeping in forepeaks and the only time it was bad was in really rough weather when the boat was slamming into a head sea. That doesn't happen too often. On those rare occasions when it does, move to temporary berths further aft.

We can carry this argument one step further and say that athwartship berths are perfectly acceptable in port, but rarely under way. They are found most often on powerboats. But I

Plate 23 *A forepeak berth, with good ventilation from the large overhead hatch, is one of the best sleeping berths on a boat.*

have seen some luxurious athwartship double berths on sailboats (See Plate 24). I don't totally agree with the objection to narrow sea berths, either. I would rather roll around a bit against a leeboard than feel as if I were wedged into a coffin.

Most boats with V-berths forward have removable inserts to convert them to a double. While this theoretically gives room to move around, keep in mind that when it's used as a permanent double berth the insert will rarely be removed. If it's left in place, bins with flop-down fronts give easier access to under-bunk storage than drawers. Top-loading bins are the most secure storage, but bedding and cushions must be moved to get at them.

The minimum depth for a hanging locker is 24 inches. Anything less won't allow a standard hanger to hang freely. Any more depth than two feet will probably permit adding small shelves at the back of the locker. Notice the height of a hanging locker and be sure clothes can hang straight without being bunched up at the bottom. *Sabrina* had this problem but we were able to correct it by raising the clothes rod a few inches.

For clothes storage aside from the hanging locker, I prefer drawers to shelves or bins (See Plate 25). Drawers have air space all around them and the clothes never touch the hull, so they stay dry and are less subject to mildew.

Shelves, particularly over forepeak berths in stock boats, are frequently inadequate. It's not really difficult to add shelves, however, and

Plate 24 *An athwartship berth in a great cabin aft can be a place of total luxury.*

Plate 25 *This chest of drawers on the trawler* All Hours *gives excellent dry storage for clothing.*

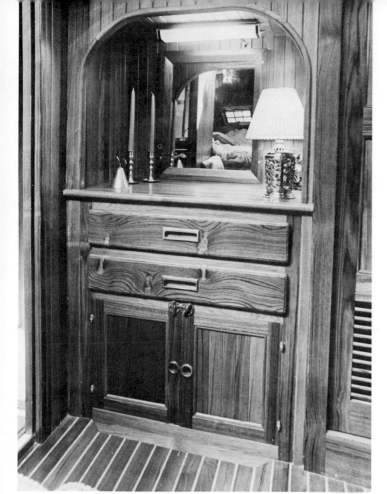

Plate 26 *This lovely dresser with drawers has a seat
directly opposite.*

you may be pleasantly surprised at just how much you can add without infringing on headroom. We'll go into that in detail in a later chapter.

If the stateroom is also a dressing room, you'll want room to turn around and space to sit down and pull off your boots (See Plate 26). The berth can double as a seat if it's not too high. Some boats have a seat between the V-berths or one that folds down from a bulkhead.

THE HEAD COMPARTMENT

I don't believe a boat under 40 feet needs more than one head. On a boat with two or more heads, consider converting one into a workshop and selling the toilet to buy a good carpenter's vise. It's a much better use of space. I was aboard a powerboat some years ago in California where the owner had removed the fixtures, added shelves and cabinets and

converted the compartment into a large, useful pantry.

Minimum space in front of the toilet is 18 inches and 22 inches is much better. It should be far enough from the bulkhead so you can sit on it comfortably. If the toilet is on a platform, the rim of the bowl should extend beyond the front edge of the platform. This is unimportant to women, but it does matter to men.

While a boat home will have an enclosed head, you'll sometimes find a second toilet installed forward, between the V-berths. That can be removed. I find the idea of sleeping directly above a toilet distasteful and marine heads are notoriously difficult to keep completely odor-free. When two people are sleeping forward with the insert in, then *both* must get up so the insert can be removed to get to the head. Hardly a convenience.

The shower—and a boat is not a real home without one—is ideally a separate compartment (See Plate 27). More often it's simply a hand-held shower head that fits into a bracket on the head bulkhead. This isn't as bad as it sounds. You can rig a shower curtain on a circular track to keep from splashing water on the counter and storage lockers and the push-button type shower heads use considerably less water than the usual faucet types.

Wherever the shower is, make sure there's a large drain in the sole leading to the bilge or a sump tank. Some boats have a removable teak grating over the sole and drain, giving you a level surface to stand on, while the head sole beneath it slopes down to the drain.

The head sink is worthless unless it's located so you can use it easily. That may sound obvious, but on many boats the sink is tucked under the side deck where there is barely room to wash your hands, let alone room to brush your teeth or wash your face. In such cases a pull-out sink, or one that folds down from the bulkhead and drains into the head, works much better.

Note the size of the sink. In the interest of saving space (or perhaps money) some builders install cute little sinks (often oval) so tiny one hand hardly fits under the faucet. Better a pull-out or fold-down sink.

A mirror is best located over the sink (See Plate 28), not off to one side or hung on the door. Ask any man how he likes shaving with the sink in front of him and the mirror hung on a door behind him. *At Last* had a port over the sink, so Bruce designed a mirror with hinges that was held up against the overhead with a hook and flopped down when we wanted to use it.

Shelves or cabinets in the head compartment are necessary for spare towels, toilet paper, combs, medicines, toothpaste, etc. (See Plate 29). A really nice feature is a built-in hamper for dirty clothes.

NAVIGATION AREA

Large sailboats may have a navigation area with a large chart table, electronics and repeater instruments. A recent trend is to try fitting a chart table into even the smallest sailboat. A proper chart table must be big. Little ones look nice drawn on an arrangement plan but are

Plate 27   *A bathtub and a shower is a luxury usually limited to powerboat interiors.*

Plate 28   *Ideally the mirror should be installed directly over the sink in the head, not off to one side.*

Plate 29 *This head has plenty of cabinets and shelving, an opening port and a separate shower compartment.* (PHOTO COURTESY ENDEAVOUR YACHT CORP., PHOTO BY SKIP GANDY.)

useless when laying out a chart and walking off a course with parallel rules. Most people find the dining table works better. A chart table on a sailboat must be able to do double duty as a desk, workbench or galley extension. Otherwise, it's wasted space on a live-aboard boat. One shelf can be set aside for navigation books and equipment (See Plate 30).

Powerboats (and motorsailers with enclosed steering stations) often have a chart table adjacent to the wheel that's big enough to be useful. With the instruments arranged around the wheel, the helmsman can steer, check the course and monitor the engine, depth sounder and other electronics. Large power yachts have steering stations or pilothouses that truly resemble functional ship bridges.

On smaller boats, while an inside steering

Plate 30 *Saga's navigation station is over the top-loading ice box.*

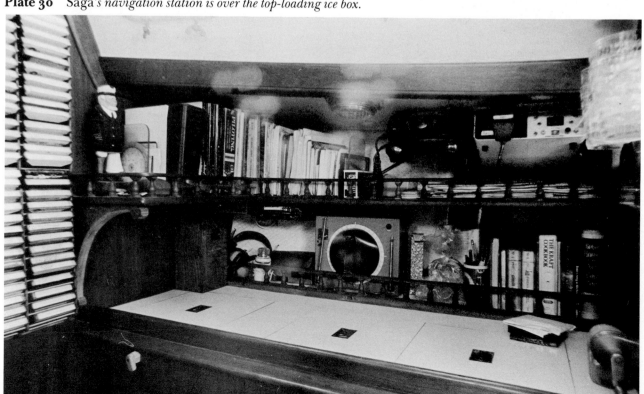

station is likely to be part of the main saloon, the saloon is generally roomy enough so the station does not intrude too much on the living space. And you may find there's just enough room close to the wheel to lay a folded chart for a quick course check, with the actual navigation being done on the dining table.

Engine Compartment

This is one area where a powerboat is superior to a sailboat. For most powerboats, engine *room* is a better term than engine *compartment*. While full standing headroom is only found on larger yachts, there's usually ample room all around the engine so the engine and all its accessories can be worked on even by those who aren't contortionists.

The engine should be accessible from the top and from all sides, with a drip pan under it to keep oil and sludge out of the bilges. It should be well insulated to prevent noise and heat from invading the living area and it must be well ventilated as well. Batteries give off poisonous, explosive fumes when they're overcharged. So they should be installed where there's a good flow of air, never under a berth or in a tightly enclosed cabinet.

Sailboats with aft cabins usually have the engine amidships where there's ample working space (See Plate 2). Probably the worst arrangement (sometimes unavoidable) is with the engine all the way aft, tucked under the cockpit and virtually in the bilge. If the engine extends into the cabin (under the companionway lad-

der or a galley counter), make sure all surrounding cabinetry is designed to be removable, preferably on all four sides and not just the front.

You'll need space to store filters, spare parts and tools, ideally with a workbench somewhere for repair projects. Dismantling a carburetor on the varnished saloon table is not the way to keep your spouse happy about boat living. I've found live-aboards tend to do more of their own repair work than weekend sailors, and sooner or later someplace on the boat becomes a permanent workspace. A locker or cabinet can be designated as the bo'sun's locker for storing paint, brushes, rags and other deck gear. Wherever the fuel tanks are located, be sure you can reach the inspection ports with enough clearance to get your hand and arm inside and that you are able to get your head and a flashlight over the port so you can look inside as well.

Storage

The more storage space you have, the better—obviously. I have yet to see a live-aboard boat with too much of it. Live-aboards have some unique storage problems—where to put the box of Christmas decorations 11 months out of the year, for example.

The boat home needs, as a minimum, one hanging locker. Two are better, a large one for regular clothes and a smaller one that becomes a wet locker for foul weather gear and boots. Again, minimum depth is 24 inches, and they should be high enough so clothes can hang straight.

Locker doors should have sturdy latches or turn buttons to keep them securely closed if a heavy object inside falls against them. Magnetic catches are too light to stand up under heavy use.

I've heard it said you can judge the quality of a boat by the number of its drawers. That may be true—drawers are time-consuming and expensive to build. I prefer them, as I said earlier, over bins or shelves for a lot of things, particularly clothes. Drawer fronts should be notched so you must lift up to pull them out; otherwise, they'll slide open when the boat rolls.

Every person living on the boat needs at least one locker or shelf that belongs to him or her alone. Even on little *Sabrina,* where every inch and every ounce mattered, we each had a small shelf on our side of the forward bunk. I filled mine with paperback books and embroidery hoops, and he stuffed his shelf with harmonicas and kites. I never said, "Do you really need three harmonicas on this little boat?" because they were in *his* domain.

I can't stress how important this is. Storage space is always at a premium on a boat. We all move aboard with the good intentions of ridding ourselves of useless possessions, keeping only what is absolutely necessary. That's fine, to a point. But remember boat living is supposed to make life more enjoyable, not less. Leave austerity to monks and give yourself enough space for just a bit of frivolity.

Cockpits/After Decks

Most land dwellers think boat people spend most of their time outdoors. Actually, unless the boat is underway, I don't think we spend much more time outside than shore people spend in their backyards. Huge cockpits are a tremendous waste of living space. It's no surprise that live-aboards, or even people who simply use their boats a lot, inevitably add dodgers, awnings and side curtains to give the cockpit protection against the weather and make its valuable space usable all the time.

I like a boat with minimal cockpit space. Some people insist on seats that are at least 6 feet long so they can nap, sunbathe or sleep outside on balmy nights. On a sailboat with a tiller, it's a good idea to modify it so it can be lifted out of the way when the boat's not sailing.

Adding an awning with side curtains that roll up in fair weather and zip down when it's cold or raining effectively adds another room to the live-aboard boat. Leave the hatches or doors open so the boat feels less stuffy and cramped in bad weather. Likewise, the boat is many degrees cooler below on hot days.

Cockpit cushions admittedly add to seating comfort, but thought must be given to where they'll be stowed when not on deck. I think cockpit cushions are often more trouble than they're worth. Despite their vinyl covers, they cannot be left out in the rain. Once they get wet and soggy, it takes days to dry them out. The alternatives are usually stuffing them into a bunk or living with them stacked on a settee in the main saloon until the rain stops. I don't like them in the cockpit underway, either. They're slippery underfoot and are apt to slide off the seats when the boat heels. The vinyl-covered life preserver-type cushions are almost as comfortable and much easier to stow.

A Word About Houseboats

All the preceding comments apply to houseboats, too, but only to a slight degree. Houseboats are just that: houses that float. Most of them, particularly the larger ones, are spacious enough to rival an apartment on shore. Even small models are comparable to mobile homes. It's unlikely that you'll find in them bunks that are too short or narrow, or hanging lockers that are skimpy. They do seem to have a design tendency to sleep lots of people, although this may take the form of hide-a-bed sofas—so you don't have lots of separate staterooms. Not that an extra stateroom is bad: remove the bunk and you can build yourself a private office, study, workshop, darkroom, sewing room, or what have you.

FITTING THE PIECES TOGETHER

Having read my recommendations on live-aboard interiors, remember they are still *opinions*. The following are more opinions, arrangement plans and boat profiles that strike me as good live-aboard layouts, supplied by many designers and builders.

Look through this section. Study it to see how the pieces of the puzzle fit together as elements in *your* ideal live-aboard home.

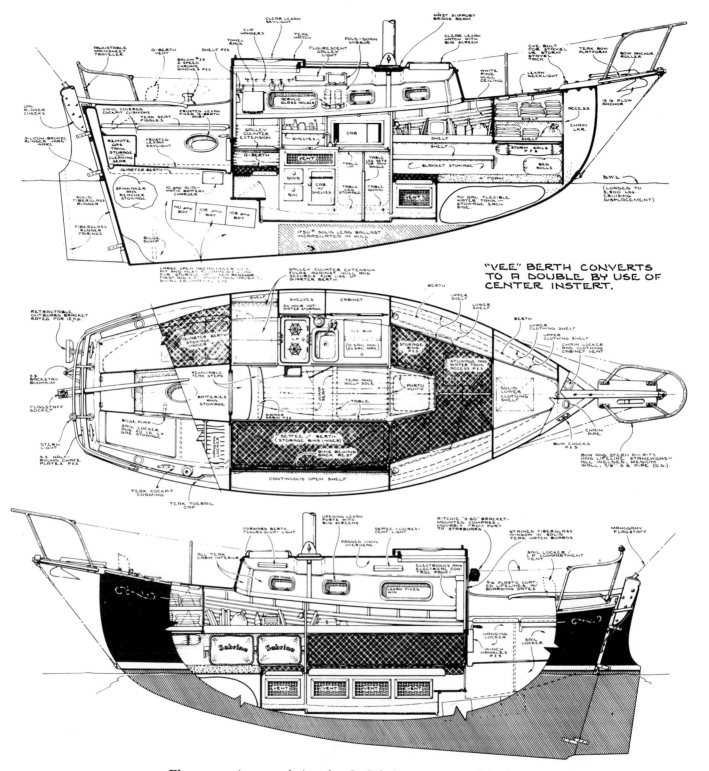

Figure 1 *Accommodation plan for* Sabrina, *a custom Flicka sloop.*

Designer: Bruce P. Bingham
Builder: Pacific Seacraft Corp.
               3301 S. Susan Street
               Santa Ana, CA 92704

L.O.A.:	23′ 7″	Draft:	3′ 3″
L.O.D.:	20′ 0″	Displacement:	5,500#
L.W.L.:	18′ 2″	Water:	40 gal.
Beam:	8′ 0″	Fuel:	Variable

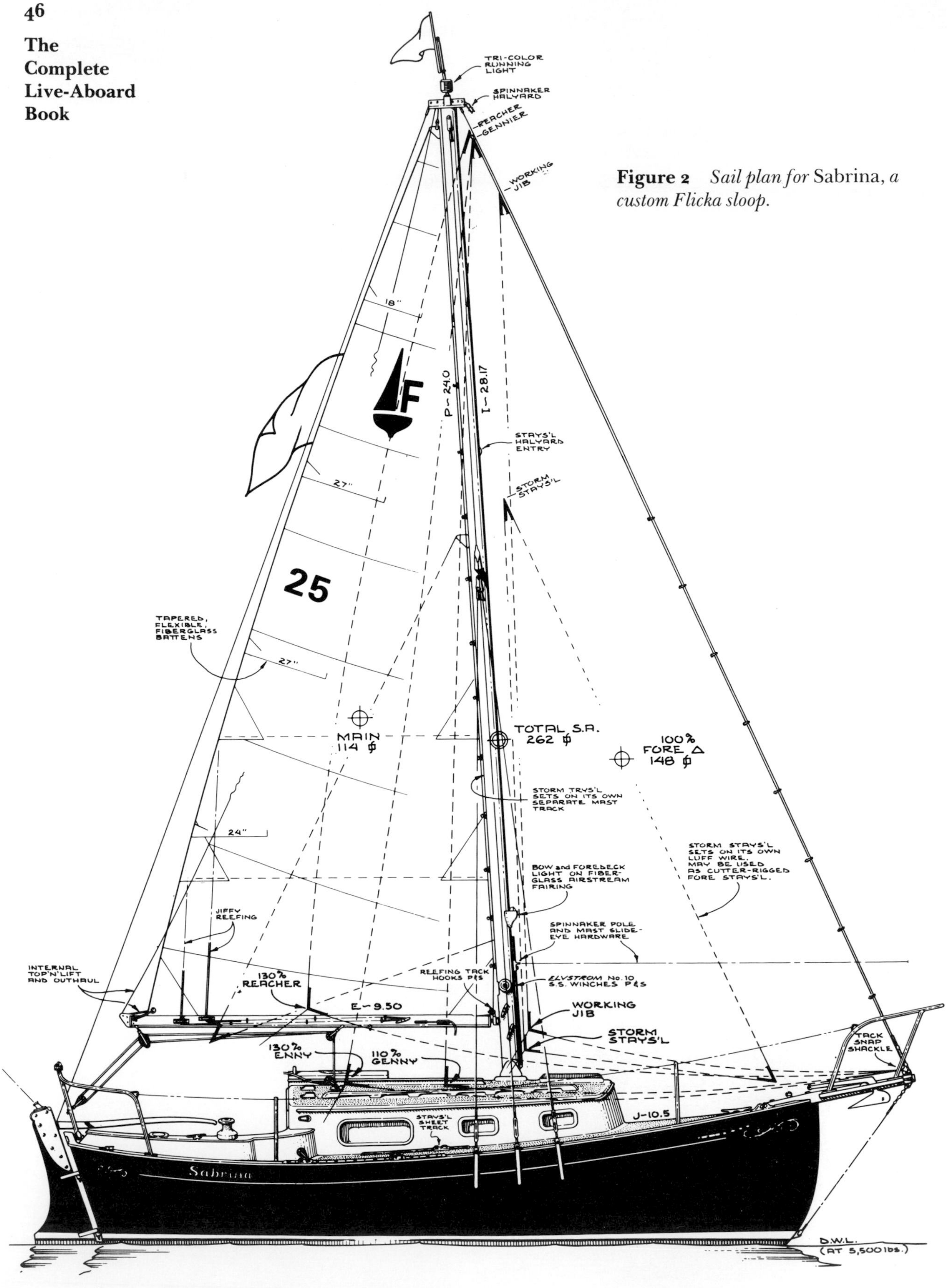

Figure 2 *Sail plan for* Sabrina, *a custom Flicka sloop.*

TRI-COLOR
RUNNING
LIGHT

SPINNAKER
HALYARD

REACHER-
GENNIER

WORKING
JIB

18"

P-240

I-28.17

STAYS'L
HALYARD
ENTRY

STORM
STAYS'L

27"

25

TAPERED,
FLEXIBLE,
FIBERGLASS
BATTENS

27"

MAIN
114 ⏀

TOTAL S.A.
262 ⏀

100%
FORE △
148 ⏀

STORM TRYS'L
SETS ON ITS OWN
SEPARATE MAST
TRACK

24"

STORM STAYS'L
SETS ON ITS OWN
LUFF WIRE.
MAY BE USED
AS CUTTER-RIGGED
FORE STAYS'L.

BOW AND FOREDECK
LIGHT ON FIBER-
GLASS AIRSTREAM
FAIRING

JIFFY
REEFING

SPINNAKER POLE
AND MAST SLIDE-
EYE HARDWARE.

INTERNAL
TOP'N'LIFT
AND OUTHAUL

130%
REACHER

REEFING TACK
HOOKS P&S

ELVSTROM No.10
S.S. WINCHES P&S

WORKING
JIB

TACK
SNAP
SHACKLE

E-9.50

130%
ENNY

110%
GENNY

STORM
STAYS'L

Sabrina

STAYS'L
SHEET
TRACK

J-10.5

D.W.L.
(AT 5,500 lbs.)

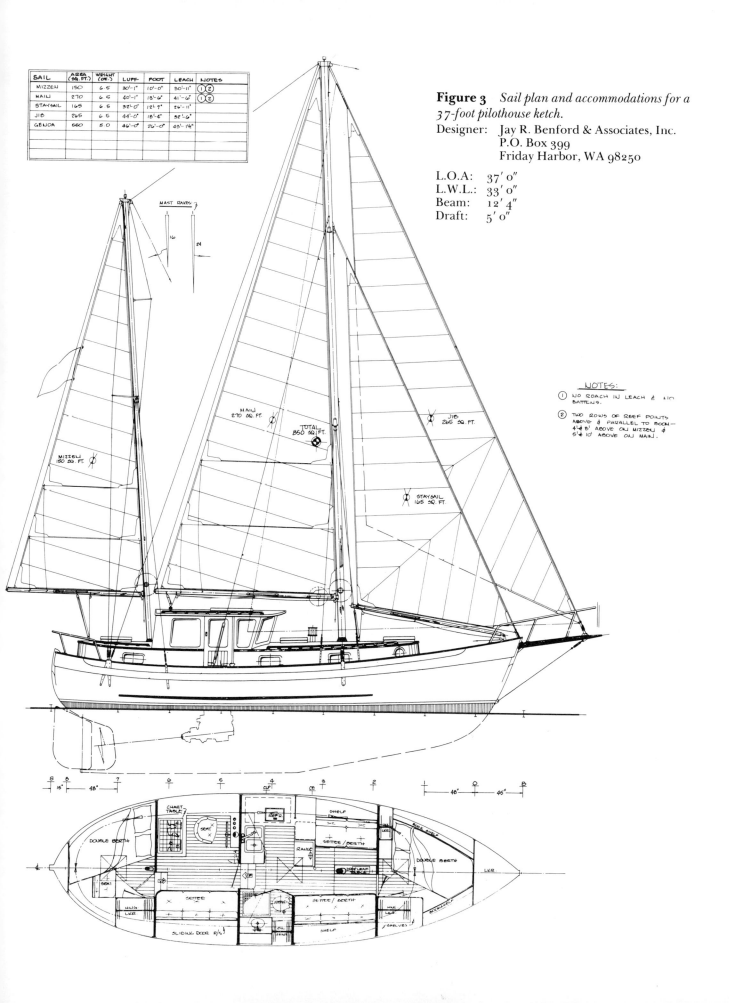

SAIL	AREA (SQ. FT.)	WEIGHT (OZ.)	LUFF	FOOT	LEACH	NOTES
MIZZEN	150	6.5	30'-1"	10'-0"	30'-11"	① ②
MAIN	270	6.5	40'-1"	13'-6"	41'-6"	① ②
STAYSAIL	165	6.5	32'-0"	12'-7"	26'-11"	
JIB	265	6.5	44'-0"	18'-4"	32'-6"	
GENOA	560	5.0	46'-0"	26'-0"	43'-1¼"	

Figure 3 *Sail plan and accommodations for a 37-foot pilothouse ketch.*

Designer: Jay R. Benford & Associates, Inc.
            P.O. Box 399
            Friday Harbor, WA 98250

L.O.A: 37' 0"
L.W.L.: 33' 0"
Beam: 12' 4"
Draft: 5' 0"

NOTES:
① NO ROACH IN LEACH & NO BATTENS.
② TWO ROWS OF REEF POINTS ABOVE & PARALLEL TO BOOM— 4'4 8' ABOVE ON MIZZEN & 5'4 10' ABOVE ON MAIN.

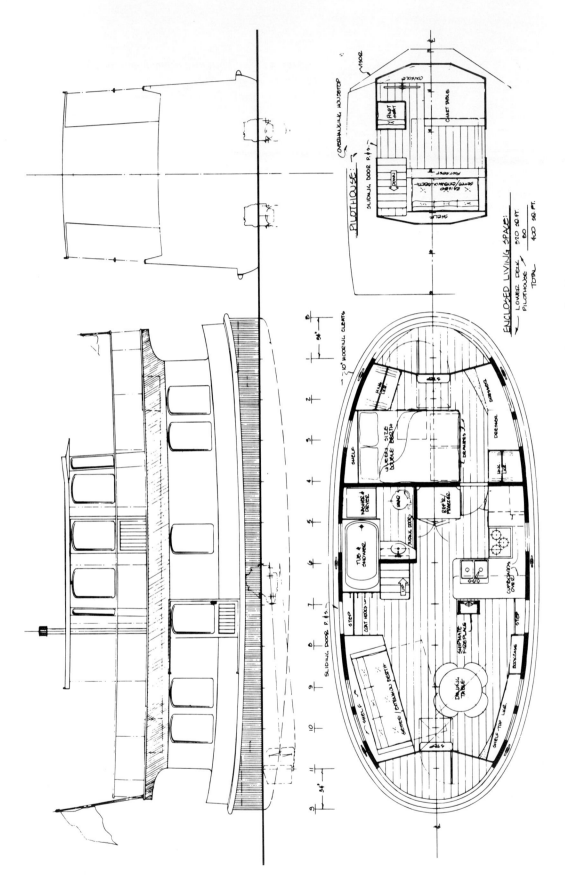

Figure 4 *Profile and arrangement plan for the Friday Harbor Ferry.*

Designer: Jay R. Benford & Associates, Inc.
P.O. Box 399
Friday Harbor, WA 98250

L.O.A.:	34' 0"	Displacement:	23,000#	
L.W.L.:	34' 0"	Water:	300 gal.	
Beam:	14' 0"	Fuel:	200 gal.	
Draft:	2' 3"			

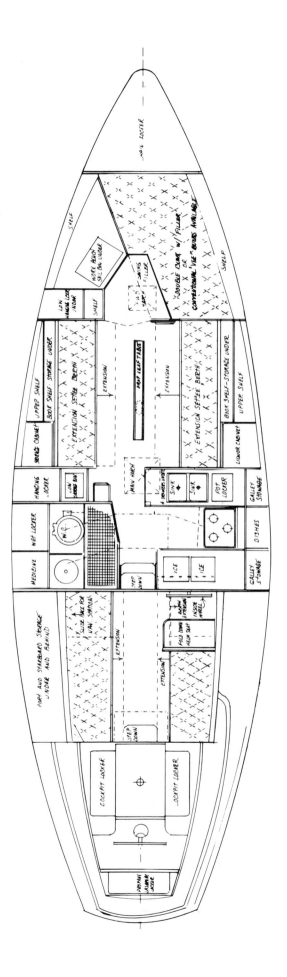

Figure 5 *Arrangement plan for the Shannon Pilot 38.*

Builder: Shannon Boat Co., Inc.
Box 388
19 Broad Common Road
Bristol, RI 02809

L.O.D.:   37′ 9″
L.W.L.:   30′ 10″
Beam: 11′ 6″
Draft: 5′ 0″
Displacement: 18,500#

Figure 6   *Profile and sail plan for the Shannon
Pilot 38.*

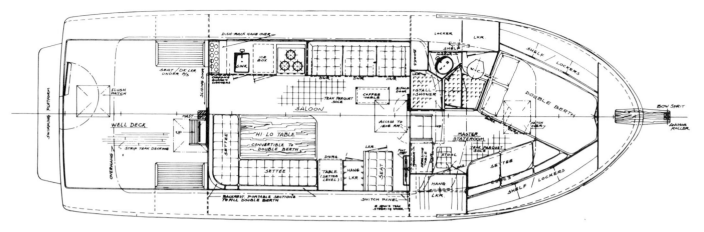

Figure 7 *Accommodation plan for Cheoy Lee Trawler 35.*

Builder: Cheoy Lee Shipyards, Ltd.
                P.O. Box 10040 Cheungshawan
                Kowloon, Hong Kong

L.O.A.:	34′ 11½″	Displacement:	21,000#
Beam:	12′ 0″	Water:	210 gal.
Draft:	3′ 7″	Fuel:	650 gal.

Figure 8 *Profile of the Cheoy Lee Trawler 35.*

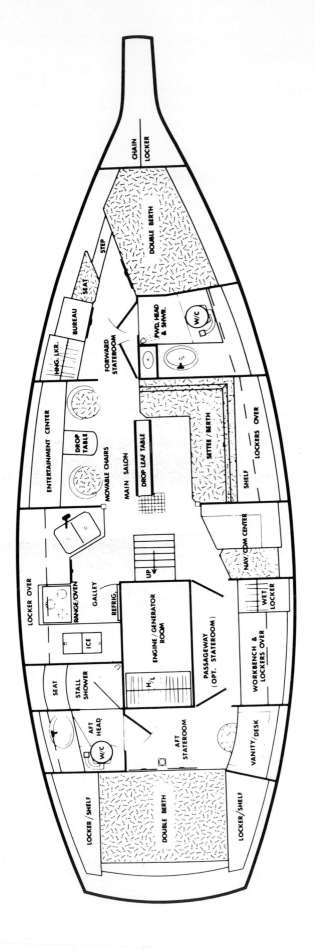

Figure 9 *Arrangement plan for the Endeavour 43 center cockpit version.*

Designer: Robert K. Johnson, N.A.
Builder: Endeavour Yacht Corp.
11700 So. Belcher Rd.
Largo, FL 33540

Figure 10   *The Endeavour 43 under sail.*

Figure 11 *Arrangement, inboard profile and sail plan*
for the Gulfstar 44 cruising sailboat.

Builder: Gulfstar, Inc.
                 6101 45th Street North
                 St. Petersburg, FL 33714

L.O.A.:   44′ 8″
L.W.L.:   35′ 6″
Beam: 13′ 2″
Draft: 5′ 6″
Displacement: 26,000#
Water: 160 gal.
Fuel: 80 gal.

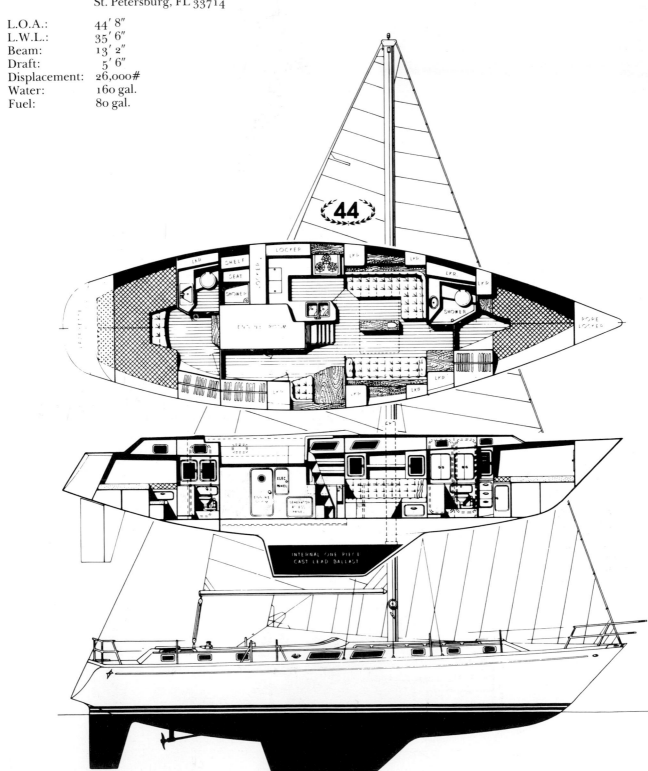

Figure 12 *Profile, inboard profile and arrangement plan for
Bluewater Yachts' 35-foot tri-cabin.*

Builder: Bluewater Yachts
                JEK Industries, Inc.
                Mora, MN 55051

L.O.A.:   35′
Beam: 13′
Draft: 34″
Displacement: 19,000#
Water: 82 gal.
Fuel: 360 gal.

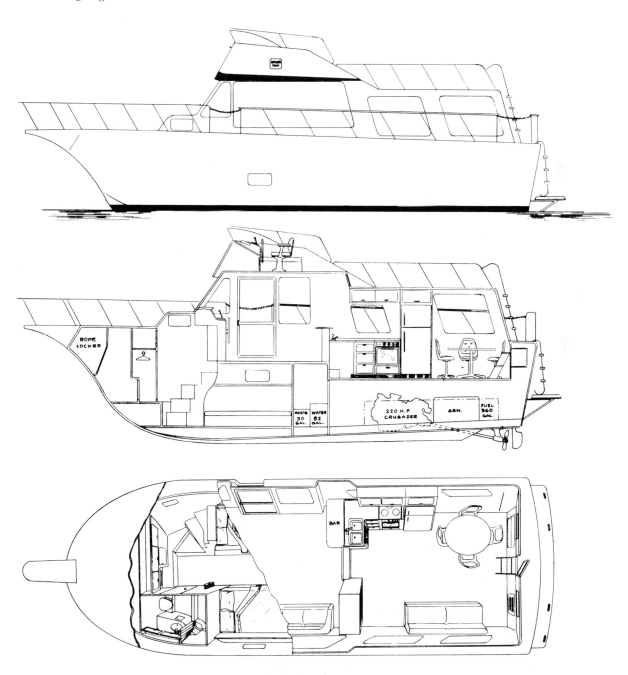

Figure 13 *Inboard profile and arrangement plan for the Niagara 35.*

Designer:	Mark Ellis Design Ltd.
	Oakville, Ontario, Canada
Builder:	Hinterhoeller Yachts Ltd.
	8 Keefer Road
	St. Catharines, Ontario
	Canada L2M 7N9

L.O.A.:	35' 1"
D.W.L.:	26' 8"
Beam:	11' 5"
Draft:	5' 2"
Displacement:	14,000#
Water:	80 gal.
Fuel:	30 gal.

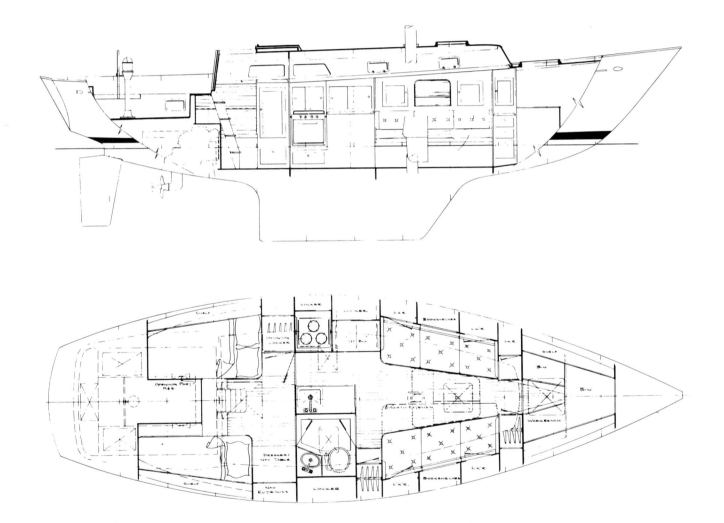

Figure 14 *Profile, inboard profile and arrangement plan for Bluewater Yachts' 40-foot tri-cabin.*

Builder:	Bluewater Yachts
	JEK Industries, Inc.
	Mora, MN 55051

L.O.A.:	40′
Beam:	13′
Draft:	34″
Displacement:	23,000#
Water:	130 gal.
Fuel:	360 gal.

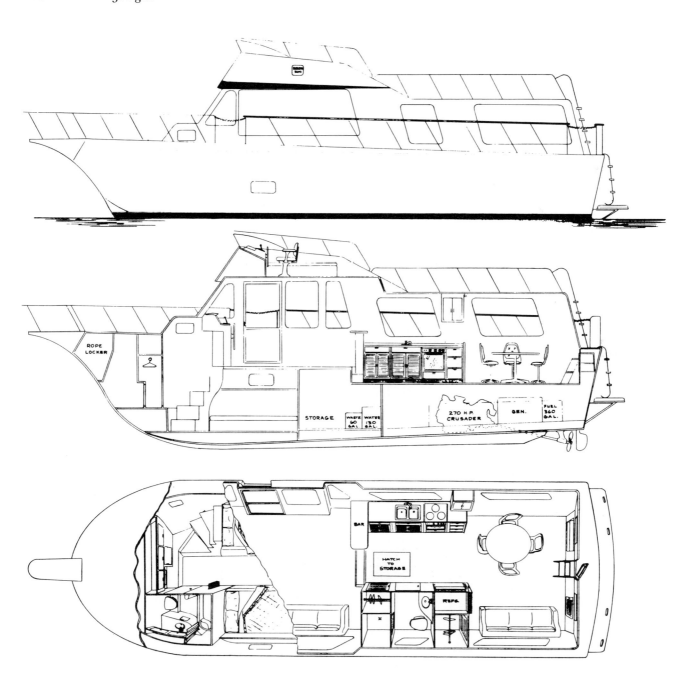

Figure 15 *Sail plan and accommodation plan for the Magellan 39.*

Builder: Magellan Yachts, Ltd.
          1900 S.E. 15th Street
          Fort Lauderdale, FL 33316

L.O.A.:   39′ 9″
L.W.L.:   34′ 0″
Beam: 11′ 10½″
Draft:
   Board up   3′ 6″
   Board down 8′ 6″
Displacement: 18,000#
Water: 130 gal.
Fuel: 140 gal.

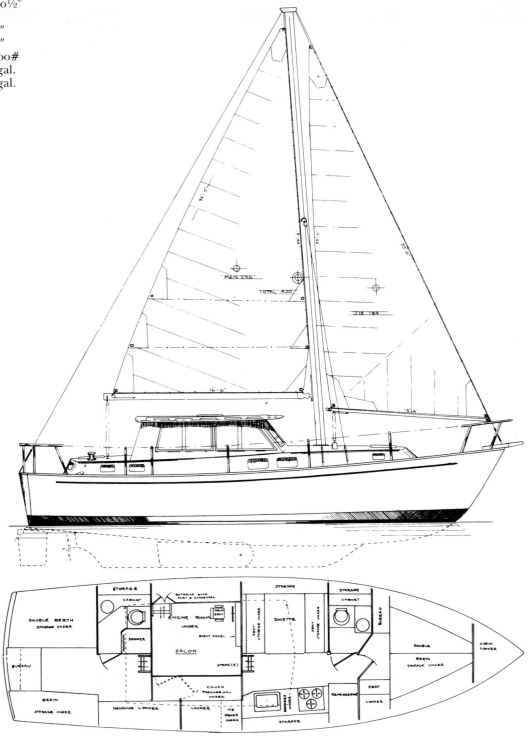

Figure 16 *Sail plan, accommodation and inboard profile of*
Independence 31.

Designer: Bruce King
Builder: Ericson Yachts
1931 Deere Avenue
Santa Ana, CA 92705

L.O.A.: 30′ 11″
L.W.L.: 23′ 11″
Beam: 10′ 5″
Draft: 4′ 11″
Displacement: 11,400#
Water: 45 gal.
Fuel: 35 gal.

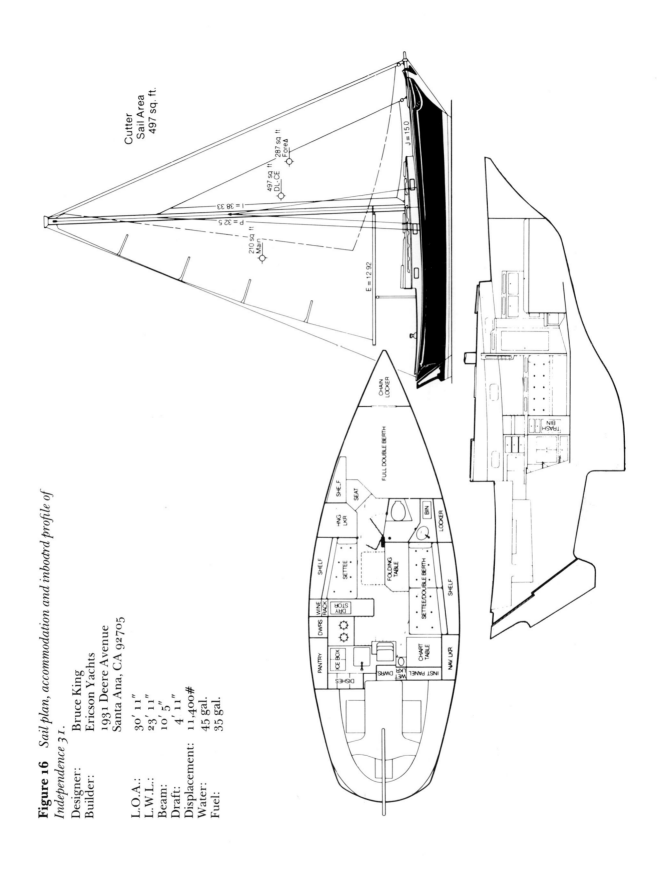

Cutter
Sail Area
497 sq. ft.

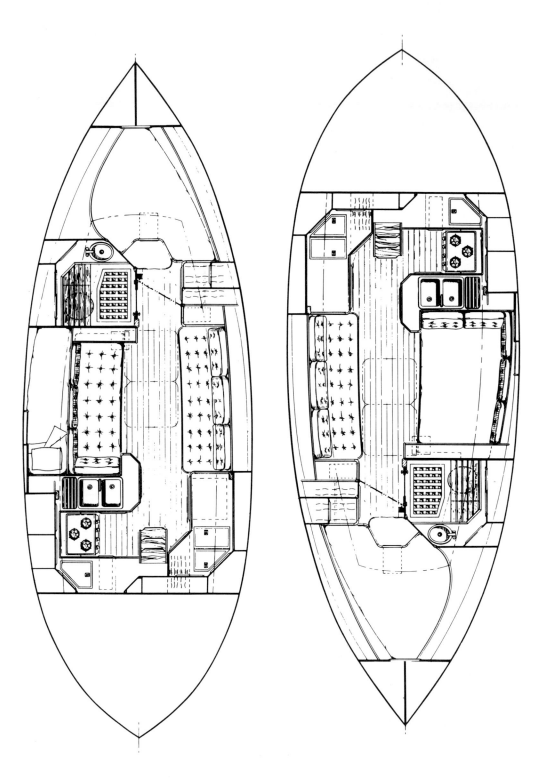

Figure 17 *Two accommodation plans for the Pacific Seacraft Mariah.*
Builder: Pacific Seacraft
            3301 S. Susan Street
            Santa Ana, CA 92704

L.O.A.: 36' 0"   Beam: 10' 8½"
L.O.D.: 30' 11"   Draft: 4' 5"
L.W.L.: 25' 0"   Displacement: 16,000#

Figure 18 *Sail plan for the Pacific Seacraft Mariah.*

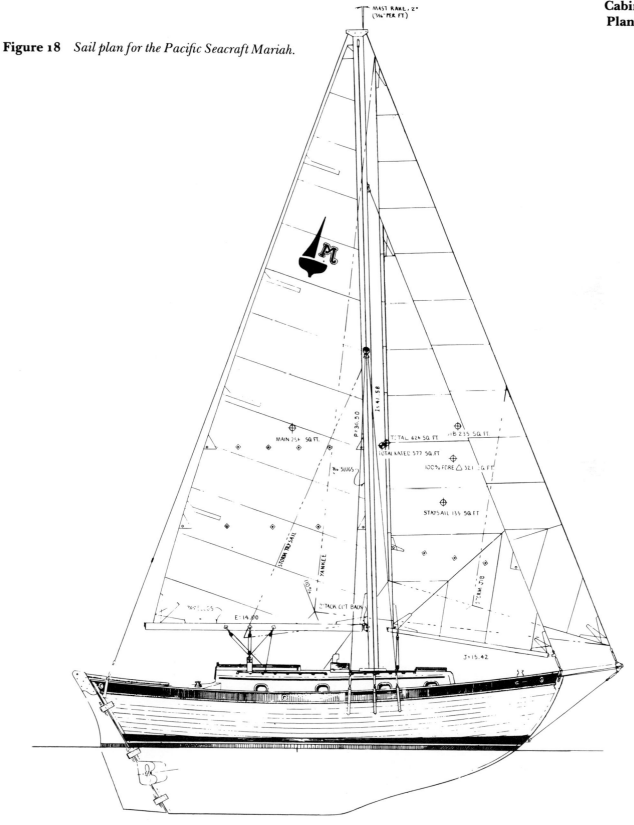

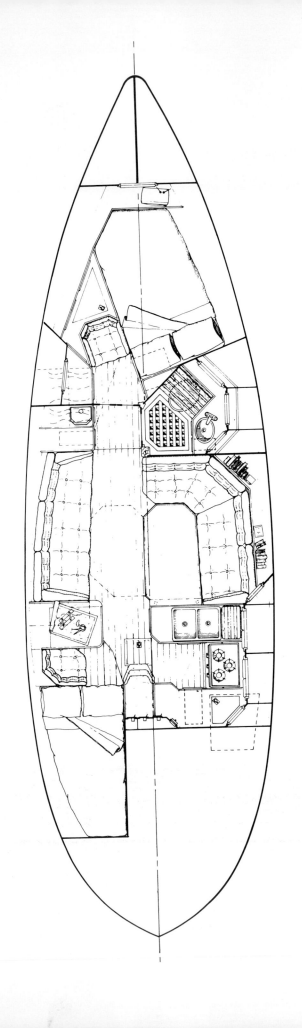

Figure 19 *Accommodation plan for the Pacific Seacraft Crealock 37.*
Designer: William Crealock
Builder: Pacific Seacraft Corp.
3301 S. Susan St.
Santa Ana, CA 92704

Figure 20 *Sail plan for the Pacific Seacraft Crealock 37.*

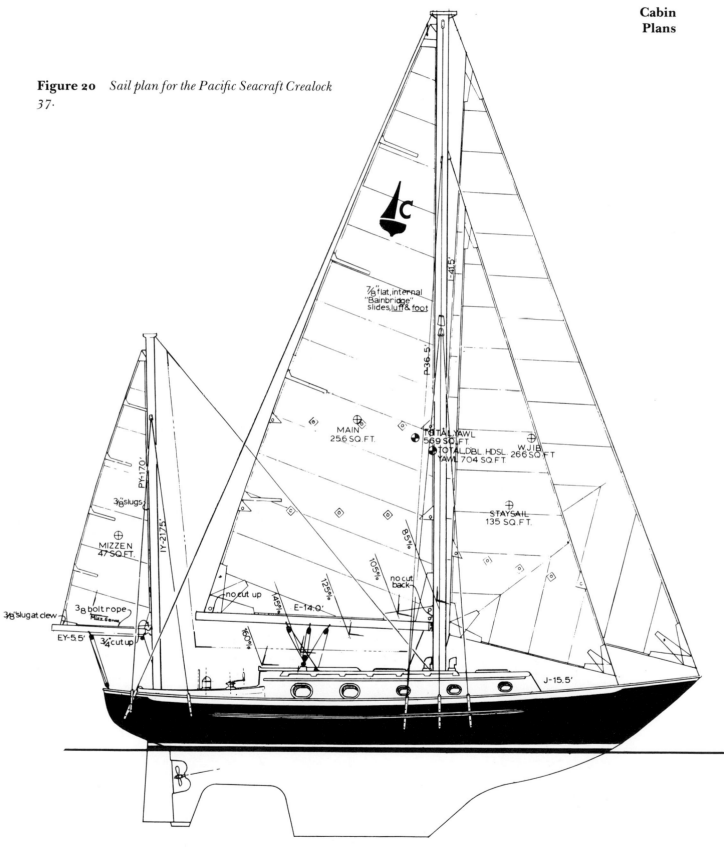

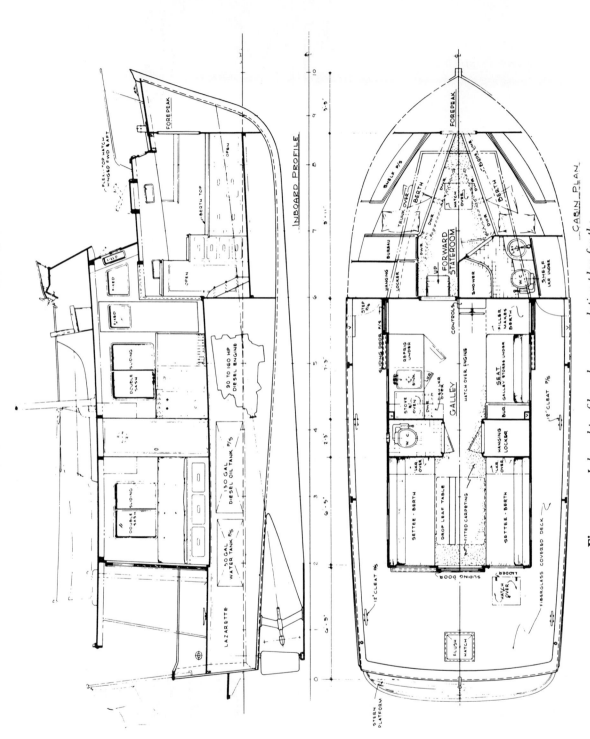

Figure 21 *Inboard profile and accommodation plan for the Meneely 36-foot diesel cruiser.*

Designer: Charles W. Wittholz
Builder: Henry T. Meneely
              616 Third Street
              Annapolis, MD 21403

L.O.A.: 36′ 8″   Displacement: 17,000#
Beam: 13′ 1″   Water: 100 gal.
Draft: 3′ 8″   Fuel: 400 gal.

Figure 22 *Outboard profile of the MeNeely 36-foot diesel cruiser.*

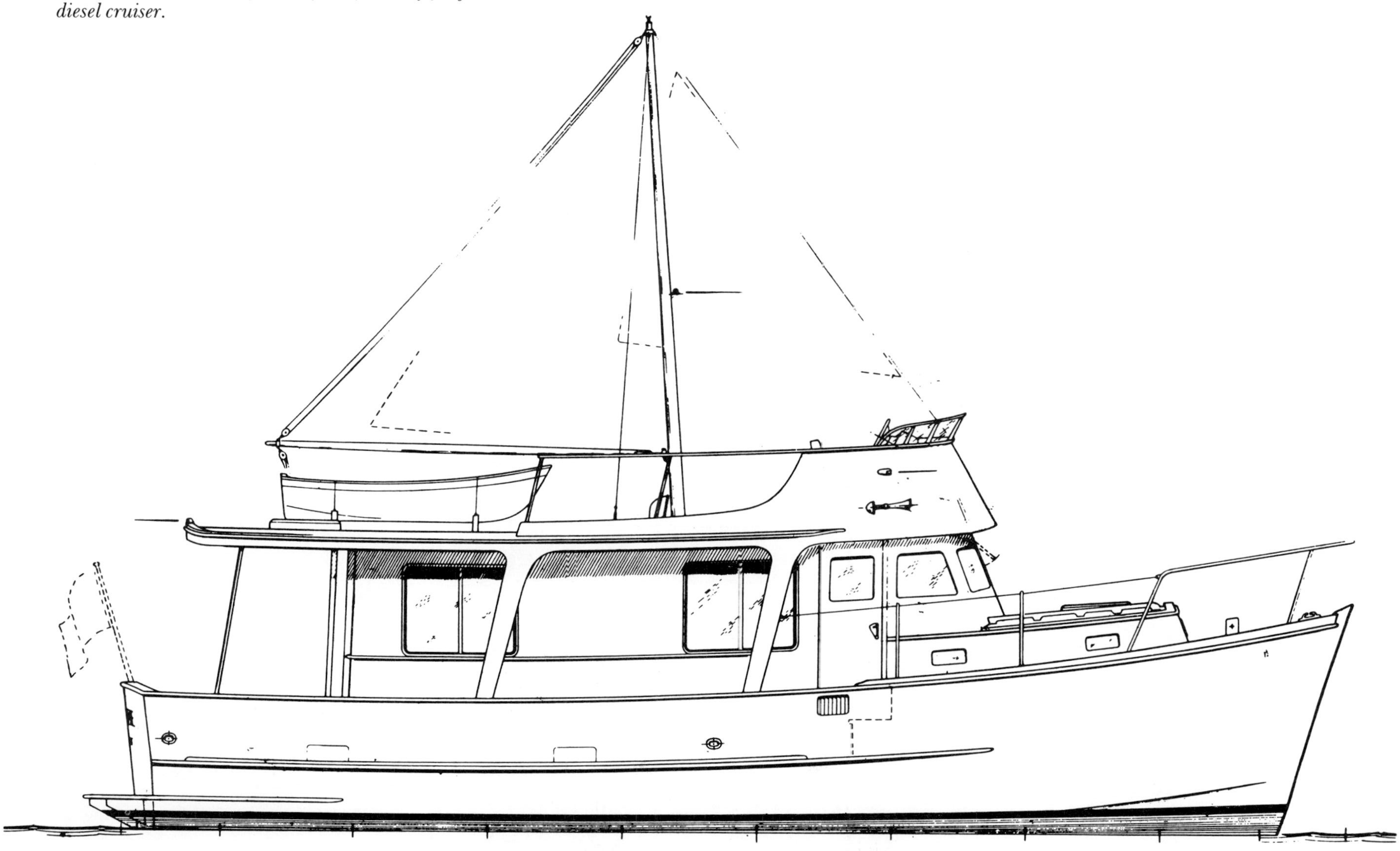

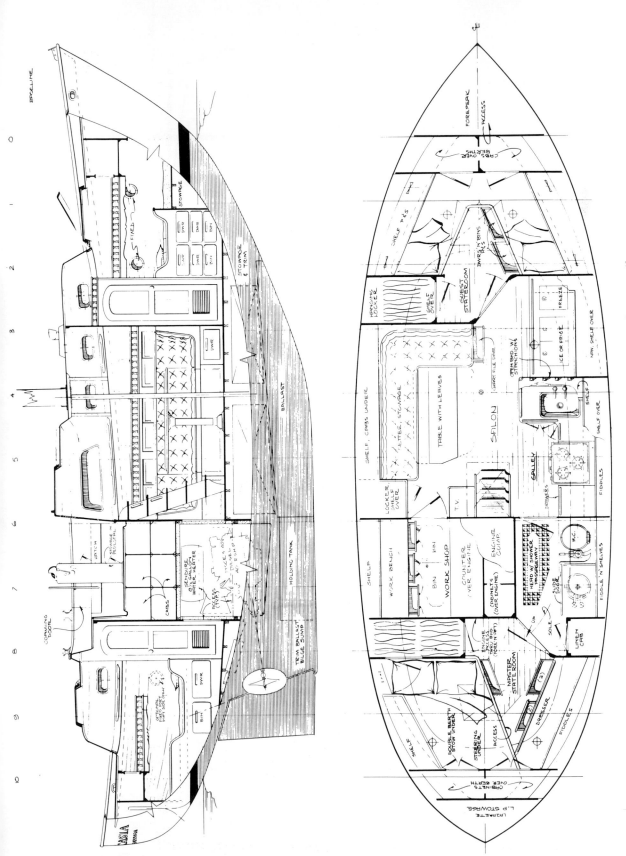

Figure 23 *Accommodation plan for Saga, a 34-foot, 6-inch motorsailer.*

Designer: Bruce P. Bingham

L.O.D.:	34' 6"	Displacement: 23,000#
L.W.L.:	29' 0"	Water: 220 gal.
Beam:	11' 0"	Fuel: 110 gal.
Draft:	5' 5"	

Figure 24 *Sail plan for Saga, our 34-
foot, 6-inch motorsailer.*

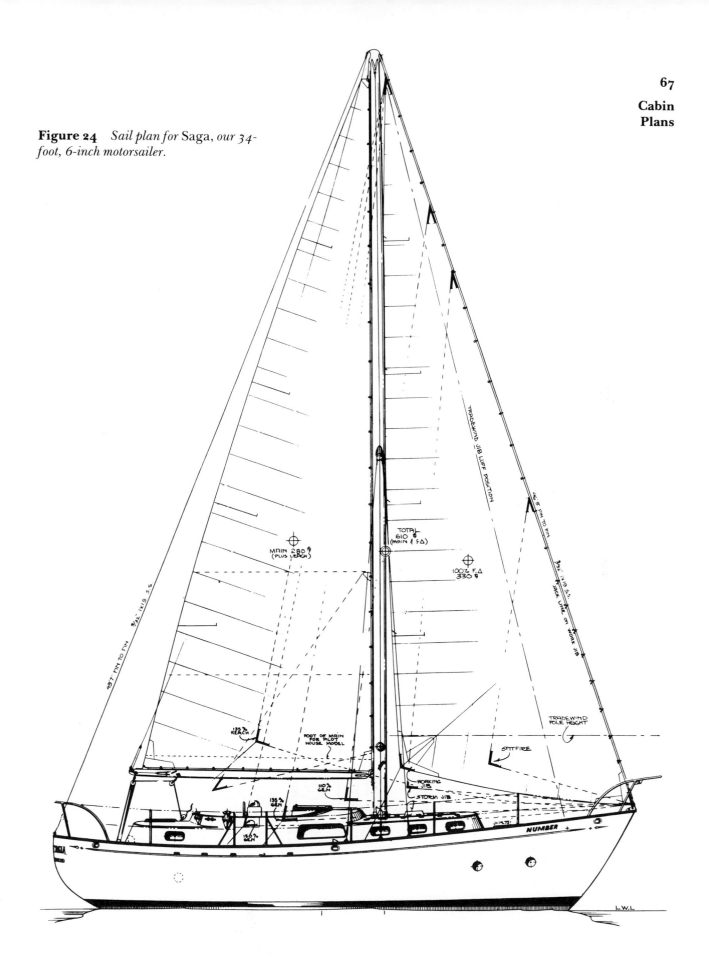

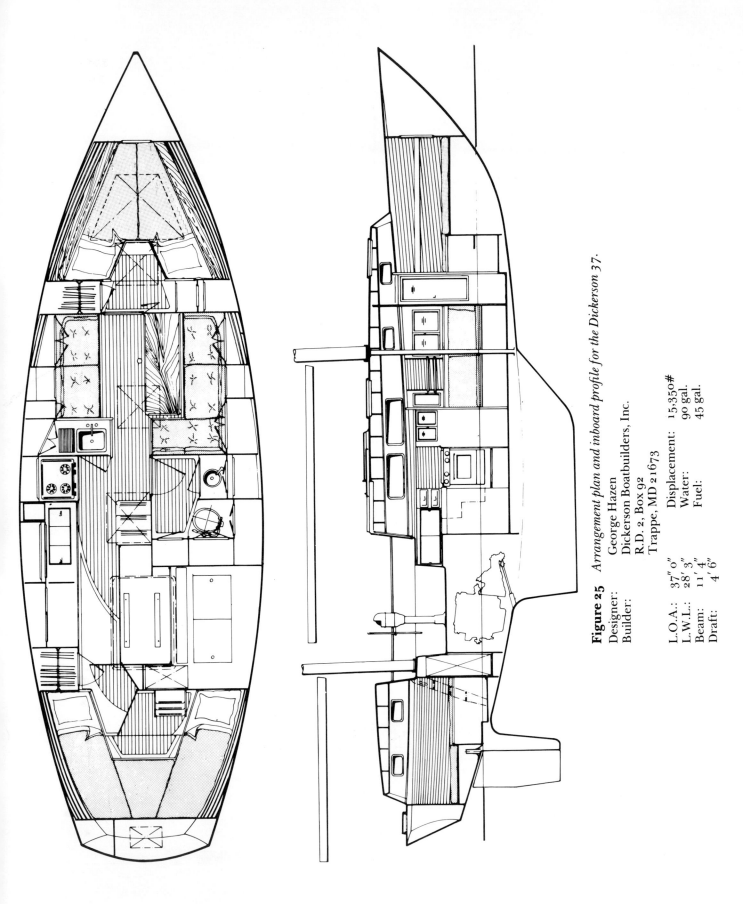

Figure 25 *Arrangement plan and inboard profile for the Dickerson 37.*

Designer: George Hazen
Builder: Dickerson Boatbuilders, Inc.
            R.D. 2, Box 92
            Trappe, MD 21673

Displacement:	15,350#
Water:	90 gal.
Fuel:	45 gal.

L.O.A.:	37" 0"
L.W.L.:	28' 3"
Beam:	11' 4"
Draft:	4' 6"

Figure 26 *Sail plan for the Dickerson 37.*

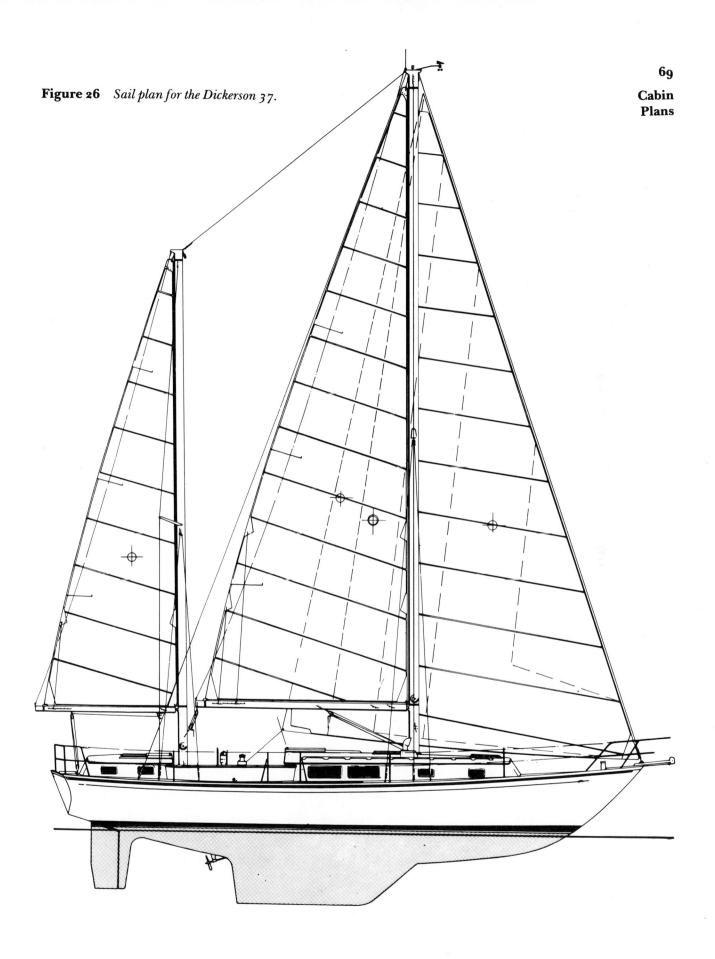

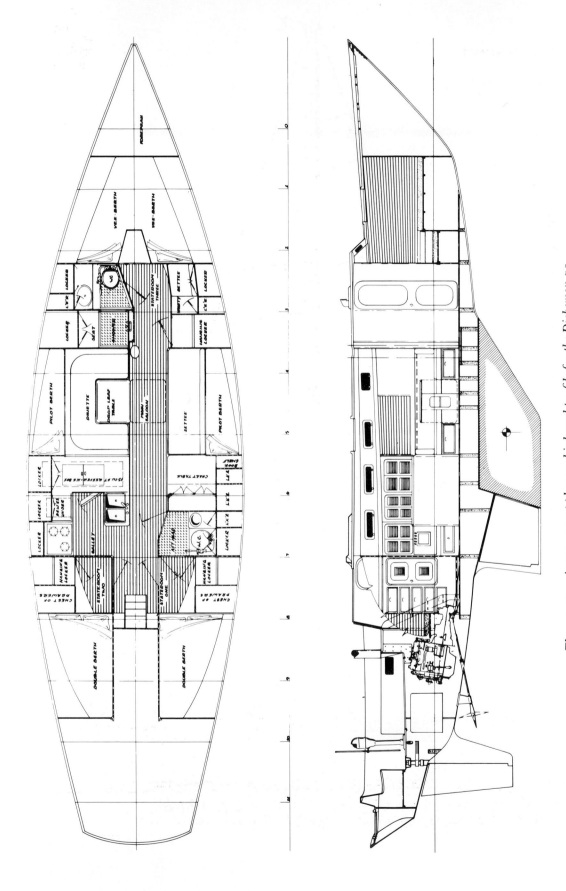

Figure 27 *Arrangement plan and inboard profile for the Dickerson 50.*

Designer:	Kaufman & Associates, Inc.		
Builder:	Dickerson Boatbuilders, Inc.		
	R.D. 2, Box 92		
	Trappe, MD 21673		
L.O.A.:	50' 0"	Draft (CB):	5' 2", 11' 0"
L.W.L.:	38' 9"	Displacement:	33,900#
Beam:	13' 9"	Water:	200 gal.
Draft (keel):	6' 6"	Fuel:	135 gal.

Figure 28 *Sail plan for the Dickerson 50.*

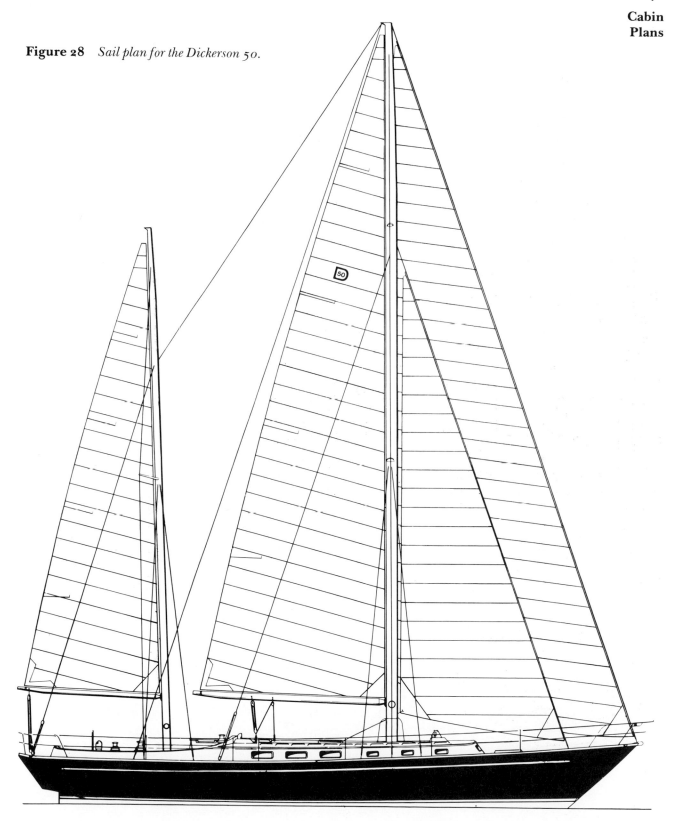

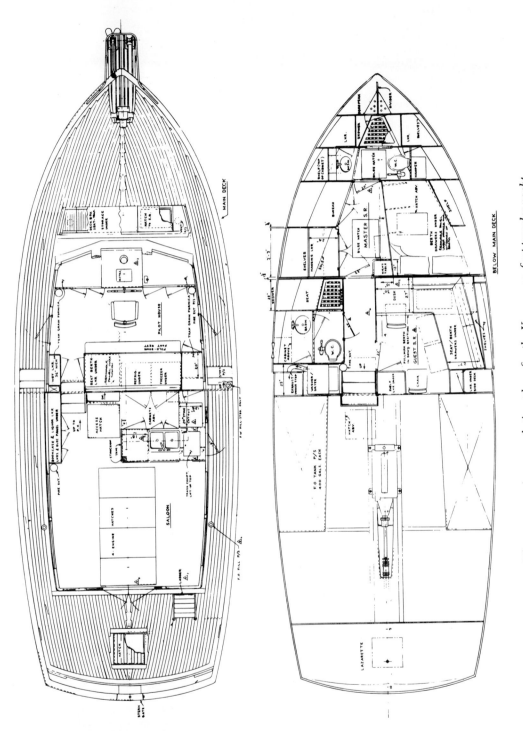

Figure 29 *Accommodation plans for the Krogen 42-foot trawler yacht.*

Designer: James Krogen
Builder: Kadey-Krogen Yachts, Inc.
3333 Rice Street, Suite 7
Miami, FL 33133

L.O.A.:	42' 4"	Displacement:	39,500#
L.W.L.:	39' 6"	Water:	400 gal.
Beam:	15' 0"	Fuel:	700 gal.
Draft:	4' 7"		

Figure 30 *Inboard profiles for the Krogen 42-foot trawler yacht.*

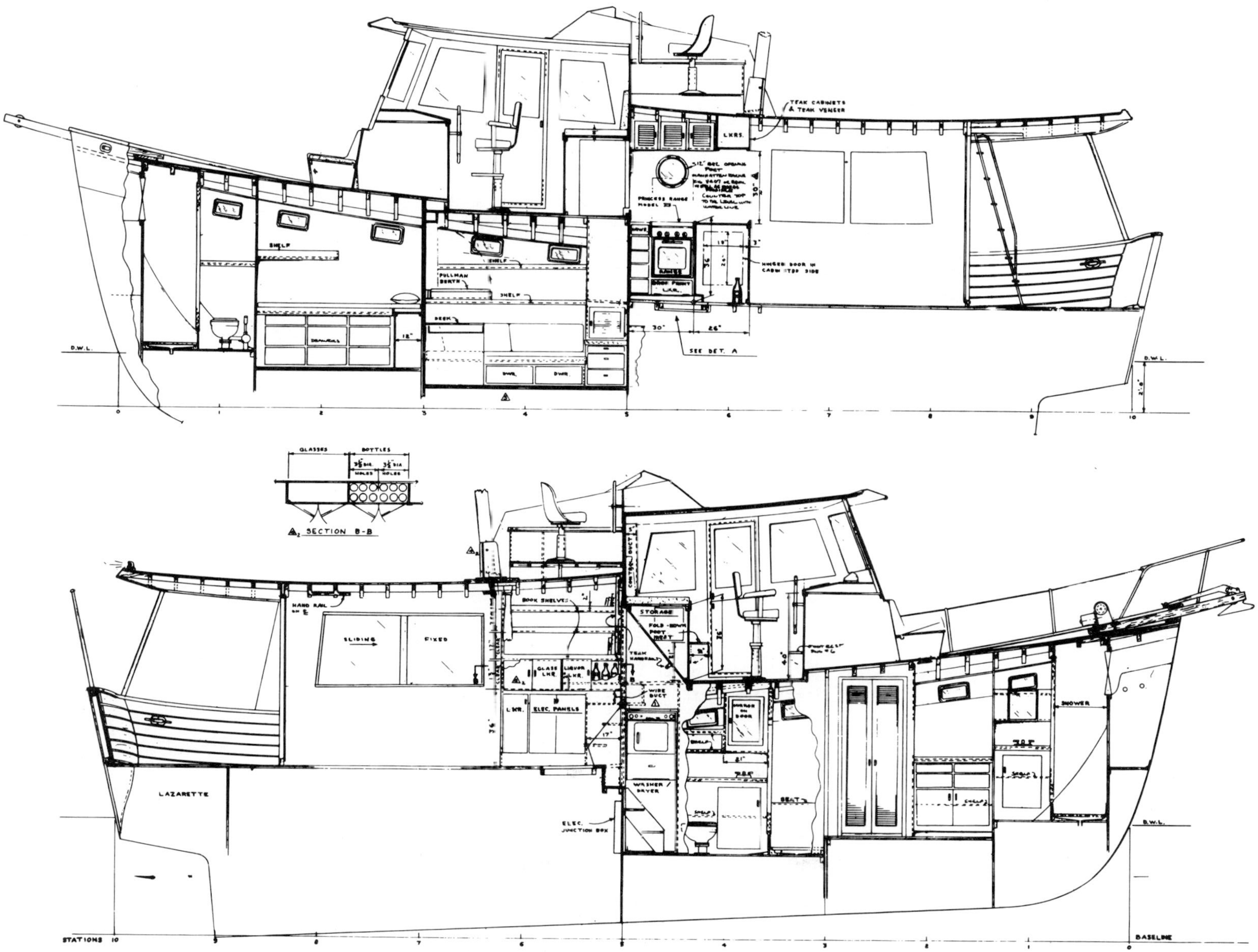

3

Taking the Plunge

"Don't fall overboard in the broker's office"

IF YOU ALREADY own the boat of your dreams you can skip this chapter. But if, like most people, you're looking for a larger or different boat to live aboard, it's important to know how to find it and what pitfalls to avoid.

SHOPPING AROUND

The obvious places to start boat hunting are your local newspapers and in boating magazines. Check display advertisements for new boats and the brokerage sections for used boats. Don't forget the classified sections. On the east coast, one of the best places to look for a used boat is in a monthly newspaper called *Soundings*—a hefty publication with hundreds of listings in every issue.

Another way is to explore the docks at local marinas, talking to people, looking for FOR SALE signs or watching someone sitting in their cockpit looking disgruntled. You also can talk to new boat dealers and check out the listings at brokers' offices (we'll go into this in detail later on).

One rather remote possibility is buying a boat at an auction. This sometimes happens as part of an estate sale (usually listed in a news-

paper) or when a boatyard auctions off a boat on a court order because the owner has failed to pay his yard bill. Of course, the boat may have been neglected for a long time and need extensive work, but sometimes the price makes it worthwhile. With the increase of drug traffic on the high seas, large boats confiscated by federal and state authorities are appearing frequently on the auction block—often at surprisingly low prices.

In areas with a year-round boating season (southern California is a prime example) boat values remain basically stable from month to month. But in places with a real winter, you can often save considerable sums in the off season. We bought *At Last* in Massachusetts in January—covered with snow and stuck in the ice —and saved several thousand dollars over what she would have cost in the spring. Admittedly, it was not much fun boat hunting in freezing weather, and we could not take her for a trial sail. But her bargain price made it worthwhile and more than offset our plane fare from California.

It's best to check out every possibility close to home before going to the expense of traveling around the country. But if you do travel—and frequently it's worth it to find the right boat—

line up as many boats in one area as you can and try to obtain photos and detailed specifications before you board a plane.

Wherever you go to look for a boat, do your homework first. Write for brochures, read all you can about construction materials and methods and check listings or ads in boat buyers' guides so you'll have a good idea of existing market values. Be clear in your own mind about what you want and the top price you can pay. Don't let a smooth-talking salesman push you into a boat you can't afford or one that's too big to handle and maintain. Be realistic about values. There still are bargains around, but not as many as most of us think. Actually, most boats are either fairly priced or overpriced. Those rare birds who will sell a good boat at a low price just to make sure "she gets a good home" are few and far between. An inexpensive boat is most likely going to need a great deal of work—and money—to get her into shape.

Keep in mind that the price of the boat is not your only initial expense. You'll be paying taxes that may vary widely from state to state, documentation and/or registration fees, survey and haul-out costs and travel expenses or cost of delivery if the boat must be moved. When you look at the price of a boat, add *at least* 10 percent to the buying price to reach the true final cost.

Buying a New Boat

When you buy a new stock boat, most likely you will purchase it through a dealer who represents the manufacturer. Once a company establishes a dealership network, it will not undercut a dealer and sell directly to you. In my opinion (and some will disagree) dealers are a pretty nefarious lot. I've known a few who were conscientious and cared about their customers, but they seemed to be the exception, not the rule.

Boat shows are among the best places to inspect and compare what manufacturers are offering. They can be fun if you are slightly deaf, have a well-honed sense of humor and are rea-

sonably sure of your buying goals. They are no place for a babe-in-the-woods with a fat checkbook and an eager heart. List beforehand in a notebook all your requirements and all the questions you need to ask. Don't trust your memory! Many questions will answer themselves as you poke around inside lockers and lift the sole to inspect the bilges. If anyone objects to a close scrutiny, your next question should be, "What are you trying to hide?"

Some manufacturers send company representatives to boat shows who are generally more knowledgeable than the local dealer about technical details and construction methods. Try to talk to him if you can. A dealer is apt to ask how you plan to use the boat so he can convince you that his boat line is perfect for you. You can count on every boat you look at being "an ideal live-aboard boat." If it's a sailboat, it may also be touted as a "world cruiser."

I hate to sound negative about dealers, since some are hard-working, honest people. But even they admit that many dealers could just as well be used car salesmen for all they know and care about boats. Several manufacturers have told me they have difficulty finding good dealers. So be careful. Don't let a smiling wheeler-dealer talk you into something you really don't want.

One couple in North Carolina bought a lovely new sloop from a dealer in Annapolis, Maryland. He was friendly and helpful up to the moment he had their check. Then he informed them that since their boat was the least expensive model he carried, he "couldn't waste any more of his time talking to them." And he didn't! They wanted the boat badly enough not to cancel the order and were able to work directly with the company, although it cost them a small fortune in telephone calls since the builder was in California. If you do have problems with a dealer, don't hesitate to contact the manufacturer. It is your money, and in the final analysis it's the builder's reputation that's on the line.

In theory, the dealer is the link between you and the company. He should make sure the boat is delivered the way you've ordered it and it's up to him to correct any mistakes. If the boat arrives with the wrong bilge pump installed or the wrong color gelcoat on the decks, the dealer should take care of it himself (and it's *his* responsibility to deal with the company) —or at least give you a credit on the final payment.

Note that I said "in theory." In practice, it may be a different story, depending on the integrity of the dealer. The best advice is to make sure everything agreed upon is in writing. Be sure to stipulate that the final payment is subject to the boat passing a survey and meeting your stated requirements.

Not all new boats are on display at boat shows, of course. Many models can only be seen at dealer showrooms or at the builder's shop. A few companies only sell directly to the customer, which eliminates the expense of the dealer/middleman. It's a good idea to visit the factory anyway, if it's possible. Most companies welcome the chance to show you around the plant. Beware of those who don't. It's an excellent opportunity for you to see first-hand how the boats are built, what methods are used, how much quality goes into assemblies that are often hidden in the finished boat and to have your questions answered by a "knowledgeable" company representative.

Determining the actual price of a new boat for purposes of comparison is always difficult. Base price and sail-away prices are meaningless until you know exactly what is included. Definitions of "base" and "sail-away" vary widely from company to company. Even if you narrow it down to basic components, price alone doesn't tell the whole story. Two boats that appear similar in their brochures may vary in price by several thousand dollars. The difference may be in quality of construction and gear or may be that one company is waging a worldwide advertising campaign and has high overhead, while the other is relatively small with no dealer network and minimum advertising. Only a close inspection of each boat will demonstrate which is the better value.

Deciding on options is another difficult task. Sometimes you can start out with what appears to be a reasonably priced boat and double the cost by the time you've waded through the options list, choosing one item after another. Proceed slowly and think carefully about each option before you make that little checkmark! Decide if you can easily install the item yourself at a considerable savings.

Cockpit winches on a sailboat, for example, are expensive but necessary little devils. Installing them is a matter of drilling holes in the cockpit coaming, applying bedding compound and through-bolting the winch.

This means someone must crawl around inside a cockpit locker or quarterberth in an uncomfortable position to tighten up the bolts. But it's a job most people—even with modest skills—can handle. Your cost is the winch, the nuts and bolts, a tube of compound and a few hours of your time. If the company installs the winches you're probably paying retail price for the winch and an inflated rate for installation, including the worker's salary as he walks to the parts room to pick up the winch, carries it back to the boat, returns to the shop for bolts he forgot and stops for his coffee break.

Another example might be the anchor and

line—it will undoubtedly cost more on the options list than it costs off the shelf at a chandlery. And often, by shopping around or buying the bulk of your gear at one place, you can wrangle a discount of 25 percent to 30 percent, even though you're a retail customer.

On the other hand, if you want something like a teak cap rail around the bulwarks—a very difficult piece of joinerwork (See Plate 1) it's better to let the company do that job, overhead and all, than attempt it yourself.

Probably the biggest disadvantage to ordering a new boat (unless you buy one on a dealer's lot or take home a boat show demonstrator) is the waiting time between placing the order and taking delivery. This can be as long as a year, even two years. Anyone who's been through it will agree the waiting is the hardest part of all. You will have to put down a deposit to ensure your place in the assembly line. This is where trouble can start.

The boatbuilding industry is a tough business. Seemingly healthy companies go bankrupt with alarming frequency. The company starts having financial difficulties, sometimes using deposits on future boats to complete the ones already on the production line, hoping that more deposits will come in to cover the next batch of boats.

People have lost their deposit money that way when the company went belly-up. Instead of enjoying their new boat, they had to spend money on lawyers and time in court. When placing a deposit, make sure the money is held in a trust or escrow account so the company cannot touch it until construction on *your* boat has begun. It's not a bad idea to have your attorney look over the contract before plunking down any hard-earned cash.

Charter First

Bruce suggests anyone buying a new boat should charter it—or one like it—for at least a weekend. A two-hour demonstration sail is better than nothing, but it doesn't give you enough time to put the boat through any kind of testing. A weekend or longer will allow you

Plate 1 *Some tasks are better left to the builder, like this intricate bulwark cap on a Cherubini 44.*

to put your prospective boat through her paces in a variety of conditions. It'll also give you enough time to poke around, see how things work and to learn if she still feels comfortable and "right" after a few nights aboard.

Are the bunks wide enough at the foot? Is the settee back at a comfortable angle? Is the galley counter at a convenient height? Is the head large enough to be functional? Is it possible to turn around in the head without opening the door?

Hundreds of little things will become apparent after you've spent some time on the boat—things you probably would have missed in only a few hours with the dealer blowing smoke in your ear about what a perfect little vessel she is.

The money spent on a charter will be worth every penny and some dealers even discount the charter fee from the purchase price. As a rule of thumb, expect to pay about one percent of the boat's price for a weekend charter.

Buying a Used Boat

As noted earlier, my experience is you get more boat for your money by buying a *good* used boat. Its initial cost is considerably lower than a new boat and you usually get many extras included in the price—electronics, a spare anchor, docklines and fenders, screens for ports and hatches, cockpit awning, etc. Buying such a boat without a broker requires a good working knowledge of existing market values. Unless you're very sure of the marketplace and can handle the paperwork, you're probably better off using a broker than going it alone.

A broker handles used boats (as opposed to a dealer, who sells new ones) and serves as a go-between for you and the seller. Like dealers, there are good ones and bad ones, although I think the proportion of good ones here is much higher.

Tell the broker you want a live-aboard boat and how much money you are willing to spend. He will provide several listing books for you to look through. He should be familiar with the listed boats that are local. Many brokers are associated with a large firm or listing service that has several offices up and down the coast or throughout the country. This is a real advantage since it expands your choices considerably.

The broker will set up appointments for you to see boats, make phone calls to check the status of any listings, present your offers to the owner and handle all the necessary paperwork for transfer of title, documentation, etc. Most brokers can help you arrange financing and insurance. A good broker *earns* his commission (which is paid by the seller). He can probably suggest several surveyors in the area for you to choose from.

Remember, the survey is *your* responsibility and *your* expense. It's not the broker's job to guarantee the condition of the boat. He can give advice and act as a buffer between you and the seller should problems arise, but the final decision must be yours.

PAYING CASH

There's much to be said in favor of paying cash for a boat—even if it means buying a smaller, less expensive and, most likely, a used boat. The freedom of not owing anybody anything and the knowledge that she may be a bit creaky but she's all yours is worth the sacrifice. Bruce and I never financed a boat and we never will.

When we moved aboard we paid off all our debts and decided not to take on any new ones. I've always been glad we stuck by that decision. It's a good satisfying feeling—one you can't place a dollar value on.

FINANCING

It's easier to finance a new boat than a used one. But it's not always easy. Your credit rating must be solid and well-established. It's easier to finance "necessities"—a house, a car or furniture—than a "luxury" like a boat. Make no mistake, it *is* considered a luxury. Tell a banker you're going to dump the apartment and your old lifestyle to live on a boat (especially if you're young) and he will instantly see you disappearing over the horizon with his collateral.

If you are able to get financing, be careful not to get in over your head. Make sure you can afford the boat payments on top of slip rental and maintenance. While it will tie you down for several years, it is a way of getting the boat you want and living aboard it *now*.

In order to finance a boat, you must also insure it. No bank or finance company will settle for less. This is yet another expense that must be absorbed. Marine insurance policies are valid only within certain geographical areas during specified seasons. For instance, it's virtually impossible to get insurance for a boat that will be in certain areas of Baja California during the chubasco or hurricane season. The policies state in which harbors the boat must stay in in order to remain covered. As long as the boat is financed—and therefore insured— you will be limited in your cruising range.

You can arrange financing through a bank or a finance company that specializes in boat loans. Interest rates may be slightly lower at a bank, but banks tend to be more conservative about making boat loans; most will not lend as much money as a finance company and then only over five to seven-year terms. Finance companies will give up to 10 years and some even 15 years.

Banks may take several weeks to process a loan; most credit companies specializing in boat loans will give you an answer within two days. It's a good idea to get a line of credit approved in advance. Once approved for a loan, you can get a letter of intent that will guarantee the stated interest rate for 30 days.

Interest rates can vary. When you start shopping for a loan, you will hear the expression "Rule of 78" bandied about. Companies using the Rule of 78 will quote you an annual percentage rate that is the average interest rate you will pay if the loan goes to its full term.

However, statistics show that boat loans are usually paid off early. Under the Rule of 78, the interest rate is much higher in the early years, decreasing towards the end of the term. That's a way of charging a pre-payment penalty without actually calling it that.

Simple interest is a fixed percentage paid on the unpaid balance. The interest rate remains the same, although the amount decreases with the principal balance. If the bank or finance company has a pre-payment penalty and you pay the loan off early, the cost will be about the same as if you had gone to a company using the Rule of 78. A simple interest loan at a competitive rate with no pre-payment penalty is your best bet, although it will take some shopping around to find such financing.

The down payment on a new boat is generally 20 percent. A used boat will require 25 percent to 30 percent down. Loan terms are usually shorter for used boats but in any case will vary, depending on the particular boat and your personal credit rating.

INSURANCE

If your boat is financed, then it must be insured. If you own her free and clear, insurance becomes a personal decision. I believe most land dwellers are over-insured.

Any insurance is expensive and yacht insurance is near the top. I would not try to dissuade owners from insuring their boats if they feel uncomfortable without it. But I should point out that a surprising number of live-aboards and cruising people do not carry insurance. The *majority* of people making world cruises in small boats carry no coverage at all. Coverage beyond coastal areas is frightfully expensive and sometimes impossible to obtain.

If the choice is between staying home and keeping the boat safely insured or going on an adventure with the risk of being uninsured, I'll take the adventure every time! Many do try to keep a small fund set aside for emergencies— a form of "self-insurance." Many put the money they would ordinarily spend on insurance in a high-yield savings or money market fund and beat the insurance companies at their own game.

If you do insure, it's best to buy a yacht policy from an agent or company specializing in marine insurance. Many large companies have a small marine department that mainly handles outboard runabouts, ski boats and small sailboats. In a total loss, these policies usually pay Blue Book value, likely to be far below the actual value of a live-aboard/cruising boat loaded with expensive gear. Be sure your boat is insured for a specific amount and not simply "current market value."

A general liability policy will cover claims in a civil court, but it may not cover you in a suit under the admiralty laws—under which most water-related claims will be filed. It probably won't cover the cost of removing a sunken boat from the center of a channel, for example. The best coverage is "P&I" (Protection and Indemnity) insurance, written specifically for a yacht. "Protection" means the insurance will cover legal fees for defense in an admiralty court, "Indemnity" means the policy will pay the court award.

Yacht insurance, as explained earlier, is always limited to certain geographical boundaries. Riders to cover additional areas may or may not be given, depending on where you want to go. You will be charged additional premiums for extending the limits of navigation.

Be sure you get all the credits or discounts you deserve. Most companies charge lower rates for completing a Coast Guard or Power Squadron safety course, for having a diesel instead of a gasoline engine and for equipping the boat with safety gear such as VHF radio, radar or Loran.

Virtually all insurance companies insist on a survey. They will either send out their own surveyor or give you a list of surveyors whose reports they will accept. Most will require a new survey every couple of years to be sure the boat is being cared for properly and holding her stated value.

YACHT SURVEYS

Before putting money down on any boat, have it surveyed by an independent yacht surveyor *you* have hired. It's accepted practice to make an offer for a used boat contingent upon the boat passing a survey. Your deposit is put in escrow or held by the broker until the boat is hauled out and checked over. If the surveyor finds major problems that will be expensive to remedy, you may decide it's not worth it. Or you may obtain a repair estimate and make a new, lower offer.

It's not wise to survey a boat yourself, no matter how knowledgeable you may be. Since you've already decided you want her, you're no longer an impartial judge. A surveyor is impartial and is trained to search for potential trouble spots you're likely to overlook.

The broker, the bank or the insurance company can probably recommend several local surveyors. Ask around the docks and boatyards to find out who's highly regarded and who isn't. When you decide on a surveyor, ask to see copies of other surveys he's done. They will be a good indication of how thorough he is.

It's a good idea to have the boat hauled for the survey, particularly if it's a wooden boat. The condition of the bottom planking and keel can be checked and, in the case of a wood boat, an inspection for worms can be made. Once hauled, a surveyor can inspect the boat's rudder, propeller and shaft bearing and/or struts, the condition of the zinc anodes and look for signs of electrolysis in any metal fittings below the waterline.

Surveying should not be limited to used boats. Even a brand-new boat may have trouble spots. The surveyor can check the hull-to-deck attachment, through-hull fittings, chainplate installation, the attachment of deck hardware and the wiring installation—to name just a few things. Ask the dealer to have the builder save the plugs from holes cut for through-hull fittings so the hull thickness and fiberglass layup can be examined.

The surveyor will give you a written report stating the overall condition of the boat and a list of defects or problems he has found. Some surveyors will state what they believe to be a fair market price. Occasionally a surveyor will quote you a flat fee for a survey. More likely he will charge you on an hourly or daily basis that will include writing his report. If he must travel out of town to get to the boat, expect to pay his time and traveling expenses as well.

Some people will balk at the cost of a survey, believing they can save money by doing it themselves. This usually is a mistake. If you do buy the boat, it will be easier to finance or insure with a comprehensive surveyor's report. And you will know at the outset the boat's deficiencies—major and minor—and what maintenance expenses you must anticipate.

In my opinion, money spent on a good survey is *always* well spent. If you don't buy the boat because of the surveyor's report, it may seem like "lost money" to pay his fee. But the only sensible attitude is that it was a small price to pay for avoiding a possibly disastrous investment.

Marina or Mooring?

"Home is where you hang the hook"

4

"SORRY, NO LIVE-ABOARDS!"

As more and more people forsake hearth and home and take to their boats, those words are being uttered with increasing frequency. While moving aboard generally implies going cruising, it "ain't necessarily so." A considerable number of live-aboards hold shore jobs and save their money until they *can* afford to cut the dock lines permanently. Some, who have been cruising for several years and are ready to settle down for awhile, are not ready to move back ashore. Others cruise for part of the year and spend the balance of their time in one place.

Most of us maintain at least a post office box or some kind of an address that we call "home port." Everybody has to be somewhere and live-aboards have three basic choices: at a marina, on a mooring or on our own anchor. Let's explore the advantages and drawbacks of each choice.

MARINAS

The primary hurdle is finding one that allows live-aboards in the first place. One state, Ha-waii, has passed a law banning *all* live-aboards, period. Other states haven't gone that far, but most marinas have at least some restrictions when they do allow living aboard. Generally speaking, the bigger and poshier the marina, the less inclined it is to permit live-aboards. Smaller, "homey" marinas are usually more lenient.

My preference is for a small marina, anyway. While we try always to keep our boat looking shipshape, occasions arise when we're working on a big project requiring more space than deck or cabin allows. It's nice to use part of the dock as a work platform. Some fancy marinas simply won't tolerate this sort of activity, even for a few hours.

Southern California seems to be one of the most crowded and most expensive boating areas in the United States. Santa Barbara's one marina had a three-year waiting list when we were there and I understand it's now up to five years. One marina in Dana Point restricts the number of slips they make available to live-aboards and you must pass a stringent interview before you'll even be considered. Bruce's brother lived aboard a *Mariah* in Newport

Beach and it costs him almost twice what we paid in Florida for transient dockage. (Transient dockage is invariably higher than monthly or yearly dock space.)

Along the Intracoastal Waterway on the East Coast are numerous small, friendly marinas and boatyards that welcome live-aboard people. Often they're located on attractive side creeks off the main channel. We found this true as far south as central Florida, after which slip space becomes harder to find on a permanent basis.

From New Jersey north, dockage becomes quite expensive, often rivaling California. However, there doesn't seem to be much objection to live-aboards in the Northeast. It's still regarded as more of a novelty than anything else, possibly because there are simply fewer people doing it.

Many marinas levy a flat extra charge for live-aboard boats and/or have metered electricity. I really can't fault them for charging more, particularly for electricity. Those living aboard dockside are more apt to use electrical appliances such as space heaters, toaster/ovens and electric skillets on the theory that as long as the power is available you might as well use it and save your kerosene or propane for cruising. This makes sense, but don't expect service without paying for it.

The objections to live-aboards of some marina operators are understandable. Live-aboards are more inclined to spill out of their confined cabins. For instance, we are more likely than the average weekend sailor to rinse out a few things and hang them out to dry on our life lines.

But this can escalate to the point where some boats really do become eyesores, with boxes and bags full of junk littering the decks and rusty refrigerators, bikes and assorted boat parts all over the dock.

The marina owner will naturally cast a jaundiced eye at the next fellow who comes along looking for dock space and says he lives aboard his boat. It's true that we all make messes at one time or another, but we shouldn't make a *habit* of imposing the mess on our neighbors.

Many advantages exist to staying in a marina. Shore power, even telephone service is possible. Most marinas have showers. Even though you may have a shower on your boat, it's often less of a hassle to use theirs. Many marinas are installing coin-operated washers and dryers, saving you a long trudge to the local laundromat.

Being able to step off your boat and walk ashore whenever you feel like it can be a big advantage, especially when the weather's rotten and you have to get to work every day—or when you realize there's no more toilet paper and must get to the store immediately! If you have a dog, it's easy to get Rover ashore for his daily run.

High wire fences and locked gates are becoming more prevalent, especially in big-city marinas. They're generally locked only at night, however, and some marinas even have night guards on duty. This gives you peace of mind when the boat is unattended. All your worldly goods are aboard and, unfortunately, most cities are high-theft areas.

Aside from rules and restrictions, probably the biggest drawback to a marina is a lack of privacy. If you're a gregarious type you may not consider this a drawback, although it can wear a little thin after a while. Curtains or shades for all ports are an absolute must. There will always be some rude character who thinks it's his right to "see what the inside of the boat looks like." Sometimes it's like living in a goldfish bowl. One friend had just stepped out of the shower and was rummaging through a forward locker looking for a pair of shorts, when he realized a woman was on her knees staring at him through an open port. What my friend did next wasn't very polite, but the woman asked for it.

Ports made of a tinted acrylic plastic function somewhat as one-way mirrors, allowing those aboard to see out, but preventing passersby from seeing in. Of course, they must be closed for privacy and that may not be pleasant on a hot day. Also, they do darken the boat's interior. For large fixed ports you could install shades or very sheer curtains that allow light to filter through but screen out glaring sunlight and Peeping Toms.

Extremely attractive or unusual boats attract attention and questions. Admittedly, we have met some very nice people among the dock-walkers and even formed some long-lasting friendships. In the days before I had a boat I, too, tramped up and down docks, and I remember how pleased I was when someone invited me aboard. Whenever someone appears genuinely interested, Bruce or I usually ask them if they'd like to come below and look around. Meeting new and different people is as much a part of living aboard as of cruising; if you choose to live in a marina you might as well learn to relax and enjoy it. Otherwise, you'll be happier on a mooring or anchored out.

During stormy weather you'll be glad you're tied securely to a dock, instead of being "out there." You can double-check your dock lines, put out extra warps and fenders and jump below to wait it out without worrying about dragging an anchor. In a hurricane, however, the last place to be is tied to a dock. In extreme high tides, floating docks are often lifted right off their pilings and carried away, taking attached boats with them.

Even the strongest dock is not likely to withstand the strain of a heavy cruising boat in hurricane-force winds. Your boat may take an incredible beating, may even be smashed to pieces. In fact, many marinas will not allow boats to remain in their slips during hurricanes, so be prepared to move to a safer area.

Bruce recalls visiting a marina in Dinner Key, Florida, after a hurricane and seeing hundreds of boats, including 30 and 40-footers, piled up like so many bathtub toys in the parking lot. That's a pretty frightening scene when the bathtub toy happens to be your home!

In order not to be dazzled by the pretty palm trees at the end of each finger pier, let's make up a marina questionnaire:

1. What is the condition of the dock wiring? Is it fairly new and adequate to meet the power requirements of every boat? If a fuse blows every time you plug in your toaster while your neighbor's running a hair dryer, it could get to be a hassle. Can you use a standard three-prong extension cord or will you have to buy an expensive Hubbell cord or adapter?

2. Are the docks in good shape or are they sinking under your weight? Are the cleats large, heavy and well-bolted or do they look as if they would pull loose if a heavy strain were placed on them?

3. If the marina is located in an area with a high tidal range, are the docks floating or fixed? We've had transient dockage at marinas where we had to climb a nine-foot ladder at low tide. It wasn't too bad for a day or so, except it was tough on our Labrador. But I wouldn't want to face that challenge on a permanent basis.

4. Are there dock boxes available for each boat or lockers on shore you can rent? If there are no dock boxes, will the marina allow you to install one?

5. Are there telephone jacks already installed if you should decide you want a phone?

6. What are the marina's rules and restrictions? Do they allow you to work on your boat? How strictly do they enforce "clean dock" rules? Ask to see a copy of their standard agreement or

contract and carefully read all the fine print. I remember one marina in San Diego, California, that required all guests to register at the office before visiting. It wasn't enforced but it could have been. What's important is there was a rule and we agreed we could live with it when we signed the rental agreement.

7. Is there parking space for your car or for a guest's car if you have visitors? Is there a place where you can securely lock up your bike?

8. Is the marina close to shopping centers, grocery stores, banks and the post office? This is critical if you don't have a car. Are buses or other forms of public transportation available nearby?

9. Are there showers? How clean are they and are there enough? If you plan to take one every morning before going to work and 14 other people have the same idea, you'd better hope you have an understanding boss! Don't laugh. I watched the line form every morning at 7:15 sharp at a marina in Annapolis, Maryland. Bruce and I switched to showering in mid-afternoon when the crowd had thinned out.

10. Is there a laundromat? How much more expensive is it than the one in town? It may not be worth it just for the sake of convenience. If there isn't one at the marina, how far is the nearest one?

11. Are gates locked or is there a guard at night? Depending on the area, security may be necessary. But if you're the type who keeps losing keys, you might find the locked gate more of a pain in the neck than anything else.

12. Do they allow pets? If they do are the animals pretty much under control? Where can you walk your dog and how long a hike is it for you and Fido before he can take a real run?

13. Taste the water coming through a hose on the dock, Some parts of the southeast have a high sulfur content in their water that makes it taste terrible. I've known live-aboards who carried water in jugs from town or even had bottled water delivered to their boats because the marina's water was virtually undrinkable.

14. Last, but by no means least, what kind of surge is there in the slips? Be sure to check this out on a sunny weekend. We spent a few days at a beautiful marina in Miami, Florida. The people who ran it were delightful, the docks were spotless, there was a long row of washers and dryers and huge shower rooms. A great place to be, except for one thing: the wakes that came rolling in from the continuous waterway traffic caused a tremendous surge. The boats, particularly those along the outermost row of slips, where *Sabrina* was berthed, were in constant motion—rolling, bouncing, straining and jerking at the dock lines. It was impossible for me to write or for Bruce to draw. The surge abated only slightly at night. Many marinas along the Intracoastal Waterway have erected breakwaters, bulkheads or "fences" to cut down on the surge. In heavily traveled areas, make sure there's *something* between you and the traffic.

Another place to look for dockage is at waterfront homes whose owners have a dock but no boat. Sometimes these homeowners will rent out their dock for some extra income, usually well below local marina fees. You will generally get electricity, water and a prestigious address—but not showers, a laundromat and other amenities a marina might offer. And your landlord may not appreciate your dog or cat running roughshod over his rolling green turf. The peace and quiet of a residential area might appeal to you, however. Look for this type dockage in the classifieds of local newspapers.

MOORINGS

A mooring can be a heavy mushroom anchor, a big chunk of concrete or granite or even an old engine block. A length of heavy chain leads to a length of lighter chain with a swivel coupling, leading to a mooring buoy. The boat is

BOAT		MUSH-ROOM lbs.	HEAVY CHAIN		LIGHT CHAIN		PENDANT (NYLON ONLY)	
DISPLACE-MENT, lbs.	LENGTH		SIZE	LENGTH	SIZE	LENGTH	SIZE	LENGTH
TO: 5,000	TO: 25'	250	3/4"	30'	5/16"	DEPTH OF	7/8"	3 TIMES
15,000	35'	350	1"	40'	3/8"	WATER	1"	FREEBOARD
35,000	45'	450	1"	50'	7/16"	AT HIGH-	1 1/4"	AT
60,000	55'	550	1"	60'	9/16"	EST TIDE	1 1/2"	BOW

Figure 1 *A permanent mooring offers greater security than the boat's own ground tackle. Using the boat's displacement is a better guide than length in determing the size of anchor and chain.*

attached to the buoy by a heavy nylon pendant (Figures 1 and 2). The pick-up buoy is secured by a piece of light line.

Once a mooring gets dug in it is highly unlikely it will ever drag. A regular anchor, however, is set according to the current or prevailing winds, causing worry when the tide or wind shifts. But a mooring has no preset directional pull, so the boat can swing around on it in any direction.

Installing a mooring is not difficult, but pulling it is. Most people put moorings in themselves, then hire a yard to retrieve it. Moorings can, of course, be left in the water for several seasons. But in that case a diver should be sent down periodically to inspect the condition of the chain, swivels and shackles.

Not too many years ago it was possible to pick a spot outside of a channel, drop a mooring and tie up. As harbors get more crowded however, this is becoming less and less possible. Most towns now require at least a permit and many charge a mooring fee. In effect, you're renting a small section of the harbor. In some

Figure 2 *A typical mooring setup. To prevent noise and hull damage caused by the mooring buoy hitting the boat, an innertube may be placed aroud the buoy as shown.*

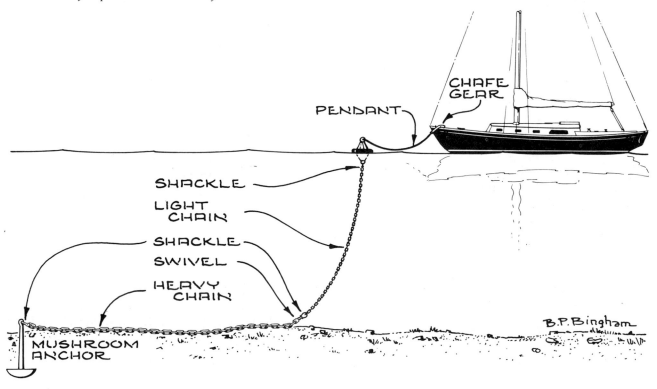

CHAFE GEAR

PENDANT

SHACKLE

LIGHT CHAIN

SHACKLE

SWIVEL

HEAVY CHAIN

MUSHROOM ANCHOR

B.P.Bingham

areas where there are a great number of moorings (like Oyster Bay, New York, where we once lived) each mooring space is assigned and each mooring must be approved by a town inspector before it goes into the water.

Despite these such problems, mooring out is still a good deal less expensive and trouble-free than living in a marina. On a mooring you can pretty much do as you please—make noise, sand the cabin trunk, whatever. And you can do it with a great deal more privacy. No dockwalkers to contend with. People might sail by, but they're not likely to stop and peer in your ports. If someone wants to visit it will require some effort on their part to reach you. Moorings cut down casual visiting considerably, which may or may not be an advantage.

Living on a mooring is a quiet and peaceful existence and might come closer to meeting your expectations of what living aboard was all about. You're surrounded by water, quacking ducks, soaring sea birds and jumping fish—as opposed to talkative people, rattling dock carts and boats a few feet away on either side. During sultry summer weather you're more likely to catch a cooling zephyr if you're away from land and surrounded by water.

Such serenity and privacy is not without its price, of course. You still have to get ashore occasionally. Most towns with a large population at moorings have launch service of some type, most often operated by a boatyard or marina. Yacht clubs generally run launches, but often the service is only for members. Usually you buy the service on a monthly or seasonal basis, or pay a fee each trip. Estimate how many trips per week you think you're apt to make,

then figure out which method of payment will be most economical.

Getting the launch's attention can sometimes be a hassle, particularly if you're in a hurry, in which case they always seem to be at the other end of the harbor. Most launch operators monitor a specified VHF or CB channel, respond to a certain horn signal or will respond when you hoist the T-flag—the "universal" launch pick-up signal.

It's rare to find a launch service that operates 24 hours a day, so you must work around their schedule. On several occasions when we were using a launch service we would be ashore enjoying an evening with friends, forget what time it was, and end the festivities with a frantic rush back to the yacht service to catch the launch operator before he locked up the boat for the night.

The alternative to a launch service is simply using your own dinghy. While my personal preference is for rowing, an outboard engine is certainly handy if you are a considerable distance from shore. I should mention that if you plan to row on an almost daily basis, you need a dinghy that rows well. Inflatables, for all their virtues, are cumbersome and tiring to row. Get a hard dinghy for rowing. A small outboard (3 hp.) is probably all you need to power an inflatable. Also, an inflatable is not apt to withstand repeated beachings and draggings across sand. Be prepared to carry an inflatable.

With several people on board and only one dinghy, shore trips have to be carefully coordinated so that no one gets stranded on the boat or on shore. Shore excursions demand some measure of planning, anyway. It's not always simple to run back to the store for something you forgot. If you've never been a list maker, you *will* become one after living on a mooring for awhile.

Weather also will play a big part in your trip planning. Carrying paper bags of groceries and clean, dry laundry on a boat ride in the rain is less than fun. (Where would we be without big plastic trash bags!) If your dog is not boat trained, count on going ashore at least twice a day, rain or shine.

The dinghy must be large and stable enough

to carry a heavy load and strong enough to withstand constant daily use. Our own Trinka dinghy (Bruce designed her and we built her ourselves) is only 8 feet long, yet she is extremely stable and we have on occasion crammed four people, a large dog and several heavy sea bags into her without sinking. Over seven years of continuous hard use, she's still going strong.

Once ashore, a safe place must be found to land and leave the dinghy. Some towns, and occasionally a marina, provide a dinghy dock. Most marinas will allow you to land there—check with them and find out where you can leave the dinghy so it won't be in the way of larger boats coming and going.

Without a dock, you'll have to find a beach or a seawall. In an area with a large tide range, this may mean dragging the dinghy several hundred feet through sand or muck (usually muck) at low tide. We added a thin stainless steel plate to Trinka's skeg to keep from wearing a hole through the bottom. She has wooden runners on each side of the keel for further protection.

An alternative to dragging the dinghy up a beach is rigging a "clothesline" between something permanent on the shore and a stake or small anchor off the beach. Splice the line so it will run as a continuous loop. Haul the dinghy out into two-three feet of water, remembering to allow for any rise or fall of the tide. This arrangement is also good if you have to leave the dinghy where it might bang on rocks or against a rough seawall or pilings in your absence (See Figure 3).

In a residential area, it's nice to make friends with someone on shore and get permission to

Figure 3   *This mooring is a nifty arrangement for leaving the dink in areas with a wide tidal range. It keeps her safely afloat while you're away and eliminates the chore of dragging her up or down the beach when the tide is out.*

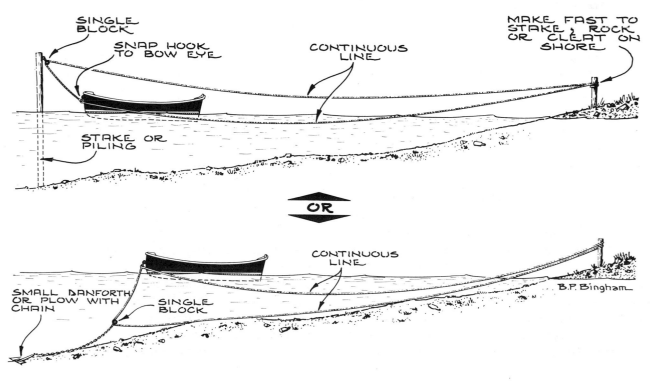

leave the dink at their beach or dock. While legally their property doesn't extend past the high water mark, bad feelings can develop if you try going through their backyard and over their fence to reach a public road.

In some places dinghy theft is a problem. You should have some means of securing the dinghy with a lock and chain. Either take the oars with you (a real pain), stow them in a locker ashore if you have one or chain and lock them in the dinghy. The same is true of an outboard, especially a small, lightweight motor. Figure out some way of locking it securely to the transom if there's reason to be concerned about theft.

Unless you're lucky and find a quiet corner with little traffic, another potential problem on a mooring is motion of the boat itself. We were on a mooring in the beautiful Annisquam River in Gloucester, Massachusetts, for over a month. It was lovely and peaceful except for an hour in the morning and an hour in the evening when the fishing fleet would go zooming by, rolling us unceremoniously out of our bunk and/or knocking over anything we had forgotten to tie down.

Some boats are livelier than others and seem to dance around their moorings, while others lie there sedately. A riding sail to steady her down (See Figure 4) is useful, as are a set of "flopper-stoppers," which are rigged outboard on each side of the boat. Flopper-stoppers dampen rolling often by as much as 30 percent-40 percent (See Figure 5).

Bruce's idea for people who keep their boat permanently on a mooring is to build a mooring platform. It is basically a floating dock, similar to the swimming platforms seen in resort areas. The platform is attached to the mooring and the boat tied up to the platform, just as though it were a marina dock. You need a heavier mooring to take the additional weight of the platform. In heavy weather you probably should let the boat ride away from the platform to prevent the two from slamming together.

We stayed on such a mooring recently in Boston, Massachusetts. Even though the platform was quite small (3 feet by 8 feet), it was delightful to be able to step off the boat whenever we felt like it; we were able to clean the topsides and boot top much easier than from the dinghy. It did confuse our dog Natasha, however, when she jumped onto the dock and discovered it didn't lead anywhere!

A larger one (8 feet by 12 feet, perhaps) would be more useful (See Figure 6). You could build a dock box or small shed for extra gear, paint and varnish, etc. Rig up an awning over a couple of deck chairs and set up the hibachi and picnic table when guests come for dinner. All sorts of possibilities come to mind. Actually, I get visions of improving the platform until eventually it becomes a houseboat with our cruising boat—tied alongside.

Despite the drawbacks, I still prefer a mooring over a marina. Peace and quiet, being able to work for hours on end without interruption —these are the principal reasons I moved aboard a boat in the first place. Occasionally marinas and civilization beckon, but it's never very long before we're ready again for the soothing effects of flowing water, birds and sealife.

POWER AFLOAT

You will need some way of generating power when you're living aboard on a mooring. How much power depends on how many electrical accessories you use. Running the engine a few hours a day or every couple of days may be sufficient to charge your batteries. Other methods could be a generator (if you require

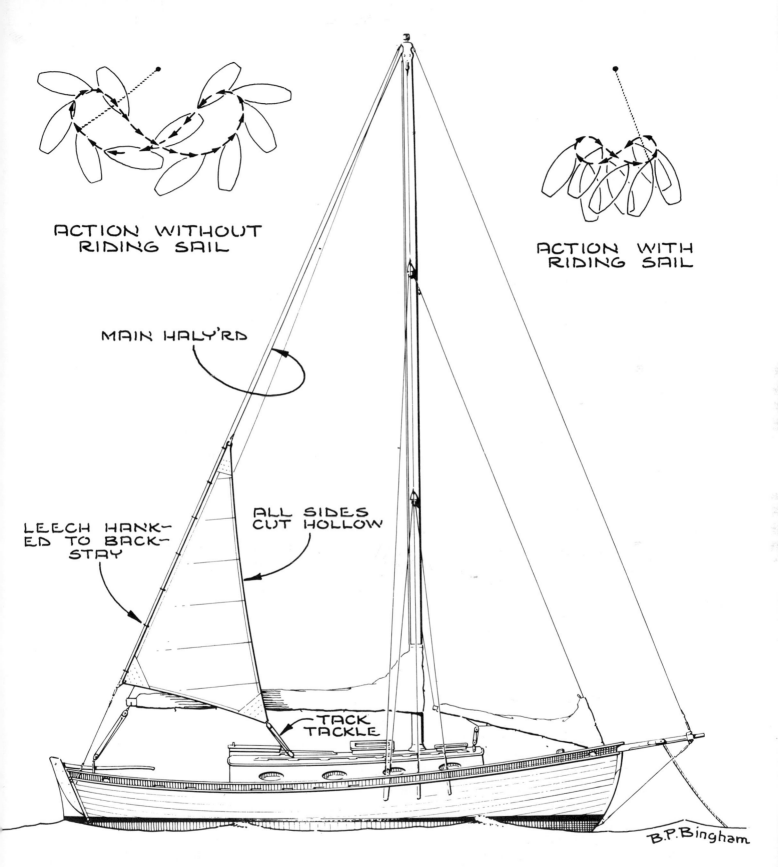

ACTION WITHOUT
RIDING SAIL

ACTION WITH
RIDING SAIL

MAIN HALY'RD

ALL SIDES
CUT HOLLOW

LEECH HANK-
ED TO BACK-
STAY

TACK
TACKLE

B.P.Bingham

Figure 4 *Riding sails are effective in steadying boats that tend to "dance" around their moorings or anchor. The sail helps the boat stay head-to-wind. Cutting the sides hollow eliminates battens or noisy flapping.*

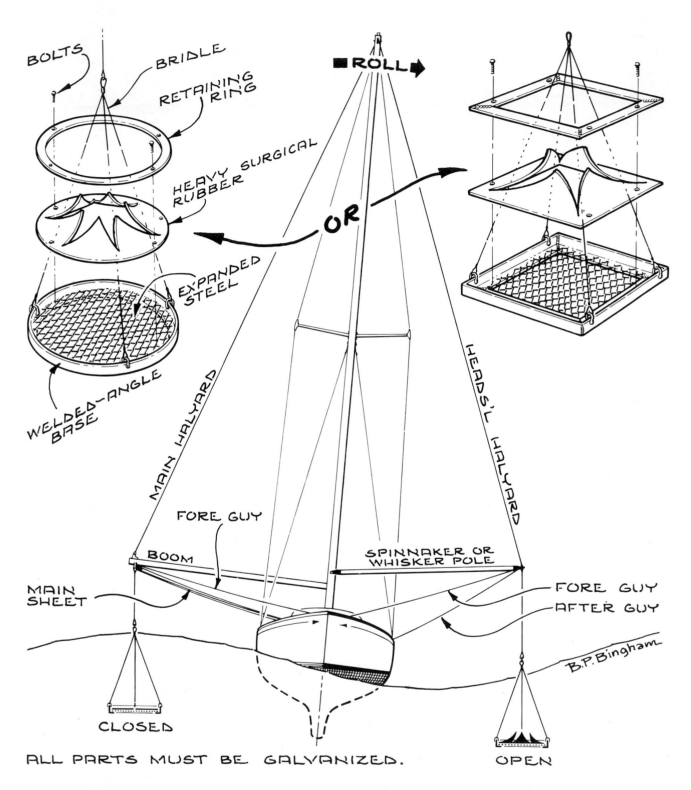

BOLTS
BRIDLE
RETAINING RING
HEAVY SURGICAL RUBBER
EXPANDED STEEL
WELDED-ANGLE BASE

ROLL

OR

MAIN HALYARD
HEADS'L HALYARD
FORE GUY
BOOM
SPINNAKER OR WHISKER POLE
MAIN SHEET
FORE GUY
AFTER GUY
B.P. Bingham
CLOSED
OPEN

ALL PARTS MUST BE GALVANIZED.

Figure 5 *Flopper-stoppers can be extremely useful in cutting down the rolling of an anchored or moored boat.*

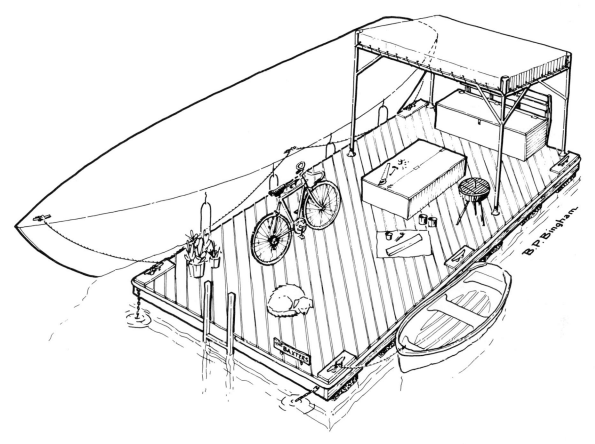

Figure 6 *People on shore have patios, sundecks and back porches. People who keep their boats on a permanent mooring can have a "back yard" too, in the form of a mooring platform. It can be small and simple or as elaborate as you want, a place for building and painting projects, for sunbathing, barbequing—the possibilities are endless.*

110 power), solar cells (expensive but an excellent source of power) or a wind generator.

I'm partial to the idea of a small, portable generator. We had one aboard our schooner *At Last* and found it invaluable when we had to use power tools. Of course, we were doing a lot of rebuilding and probably needed power more often than most live-aboards.

ANCHORING

The advantages and disadvantages of living aboard at anchor are basically the same as being on a mooring—with a few exceptions. Since *any* anchor is likely to drag in a wind shift, particularly when it's blowing hard, anchoring is not "permanent" in the same sense as mooring.

I'm always reluctant to go off and leave the boat unattended when she's *only* anchored. We never leave even if it just *looks* like the weather is starting to make up.

Some harbors place restrictions on anchoring. They will let you stay for a few days, but if authorities see you're still there after a week, they will ask you to either move on, rent a mooring or hire dock space at a local marina. Some cities, such as Ft. Lauderdale, Florida, have passed ordinances banning anchoring anywhere within the city limits for any length of time, and issue fines to offenders.

Anchoring out can be a real pleasure and it is certainly a very real part of cruising. But, for a long stay in one place, I think you'll find more peace of mind in a marina or on a heavy mooring.

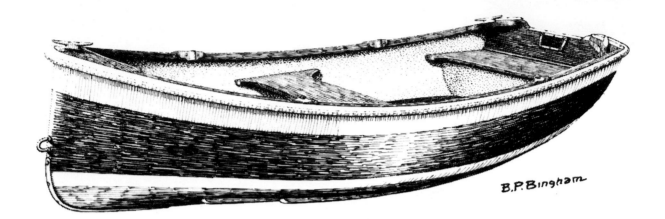

The Trinka Dinghy
Illustration Courtesy of Knock on Wood

The Dinghy

5

"Your link to the land"

Go CRUISING, STAY anyplace but a marina and the dinghy becomes one of the most vital pieces of boat gear. Unfortunately, it's too often an afterthought, purchased on the basis of price alone: "Get the cheapest one you can; it's only a dinghy!" (See Plate 1).

It's *not* "**only** a dinghy." It's your taxi, at times your *only* link to land. It had better be seaworthy enough to get you ashore or—even more importantly—back to the boat in foul weather. It will often be in daily service. It will carry people, kids, groceries, bicycles, laundry and the dog (See Plate 2). It must be rugged, it must be stable, it must row well and tow well and it should also be attractive and complement the mother ship.

RIGID VS. INFLATABLE

I'll say it right up front: I am 100 percent in favor of a good, rigid dinghy. Bruce recently wrote an article about the subject. I excerpt from it here, since it reflects my own viewpoint so well:

Plate 1 *Rigid dinghies come in all shapes and sizes, some good and some awful.*

Plate 2 *The cruising tender frequently will be loaded to capacity and must be stable enough to carry the load.*

If you ever stepped from your boat into an inflatable and had it skid out from under you, you may be among the thousands of seasoned sailors who've ended in the drink instead of the dink. A rigid tender is far less susceptible to this tendency. And, when your feet touch the seats, you're on something distinctly solid, not dangerously flexible.

A solid dinghy with solid seats provides for an efficient and comfortable rowing position—legs extended and braced, knees clear of the oars, hands and body height at the best rowing angle.

The oars of an inflatable are usually short, flimsy aluminum affairs with plastic blades, pivoting in plastic or rubber oarlocks attached to the flexible boat. Of course, you can replace them with a more efficient pair but you still have to deal with the same oarlocks and ridiculous rowing position.

A rigid tender can be sanded and bottom painted as well as easily scraped when she becomes fouled after long service in the water. Try that with an inflatable!

A rigid dinghy can abrade on sand, coral, rocks, barnacled pilings and docks, be dragged up and down beaches for years with minimal damage. An inflatable can't.

Leaks in a rigid dinghy (extremely rare) can be permanently repaired with a little resin and glass tape. Leaks in an inflatable (the rule rather than the exception) are fixed with a flexible patch and adhesive that rarely holds over the long term.

Strong winds (more than 30 knots) can, and usually do, flip an inflatable over. With it go the outboard, oars, bailer and inflation pump.

That's not the case with a rigid tender. Winds in excess of 100 knots, with accompanying seas, are normally survived upright by most rigid tenders.

In wind over 15 knots, an inflatable becomes difficult to row and power by outboard, while a rigid tender is relatively unaffected. In winds stronger than 25 knots, the inflatable is essentially unmanageable while the rigid yacht tender forges ahead under complete control. If winds reach 40 knots, even the best rigid tender is a handful under oars or power. But the inflatable becomes an impossible vehicle to handle. On breezy days, you'll see most inflatables skidding sideways with little or no directional stability while most rigid dinghies are still going where they are told.

The inherent bulbous shape of an inflatable is a very inefficient hydrodynamic form, hence is difficult to propel into a chop. A well-designed rigid tender is far more easily driven.

There is no such thing as an attractive inflatable. Rigid dinghies, even the worst of them, are aesthetically more pleasing. A good rigid tender is usually handsome and complementary to the mother ship. Did you ever see an inflatable that didn't all but destroy the appearance of its host vessel?

Many sailors have been sold the concept that an inflatable solves the dinghy storage problem. It's true that an inflatable can be deflated, packed and stowed, but this is difficult and time-consuming. To struggle through this procedure every time you get under way is really impractical and such a bother that hardly any inflatable owner does it.

Much more often an inflatable ends up tied onto the foredeck, lashed against the shrouds, bow-tied to the stern pulpit or, occasionally, stowed on the cabin top. So, the inflatable normally causes the same stowage problem as the rigid dinghy.

Additionally, if an inflatable has been deflated, it follows that it must be reinflated. The stowage of a rigid dinghy, then, is no more trouble than the inflatable in either form. In fact, it's more a matter of how the dinghy is lifted and stowed than the type of dinghy being carried. Most often, the rigid dinghy can be safely towed in conditions that would be impossible with an inflatable, even rough ocean conditions. Given a well-designed, well-built rigid dinghy, only extreme offshore mayhem would require its hauling and stowing aboard.

Leaving an inflatable on a beach unattended or untied on a windy day is asking for trouble. A rigid dinghy, hauled clear of the surf, stays put.

If you think an inflatable is less expensive than a rigid tender, you're in for a real shock. In fact,

you won't save a single nickel. Given a really good rigid dinghy, perhaps slightly more expensive initially, the gain through longevity becomes a bonus. Ever heard of an inflatable lasting 10, 20 or 30 years?

Thank heavens no one has come up with an easily stowed inflatable yacht.

Figure 1 *After 13,000 miles of towing, the Trinka now lives on* Saga's *davits. Here, our former home* Sabrina *rafts alongside.*

had piped up and their inflatable couldn't handle the rough seas. Our Trinka, with her 7½-foot spruce oars and correctly-positioned seats and oarlocks, is a pleasure to row (See Plate 3). With her sailing rig, she's also given us many afternoons of delightful relaxation.

The major reason we're so adamant about all this is undoubtedly the good experiences we've had with our own rigid dinghy. Our 8-foot Trinka is more than eight years old and is still going strong. We have towed her without problem thousands of miles, even offshore in 15-foot seas.

More than once, we've given someone a lift back to their boat in Trinka when the weather

CHOOSING THE DINGHY

The trade-offs in dinghy design are many, making it difficult to find a good all-around, multi-purpose dinghy. Jeff Spranger, editor of *The Practical Sailor,* said he couldn't find a good dinghy, so he had to build his own. His design choice was a Trinka. There are a number of things to consider.

If a dinghy is long, narrow and rows superbly, it will probably be at the sacrifice of stability and carrying capacity and will likely be

Figure 2   *Having survived 15-foot ocean seas behind our 20-foot home* Sabrina, *the Trinka dinghy liked the protected waterways best.*

Plate 3 *Live-aboards George Cranston and Gainor Roberts try rowing our Trinka dinghy.*

hard to stow because of its length. Eight feet is about the maximum length that most average-size yachts can accommodate easily. We did see a lovely fiberglass lapstrake rowing dinghy that

neatly addressed this stowage problem. The 10½-foot Whisper, built by Clone Boats, can be broken down into two nesting sections that occupy a space of only 5 feet, 9 inches in length and by 2 feet, 2 inches high (See Plate 4).

Another alternative is the 10-foot Portabote (See Plate 5). The seats can be removed in minutes and the polypropylene dinghy folds lengthwise to four inches in thickness so that it takes up about as much room as a surfboard.

Plate 4 *Whisper, a fiberglass "lapstrake" Whitehall, can handle any load and any sea condition easily because of her 10½-foot length. But it can be nested in two sections for easy stowage.*

Plate 5 *John Chille demonstrates his folding Portabote that can be collapsed to a thickness of about four inches.*

A fine entry or one with a slight hollow, will make the dinghy easier to row (See Figure 3). A long, straight run and straight underbody profile will help her tow straight and level (See Figure 4A). Boats with "swoopy" underbodies don't track well and stand on their transoms,

digging in terribly when towed at any speed. They are also notoriously unstable. I call them banana boats since that's what they resemble (See Figure 4B). The dinghy should have enough beam to make her reasonably stable and enough freeboard, especially at her ends, to carry a load and remain fairly dry in a chop (See Figure 5A). Low end sheers are notoriously wet (See Figure 5B).

A figerglass dinghy will be very strong for its weight, and is by far the easiest to maintain. A simply built wood dinghy requires low maintenance, certainly, but I don't think it will hold up to rugged use as a fiberglass dink will.

A flat-bottom pram (See Figure 6A), like the Naples Sabot and the Optimist (See Plate 6), is very stable. They sail decently, are acceptible rowers (but not in seas) and they can carry a

Figure 3 *A fine entry, or one with a slight hollow, will make the dinghy easier to row.*

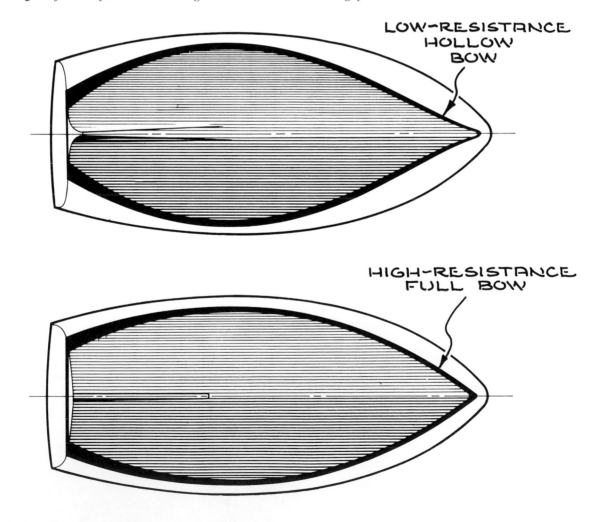

LOW-RESISTANCE HOLLOW BOW

HIGH-RESISTANCE FULL BOW

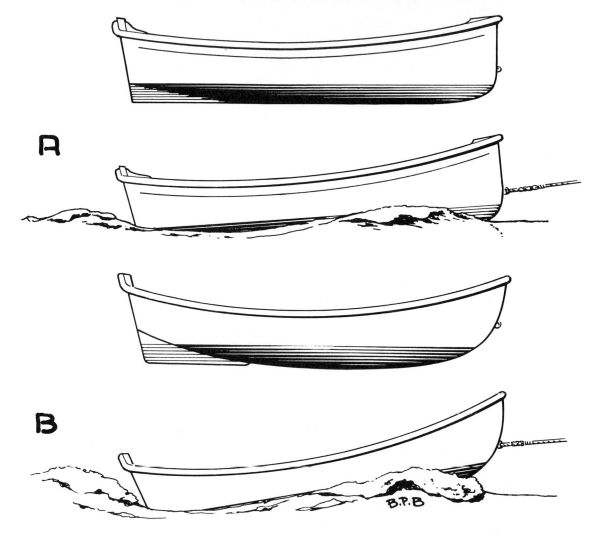

Figure 4 *A straight underbody (A) will help her tow level. A swoopy underbody (B) will dig in and cause the dinghy to stand on her transom.*

Figure 5 *A dinghy with high freeboard at her ends (A) will be relatively dry compared to one with low ends (B).*

Figure 6

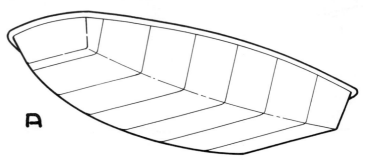

A flat-bottom pram

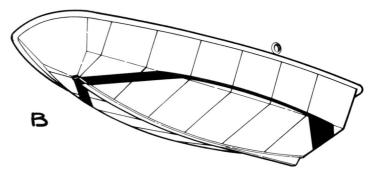

A V-bottom pram

Plate 6 *The Optimist pram is a stable, flat-bottomed dinghy that can be sailed or rowed.*

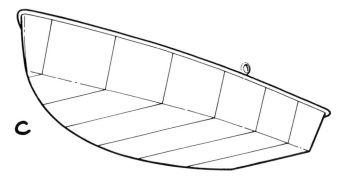

A flat-bottom skiff

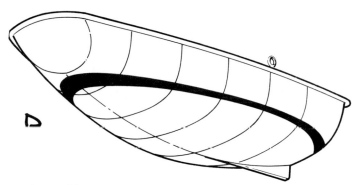

A round-bottom pram

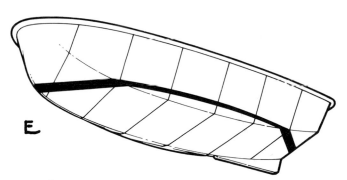

A V-bottom dinghy

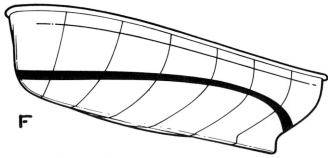

A round-bottom dinghy

reasonable load. (The Optimist is also available in fiberglass.) In the pram family, the flat-bottoms are the best under tow. In wood, they are easiest to build.

A V-bottom pram (See Figure 6B) is a prettier boat, a better rower (especially in a sea), a better sailer, but it is usually "thicker" or "taller," and thus harder to stow. It is also difficult to tow because of its swoopy underbody. It also will carry less load than a flat-bottom pram. If wood, it will be heavier because of the more complicated construction.

The flat-bottom skiff (See Figure 6C), is one of the most rare and underrated of all the dinghy types. It is extremely stable, excellent to tow, a good rowing boat even in a chop and simple to construct in wood.

A round-bottom pram (See Figure 6D) is essentially equal to the V-bottom pram, but complicated and difficult to build in wood. Several models are produced in fiberglass.

V-bottom dinghies (See Figure 6E) are the most popular type on the market. Their flat sections, however, render them somewhat weak and their sharp corners are vulnerable to damage. They are better rowers than the types mentioned previously, but are not particularly good to tow.

The round-bottom dinghy (See Figure 6F) has the most potential for good performance, whether rowed, towed or sailed. Its stability must be sacrificed slightly for this performance. They are difficult to build in wood but hundreds of models are available in fiberglass. Their compound-curved surfaces render them very strong. For daily service involving long distances, strong headwinds or choppy waters, the round-bottom dinghy is your best bet.

Weight is another trade-off. Heavy construction (within reason) equals longevity, but also makes a dinghy that's harder to haul up a beach or lift aboard, although lifting a dinghy aboard, even a heavy one, should not be a problem, particularly on a sailboat, since you have a built-in "cargo" boom, block and tackle as well as winches to make the task easier.

Wood lapstrake construction is a very strong building method. A fiberglass dinghy, molded to look like wood lapstrake, is also very strong because of the longitudinal "ridges" (See Plate 7).

Danny Greene, of *Cruising World* magazine, sells plans for Two Bits, a 9-foot, 4-inch two-piece dinghy to be built in plywood. One half fits snugly inside the other and it will stow in only a 4-foot by 5-foot space. It can be built with daggerboard and sailing rig. While you may not be interested in building your own dinghy, Two Bits appears simple enough for most amateurs and is a solution for the owner of a pocket-sized cruiser who wants a dinghy he can store on deck.

Theoretically, cost should not be an issue with something as important as a dinghy. But it is. Don't be dismayed—buy a good, well-built, basic dinghy and add extra features yourself, a few at a time, as your pocketbook allows. The following are some of the features I like to have in a dinghy (See Figure 7):

A. A stainless steel plate on the skeg, the area most vulnerable to damage by rocks and coral.

B. A transom or keel self-bailer, like the ones made by Elvström.

C. Wooden runners on the bottom to protect the hull when dragging it onto a beach.

D. A stout stainless towing bail, not just an eye bolt, through-bolted to a metal backing plate and heavily glassed in place.

E. A stainless steel strip on the stem to prevent damage when beaching or towing at high speeds.

F. A stout breast hook to strengthen the dinghy longitudinally and increase impact strength.

G. Cleats through-bolted at bow and stern.

H. Heavy bronze oarlocks, not cheap little pot-metal ones, with two rowing positions—one amidships and one in the bow.

I. A thick, hefty gunwale guard, such as a canvas-covered rubber half-round or a ship-sized rope, laced or screwed at close intervals all around.

J. A stout wooden gunwale, not just a fragile fiberglass flange.

Plate 7 *The fiberglass Halcyon dinghy derives its strength from the "lapstrake" ridges.*

K. Floorboards, to keep shoes, fresh laundry and grocery bags out of those little puddles that always seem to live in a dinghy.

L. The transom correctly shaped to receive an outboard engine should you want to use one.

M. Stout quarter knees to add longitudinal strength and to absorb outboard motor thrust.

N. Protective outboard mounting pads mounted inside and outside the transom.

O. Stainless steel half-oval across the top edge of the transom to protect it when doing a rough job like rowing out a storm anchor.

Figure 7 *Dinghy features, courtesy Knock on Wood*

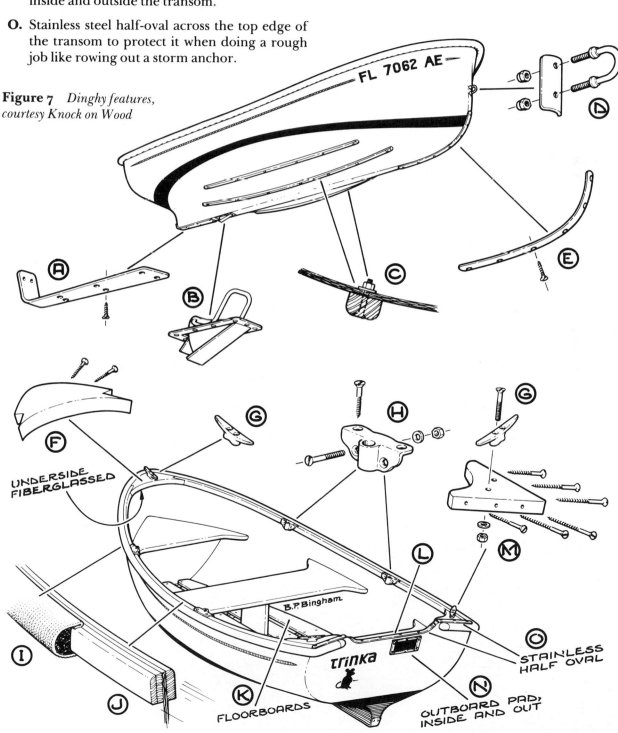

DINGHY EQUIPMENT

It's amazing how much gear we carry around in the dinghy. I think oars should be as long as possible and still fit completely inside the dink. Trinka is 8 feet long, and her 7½-foot oars just fit inside.

One of the handiest items we keep in the dinghy is a little 2½-pound anchor with about 30 feet of line. While she's hardy enough to withstand some banging around, we feel better if she doesn't. Set and tied to a stern cleat, the little anchor holds her off rocks and coral and keeps her away from other boats at a crowded dinghy dock.

The collapsible Norwegian anchors are ideal for a dinghy. They take up almost no room when folded and are usually sold with their own canvas storage bag.

Setting a dinghy anchor is not difficult. Drop the anchor from the stern and paddle or drift in to shore in a straight line. Step out with the painter in hand (See Figure 8A). Tie the painter so that it holds the dinghy at an angle to the shore (See Figure 8B). This will keep the bow safely away from rocks or a seawall, but you can retrieve her by pulling straight in.

Dinghy theft and theft of oars and outboards is big business in some areas. It's a good idea to have a chain and padlock to secure the dinghy and some means of chaining the oars and outboard to the dinghy. Keep a record of the serial number of the outboard. Paint the name of the boat on the dinghy *and* the oars. Better yet, carve them in so they can't be easily removed or painted over (See Plate 8).

In most areas, a rowboat or a sailing dinghy under a certain size does not require registration. However, if you add an outboard, you will then have to register it and apply registration numbers to the bow.

An outboard on the dinghy usually means additional gear—a jerry jug of pre-mixed fuel, a funnel and perhaps a handle extension so you can keep the dink in trim when single-handing.

The Coast Guard requires a personal flotation device for each person on board. In a dinghy, flotation cushions are acceptable, but that's something else to flop around. Now that we carry Trinka in davits when underway, Bruce hit upon the idea of stowing our life jackets in the dinghy. I made two rectangular canvas bags and we stow a pair of jackets on each side of the centerboard trunk under the center thwart. This not only complies with regulations, but it puts the life jackets in a handier spot aboard the mother ship than any other place we've ever stowed them.

Other items to carry are a bailer and/or a

Figure 8 *Set a dinghy anchor by dropping it and rowing in a straight line to shore (A). Step out and tie the dinghy at an angle to shore (B).*

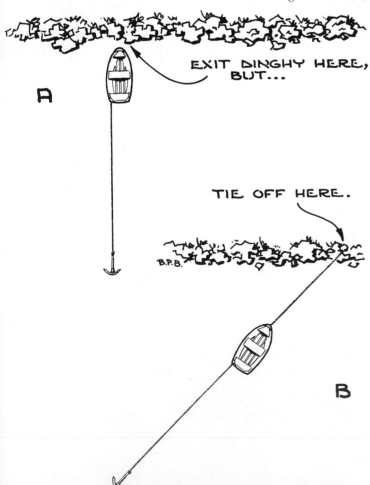

Plate 8 *John Chille carved the dinghy's name right into the seat. A potential thief would probably think twice before rowing off with a dinghy identified in this manner.*

Plate 9 *Bruce Morrison shows off the lovely lines of his 12-foot Whitehall. The leg o' mutton rig will stow completely inside the dinghy.*

hand pump, a small fender, a whistle, horn or bell and a flashlight. The Coast Guard now requires that flares and other safety equipment be carried in all boats, including dinghies.

A Sailing Dinghy

Here again, we face more trade-offs. I believe sailing to the store or sailing to work is a romantic idea, but generally not that practical. We do, however, know one 75-year-old gentleman, Bruce Morrison, who rows his 12-foot Whitehall about four miles upwind to the grocery store several times a week, then raises his leg 'o mutton rig and sails the downwind run back to his live-aboard powerboat at the marina (See Plate 9).

For pure pleasure and recreation it *is* fun to have a sailing rig for the dink. With children aboard it is almost a necessity. However, it means a lot more gear to stow—spars, sail, rudder and tiller, plus a daggerboard or leeboard if you don't have a built-in centerboard. Most dinghy rigs collapse and stow neatly inside the dink (See Plates 9, 10 and 11), but this is only practical when under way.

With the dinghy in daily use, you don't want to be tripping over all that stuff, so you will have to find a storage place outside the dinghy. Remember, you are permanently losing some space in the dinghy when it's built with a dag-

Plate 11 *Morrison's Whitehall with the leg o' mutton rig collapsed and stowed.*

gerboard or centerboard (more with a centerboard).

Bruce Morrison's solution is interesting. He did not care to give up any of the rowing qualities of his Whitehall by adding a daggerboard or centerboard, so he chose to sail in one direction only (downwind) and keep the boat intact for her designed use: rowing.

THE DOCILE DINGHY

Dinghies have been known to sneak up and give a resounding whack! to the mother ship, usually when anchored in currents or when wind is against the tide. That's not always bad. If everyone is snug below, the dinghy banging alongside may be telling you your boat is dragging anchor.

To keep the little one quiet and well behaved (short of bringing her aboard), you might want to trail her off the bow instead of the stern until the tide turns or the wind shifts. This sometimes works if the current has the big boat heading one way and the wind is carrying the lighter-weight dinghy in the other direction.

Plate 10 *A sliding gunter rig will stow neatly inside the dinghy.*

Or you can lash the dink amidships with several fenders between little ship and big. Another alternative is to stream a small sea anchor (the kind sold for use with life rings) off the dinghy's stern.

When we lived aboard *Sabrina,* Bruce would sometimes rig the spinnaker pole as a dinghy boom. He secured the pole at right angles to *Sabrina,* with the dinghy streaming from the outboard end. A line from *Sabrina* to a stern cleat on the dinghy would allow us to haul her in (See Figure 9).

On-deck dinghy stowage is fine for a long passage, but I think it's too much trouble as a day-in day-out practice. If it's stowed upright, it should have its own cradle. A cover makes sense to keep out rain and to protect all the gear that inevitably finds its way into an up-

right dinghy (See Plate 12). A bilge drain is a must.

A dinghy stowed upside down over a foredeck hatch or skylight can act as an effective rain shield, allowing the hatch or port to be left open in bad weather. We saw one fiberglass

Figure 9 *Rigging a boat boom.*

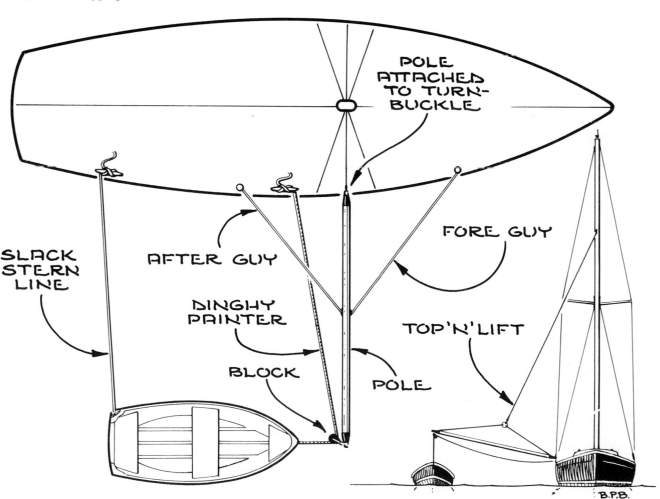

When towing Trinka offshore or in rough weather we used two painters, one secured to the dinghy's towing eye, the second secured to her bow cleat and both lines leading to separate stern cleats on our boat (See Figure 9). This system reduces the tendency of the dinghy to wander or charge wildly from side to side. It also provides a backup should one of the painters part. Everything stowed in the dinghy was securely lashed and we sometimes tied three or four fenders to the center thwart. They gave her enough negative bouyancy (when in the inverted position) to allow her to right herself if she were capsized (See Figure 10). That happened only once—in the Gulf Stream—in seven years of towing.

Choosing a dinghy deserves every bit as much practical and financial consideration as buying the live-aboard boat itself. I believe once you have owned a rigid dinghy that is an able performer and once the choice has been made based on practical reasons such as handling characteristics, stability, size and construction, you will find she's not *only* a dinghy,

Plate 12 *A dinghy stowed upright should have its own cradle and a cover. The ribs shown here allow rainwater to run off instead of puddling in the center.*

dinghy stowed this way that had been made without a gelcoat to allow light to filter through.

We prefer davits if the boat is large enough, since they keep the dinghy secure but completely out of the way (See Plate 13). Davits are not the perfect answer, of course. One sailor neatly wrapped a davit around a piling when he turned too sharply when leaving a fuel dock.

In Charleston Municipal Marina, South Carolina, where docked boats are rafted and stacked like so much cordwood alongside fixed docks, we spent an inordinate amount of time keeping Trinka from fouling neighboring dock lines as the floating mass rose and fell with each 10-foot tide.

Plate 13 *Davits keep a dinghy secure but out of the way.*

Figure 10 *Two painters help the dinghy track in a straight line and provide a backup should one part. Three or more bumpers tied to the center thwart will right most capsized dinghies.*

but a second boat, a good friend and just plain fun to mess around in.

SOURCES OF DINGHY INFORMATION

HALCYON
Halcyon Boat Corp.
1155 Mueller Lane
Melbourne, FL 32935

PORTABOTE
Portabote Inc.
P.O. Box 2287
Menlo Park, CA 94025

TRINKA
Knock on Wood
P.O. Box 331135
Miami, FL 33133

TWO BITS
Danny Greene
Colebrook Road
Little Compton, R.I. 02837

WHISPER
Clone Boats
2090 Main Road
Tiverton, R.I. 02878

6

Living Expenses

"Making ends meet"

ANY LIVE-ABOARD WILL tell you living on a boat is much cheaper than living on shore. How much cheaper depends on several factors—the size and age of your boat, whether you spend most of your time dockside or at anchor and your own definitions of necessities and luxuries.

During our first year aboard our 36-foot schooner *At Last,* our expenses averaged about $200 a month. That was below poverty level, even in 1976. Most of the money went for food. We bought no clothes, we never went dockside and we never went out to dinner or hired a taxi. We did do a lot of sailing (*At Last* had no engine) and a lot of sightseeing by boat and by foot ("freebies" like lighthouse tours and outdoor concerts) and managed to have a wonderful year of cruising and good times without ever feeling deprived.

Having proved it could be done, I'm the first to admit I don't want to do it again. We were so enthralled with our new lifestyle and so pleased to have finally and actually cut ties to land, that I think we would have endured just about anything—and enjoyed it—to keep from going back to the pressures of our previous existence.

Aboard *Sabrina* in 1979 our expenses averaged about $700 a month. That year included a round trip from Gloucester, Massachusetts, to Miami, Florida, via the Intracoastal Waterway—with quite a bit of powering—and a cruise to the Bahamas. We "bought" overnight dockage every two weeks to charge the batteries. We ate out occasionally, went to movies and visited some tourist attractions. We bought souvenirs, clothes and equipment for the boat. *And* our grocery purchases included fewer canned goods.

On *Saga* in 1980 we spent about $1,000 a month. Part of the increase, of course, was due to inflation—boat people are affected just like everyone else! Also, our spending had increased right along with our income. *Saga* is a much larger boat, so the cost of both new equipment and routine maintenance was proportionally higher.

In 1981, despite continuing inflation, our monthly spending remained about the same. Two factors accounted for that: we remained south the entire year, where the cost of living is generally lower than in the Northeast, and we made fewer major purchases.

Don't be misled by the $1,000 a month. That figure is an average. Our "normal" expenses (food, laundry, postage, etc.) was much lower.

The $1,000 includes once-a-year expenses like haul-out and bottom paint and major expenses like new chain and anchor rode, all averaged over a 12-month period.

Housing—rent or a mortgage payment—is a major land expense that is eliminated when you move aboard. I'm assuming, of course, that your boat is paid for. If it has been financed, the payments may equal that of a house, although for a shorter period of time. If you're cruising and/or anchoring out much of the time, you'll still be paying for occasional dockage. Even if you keep a permanent marina slip, the cost will be a fraction of what you'd pay for rent ashore. Consider too, that your boat home is waterfront property, often in a resort area—the most desirable and expensive of locations. For example, we spent several weeks on Hilton Head Island, South Carolina, a renowned tennis and golf resort. We paid several nights' dockage at $5 a night and anchored out the rest of the time. Some friends had permanent dockage there that cost them less than $100 a month for a 38-foot boat. One night in most Hilton Head hotels cost that much and waterfront homes were in the six- and seven-figure brackets.

Most live-aboards have some means of generating their own electricity. Electricity and water is almost always included in docking fees, with occasionally a small surcharge for full-time live-aboards. Fuel for cooking, lighting and heating is minimal compared to the cost of utilities on shore. Even heating a boat through a northern winter is much cheaper than heating a house or apartment, primarily because the volume of space being heated is so much less.

Government statistics show that someone with an average income spends 25 percent of his earnings on an automobile and related expenses (fuel, repairs, insurance, etc.) I find that figure staggering.

A strange metamorphosis seems to occur in people when they become live-aboards: the majority, in an effort to minimize monthly expenses, sell their cars. The few who do own cars drive clunkers. I can't think of one live-aboard who owns a new car or is making monthly car payments. The automobile ceases to be a status symbol and becomes instead a means of getting from point A to point B. That 25 percent goes into our pockets, into our boat-home or into a cruise.

Our transportation expenses for 1979 averaged $11 a month. That included bus and train fares and occasionally a taxi.

If the boat is financed, then it will be insured. Other than that, I know of few live-aboards who carry any kind of insurance at all. People on shore often carry mortgage insurance, fire and theft insurance, car insurance, medical insurance and life insurance—all with monthly or quarterly payments. Our total cost for insurance for the past six years adds up to a big fat zero! The need for insurance is debatable. Some people simply don't feel comfortable without it and that's understandable.

We have had a few major expenses that we hadn't planned for, but somehow we always managed to handle them. Sometimes it meant taking on an extra job for awhile, or hocking the sextant. But we found a way. Most of us try to pile up a little nest egg to cover emergencies. Moving aboard signifies new feelings of independence, of relying on ourselves. We decide we can take care of ourselves and, sure enough, we do.

Self-sufficient or not, we still have to pay our dues to society, in one form or another. Income tax is ever-present, even if you've quit a high-paying job. Property taxes vary from state to state, a few not having any at all. In states (and sometimes cities) that do, it is generally levied on boats that are in the state on a specified date. When I lived in southern California,

I was always amused by the annual mass exodus of boats leaving for a Mexican cruise the weekend before "tax day." In other states your boat becomes taxable if you stay for a specified length of time, regardless of where the boat is registered.

The trick is to stay up to the limit, leave on a cruise and then return. There are advantages to the mobility of a boat-home. If you have children, however, you can count on being taxed in most areas as soon as you enroll the kids in a public school.

Sales tax is a one-time fee paid in most states when you buy a boat. It can sometimes be avoided by documenting the boat in a non-sales tax state. This usually involves incorporating (often in Delaware, sometimes in New Hampshire or Louisiana) and having the corporation own the boat. Some states will tax you anyway, incorporated or not. Incorporating requires the services of an attorney and certain fees must be paid, so the cost of incorporating must be weighed carefully against the amount due in taxes. For anyone with a high income or planning to buy an expensive boat, it would be worthwhile to discuss it with an accountant or attorney beforehand.

Our schooner *At Last* was documented. We renewed the documentation each year by simply filling out the forms and mailing them to the Coast Guard. *Sabrina,* on the other hand, was registered in a state, so we paid a considerable sum in sales tax when we bought her and a fee each time the registration was renewed. It's one of the few instances where the smaller boat cost us more money than the large one. Several states now require even documented boats to be registered.

We've found our grocery bills run about the same afloat as they did on shore. Assuming that the boat has an icebox or refrigeration, eating habits rarely change as much as most people think. If any money is saved, it's because we become better planners—you can't just run down to the corner store for an item you forgot or because you get a sudden yen for something. We plan our menus more carefully and, since space in an ice box is at a premium, we tend to eat up our leftovers instead of throwing them away.

One fellow says, "If it's not eaten at dinner, it gets scrambled with eggs the next morning." He has some pretty strange breakfasts, but he rarely wastes anything. These small savings are generally offset when coastal cruising by having to shop occasionally in "Mom 'n Pop" stores or at marinas that stock a few staples and where prices are invariably higher. Long-distance voyagers sometimes save money by buying case quantities of items, although I've found that not all markets will give a discount for this. It's necessary to find a wholesale outlet that specializes in discounts for volume purchases.

Some live-aboards claim to save a lot of money by fishing for a lot of their food or by gathering clams and mussels.

Those who move aboard but keep regular shore jobs will be buying as many clothes as ever. Stowing all the clothes and keeping them presentable will be the real problem. For those who don't have dress-up jobs, clothing ceases to be much of an issue. On shore I had a closet full of dresses, pants suits, shoes and handbags—something for every occasion. Bruce had suits, dress shirts, sport jackets and dress shoes. Now we each have one outfit for those rare times when we dress up. I've always disliked formal affairs, anyway, so it doesn't bother me at all to pass them by if I don't have anything to wear.

The consensus among live-aboards, I've discovered, is that comfort comes first, followed by selection of easy-care, washable fabrics. No one seems to care much about being stylish. Along the waterfront, jeans and T-shirts are always acceptable. As a consequence, we wear our clothes until they become paint rags instead of until they go out of style. We spent less than $100 in 1979 for clothing, although when our foul-weather gear wore out that figure more than tripled.

Another reason we spend less on clothes is simply lack of stowage space. We rarely add to our clothing inventory; when we buy something it's to replace an article that's worn out.

I can't say with any authority that live-aboards get sick any less often than shore people, although it seems that way. Perhaps it's because we get more fresh air and more exercise or because our lifestyles are more relaxed, without the stresses involved in climbing up business or social ladders. It came as no surprise to discover that several live-aboards I've met had previously suffered heart attacks and moved aboard as a way of easing tensions and pressures. Many live-aboards are more isolated from the general public and thus less likely to catch colds or the flu.

Live-aboards, particularly those who are cruising, become more self-sufficient at treating themselves for minor ailments. It's no longer as convenient to visit the family doctor for every little ache and pain, so we fall back on Grandma's old-fashioned remedies.

Boat maintenance and buying gear are a part of boat ownership whether you live aboard or not. Live-aboards, however, are generally more inclined to do their own work instead of hiring a boat yard to do it. This may be because we have more time once aboard and/

or because we care enough to do the job correctly and take pride in having done it ourselves. It also saves money!

Northerners who move aboard to "follow the sun" may be surprised at how cheaply they can live. The money saved in heating costs alone can more than offset the price of engine fuel, charts and other travel expenses. You'll also buy fewer and less expensive clothes. Compare shorts and T-shirts to parkas, wool pants and fur-lined boots!

Other, more subtle ways exist to save money without really making a conscious effort to do so. The pressure of keeping up with the Jonses is gone. We spend less on entertainment and we don't buy on impulse very often. We may window shop and admire goodies, but we can't buy all those marvelous knickknacks simply because there's no place to put them.

7

Lighting Afloat

"Let there be light"

LIGHT IS CRUCIAL in determining whether a live-aboard boat is homey and comfortable or miserable and cave-like. Second is proper ventilation and frequently the two can be combined. I wouldn't pass up a good buy on a used boat if the only thing wrong with it was poor lighting. Much can be done inexpensively to remedy that problem. Even new boats usually require some lighting modifications to turn them into true boat homes.

LIGHTING BELOW

A visit to a boat show will convince anyone that manufacturers of stock fiberglass boats are getting away from all-plastic construction. They're starting to put back a little warmth with teak trim, teak bulkheads and teak-and-holly cabin soles. Some of them are even installing all wood (usually all-teak) interiors, finished bright. My first reaction when I step aboard one of these floating lovelies is, "Isn't this magnificent!" as I caress the satiny swirls and curves of real, honest-to-goodness wood.

PAINT OR VARNISH

Yet, like most things in life, you can have too much of a good thing. The cozy warmth of bright finished interiors, especially when coupled with upholstery fabrics in warm colors like orange, rust and beige, can turn the most comfortable boat into a gloomy dungeon if you're couped up below over a three-day rainy spell (See Figure 1A).

Sailboats, particularly, tend to have small ports, with much of their light provided by the open companionway. But, put in the hatch slides, slide the hatch closed and after a few days a brown interior can take on all the aspects of cave dwelling. Add to this that sticky damp feeling that comes with prolonged rainy weather and it'll really seem like the stone age.

The first and most obvious solution is to paint some of that wood and leave the trim bright (See Figure 1B). Already I can feel you cringe! Considering the price of teak, $12 a board foot in some areas, I'll admit it's painful to deflower it with white paint, regardless of how nice it's going to look when you've finished. But, if you're ordering a new boat, build-

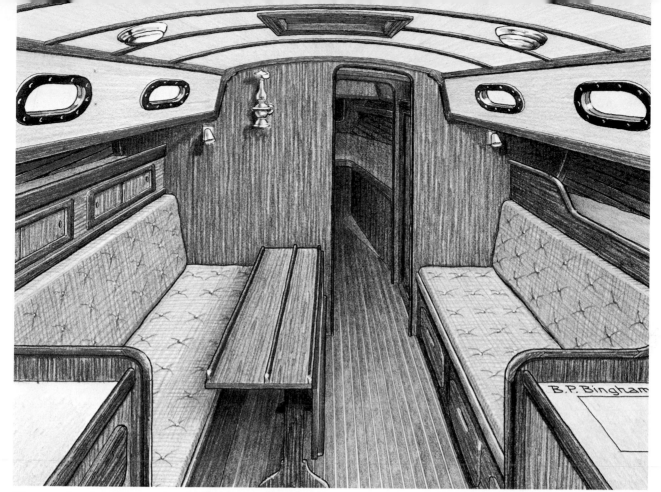

Figure 1A   *An all-natural wood interior can make a boat dark and gloomy, especially on rainy days.*

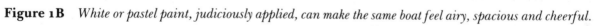

Figure 1B   *White or pastel paint, judiciously applied, can make the same boat feel airy, spacious and cheerful.*

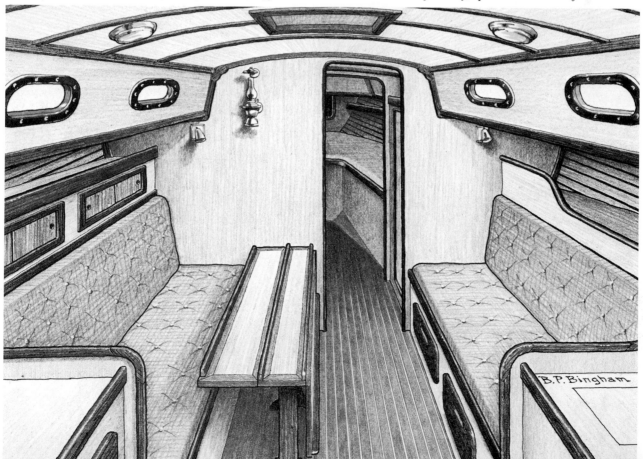

ing or re-building one yourself, you should seriously consider the advantages of painting major surfaces and leaving wood trim varnished or oiled. The trim alone can include bulkhead edgings; shelf and counter fiddles; moldings around doors and drawers; locker doors and drawer fronts; small, bulkhead-mounted shelves; and even varnished pine ceiling on exposed areas of the hull. That's a considerable amount of brightwork!

The large, major surfaces, such as bulkheads, berth and counter fronts, can be painted—either white or a pale pastel. Contrary to what many people believe, that is the traditional type of yacht interior—not one with all the wood finished bright.

The dark colors of most woods absorb light and makes an interior feel smaller than it really is. Remember, too, that any wood will darken with age. Anyone who has ever tried to match a piece of brightwork with new wood knows what I mean. Light colors reflect light and give a nice feeling of spaciousness. The use of mirrors to reflect light will extend your apparent field of vision and make a cabin appear even larger.

Some manufacturers are installing wood planking to the underside of the cabin top. It's very attractive, but if it's combined with an all-wood interior, the total effect can be pretty gloomy. A white painted wood, formica or a vinyl liner overhead will give the appearance of more headroom as well as reflecting light. A good idea for the overhead is using acoustical tiles. They are white, lightweight and an excellent insulating material for both sound and heat.

Choosing fabrics for cushions, pillows and curtains from the cool family of colors—such as light blues and greens—will also brighten a dark interior. It's true that light colors show dirt faster than dark colors. However, I think the bother of more frequent cleaning is a small price to pay for the light and space-enhancing qualities of pale colors. All fabrics used on a boat should be Scotchgard treated. Plaids, stripes and prints can be of light colors. They'll look cleaner longer than a solid light color.

One of the most pleasant boat interiors I've ever seen is Ken and Nancy Day's 28-foot-sloop, *Cero II*. Virtually all the wood below is painted white, including cabin trunk sides, the overhead, berth and counter fronts, and all bulkheads. The cushions are a white, blue and green plaid, and the sole in the main saloon is carpeted in a pale beige. Bright blue-and-green pillows pick up the colors of the cushions. Only a few cabinet doors and fiddles were left natural. The resulting atmosphere is light, airy and inviting, and I always have the feeling that I'm on a boat much larger than 28 feet.

One area in a boat where I do like all brightwork and warm colors is an enclosed stateroom used exclusively for sleeping. The impression of darkness and warmth can be quite conducive to slumber (this is especially true when you're trying to catch a nap during the daylight hours following a long night watch). I like the warm cozy feeling of snuggling down into a bunk surrounded by the soft glow of varnished wood and rich dark-colored fabrics.

NATURAL LIGHTING

If you can't bring yourself to paint over natural wood, there are other ways to lighten a dark interior. Many stock boats have clear or tinted acrylic forehatches, but the main companionway hatch is invariably solid wood or fiberglass. When we first moved aboard *Sabrina*, we had a long stretch of rainy weather. After a week cooped up below, the continuous gloom was affecting our usual sunny dispositions.

When the sun finally popped out, Bruce in-

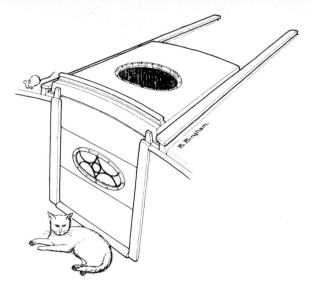

Figure 2 *Sabrina's companionway hatch decklight admits a tremendous amount of light even when it's buttoned up during inclement weather.*

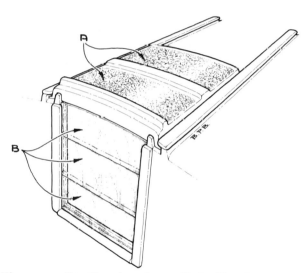

Figure 3 *Sanding the gelcoat off of a fiberglass hatch will make it translucent (A), and cribboards can be replaced with pieces of Plexiglas cut to size (B) for even more light.*

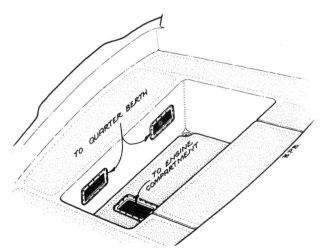

Figure 4 *A decklight installed at the aft end of a cockpit sole will light the compartment beneath. Ports in the cockpit side will brighten the quarterberth. If they're opening ports you'll get ventilation as well.*

stalled a large oval decklight of ¼-inch Plexiglas in the teak companionway hatch and I painted the remaining wood of its underside an off-white to match the vinyl overhead (See Figure 2). What a difference! *Sabrina* became almost as bright below with the hatch closed as when it was open.

If your boat has a fiberglass hatch, it isn't necessary to install a decklight. Using a belt sander, grind off the gelcoat and make the hatch translucent. This won't weaken the hatch as long as you're careful to remove *only* the gelcoat (See Figure 3).

Sailboats usually have hatch slides instead of doors. They, too, can receive small decklights or be replaced entirely with slides of Plexiglas cut to size (See Figure 3). You can install decklights or windows in solid wood doors or replace one of the panels with Plexiglas. Where loss of privacy is a problem when installing Plexiglas, it can be converted from transparent to translucent by sanding until it has a matte finish.

Decklights can be installed almost anywhere in the deck or cabin top. Even very small decklights will let in a surprising amount of light. In a boat with the engine under the cockpit, a decklight installed at the aft end of the cockpit sole will shed light on what is always a dark and mysterious place (See Figure 4).

Decklights can be either Plexiglas or Lexan. In places with a considerable curve, such as the cabin top, Lexan is the best choice as it's quite flexible. Plexiglas is likely to crack if you try to force it around a bend unless you have some method of heating it. A translucent decklight will provide more light below than a clear one,

Figure 5 *If headroom will allow for their use, prism decklights bring in more light than any other type.*

something to consider if you're putting a decklight in the head compartment. And, since the light is diffused, you never get blinding light in your eyes or hot spots of direct sunlight. We installed six decklights in *At Last* and I made half of them translucent by wetsanding the Plexiglas with a very fine grit of wet/dry sandpaper.

Prism decklights will let in the greatest amount of light. But you consider headroom when installing them in a passageway (See Figure 5). Prisms are expensive and sometimes hard to find, although you can still order rectangular ones from Jay Stuart Haft in Milwaukee. I personally feel they are worth the money, since they really do bring in an inordinate amount of light. One firm—Palmer Johnson—has started producing prism decklights in Lucite.

Dorade vents can be converted to decklights by replacing the wooden tops with Plexiglas so they let in light as well as air (See Figure 6).

Portlights can be added to many boats. I wouldn't install additional ports to a cabin trunk side if it would affect the appearance of the boat, but they can be added to the forward or aft end, or both. An excellent place for an opening port is in the side of the cockpit on a sailboat that opens into the quarterberth. This gives both light and ventilation to what is always a shadowy, stuffy area (See Figure 4). Curtains over ports should open wide enough to expose the entire port.

Hull ports also can be added. But for obvious reasons I wouldn't want them to be opening. We installed two 5-inch round ports on each side of *At Last*'s forepeak berth. Hull ports

should be added with careful thought given to their external appearance (See Figure 7). We taped 5-inch circles of paper to *At Last*'s hull, then rowed off to look at her and readjusted the paper circles until they looked right. Since *At Last* is wood, we had to be sure we were locating the ports between frames. Aside from the light they allow in, I've always thought that hull ports give a nice "shippy" look to a yacht, either sail or power, and create the illusion that the boat is much longer than she really is.

Hull ports can fit into a rabbetted opening on a wood boat so they're flush with the planking, although the rabbet really isn't necessary. Most fiberglass hulls aren't thick enough to allow a rabbet unless you are able to build up the hull with additional layers of glass on the

Figure 6 *Substituting Plexiglas for the top of a wood dorade box will let it do double duty as a decklight and as a ventilator.*

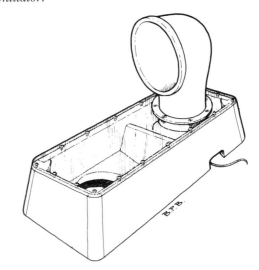

inside. The ports should be fitted on the out-side of the hull so that water pressure (especially on a sailboat heeled over) has the effect of pressing the Plexiglas against the hull, and making the seal tighter. The ports should be well bedded and fastened with bolts and lock washers.

When we installed the ports in *At Last* I was a little concerned because we only used ¼-inch Plexiglas, but I shouldn't have worried. We were caught in a gale off the New Jersey shore and our 50-pound anchor tore loose. It bashed against the hull and the port for several minutes before we figured out what was causing that clanking noise. An inspection showed deep gouges and chunks of wood torn out of the hull, but only a few scratches in the Plexiglas port. We always walked on the large deck-light in *Sabrina*'s hatch while we were furling sails and I've never felt it give the slightest bit under our weight.

ARTIFICIAL LIGHTING

Once the sun dips below the horizon, it's time to think about artificial lighting. This can be electric, kerosene or even candles. First let's talk about the location of lights, regardless of type.

One dome light, located in the center of a cabin, is a simple way of lighting a general area such as the main saloon or the forward cabin.

It's a waste of power, however, if it's the only light source for individual tasks like reading, navigating or beard-trimming. The dome light is then usually too far from the work at hand to illuminate it properly and chances are you or some object will cast a shadow where you don't want it.

When we're underway at night, I like to keep a small light on below so I can find my way around quickly and without stumbling. It doesn't have to be much—a kerosene lamp turned very low or a small bunk light with the shade turned towards the hull. It's important that this light not interfere with the helmsman's night vision. If it's electric, you might consider making a night shade of red acetate or painting the bulb with red nail polish. There is also a commercial red plastic dip available for this purpose. If you like to navigate from the cockpit—even at night—flashlights are available with red lens inserts. Or, you can make

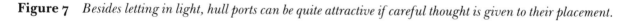

Figure 7   *Besides letting in light, hull ports can be quite attractive if careful thought is given to their placement.*

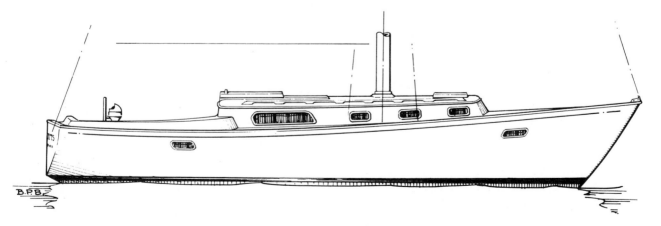

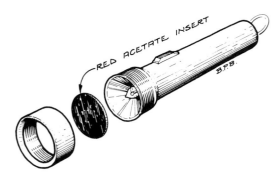

Figure 8 *A red acetate insert for a flashlight will provide nighttime illumination without destroying the helmsman's night vision.*

Figure 9 *A small, inexpensive, low-draw dashboard rally light can be installed anywhere a minimum amount of light is required.*

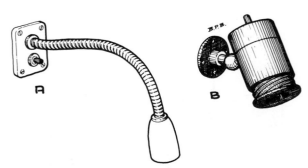

Figure 10 *A gooseneck navigator's light (A) provides a concentrated beam of light that can be aimed in any direction. A variable-width beam light (B) allows adjustment from a wide circle of light for general use to a narrow beam for closeup work.*

your own (See Figure 8) out of red acetate purchased from either camera or art supply stores.

There is a very small light that can be ordered through sports car magazines called a dashboard rally light (See Figure 9). They are inexpensive, can be loaded with low-wattage bulbs and can be used all over the boat. They work well anywhere a minimum amount of light is needed at night: at the aft end of the cabin trunk for soft companionway illumination; over the galley so the night watch can make a cup of coffee or fix a sandwich without disturbing the off watch; inside lockers and cabinets; in the head; or over the chart table for a quick glance at the course.

The gooseneck navigator's light is also an excellent investment, since you can aim the concentrated beam in any direction (See Figure 10A). They are available at marine hardware stores and by mail and from auto supply outlets and at aircraft supply stores. Some manufacturers make a variable-width-beam light on a gooseneck base so you can adjust the lamp from a wide circle of light for general use to a narrow beam for closeup work (See Figure 10B).

With electric lighting on a boat, the major concerns are the drain on the ship's batteries and the complications of a wiring system. I think the best wiring system is one with separate circuits for port and starboard (See Figure 11). That way, if something goes wrong with one circuit, you still have the lights on the other side of the boat as a backup system. But it's not wise to have a boat dependent entirely on electric lighting. Even if electricity is the primary source, there should be at least one or two kerosene lamps for emergency use.

Fluorescent lights put a very low drain on the batteries—compared to the high draw of an incandescent bulb. The only objection, for some people, is the cold light produced by fluorescent bulbs. You can buy yellow fluorescent lights, but they're not easy to find. My own preference is for fluorescent lighting in work areas, such as the galley, the navigation area and the head, and incandescent lamps in relaxation areas—the main saloon and sleeping quarters, for example.

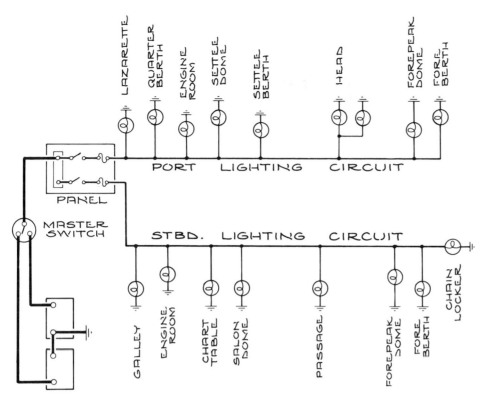

Figure 11 *A port/starboard wiring system provides compartment lighting backup if something fails with one of the circuits.*

We've found the best place to buy fluorescent bulbs is at trailer supply stores, where they have a wide choice of sizes and styles. It's a good idea to purchase extras, since they're not easy to find of the right size. However, the life of a fluorescent tube is *so much longer* that replacement isn't required often.

Aside from permanently mounted electric lights, there's a large variety of self-contained battery-powered lamps on the market (See Figure 12), including fluorescent lanterns. Their great advantage is that they can be moved around wherever temporary light is needed. We have one that invariably ends up hanging from the boom to light up the cockpit for after-dark gatherings at anchor.

The disadvantage to self-contained lights is the need to carry extra batteries, especially if they are used as a primary lighting system. We once used our cockpit lamp as an anchor light when we ran out of kerosene. After a night of continuous use (about 10 hours) the large 6-volt lantern battery had to be replaced. Hardly an economical application.

They're best used as backup lights or for handy temporary lighting. We mounted one in *Sabrina*'s forward clothing locker (See Figure

13). The original D-cell batteries lasted well over a year, since the light was only used briefly when searching for something in the locker at night. These lamps are inexpensive and are available at most hardware stores and large department stores such as Sears.

The old tried-and-true lighting system for yachts remains kerosene lamps. Despite the wonderful convenience of flicking a switch, I

Figure 12 *Self-contained battery-powered lamps: incandescent (A) and fluorescent (B).*

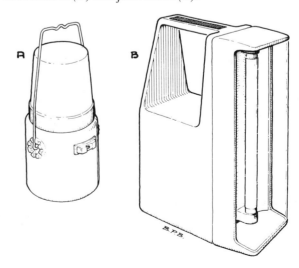

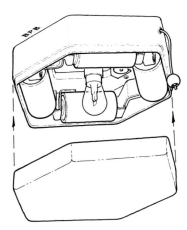

Figure 13 *A self-contained light, powered by four D-cell batteries, is ideal for lockers, bins and small compartments.*

still feel that nothing compares to the cheery glow of a cabin lit by the soft light of a kerosene lamp. *At Last* used kerosene lighting exclusively for two years until we installed wiring circuits. Since the kerosene lamps were in constant use, the wicks were trimmed and the globes cleaned daily, a routine we did not find bothersome. We never used the expensive "odorless" kerosene, although we always bought a good grade. The best is sold as "range oil" and is crystal clear. Always check the color of the kerosene—if it has a yellowish tinge it will smoke and smell.

One thing we learned quickly was that it's not the size of the lamp that's important, but the size of the wick. Many of the pretty gimballed brass marine lamps have ½-inch wicks. A ½-inch wick won't produce enough light to read or work by. About all they're good for is a night light or for atmosphere. Disappointed in them, we bought two simple kerosene lamps with

1-inch wicks for $5 each at a local hardware store. I covered their glass bases with macramé and Bruce made brackets so we could hang them up when underway. The light given by their 1-inch wicks was a big improvement, and their tall globes produced a cleaner and brighter flame than the short chimneys of their marine counterparts.

Lately I've been seeing some lovely brass lamps with wide wicks, usually in marine gift shops. One of the best marine lamps is made by West Products—it has a wide wick, a double-gimballed bracket and a *large* smoke bell. That's important if you have a white overhead.

Kerosene lamps must be gimballed to keep the kerosene from spilling when the boat heels and to prevent the overheating and smoking that happens when the lamp is not level. A reflector plate mounted on the bulkhead behind the lamps will make them appear brighter by reflecting light, in addition to making it easier to keep the surrounding area clean.

The brightest kerosene light is produced by lamps like the Aladdin, which burn with a mantle. One drawback is that these lamps are generally cumbersome and hard to stow on a small boat. They also generate a good deal of heat, which can be nice on a chilly evening, but may drive you right out of the cabin on a hot summer night.

No discussion of interior lighting is complete without at least a mention of candles. I wouldn't consider them for reading or general use, but they do add a festive touch when entertaining. The short, fat ones work best on a boat. And I wouldn't be without a couple of citronella candles to help keep the bugs away in the summertime. The ones we use are in glass containers, but are covered with netting and we've yet to break one. Remember to store candles in a cool place. I left one under a deck-light one hot afternoon and had a melted-wax mess to clean up.

LOCKERS AND CABINETS

When planning interior lighting, thought must be given to lighting the dark recesses of lockers and cabinets—any hard-to-reach storage areas. I've already mentioned the battery-powered light in *Sabrina*'s clothing locker, but natural lighting is even more important. The more natural light you let in, the less chance of mildew forming. This is especially important in sail and clothing lockers. Installing small translucent decklights over such lockers is an excellent idea; even better would be a dorade vent with a translucent top to let in fresh air and light.

Lockers that don't reach the deck and storage areas under berths and counters benefit from open grillwork panels and doors to let in both light and air. Stock louvered vents, available in several different sizes, can be installed. Cut-out panels are easy to make with a drill and jigsaw.

On both *At Last* and *Sabrina* we painted the inside of all lockers, including the chain lockers, with a semi-gloss white paint. This paint reflects the merest bit of light, so it's easier to locate gear and easy to clean. While painting the chain locker in *At Last* I needed a flashlight at first. But by the time I was halfway through I was able to turn off the flashlight since the small amount of light coming through the deck pipe was reflected well enough by the new paint to finish the job in natural light.

ABOVE-DECK LIGHTING

So far we've been talking about interior lighting. But obviously light is needed on deck after dark. With the exception of engineless houseboats, I have to assume that a live-aboard boat will at least occasionally be used for cruising, and sooner or later that cruising will include running at night.

SIDE LIGHTS

Port and starboard running lights are often mounted on the sides of the cabin. Although this may be a convenient spot and handy for wiring, it's *not* the best location. The running light on the leeward side may be no more than a foot above the water when the boat is under sail, while the windward light may be shrouded by the deck, toerail or bulwark. Furthermore, such a light can be hidden by a deck-sweeping genoa. This arrangement is illegal *and* unsafe.

Quite a few stock boats are being molded with recesses in the stem just below the toerail. It's questionable whether this really raises the lights any higher off the water than the cabin-side position. And since this location is at the end of the boat, its height above the water is constantly changing when the boat is pitching. In rough weather, the light may actually be below the mean wave level half the time, even though it's not submerging. An even greater flaw to bow-mounted side lights is that sooner or later they *do* become immersed and, regardless of how well the light bases or lenses are bedded, water seeps into the unit and trouble is not far behind. Water only needs a hairline route to find its way to the bulb socket or wiring connection, then pfftt!

A better arrangement is pulpit-mounted side lights. This raises the light position about 2½ feet. Connections are more accessible and the lights are far less likely to become doused in a seaway. They're still at the end of the boat, of course, and subject to pitching motion. But the added height helps. They should be mounted as far forward as practical to prevent them from snagging headsails and sheets.

Owners of traditional boats love light boards in the rigging. We like the look of them, too. But more than once we've seen one washed up on the beach, having been torn loose by a flogging headsail or snarled sheet. I hate to think what these lights did to the sails in the process.

Keep in mind, too, that light boards with kerosene lamps are now illegal (except in emergencies). If light boards are used, the lights must be visible slightly across the bow, that is, not be covered by a headsail when viewed from dead ahead. This is a particular problem when a boat is on a reach.

On *Sabrina* we installed a trilight at the masthead and used it almost exclusively, keeping the cabin-mounted running lights and stern light as a backup system. We prefer the trilight for several reasons (See Figure 14). For one thing, it's almost 32 feet above the water, making it visible at a considerably longer distance, particularly in heavy seas. We have sailed at night when other sailboats were around and only caught an occasional glimpse of them as their running lights kept appearing and disappearing in the trough. I like the idea that

Figure 14 *A masthead trilight allows greater visibility than cabin or hull-mounted running lights, with the added bonus of using one light bulb instead of three.*

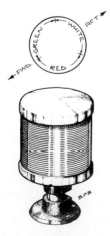

especially a large ship will be able to spot us more easily when we're using the trilight. And with it, we're only using one light bulb instead of three, so the drain on the battery is considerably reduced. Remember that under existing Coast Guard regulations a masthead trilight is only legal while under sail. When motoring—even with sails up—standard port and starboard side lights are required.

STERN LIGHTS

The stern light is possibly the most important light on the boat. The highest risk of collision is from the stern simply because you're almost always facing and looking forward. A stern light mounted on the taffrail becomes the lowest running light aboard the boat and is subject to the same pitching and dousing problems of hull-mounted side lights.

While the white sector of a masthead trilight is our first choice to fulfill the stern light requirement, if a hull-mounted stern light is used (even a secondary one) it should at least be mounted on the pushpit instead of the taffrail. A boom gallows mounting is even better, as several additional feet of height are gained that way.

A stern light should never be mounted on the top of an outboard rudder since it causes the critical light angles to change constantly, and may confuse vessels approaching from astern. If your boat has an outboard rudder, make sure that if the light is taffrail mounted the rudder head does not obstruct the stern light in any way. An alternative is to install a pair of stern lights, one on each side of the rudder head, but as close as possible to each other so they always will appear as a single light from dead astern. I saw this done on a Nor'Sea 27 and it worked surprisingly well. It does, however, increase the drain on your batteries.

FOREDECK LIGHTS

When sailing to weather we sail "by the wind" using the telltales on the headsail rather than a set compass course. So it's vital that we can see the woolies—and that's always a problem at night.

Donald Street came up with a great solution in his book, *The Ocean Sailing Yacht: Volume II.* He suggests cutting off the metal visor portion at the top of the bow light so it will light up the foretriangle (See Figure 15). Bruce did this on *Sabrina,* and went one step further. He lowered the bow light from its position near the spreaders so that it lights up the foredeck as well as the headsails. That worked out very well, especially for me. Bruce can usually see the tell-

Figure 15 *The foretriangle can be lighted by cutting off the metal visor portion of the top of the bow light. Lowering its position will illuminate the foredeck as well.*

tales if there's any moonlight at all; my poor eyesight makes it impossible for me to sail at night without the altered bow light.

In addition to the bow light, a stern light could be mounted upside down on the mast to function as a foredeck light (See Figure 16A). It could be used instead of—or in addition to—the high-watt and high-drain spreader light. There is a bow light/foredeck light combination on the market that is used in conjunction with a three-way switch (See Figure 16B). The light is compact and uses only a fraction of the power of a sealed-beam spreader light.

A spectacular gimmick most often seen on ocean-racing circuits is using a 12-volt fluorescent black light, mounted on the forward side of the mast. Fluorescent tape, or fluorescent woolies, are applied to the headsail, illuminating its shape at night without using blinding white lights. The fluorescent bulbs draw less than 2 amps, yet their lighting power is amazing. The tube, of course, must be protected by a Lexan cover.

It also is possible to take advantage of the loom of a headsail black light on a dark foredeck for locating cleats, blocks, genoa track locations, winches and winch handles by applying short strips of flourescent tape to them. Such an application will prevent a lot of stubbed toes and reduce fumbling a lot.

Anchor Lights

Anchor lights can be electric (wired into the ship's system), kerosene or the type that use a self-contained battery. The electric ones do drain the boat's batteries. I know at least one firm that makes a masthead trilight that includes an anchor light and a strobe. Kerosene anchor lights, just like cabin lamps, must be filled, have the lenses cleaned and the wick trimmed before each night's use.

We have a small Perko brass anchor light and have *never* had problems with it blowing out. I've never used a battery-powered anchor light, but I understand from people who own them that they are quite efficient and the batteries *do* last a long time. Check the lantern to make sure it comes with a low-watt bulb rather than a high-watt bulb designed primarily for interior lighting.

Afterdeck Lighting

Kerosene lanterns (as opposed to cabin lamps) work especially well for cockpit or afterdeck lighting at night. The fuel is inexpensive and their warmth is usually appreciated on a chilly evening. Another idea (if battery drain is not a consideration), is to purchase a 32-point white masthead light (wingtip variety) and mount it on the underside of the boom over the cockpit. It can be used as a cockpit light when dockside or at anchor.

Figure 16 *A standard stern light (A) can be inverted on the mast to serve as a foredeck light. A bow/foredeck combination light (B), when hooked to a three-way switch, uses a fraction of the wattage of a sealed-beam spreader light.*

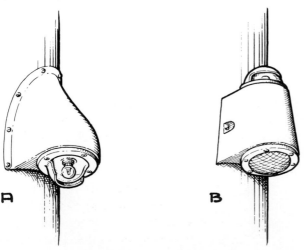

A   B

Citronella candles give a nice soft glow for evening entertaining as well as driving summer bugs away. If there's enough breeze to blow out the candles, it's probably enough to keep the bugs away, too.

Flashlights

We've all had trouble with flashlights. Granted, sometimes the cause is simply cheap construction. More often, however, they go on the fritz due to corroded connections or battery-end terminals. An occasional sanding of all connecting surfaces using fine-grit sandpaper is an excellent preventive, followed by a light application of electrician's silicone grease—just a dab.

We have learned over the years it just doesn't pay to buy cheap flashlights. In our opinion, one of the best on the market today is the "Pro-Light", made by ITT Jabsco Products. This flashlight is available in several beam types and voltages. The key to its superiority is its construction: an anodized aluminum pipe body with anodized cast aluminum end fittings. The connection threadings are machined to very exacting tolerances, in addition to having neoprene O-ring seals—making them virtually vapor-tight. This type of flashlight is frequently seen in use by police and the military. The large ones also would be useful for repelling unwelcome boarders.

Penlights are made in a variety of hermetically sealed throw-away sizes and shapes and are quite inexpensive. Some are about the size of a cigarette lighter and others resemble a ball-point pen. One will fit in your pocket and you'll find it invaluable for a quick glance at the chart, untying a knot at night or for other jobs that don't require broad illumination. Paint the bulb with red plastic dip and you can use the penlight without spoiling anyone else's night vision.

Searchlights

We don't think any boat should be without a hand-held, high-powered, sealed-beam searchlight. They are generally offered with plugs that fit into a cigarette lighter receptacle, which should be located just inside the companionway hatch so it won't be shorted out by rain or salt spray. The lights generally offer a pinpoint range of about 100 yards, and a reflective range double that when aimed toward a fluorescent-taped object—such as buoys or waterway markers.

These searchlights also are able to penetrate relatively clear water for surprising depths, an important consideration if navigating at night in poorly marked, coral-infested waters like some of the out-islands in the Bahamas.

Strobe Lights

Almost all boats heading offshore carry a bright, flashing man-overboard strobe light. Those that don't should. The strobe light can be used for emergencies other than a man overboard, since it is undoubtedly the strongest light on board.

Bruce was at the helm crossing the Gulf Stream between the Bahamas and Miami in very light air one night, when he noticed we were being approached by a ship steering an extremely erratic course, although her bearing essentially remained steady. He decided to begin taking evasive action, despite our right-of-way position. It seemed almost as if the ship was actually *trying* to run us down. She continued to alter her course toward us.

At first Bruce thought she might be a Coast Guard patrol vessel. When we were less than a quarter of a mile apart, he yielded to his instinct for self-preservation, grabbed the man-overboard light, snapped it on and held it as high as he could.

We both breathed a sigh of relief as the vessel instantly turned her bow away from us.

A strobe light also could be very useful to a boat that's disabled and awaiting rescuers. Flares could be used as well, of course, but the strobe provides a *continuous* brilliant flashing light to indicate position. It can be hoisted to the masthead to increase its visibility.

If the boat is equipped with only one man-overboard strobe (and we recommend two), it should be attached by a lanyard to the overboard flagpole and life ring. This should be within reach of the helmsman. But it also can be rigged so it's retrievable by someone in the water. This is done by trailing a long buoyant line astern attached to the strobe. Even if the boat is traveling fairly fast, you'd be amazed at how quickly someone can get their senses together, swim to the trip line and grab it.

Small strobe lights are available (about the size of a pack of cigarettes), that can be attached, along with a whistle, to a life jacket. It's an excellent idea, but how often do you actually wear a life jacket? I'd rather see the strobe stuffed in a pocket or attached to a belt so the person on deck at night always has it with him. At very least, when the weather gets rough and safety harnesses are worn, personal strobe lights should be carried as well.

LIGHT UP YOUR BUILDER

Production boats are usually manufactured with "first impression impact." Little thought is given to actual live-aboard or underway conditions.

If you're ordering a new boat or having one built, however, then you're in a position to "ride herd" on the builder to ensure the boat's lighting arrangements are done right and that she is delivered in such a way as to make her most habitable. Make sure lights of your choice are installed where you want them. You might have to supply the builder with any lights that are different from his stock ones, of course, but it's easier to have him install what you want to begin with than have to replace them later.

On an older boat, don't be hasty about removing existing lights—particularly topside. It may be easier to add what you want and simply use the original system as a backup, as we did with *Sabrina*'s running lights when we added the trilight. In the same vein, kerosene side lights may be illegal, but I still consider them a good backup system if something goes haywire with the electrical connections or the batteries go dead.

The total lighting system—interior, topside, natural, artificial and emergency—is of vital importance on the live-aboard and cruising boat. Careful planning can result in a boat that's bright, cheery and comfortable, as well as being safe and economical to operate—one that's a pleasure to call "home."

SOURCES

JAY STUART HAFT CO. INC.
   8925 North Tennyson Drive
   Milwaukee, WI 53217

ITT JABSCO PRODUCTS
   1485 Dale Way
   Costa Mesa, CA 92626

PALMER JOHNSON
   61 Michigan St.
   Sturgeon Bay, WI 54235

PERKO INC.
   16490 N.W. 13th Avenue
   P.O. Box 64000D
   Miami, FL 33164

Ventilation

8

"Airy opinions"

GOOD VENTILATION IS necessary—even vital. It prevents mildew and condensation, rids cooking fumes and musty odors, and generally makes conditions below pleasant, dry and comfortable in any weather.

HATCHES

Ideally, a hatch (other than a sliding companionway hatch) should open either fore or aft. Several boat manufacturers include double-opening hatches as stock items. With a little ingenuity, many hatches can be made to open in all four directions (See Figure 1). This allows you to open the hatch towards the wind (for intake) or away from the wind (for exhaust) regardless of the boat's heading and increases the chances of being able to leave the hatch open in the rain.

Most existing hatches can be made multi-directional by adding a set of hinges for each direction. Some hatch risers will work in two directions so you may be able to get away with installing only one additional riser.

A hatch that opens fore and aft is probably all you need if you anchor out most of the time. But for anyone living aboard dockside all the time, a four-way hatch is probably worth the extra investment.

For maximum air flow, a hatch should be opened to about a 45-degree angle. If it's wide open most of the air will simply pass over it. Side flaps can be added to increase the hatch's "scooping" effectiveness. They can be canvas or Dacron sailcloth and attached with Velcro

Figure 1 *Hatches often can be made to open in four directions by adding an extra set of hardware for each direction.*

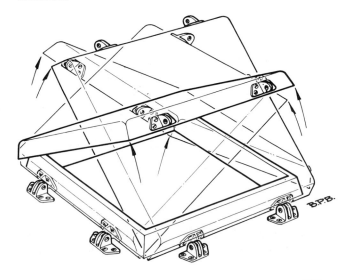

131

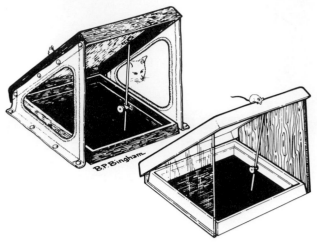

tape, snaps or buttons. Or, wedge triangles of ¼-inch plywood, or any other suitable material, into the wedge-shaped openings at the sides of the hatch (See Figure 2).

Canvas hoods or dodgers that completely enclose the hatch on three sides will be more watertight than simple side flaps (See Plate 1), particularly if they extend *forward*, past the edge of the hatch (See Figure 3). Bruce designed a hatch hood using a spreader to increase the "scoop effect" of the opening (See Figure 3). This spreader can be as simple as a wooden dowel with brass pins epoxied onto each end.

Figure 4 shows a more sophisticated version of the canvas hatch hood. The canvas baffle sewn inside the hood makes it virtually rainproof while still allowing a strong flow of air. Also shown in Figure 4 is a wood and plastic hood that replaces the existing hatch. Since the top piece of acrylic (or Lexan) would have to be heated to conform to the curve, that part of the project probably has to be done professionally. But the rest you can do yourself. This type of permanent hood, if fitted with hardware to match the replaced hatch, would be of tremendous value to boats left unattended during sweltering weather. To reduce heat builup and give a filtered light, use a translucent plastic or wet-sand with a very fine grit wet/dry sandpaper. A foredeck awning can also offer protection (See Plate 2).

Several "wind sails" or air scoops are on the market designed to fit over a hatch (usually a forward hatch). These admit a tremendous volume of air, even in the slightest breeze (See Plate 3). Some of them are unidirectional and

Figure 2 *Canvas side flaps can be made with vinyl windows to let in light as well as channeling the breeze. Rigid side flaps are simply wedges cut to fit. These, too, can keep it light below if they're made of clear acrylic.*

others work no matter which way the wind is blowing. One design, called a "flying nun," has large flaps or side extensions to bring in even more air. I've visited boats with wind sails so effective there was a virtual gale whistling through the cabin—almost to the point of being ridiculous: if you have to tie down the

Figure 3 *Hatch hoods can also have "windows". The hood on the left extends forward over the rim of the hatch and uses a dowel to keep it rigid (a more effective rain shield than side flaps). The hood on the right greatly increases the size of the opening by using a dowel spreader.*

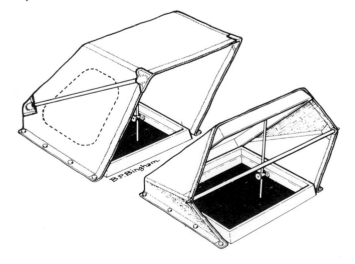

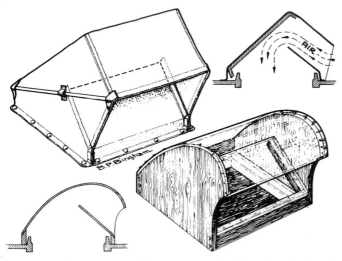

Figure 4   *Adding a canvas baffle makes this hatch hood waterproof (top view). Note, too, that the extension over the edge of the hatch angles down to a greater degree than the one shown in Figure 3. The waterproof hatch hood in the bottom view is made of wood and acrylic (or Lexan) and replaces the existing hatch. It's an excellent idea for boats left unattended in hot weather.*

Plate 3   *"Wind sails," like the familiar Windscoop, bring in a tremendous amount of air and will work in the lightest of zephyrs.* (PHOTO COURTESY OF PASTIME PRODUCTS, INC.)

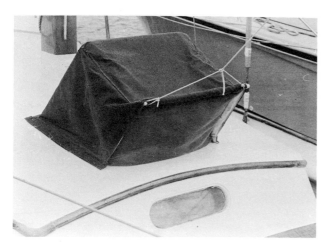

Plate 1   *A canvas dodger can completely enclose a hatch.*

Plate 2   *A foredeck awning will sometimes allow a hatch to remain open during rain as well as affording shade.*

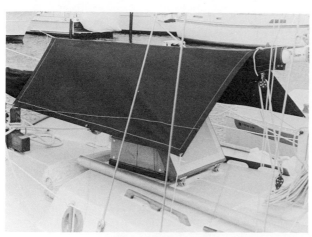

Plate 4 *This small ventilation hatch on a Cherubini 44 provides a flow of fresh air directly to the galley.*

cat, it's too much. There are enough designs and brands around to make comparison shopping worthwhile—or make your own.

Sometimes small hatches can be added in critical areas, such as over the galley or the head (See Plate 4). Several manufacturers make ventilation hatches small enough they can be installed in places where a standard hatch would not fit.

OPENING PORTS

Most opening ports in a sloping cabin trunk side will collect rainwater in the lower rim. Some manufacturers (Martec, Beckson and Nicro Fico, to name just a few) are now making ports with the lower rim angled in such a way as to eliminate this annoyance. Otherwise, the problem can usually be solved by drilling a small angled hole through the bottom of the frame so the water can run out. A very small hole will be clogged easily, so we used a short piece of brass rod on *Sabrina* for keeping them clear. If the ports can't be drilled, they can be furnished with a drip tray made of metal or acrylic (See Figure 5). One idea for a drip tray is to take a stock rainshield or hood and install it upside down under the port on the inside of the cabin trunk.

Sailing Specialties, Inc., has developed a clever, yet simple, porthole drain that works as a self-priming siphon (See Plate 5).

Bronze ports, however, even if they're drilled or fitted with a drain, will probably need a drip tray anyway to catch condensation. Ports can occasionally be left open in a light rain,

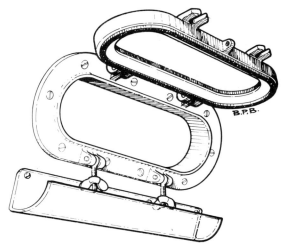

Figure 5 *A drip tray under an opening port will catch water that's collected in the outside rim (or drops of condensation). This simple tray (without end pieces) will hold a paper towel or strip of cloth that can be wrung out or discarded.*

Plate 5 *A porthole drain, made by Sailing Specialties, Inc., removes standing rainwater from port rims by a self-priming siphoning action.* (PHOTO COURTESY OF SAILING SPECIALTIES, INC.)

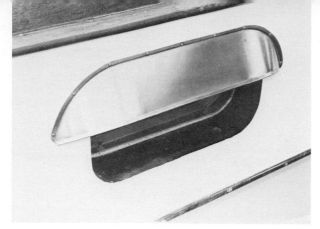

Plate 6 *Plastic, canvas or metal hoods help shield an open port from the rain. They can be purchased as stock items, or custom-made like the stainless steel one shown here.*

particularly if they are fitted with plastic, metal or canvas hoods on the outside of the cabin trunk (See Plate 6).

Beckson makes an internal rain shield for its opening ports that's a clear plastic louver combined with a screen that fits inside the port rim (the port can still be closed with the shield in place).

Bruce designed a combination hood/air scoop for opening ports, made out of a simple polypropylene plastic breadbox. Rigid plastic boxes are too prone to crack to use for this purpose. One end is cut out of the box which is then attached to the cabin trunk side using Dot fasteners (See Figure 6). Another attachment method is to install roundhead or panhead screws around the perimeter of the port, but screwed in only until the heads hold the rim of the box in place. The opening can face either fore or aft, depending on wind and weather.

I particularly like the type of opening port that consists of a rectangular piece of acrylic (not glass) resting inside a triangular-shaped box sometimes referred to as Herreshoff ports (See Figure 7). In the closed position the acrylic is held against the frame by wedges. When they're open, they are open at the top. I have been aboard boats with this kind of port and they could be kept open even in a hard, driving rain. On really hot days, the acrylic panes can be removed entirely. Since they often are removed, it's a good idea to build a small stowage rack near each port, preferably against the overhead. This can simply be a pair of L-shaped wood brackets and a turn-button, or

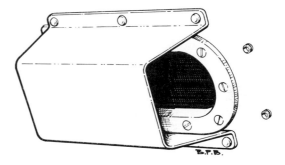

Figure 6 *A combination hood/air scoop can be made for an opening port by cutting off one end of a polypropylene bread box.*

Figure 7 *This simple and very effective port can be left open in a driving rainstorm. The wedges hold the acrylic secure in either position, or the acrylic can be removed for a wide-open port.*

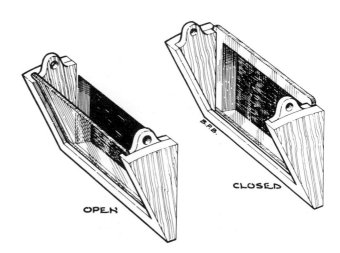

short lengths of shock cord criss-crossed over the acrylic.

Quarterberths are often stuffy airless tombs —not a pleasant place to sleep on a summer night. Adding a large port, opening into the cockpit, can make a tremendous difference.

VENTILATORS

Cowl vents work best in pairs, with one facing into the wind and one facing away. The first will bring air below. The vent facing away from the breeze will create a vacuum, expelling stale air from the cabin. Cowl vents installed on dorade boxes can be left in place in almost any kind of weather, since the design of the box prevents water from getting below (See Plate 7).

Sabrina had three cowl vents, none of which were on a dorade box. We found we could leave them in almost all the time, as long as we

Plate 8 *The Martec Dri-Vent has two internal baffles that channel any water out through drain holes in the back of the vent. This type of vent eliminates the need for a dorade box.* (PHOTO COURTESY MARTEC ENGINEERING CORP.)

turned them away from the wind when it rained. Several manufacturers offer cowl vents with an integral baffle that keeps out water and eliminates the need for a separate dorade box (See Plate 8).

Turbine ventilators (See Figure 8) are rarely seen any more, for several reasons. They are large and rather cumbersome for a small boat and must be located with care so lines are not fouled by them. Besides being hard to find,

Figure 8 *Turbine ventilators, while most suitable for large boats, will turn in the lightest airs and are an excellent choice for the galley.*

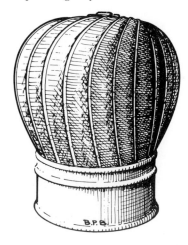

Plate 7 *Using a baffled dorade box means a cowl vent can keep working in almost any weather.*

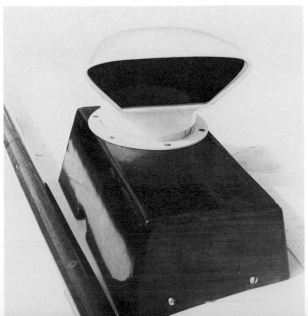

they're usually made of galvanized steel and must be kept painted to prevent rusting. I did see one recently (in a Manhattan Marine catalog) that was made of stainless steel. Despite their drawbacks, they are an excellent choice if you have the room for a galley vent. They will turn in the slightest breeze, drawing out cooking fumes, odors and steam to keep the galley fresh and dry. Water cannot enter as long as the vent is spinning even a tiny bit. And, a turbine ventilator is more efficient than a cowl vent.

Mushroom vents (See Plate 9) are handy where the height of a cowl vent will be a problem or where only occasional ventilation is needed. The basic no-frills type will take in water and must be screwed down tightly when it rains. You seldom have to go on deck to do this—most of them have an adjustment knob operated inside the boat. Some newer models have an additional rounded cover that lets in air and repels water. A mushroom vent is a good choice for exhausting a head or shower compartment, for venting a galley stove or, sometimes in a hatch top for airing the lazarette.

One ventilator that's been around for a long time (and with good reason) is the Sudbury Sky Vent (See Plate 10). Generally mounted on a hatch top, it has an internal baffle that keeps out even a pelting rain, while the transparent domed top admits light as well as air.

Vents needn't be limited to living spaces. Sail lockers, hanging lockers (especially ones used for foul weather gear), the forepeak (where chain and wet anchor rode is stowed), the bilge and the lazarette—all are areas particularly susceptible to dampness and mildew and should be vented. A stock metal louvered vent sometimes can be installed in the side of the cockpit or cabin trunk to get air to a sail locker or hanging locker. If the vent is painted to match the surrounding area it will hardly be noticeable.

Saga has such a vent located in the head that is quite effective. The metal ventilator is on the outside, with the vent then covered by a vinyl clam shell vent that acts as an air scoop. Louvered vents also can be installed in the compan-

Plate 9   *A mushroom vent, such as this Vetus vent, could be used in areas where only occasional ventilation is called for.* (PHOTO COURTESY W. H. DENOUDEN (USA) INC.)

Plate 10   *The Sudbury Sky Vent has an internal baffle to keep water out while the transparent top brings in light as well as air.* (PHOTO COURTESY SUDBURY LABORATORY, INC.)

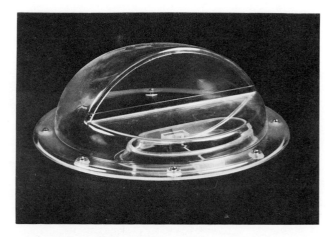

ionway cribboards to help air circulate when
the main hatch must be closed up tight (See
Plate 11).

Flexible vent hose sometimes can be used to
bring fresh air to hard-to-reach areas, and T
fittings can be added to reach several compartments (See Figure 9). As an example, a 3-inch
cowl vent on deck could be ducted with flexible
hose through a hanging locker or shelf behind
the settee and led down to the bilge. Additional
hose could be added, using a 3-inch PVC pipe
T, and led elsewhere—forward, perhaps, to
under-berth storage compartments.

On cold, blustery days you may wish to close
off one or two cowl vents. You can, of course,
remove the vents and snap in the covers. But I
would rather control the air flow from below.

The obvious, although unsightly, solution is to
stuff a towel in the vent. A more permanent
and attractive method is to cut a disk of the
same diameter as the vent's covering ring (See
Figure 10). Attach the disk by using one screw
in common with the ring so the disk can be

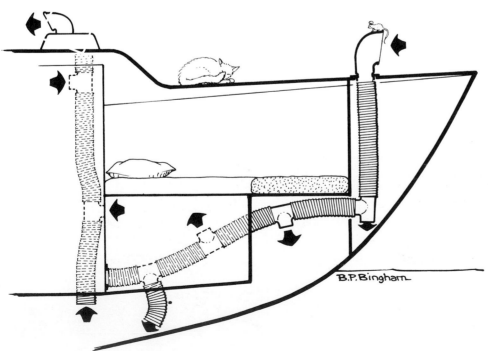

Figure 9 *Hard-to-reach
areas (under berths, lockers,
the bilge, etc.) can be vented
using cowl vents and flexible
vent hose. One cowl can reach
several compartments by
using PVC pipe Ts and
additional hose.*

swung around to partially or completely cover the opening. The disk could be plywood (painted to match the overhead) or clear acrylic (or any other rigid material). Either way it will scarcely be noticeable.

Another method is to build a narrow framework that holds a sliding panel that covers and uncovers the opening (See Figure 10).

You can close the vents from outside without actually removing them. Remember those elasticized bowl covers your Mom used when she was storing leftovers? You can still find them in some dime stores or hardware stores. Or you can make your own out of light canvas and elastic.

FANS

On sweltering summer days, you might consider a cabin fan. Several small 1.5 to 2-amp 12-volt models are designed specifically for boats and recreational vehicles.

If you're dockside and have 110-volt power, measure a hatch and buy an electric fan that will just cover the opening. This arrangement is a familiar sight in Florida marinas. A fan also can increase comfort when you're operating a cabin heater. Heat rises, making your forehead sweat and your feet freeze. A small fan will get the air circulating and help distribute the heat more evenly throughout the cabin.

Bruce designed an overhead fan for *Saga* that's run by a wind-powered "squirrel-cage" blower fan mounted on the cabin top so it requires no electricity (See Figure 11). The blower fan is the type used in small electric space heaters. This fan is not meant to create a breeze like an air conditioner; it just promotes circulation, keeping stale or hot air moving.

SCREENS

Screens can be purchased or made for all hatches, ports and vents if you're in an area where bugs are a problem. Most manufacturers offer snap-in screens for their ports and

Figure 11 *This overhead fan requires no electricity. The cabin-top "motor" is a squirrel cage blower fan that's turned by the wind.*

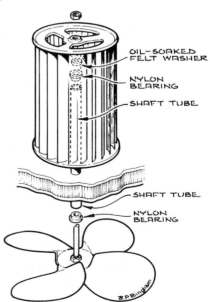

OIL-SOAKED FELT WASHER

NYLON BEARING

SHAFT TUBE

SHAFT TUBE

NYLON BEARING

Figure 10 *Two methods of controlling air flow from cowl vents. The first is a simple disk that swivels from one screw in common with the vent's finishing ring. The second method is a sliding panel held by a narrow framework.*

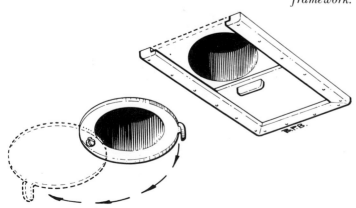

cowl vents. Velcro produces screen kits for hatches and companionways. Or, you can make your own using fiberglass screen (available at hardware stores) or mosquito netting and ¾-inch Velcro tape.

HULL CEILING

It is vital that fresh air reach every remote corner of a boat. Dead air space is an invitation to trouble, especially on a wood boat. Hull ceiling should never be solid (See Plate 12). On *At Last* the ceiling was 1½-inch strips of pine with a ½-inch to ¾-inch space between each two strips. If the ceiling *is* installed solidly, the top strip should be eliminated or at least drilled with rows of holes so air can circulate behind the ceiling and down into the bilge.

Every storage compartment needs ventilation if the contents are to remain dry and mildew-free. Solid cabinet doors can be drilled or cut with a jigsaw in a "personal" pattern. If the doors are framed with plywood panels, the panels can be replaced with caning (See Plate 10), grillwork, woven strips of wood or perforated Masonite. Be careful not to use cane for a large area as it's not strong enough to withstand the weight of a person falling against it. Some builders back up the caning with perforated masonite, but this so restricts air flow that it almost defeats the non-aesthetic purpose of the caning.

Many sliding cabinet doors have horizontal slots that are about ¼-inch wide. These can be replaced with sliding panels of ¼-inch, tempered, Masonite perforated in a pleasing pattern.

Even drawers can be vented. If the "handles" are finger holes drilled through the front of the drawer, the holes will function as vents as well.

Counter fronts and berth fronts (with top-opening bins) can receive cutouts or openwork panels (See Plate 13). These could be "false doors" constructed to match the rest of the interior woodwork or, as mentioned earlier, stock metal louvered vents installed and painted to blend in with the decor.

Plate 12 *Hull ceiling should have spacing between each strake, like the forepeak on this Cherubini 44. Caning on the cabinet doors is an excellent means of ventilation.*

Plate 13 *We used perforated masonite and teak frames to make attractive ventilation panels for Sabrina's under-settee storage.*

Louvered doors have long been a favorite of mine. Not only are they excellent for ventilation, but they're attractive and give a warm, homey feeling to a yacht interior (See Plate 14).

Settee and berth tops are usually solid plywood or fiberglass. If the cushion bottoms or the berth top become the slightest bit damp (and they often seem to) mildew will form quickly. You can riddle the plywood or fiberglass with holes so that air circulating in the lockers can get to the cushions and allow them to "breathe." We did this to *Sabrina*'s berth

Plate 14 *Saga's louvered doors are attractive as well as functional.*

tops, cutting 3-inch holes about 2 inches apart. As long as the holes are round they will not weaken the berth top.

ICE BOXES

No, you don't need to ventilate an ice box or a refrigerator, but they may work better if you ventilate the spaces around them (See Plate 15). If the ambient temperature can be reduced by venting away hot, stagnant air from the nearby engine room, stove recesses or the dead space between ice box and the hull, ice will last longer and mechanical refrigeration will operate more efficiently.

ENGINE ROOM

The Coast Guard has regulations covering engine compartments and bilge ventilation—or *any* area where flammable or combustible material is stored.

Basically, the boat should have at least two ventilators routed from the engine area to the outside. The openings must be fitted with cowls and ducting must be used to channel the flow of air in and out. The intake hose should extend from the cowl at least half-way to the bilge (or below the level of the carburetor air intake). The exhaust hose should start from a point *lower* in the bilge, but not so low as to ever be under water.

The Coast Guard also recommends a mechanical blower, with its own separate exhaust duct. The blower, of course, should be a sealed or arc-less type with non-sparking blades and impeller. The manufacturer's plate should state that the blower meets Coast Guard safety standards.

DANGER ZONES

Everyone is aware of the importance of venting an engine compartment, particularly for a gas-

Plate 15 *Open grillwork vents the galley space next to the ice box (located forward of the sink), reducing the ambient temperature and helping ice last longer.*

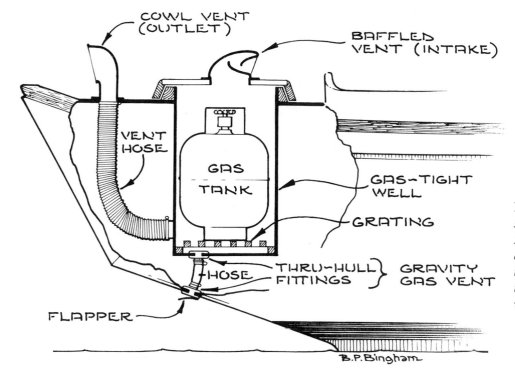

Figure 12 *Lazarette stowage of a propane tank. Note both the gravity gas vent at the bottom of the well and the ventilation system similar to an engine room, using cowl vents and flexible vent hose.*

oline engine. Yet I'm always surprised when I see a boat with the batteries tucked away in an unvented locker, usually under a settee or quarterberth. A charging battery gives off explosive fumes. Batteries *must* be kept in a well-ventilated area.

LP tanks arc stored on deck or in a recessed compartment or deck well totally separate from the cabin area (See Figure 12). Since propane is heavier than air, the well must have a vent at the very bottom, leading overboard. Obviously the bottom of the compartment must be some distance above the waterline. You can also ventilate the compartment with a pair of cowl vents and ducting to direct the air flow, in much the same manner as an engine room. On boats using propane (regardless of the engine fuel), a mechanical blower with separate exhaust duct is an excellent idea.

SOURCES

BECKSON MARINE INC.
 Box 3336
 Bridgeport, CT 06605

W. H. DENOUDEN (USA)
 P.O. Box 8712
 Baltimore, MD 21240

MANHATTAN MARINE
 116 Chambers St.
 New York, NY 10007

MARTEC ENGINEERING
 2257 Gaylord St.
 Long Beach, CA 90813

NICRO FICO
 2065 W. Ave. 140th
 San Leandro, CA 94577

PASTIME PRODUCTS INC.
 P.O. Box 843
 Madison Square Station
 New York, NY 10010

SAILING SPECIALTIES INC.
 P.O. Box 527
 Lexington Park, MD 20653

SUDBURY LABS
 572 Dutton Road
 Sudbury, MA 01776

9

Stowage

"You can take it with you"

I'M ALWAYS AMAZED at the amount of gear that a boat—even a small one—can gulp down its hatch and digest in endless little hiding places, sometimes never to appear again. The trick, of course, is knowing where all the hiding places are, making careful lists of what's stashed where and keeping the lists up to date.

My biggest downfall is I am forever finding a better place for something to live and then neglecting to change the list.

I'm better about list-keeping when we're cruising then when we're staying put, since shopping trips are less frequent. Everyone seems to devleop his own methods. Here are mine.

I sketch out the accommodation plan of the boat, showing every storage bin and locker, and assign each locker a number—even numbers to port, odd numbers to starboard. In a loose-leaf notebook, I keep a page for each locker, listing *everything* it contains. If something is removed or used up (primarily from the food bins), it gets crossed off and placed on the shopping list.

Bruce remembers crewing on a large ocean racer that used this system. But they also kept a master list of everything on the boat arranged in alphabetical order with the locker number beside it, so any crew member could locate something in a hurry.

It sounds like a lot of work, but I think it's worthwhile particularly if you're having guests for any length of time. It stops those endless questions of, "Hey! Where do you keep the . . . whatever?"

MAKING STOWAGE MORE CONVENIENT

The major reason for our reshuffling routine is to move frequently-used items to within easy grasp. We've learned through sad experience that the harder something is to get at, the less apt we are to dig it out and use it. And forgotten items are the ones that get ruined.

The shirts at the front of the locker are worn, laundered and worn again. The shirt hidden at the back of the locker gets mildew. Potatoes at the top of the bin are cooked and eaten. The stray potato that gets lost under the onion and flour sacks starts to sprout. And that seldom-used chisel finds its way to the bilge and turns into a pile of unrecognizable rust.

Aside from the obvious importance of a reg-

144

ular cleaning and airing program, it's just as important that the storage be convenient in the first place—if only to make cleaning easier! One of the most common types of storage is a top-loading bin under a settee or berth. While it's secure storage, particularly on a heeled sailboat—nothing short of a capsize is going to dislodge the contents—it's also really inconvenient on a day-to-day basis. Invariably, someone is sitting on whatever you're looking for. It is possible to replace the bins with drawers, although the shape of the hull usually prevents this. A more practical solution is to make the bins front-opening as well as top-opening. Hinging the doors at the bottom so they open *down* will help prevent the contents from spilling out all over the cabin sole. And, dividing settee cushions into two or three sections in-

stead of one long one makes it easier to get into individual bins.

Cavernous lockers are more useful if they're divided into smaller compartments. They can be sectioned permanently using ¼-inch plywood or temporarily by using various sizes of

BUT YOU DIDN'T TELL ME IT WOULDN'T ALL FIT!

TAG-ALONG

B.P. Bingham

plastic dishpans or wastepaper baskets. This keeps everything orderly and prevents the contents from shifting and jumbling together when the boat rolls or heels. Pieces of flexible foam (cut up an old worn-out cushion) can be wedged into odd spaces to prevent rattles while under way.

We use plastic trays on shelves and in drawers to keep small items secure (see Plate 1). One

Plate 1 *Plastic trays and boxes will keep small items orderly and secure.* (PHOTO BY DICK PENTONEY.)

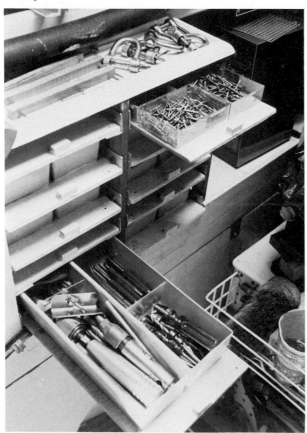

tray, for instance, holds paper clips, Scotch tape, a stapler, a roll of stamps—all the small bits of office gear. Several trays on a galley shelf keep tins of spices orderly. I've found that without a special tray or box specifically for small stuff, it has a way of sifting down through the larger items until it disappears. I could never find a rubber band, for example, until I started sticking them in a Baggie and keeping the Baggie in the office gear tray. Now I always can find one.

Runners can be added inside deep drawers to take a sliding tray and increase the usable storage capacity.

Plastic containers or trash cans are particularly useful for storage in the bilge. I was aboard one boat, a Columbia 8.9 called *C-Moon*, that had at least five trash cans wedged tightly under the cabin sole. One container held bottles of wine wrapped in foam, another held cleaners and solvents and another contained cans of engine oil. It was a tidy, efficient arrangement and if anything spilled or leaked it was held in the trash container instead of running down into the bilge.

Zip-Loc bags are invaluable, and not just for storing leftovers in the ice box. Anything that might be harmed by moisture—from noodles to cameras—gets stored in a Zip-Loc bag. And anything that might damage something else is bagged as well. A partially used can of oil, tubes of epoxy glue, grease for the winches, tack rags, anything gooey, sticky or messy—and there's always a lot of *that* on a boat—is put in its own Baggie.

All boxes or closed containers—unless they're clear plastic—should be labeled. A permanent marker (like Magic Marker) writes on most surfaces. Paper labels will last for several years if they're covered with transparent Scotch tape.

KEEPING THINGS IN PLACE

Virtually every item on a boat must have a place to live, where it's held securely until needed. You can spend a small fortune at a local hardware store on teak or mahogany racks and holders or you can make them your-

Plate 2   *Saga's clear Lexan binocular holders, mounted on the side of the companionway ladder.*

Plate 3   *Sabrina's magazine rack, made of clear acrylic.*

Plate 4   *Bruce made special racks for Saga's wine and water glasses.*

self. Bruce has made binocular holders (See Plate 2), a horn holder, magazine (See Plate 3) and glass racks (See Plate 4), and all sorts of things out of clear acrylic. I like them better than the wooden ones since they're lighter and less obtrusive (See Plates 5 through 8). It's one thing to look at a "decorated" boat in a show with the cheese board on the table and a few selected books and plants on the shelves. But in the real world shelves are filled to overflowing with not-so-pretty necessities (See Plate 9) like flashlights, air horns and winch handles. Special holders, particularly the acrylic ones,

seem to cut down on the clutter considerably— the binoculars look like they *belong*, instead of like someone tossed them carelessly on a shelf.

I've found that simple stainless steel spring clips work well for many small items. We have one in the galley for the ice pick, one inside the cockpit locker for the bilge pump handle and another near the companionway for a flash-light.

Hooks are useful, too, and not just for coffee cups, wet clothes and spare line. *Sabrina* had two along the galley front that held the table leg when it was not in use. Two hooks inside the quarterberth keep the Tillermaster auto-pilot in place. Hooks inside *Saga's* hanging locker take watch caps and mittens. Even our pet mouse's cage is held securely by two hooks screwed into the shelf that fit over the bottom rim.

Shelf fiddles should be at least 3 inches high

Plate 7 Edon II *has an acrylic shelf at the forward end of the V-berth.*

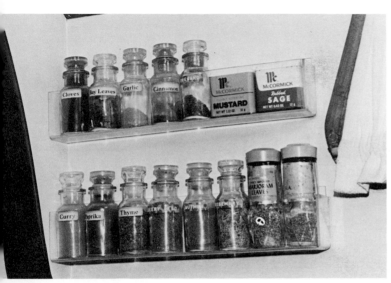

Plate 5 Saga's *acrylic spice racks seem almost to disappear.*

Plate 6 *This upper shelf on* Saga *is made of Lexan to handle the weight of heavy jars, tins and flower pots.*

to be functional. Sometimes a high fiddle on a short shelf can make retrieving a tall item difficult. We solved this problem aboard *At Last* by hinging the fiddles. They would tilt down onto the cushion back when we wanted something off the shelf and were held securely in the "up" position by barrel bolts at each end.

Gainor Roberts, who lives aboard *Endymion II,* a Camper & Nicholson 31, added high fiddles to the shelves inside a head locker to keep the normal myriad bottles, tubes and small boxes. She fashioned the fiddles out of ¼-inch clear acrylic so she can see through the fiddles and find what she's looking for with a minimum of fumbling around.

Counter and table fiddles can be lower— about 1½ inches—and removable ones are very convenient. *Saga's* table fiddles are only kept in place when we're under way. We drilled the underside of the fiddles and epoxied brass

Plate 8 Saga's *Lexan TV shelf has teak fiddles and incorporates a magazine holder beneath the shelf.*

Plate 9 *The real world on most live-aboard boats is shelves filled to overflowing.*

pegs (made from brazing rod) into the holes. The pegs fit into corresponding holes drilled in the table top.

Large items, such as books, radios, a television or folded clothing stacked high, will probably need more than fiddles to keep them in place (See Plate 10). A removable ¾-inch by 1-inch wood bar or a heavy brass rod that fits into brackets at each end of the shelf will usually do the trick. On *Sabrina*'s clothing locker shelves, and on the galley shelf that held tall canisters, we screwed hooks into the top of the fiddles and into the underside of the deck, then criss-crossed the opening with shock cord. Everything stayed in place, yet we could get at it easily by reaching through the cord.

The television set on *Sabrina* was secured while under way by a length of shock cord that went around the TV and attached to two hooks screwed into the hull ceiling.

Shock cord is one of the handiest items on a boat. I particularly like to use it with hooks for securing things to the underside of decks and shelves. *Sabrina*'s light spare anchor was at-

tached that way under the foredeck inside the clothing locker. Her storm sails were tightly rolled and held against the underside of the clothing locker over the forepeak berth, leaving ample clearance for our feet. Flagstaffs, fishing poles, even collapsible shopping carts and bicycles can often find places to live where they're secure, out of sight yet fairly easy to retrieve.

Velcro tape, in my opinion, runs a close second to shock cord in usefulness. It can be used for tying down and hanging up in much the same manner as shock cord, although it lacks the elasticity of shock cord and often isn't strong enough to hold really heavy gear. We use it to keep the cushions against the settee back and to hold the edges of the carpet against the hull. You can buy double-stick carpet tape, but that's a permanent installation and I like to be able to pull up the carpet frequently for cleaning, airing or drying.

For keeping knickknacks on shelves (shells, sailing trophies, the ceramic Gloucester Fish-

Plate 10 *Shock cord is used in addition to the fiddles to keep books in place.*

erman statue you can't bear to part with) I've had great luck with plant putty—that green clay-like stuff you can buy at florists and garden shops. It adheres to just about anything yet scrapes off easily when it's time to remove it. Double-sided foam tape works well for rooting small trinkets or hanging pictures.

Several companies are now producing a non-skid plastic shelf liner that comes in a roll. You can cut it to shape to use as placemats, shelf liner or, in small pieces, to go under individual items. It won't prevent a tall object from toppling over if the boat lurches, but it will keep small stuff from sliding about. A damp towel—either a paper towel or a hand towel—works well as a temporary skid preventer. Wet paper towels are invariably our place mats underway and then used for galley cleanup after the meal.

A lot of things seem to get hung on hooks aboard boats, but beware of hanging anything that will swing against a bulkhead—like a ditty bag on a lanyard. The constant movement, however slight, will quickly wear through the finish and start to carve a groove. And those beautiful brass lamps that look so lovely and traditional swaying over the saloon table can be a real head-banger if you've no way of securing them when the boat is underway.

I've always been partial to net bags for stowing things—from fruits and vegetables to clothing in lockers. They can be slung under shelves and put inside lockers and cabinets and tucked into odd corners where nothing else seems to fit. Bruce detests them, but I suspect it's because he tries to stuff something square and solid (like a camera) into them and then it clunks against the hull and gets tangled in the net.

Ray and Hilary Groves kept their newborn baby in a well padded hanging net—similar to a hammock—while they were sailing. Little Carolyn was absolutely secure when the boat heeled and she seemed to love the gentle swinging of her seagoing crib.

We've also found small duffle bags or ditty bags to be extremely handy. We have one for spare blocks, one for assorted shackles, another for odd lengths of line and one for assorted cleaning and polishing rags. Each bag is labeled with a permanent marker pen.

ADDING STOWAGE

Look around your boat. I'll bet all sorts of hidden spaces could be used for storage by adding a shelf or a bin to make the space accessible.

One place to start is inside lockers and cabinets. Dividing up a big locker can double and sometimes triple the amount of usable space. *Sabrina*'s forepeak clothing locker was one huge cavern—large enough for me to crawl into. I added a shelf on each side and sectioned off the bottom with fiddles (See Plate 11). Our clothes no longer wound up in a big heap but stayed neatly stacked on the shelves. And there

Plate 11 *I added shelves to* Sabrina's *forepeak locker, then sectioned off the bottom with fiddles.*

Plate 12 *Bruce added small shelves to the inside of a locker door on* Sabrina.

was still room to crawl between them to reach the chain locker.

You often can add small shelves to the inside of locker doors. Bruce made two for *Sabrina's* galley cabinet (See Plate 12) out of ¼-inch plywood, although you really don't have to *build* anything. Buy small plastic trays (the kind sold for silverware) and screw them to the back of the door. Like many engine compartments, *Saga's* had a great deal of open space around the engine. We added vinyl-coated wire racks to the inside of the access panels to hold spare oil and fuel filters. Hooks in the overhead hold spare drive belts, a 12-volt drop light and special tools. And do you remember shoe bags? They are still sold in some department stores and dime stores. Hang one on the back of the hanging locker door for rolled-up socks, underwear, bathing suits—even shoes.

The shape of the hull on a sailboat and the forward sections of a powerboat lend themselves to a wealth of additional shelves. Bruce's brother added a bank of shelves at the back of a hanging locker on *Outward Bound* without infringing on the clothing space. We did the same inside *At Last's* sail locker. If the shelves are installed at an angle, to hold things on nat-

urally, it's often possible to eliminate or lower fiddles.

Sabrina had shelves on each side of the forward berth, but there was enough flare to the hull to allow us to add narrow shelves beneath the existing ones and still leave ample room for sleeping (See Plate 13).

I would like to mention that a master carpenter is not required to do most of these jobs—particularly adding shelves *inside* lockers where they don't really show. They are not structural and they'll probably be painted. Building shelves that *do* show, and especially if they will be varnished, will require more skill, of course, so start with the hidden ones if you're unsure of your skills.

Plate 13 *Sabrina's hull had enough flare forward to allow additional shelves beneath the existing ones.*

Sabrina had a large instrument box mounted on the aft bulkhead. I added a small fiddle to the flat top and presto—a shelf! (See Plate 14). It was so handy that Bruce built a similar shelf on the opposite side of the companionway (See Plate 15).

I remember seeing a boat in California where the owner had added fiddles to each side of the top of a partial bulkhead, giving him a narrow shelf for match books, keys and other small items. He also had fitted several half-round shelves around the corner posts, although it obviously took considerable skill to get a perfect fit. Bruce drilled holes in the trim on a partial bulkhead in *Sabrina*—four small holes to hold pencils and pens and one large

one to hold the navigation dividers: simple yet very efficient.

Box bins are a great way of putting wasted space to work. They are simply that—boxes—attached to the back of a bulkhead or door, with a cutout in the bulkhead (See Figure 1). I generally leave the top off so they also act as ventilators for the compartment in which they're installed. The top of the chain locker is always unused space. I installed two box bins (to hold paperback books) on the forward side of *At Last*'s forepeak bulkhead right up near the deck, with the opening facing the berths. I attached the boxes so the bottom of the box was about 2 inches below the bottom of the opening, providing a natural fiddle without further work.

At Last also had two box bins installed at the top of a hanging locker—one opened to the galley counter, the other to the head compartment. The galley box held our dish soap, sponges and cleaning gear without using up valuable counter space.

Almost all sailboats have a companionway ladder. Ladder bins are another way of gaining storage (See Plate 16). They're especially good for tools and for extra blocks—things you may need at a moment's notice. Powerboats are

Plate 14 *A simple fiddle turned the top of* Sabrina's *instrument box into a shelf.*

Plate 15 *Bruce built a matching shelf on the opposite bulkhead.*

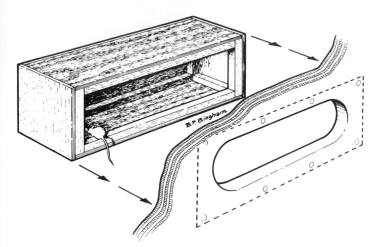

Figure 1 *Box bins are easily installed and a great way of putting unused space to work.*

more likely to have just a step instead of a ladder, but check its construction. It's possible to cut and hinge the top of the step to use the space inside. *Sabrina* had two steps, held in place by barrel bolts. The top step originally had to be removed in order to take out the bottom one. Bruce cut out a large oval in the back of the top step, giving us access to under-cockpit storage (as well as ventilation), and then hinged the bottom step so it flipped up without having to remove either step.

Chart stowage is always a problem on a crusing boat. It makes no sense to keep them rolled

—they're even *more* difficult to stow that way. And you always wind up folding them when they're in use, anyway. At first we stowed our charts flat under bunk cushions. But after a few hundred miles our berth started getting lumpy. Now we have an acrylic chart rack— just like a magazine rack, but large enough to hold a folded chart on the front of a locker door. This holds two or three charts, plus a copy of *The Eldridge Tide and Pilot Book* and a waterway guide, and the bulk of the charts are stashed elsewhere.

I've seen some pretty ingenious arrangements for chart stowage. One was a pocket made of sheet copper attached to the underside of the lift hatch in a cockpit seat. The same thing could be made of acrylic, thin plywood, Masonite or aluminum battens nailed to 1-inch by 2-inch lumber, or even heavy canvas (See Figure 2). Such pockets could also be installed

Plate 16 *Ladder bins are a great way to gain additional storage.*

Figure 2 *Pockets for folded chart stowage can be made of acrylic, copper or aluminum (A), of canvas (B), or of wood (C). They are attached under lift hatches or in the underside of a deck and take up little space.*

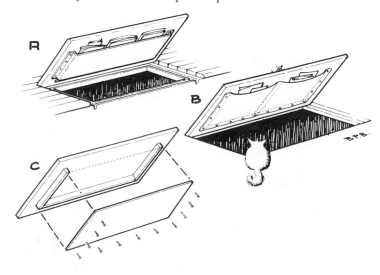

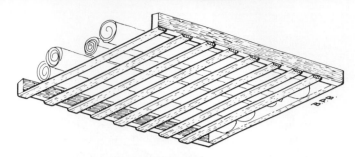

Figure 3 *An overhead rack, for rolled or folded charts, can be used if the boat has enough headroom.*

under lift hatches in berths and settees, or to the underside of shelves or decks, providing they're wide enough. Another nifty place is *inside* a settee or berth locker that only opens from the top. The chart pockets can be attached to the front face of the locker, on the *inside;* they are thin enough so they barely intrude on the rest of the stowage space.

An overhead rack can be built in boats with ample headroom (See Plate 17). To do this, wood frames are cut to the radius of the cabin top, then installed with wood dowels between them (See Figure 3). Aside from holding charts, the dowels are great for drying wet socks and gloves.

Extra pillows, blankets and bedding are gen-

erally needed aboard, but they're bulky and hard to stow. When we were aboard Ruth and Larry Penn's Chesapeake bugeye, *Quick Step,* I noticed their attractive "throw pillows" on the settee were actually zippered canvas bags, each containing a blanket, sheets and a pillow for a bunk. On *Sabrina* we made covers for standard-sized bed pillows so they could do double-duty as lounging pillows during the day and sleeping pillows at night. The cotton duck covers kept the pillow cases clean, were quickly removed at night and were easy to launder.

Increasing Existing Stowage

Quite a few stock fiberglass boats are built with molded hull liners that form the settees, berths and lockers. This gives you lockers that are smooth and easy to clean and reduces condensation problems, since nothing is actually touching the hull. Unfortunately, it also reduces the volume of the lockers. We removed the molded-in bins on *Sabrina* and almost doubled the usable space. We removed only the lower portion of each bin, leaving the flanges that were bonded to the hull.

Existing shelves sometimes can be widened. We increased *Sabrina's* outboard settee shelf four inches by extending it over the cushion back. It did not spoil the sitting comfort of the settee and, as a bonus, the shelf kept the cushion in place when the boat was on the port tack.

Stowage on Deck

We've talked about box bins below, but they also can be used on deck. Fiberglass boats made with a molded one-piece deck, cabin and cockpit unit usually have nothing but empty space

Plate 17 *These overhead compartments (stock items from Sailing Specialties) can be mounted to the underside of decks or cabin tops.* (PHOTO COURTESY SAILING SPECIALTIES, INC.)

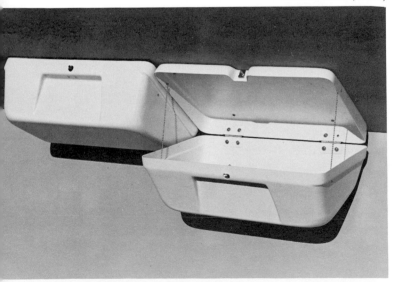

inside the cockpit coamings—a perfect place for box bins. Made of ¼-inch plywood and glassed into the coaming interior, they're handy for sail stops, suntan lotion and all the odds and ends that usually clutter up the cockpit. Be careful where you position them so you can still get at deck hardware fastenings, like winch and cleat bolts.

Winch handle holders can be made of 1½-inch diameter white vinyl tubing at a fraction of the cost of store-bought holders. Below-deck binocular holders and horn holders can be duplicated for topside use.

Shock cord and Velcro are just as useful on deck as they are below. Extension cords and water hoses can be coiled neatly and kept that way with Velcro tie-downs. These coils, or anything fairly flat (like a fender board, a bo'sun's chair or a collapsible barbeque grill) can be held against the underside of a seat locker or flush against the hull inside a locker with hooks and shock cord. Shock cord works well on powerboats for stowing folding deck furniture, bicycles and other large pieces of gear against cockpit sides when the boat is under way.

Hooks are useful on deck, too, for coils of spare line, fenders and canvas ditty bags holding spare blocks, shackles and other small items. Spring clips are just as useful—often boat hooks and windlass handles can be securely mounted on a bulwark to keep them off the deck.

Equipment also can be mounted on the cabin top, provided it's kept low enough on sailboats so nothing interferes with the helmsman's view

(See Plate 18). Add brackets if necessary, but don't lash anything to the handholds—they're for safety.

Every piece of gear on deck must be kept securely lashed down. Nothing is more irritating and dangerous as something sliding around loose on deck (See Plate 19). Equipment stored topside permanently will last longer if it's protected from the weather—either in lockers, in deck boxes or under cover. I prefer canvas covers to plastic ones, since canvas "breathes." Plastic will permit condensation inside the cover. I've seen equipment rust faster under a plastic cover than it would have with no cover at all.

The following plates (20 through 33) are a catch-all collection of storage ideas.

Plate 19 Heron's *small stern anchor is held securely in its own brackets, with the rope coiled in a bucket, ready to go in an instant.* (PHOTO BY DICK PENTONEY.)

Plate 18 *This teak LP storage box, mounted on* Rhapsody's *cabin top, holds horizontal LP tanks to keep the overall height as low as possible.*

Plate 22 *This "fancy" shelf for an anchor light is simply an inexpensive modified teak trivet purchased at an import store (like Pier I Imports).* (PHOTO BY DICK PENTONEY.)

Plate 20 *Bruce made cassette tape racks of ¼-inch mahogany plywood and ⅛-inch dowel.*

Plate 21 *A heavy sewing machine (under canvas cover) acts as a counterweight for this gimballed table.* (PHOTO BY DICK PENTONEY.)

Plate 23 *Heron's nav station: the RDF sits on its own shelf, mounted to the ice box front. The RDF and the boxed sextant beneath it are secured with leather straps and common-sense fasteners.* (PHOTO BY DICK PENTONEY.)

Plate 24 *Dick Pentoney claims "some folks just can't learn new ways." One of his just-for-fun projects was making this holder for his shaving mug and brush.* (PHOTO BY DICK PENTONEY.)

Plate 25 *A simple method for locking drawers: small bolts or nails in each end of a ¾-inch by ¾-inch length of wood drop into holes drilled in the aluminum angle runners.* (PHOTO BY DICK PENTONEY.)

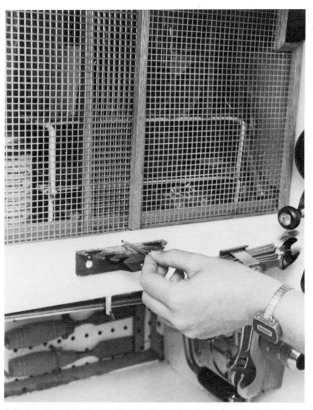

Plate 26 *Perforated metal can be used for sliding doors. A long cotter pin locks them in place.* (PHOTO BY DICK PENTONEY.)

Plate 27 *An organized shelf in Heron's workshop. Sandpaper is cut to size to fit Dick's sanding block, then stored in plastic napkin holders he picked up at a sale.* (PHOTO BY DICK PENTONEY.)

Plate 29 *Lucite was cut to hold various sizes of jars, cans and bottles. No clanging and rattling about in this locker!* (PHOTO BY DICK PENTONEY.)

Plate 28 *Simple wood brackets hold saws securely, yet they're easily removable.* (PHOTO BY DICK PENTONEY.)

Plate 30 *The underside of a shelf over a work bench and the outboard hull are lined with pegboard. Pipe clips are used extensively for securing tools. Note the ingenious use of dowels and cotter pins to hold the drill bits.* (PHOTO BY DICK PENTONEY.)

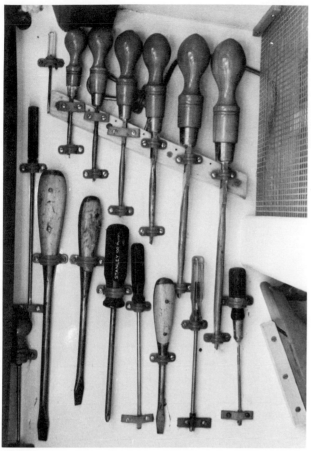

Plate 31 *More tools hung on a bulkhead with pipe clips. Leather is sometimes helpful (lower right) to hold tools or gear tightly.* (PHOTO BY DICK PENTONEY.)

Plate 32 *A cabinet front covered with pegboard. Both pipe clips and dowels are used to secure gear, as well as vinyl-coated wire shelves available at most hardware stores.* (PHOTO BY DICK PENTONEY.)

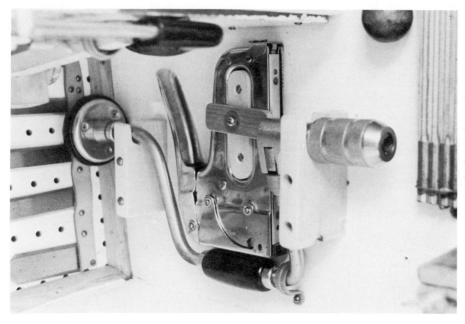

Plate 33 *Dick Pentoney made a special holder for his brace, then nested the staple gun inside. The staple gun holder is wood cut to fit the inside of the gun's handle and screwed to the bulkhead. It's held securely by a wood turn-button.* (PHOTO BY DICK PENTONEY.)

10

Home, Sweet Home,

"Be it ever so humble . . ."

At one time, yacht interiors were limited to white paint, varnished trim and cushions covered in a narrow choice of "acceptable" colors. No more! Boats are decorated in every imaginable color scheme. There's a dazzling array of fabrics, vinyls, wall coverings and carpeting suitable for floating homes. There are even interior decorators who specialize in yachts.

"Wall" Coverings

Bulkheads are usually plywood, either oiled or varnished teak ply or painted fir plywood. *Saga* has teak bulkheads. Her previous owner used Liquid Gold to preserve and protect the wood, and we continued using it for awhile. It looked lovely for the first few weeks, but seemed to need a fresh application every month or two.

I really prefer varnish, as we used on *Sabrina*. After the initial work of sanding and applying numerous coats, the finish will last for years, requiring only an occasional touch-up. We like the soft luster of satin varnish better than gloss, but that's purely a personal preference.

Too much natural wood can be dark and dreary. You may prefer a painted surface. If you choose a color instead of white, choose a very pale pastel to make the whole interior feel lighter and brighter. I still prefer a satin or matte finish, except in areas like the head or inside lockers where a gloss paint is easier to clean (See Plate 1).

Specially formulated "marine" paint is not necessary belowdecks. Any good quality household paint will work fine. Most paint manufacturers have stopped adding mildicides to paints, although you can still buy it separately and add it yourself. It's an excellent idea to do so. Actually, *one tablespoon* of formaldehyde, available at drug stores, added to *one quart* of paint, will make the paint virtually mildew-proof.

Latex paint has several advantages. Cleanup is done with water and—most importantly—it dries very fast, usually within a couple of hours. It is, however, harder to stroke out without leaving brush marks. And when it's time to repaint it's almost impossible to sand it to a smooth finish. I've always been able to achieve a much finer surface with oil-base paints.

Formica makes an attractive, easy-care bulkhead covering. It is available in either gloss, eggshell or matte finish in a wide choice of colors. (It's also quite expensive.)

I was aboard a large motorsailer that had a gorgeous (as well as practical) tiled head compartment. Tile is tricky to work with and not something that most amateurs can handle, so the cost of professional installation must be considered. The effect of ceramic tile can still be achieved by using plastic tile or simulated-tile linoleum. Both are easily applied by amateurs.

Cloth-backed vinyl wallcovering is another alternative to paint or varnish (See Plate 2). It will stand up to hard use provided care is taken in surface preparation and the proper adhesive is used. Since these wall coverings do not "breathe," they must be applied to a surface that has been sealed with an oil-based primer or sealer. The adhesive should be a synthetic that contains a mold and mildew inhibiter, as most of them do. Try a test patch first to be sure the adhesive is compatible with the primer or sealer.

The cabin trunk sides can receive the same types of treatment as bulkheads. If they are fiberglass, and you feel there is too much fiberglass below, consider covering some surfaces with a wood veneer. The veneer is generally applied with epoxy. It takes considerable skill to achieve a perfect fit around ports and windows, hanging knees or other projections, but the results can completely change the atmosphere of the cabin.

UPHOLSTERY

Vinyl cushion covers are the easiest to care for, but they are sticky and uncomfortable in hot weather, particularly against bare skin. Most live-aboards eventually replace them, or at least make slip-on covers for use during the summer months.

There's an incredible array of upholstery fabrics to choose from (See Plate 2). Look for a heavyweight, closely woven fabric, either a synthetic or a blend of synthetic and natural fibers. The best choice is a fabric that will dry quickly and resist mildew and staining. It should be treated with Scotchgard. Some materials are fire retardant as well.

Pale, solid colors will make the cabin seem larger, but will be harder to keep clean. Tweeds, muted plaids and stripes and some small patterns generally work well in a boat home (See Plate 3). Most cabins are—visually—complicated, "busy" places. So big, bold prints are often overwhelming.

The cushion covers on our schooner were

Plate 1 *Gloss-painted trim makes this head light, bright and easy to keep clean.*

Plate 2 *Cloth-backed vinyl wallcovering is an attractive alternative to paint or varnish.*

Vel-Suade. They looked and felt luxurious, but wore remarkably well. Since the material was so expensive we chose acrylic canvas for the underside (not cotton canvas, as it's prone to mildew).

Sabrina's upholstery was Herculon on top and vinyl underneath; the vinyl kept any moisture or condensation from being absorbed by the cushion.

Cushion covers are best made with plastic zippers. If you do have brass ones, however, rub them with beeswax each time they are zipped closed to keep them from corroding. Steel or aluminum zippers should be avoided.

THE CABIN SOLE

A teak-and-holly sole in most production boats is not made of solid strips of wood, but plywood with the teak-and-holly pattern a thin, top-layer veneer. The veneer must be protected. Constant foot traffic can wear through the veneer. Once dirt is ground into the holly it's almost impossible to restore to its original white. It's better to wear away coats of varnish. I like satin varnish because it's not slippery like gloss finish.

The sole can be oiled—just like a teak deck topside—but frequent applications are neces-

Plate 3 *Soft, muted plaid and warm wood tones make this stateroom restful and inviting.*

Plate 4 *A tiled sole in the head can be effective. On this Cherubini 44, the teak grating provides a non-slip surface to stand on.*

sary to keep it looking nice, and sealed from dirt.

A linoleum or vinyl flooring works well and occasionally tile (See Plate 4) particularly in work areas like the galley, engine room and head. It's attractive, easy to clean and requires very little maintenance—only an occasional

scrubbing with soap and water. Waxing or polishing would only invite a slip—and injury—if it got wet while you were under way.

For the main saloon and staterooms, my vote is for carpeting (See Plate 5). Aside from its appearance, it does have practical value. It's a good insulator that can really make a difference in chilly weather or in very cold waters. The boat is quieter and carpeting is probably the best non-skid sole covering, assuming, of course, that it's well secured to the sole.

The first time we bought carpet for a boat, we got kitchen carpet with a foam rubber backing. The carpet held up, but the backing began to disintegrate within months. When the carpet got wet, we would pull it up and find patches of foam rubber stuck to the sole.

Both the carpet and the backing should be

Plate 5 *Carpeting gives a feeling of hominess that few other additions can match. Note the pleasing window treatment with both curtains and venetian blinds.*

of synthetic materials. Check the chart (See Figure 1) for characteristics of different synthetic fibers. While backing is very often jute, you *can* find carpeting with vinyl foam or polypropylene backings that resist mildew and moisture. Action-back is a *treated* jute that wears very well.

It's rare to find carpeting on a boat laid down with padding underneath. There's often not enough room for the extra thickness and, of course, it means another layer to worry about when the carpeting gets soaked. The main reason for a cushion is to protect the carpet from the impact damage of constant footsteps.

Aside from getting wet, carpeting on a boat is subject to concentrated use. I suppose you could compare it to carpeting in a house entry hall. Carpets designed for commercial use (hotels, restaurants, hospitals) are made to take abuse. This is most often "level loop" carpet: rows of looped yarn that provides a flat, dense surface to keep spills and dirt from sinking in —they stay on the surface so you can clean up readily.

Carpeting called "twist" is also designed for hard use. A twist is an even pile carpet with the yarns twisted for a nubby appearance. Like level loop, it resists soiling.

More luxurious carpeting like plush (a velvety cut pile) or saxony (a shag carpet with shorter, denser yarn) would do fine in areas with less traffic—an aft cabin stateroom, perhaps. Whatever the weave, the important point is to choose a synthetic.

Keep in mind that medium to dark tones hide dirt best. Light colors (particularly yellows and golds), show dirt the most. Tweeds and multi-colors hide soil better than solids, while patterns are even better.

Most carpet comes in 12-foot widths. Unless

FIGURE 1.

SYNTHETIC FIBERS FOR CARPET

FIBER	TRADE NAMES	CHARACTERISTICS
NYLON	Enka®, Enkaloft®, Antron®, Anso®, Ultron®	Strongest of the synthetics. Resists abrasion and water-absorption. Easy to clean. Some, like Antron®, actually help hide soil.
ACRYLIC	Acrilan®, Zefran®	Strong, resilient, resists water-absorption. Easy to clean. Has wool-like warmth and softness.
POLYESTER	Dacron®, Encron®, Trevira®	Highly resistant to abrasion. Low moisture absorbency. Wool-like in appearance. Easy to clean.
POLYPROPYLENE (OLEFIN)	Herculon®, Marvess®, Vectra®	Durable, easy to clean. Noted for its high resistance to stains because the fiber is non-absorbing. Often used for kitchen and indoor/outdoor carpet.

NOTE: All synthetic fibers are naturally mothproof and non-allergenic.

QUOTED FROM: "Everything You've Always Wanted to Know About Carpet . . . but were afraid to ask," and "Great Beginnings," copyright Bigelow-Sanford, Inc.

you have a really large boat that will use carpeting equal to a room in a house, you may find buying carpeting quite expensive. You pay a premium for a small quantity and possibly a cutting charge as well. It's usually better to shop in carpet stores specializing in remnants.

Bruce's brother bought automotive carpeting for his boat and reports it's holding up extremely well. It does make sense—carpet in a car is subjected to extremes of grime, rain and mud. The backing is treated with a synthetic rubber to withstand such abuse. Its only drawback is it lacks the thick, cushiony feel of household carpet. For that matter, so does most commercial carpet. Also, automotive carpet only comes in 40-inch widths.

Wall-to-wall carpeting and throw rugs, too, must be well secured to keep them from sliding when the boat is rolling or pitching. I don't like double-faced carpet tape since it makes a fairly permanent installation. You have to be able to take the carpet on deck for drying or onto a dock for an occasional scrubbing and hosedown. Velcro works well to hold it down, and we've had good results using oval screws with finishing washers. We put a small throw rug on top of the main carpet at the base of the companionway ladder. I sewed the "sticky" half of Velcro tape to the corners of the rug so they grab the carpeting and the rug stays in place.

PORTS AND WINDOWS

Curtains or some sort of port covering are necessary for privacy if you spend much time dockside. And they're needed to keep blinding rays of sunlight off the book you're reading. They also are an excellent idea to discourage prying eyes when you go off and leave the boat unattended for any length of time.

Curtains for opening ports will require careful design so the rod doesn't interfere with the swing of the porthole. Sometimes it's easiest to just use a cloth or paper cutout that can be inserted between the port and its frame and is held in place by dogging down the port. Or, you could make a "shower cap" cover with elastic around the edges that snaps over the port.

Curtains can be on rods, on a special track that follows the curve of a cabin side or held in place with snaps or Velcro.

Fixed ports and windows sometimes can use shades or blinds, even venetian blinds (See Plate 5) instead of curtains. I saw one powerboat with shutters over the windows. Sunscreen blinds can be very nice in the summer, reducing glare while allowing soft natural light to enter. Very sheer curtains will do the same thing.

11

Add-Ons

"Making the boat seem bigger"

It's NOT ALWAYS necessary to buy a larger boat in order to get more room. Many ways exist to give a boat more usable space. Many of the ideas discussed and shown here are fairly simple weekend projects—but what a difference they can make in comfort and livability!

ADD-A-ROOM

We tended to think—early on—of a dodger as something to keep wind and spray off the helmsman while under way in bad weather. That was the original reason for acquiring one. But soon we discovered a dodger serves so many functions we seldom fold it down. For starters, the companionway hatch almost always can be left open when it's raining, and the cribboards left out, as well.

Consider how stuffy it gets belowdecks when the boat is buttoned up. If you're at anchor and there's any breeze, open a forward hatch and the dodger will become a huge "cowl vent," helping to exhaust stale air from the cabin. Conversely, on hot, clammy days and nights, anchoring by the stern may let the dodger act as a wind scoop.

On blustery days at anchor, the dodger will act as a windbreak, giving the cockpit more protection. The clear plastic windows in the dodger will intensify the sun's heat, making it a small solar heater for the cockpit.

You *can* add an extension to the dodger so it will completely cover the cockpit but remember, all you'll achieve—usually—is sitting headroom beneath it. Meanwhile, climbing in and out of the cockpit will be more difficult. The dodger extension idea can be carried one step further and the cockpit completely enclosed with side curtains. This, combined with comfortable cushions, can transform a cockpit into a pleasant protected outside "room" on a dreary day (See Plate 1).

Instead of a dodger extension, I prefer a cockpit awning, one that fits over the boom and gives standing headroom along the side decks. An awning can rarely be fitted *under* the boom, since mainsheets, boom vangs and other hardware get in the way.

To use the awning on a windy day (we have left *Saga*'s in place in up to 30 knots), the fit must be drum-tight (See Plate 2). Cutting the sides with a slight reverse curve helps reduce flapping, and adding a bolt-rope all around the edge stiffens it even more. Another idea is to

Plate 1   *Live-aboards Joe and Jackie Barnes added a dodger extension to completely enclose the cockpit of their motorsailer* Great Lady.

Plate 2   Saga's *awning fits drum-tight over the boom and allows standing headroom along the side decks.*

add leech lines, just as if it were a sail. On *Saga*, all the tie-down lines are cut and spliced to a set length and snap into rings on the shrouds, life lines and around the mast. Final tightening is done by a self-cleating 5:1 tackle permanently attached to the backstay. This allows us to really horse it down or to release the tension instantly. I like snaps and rings rather than tying down each line, since it makes setting up easier and, more important, the awning can be taken down fast when a squall threatens (See Plate 3).

Ridge poles can be wood, PVC pipe or tele-

Plate 3A   *Live-aboards Tim Loughlin and Shauna Steinburn can cover almost half their boat with this awning.*

Plate 3B   *One person can roll and secure the awning quickly during threatening weather.*

scoping aluminum tubes. Wood poles can be cut into two short lengths, then assembled to full length by inserting their inner ends into sleeves of aluminum tubing. On *Saga* we used 1¼-inch clothes rod dowel. PVC can be made into pole sections with threaded pipe fittings, and is quite flexible compared to wood or aluminum.

The yacht *Heron* has a tent-shaped awning that does not require ridge poles. Instead, the aft end is supported by two swab handles that are inserted at a 45-degree angle into stanchion bases mounted on the aft cabin top. A boom gallows usually eliminates the need for a ridge pole aft.

Side curtains can be added, but you should be able to roll them up tightly when they're not wanted. Even short panels greatly increase the amount of shade, particularly when the sun is at a low angle. Of course, they also restrict air flow to a certain extent. As with a dodger extension, awning side curtains can be made so they completely enclose the cockpit.

I've been saying "cockpit awning," but in reality most such awnings are as long as the boom, covering most of the cabin trunk and the cockpit (See Plate 4). This keeps the deck

cooler underfoot by preventing the sun from beating on the cabin top, making the boat interior many degrees cooler as well. You see many boats in southern waters with foredeck awnings *and* afterdeck awnings (See Plate 5) to keep the sun off virtually the entire boat.

Both awnings and dodger extensions can be rigged to act as raincatchers. (See the chapter on plumbing for several ways to rig such systems.)

The big disadvantage of an awning is that it cannot be left up while sailing. A Bimini cover, on the other hand, will shade the cockpit and the helmsman while under sail. If you plan to do considerable cruising in tropical waters, a

Plate 4 *This tent-shaped awning covers the cockpit and most of the cabin trunk, as well as the side decks.*

Bimini is an excellent investment. Because of the rigid framework required, a Bimini can be used in almost any weather, even in gale-force winds. Also, because of its framework, side curtains are generally easier to attach. Occasionally we see a dodger extension that was designed to snap into the Bimini cover, making it a total protection for the cockpit. (See Plate 6).

Powerboats often use Bimini covers for shade over the steering station on a flying bridge. These, too, can have roll-down curtains of clear plastic, which usually enclose the Bimini cover across the front and sides. Also, many powerboats have an afterdeck that is covered, or at least partially covered, by a canopy. The permanent structure makes it relatively simple to install roll-up curtains—certainly simpler and cheaper than designing and building an enclosure for a sailboat.

Almost all modern trawler-type boats can have their after decks completely enclosed. Some lessons can be learned from fine old power yachts like Trumpy or Consolidated. If the boat has side decks, as most do, when the boat is under way the wind will sweep along the boat's side and funnel into the after deck, particularly if it's enclosed. A combination of wind speed and boat speed can make the area uncomfortable. So, many of the old yachts had

Plate 5 *This small afterdeck awning uses a boat hook for its lower ridge pole. It shades the cockpit and gives privacy when dockside.*

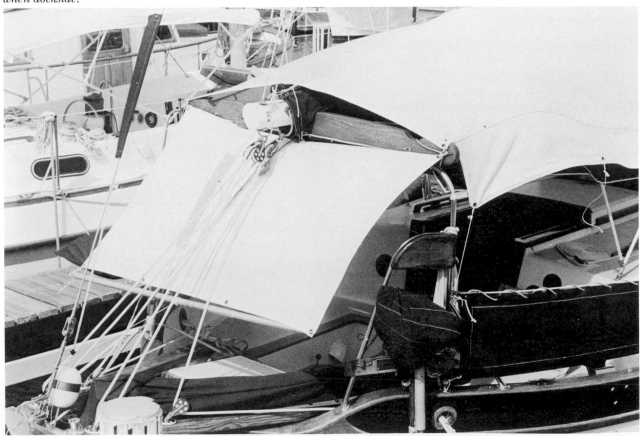

Plate 6 Edon II's *dodger/Bimini has roll-up curtains all around to convert the cockpit into an additional room.*

"weather doors" for the side decks leading aft. These doors could be added to most power-boats (See Plate 7). Even a simple canvas curtain, rolled down from the canopy and stretched taut, would be a great help.

We've been aboard several large power yachts with enclosed aft decks or canopy decks that were beautifully furnished and decorated rooms, complete with lounge chairs, dining tables, a bar, a refrigerator and potted plants (See Plate 7). The curtains were rolled up in fine weather and zipped closed in bad.

If you don't want to go to that much trouble, a canvas awning can be rigged leading from the

Plate 7 *The enclosed after deck on this Hatteras is indeed another room. The weather doors can be opened for a breeze or tightly closed in bad weather.*

Plate 8A *Sabrina's accordian-folding counter extension folds down over the quarterberth.*

Plate 8B *The galley extension in the stowed position, flush against the hull.*

canopy to the aft bulwark. It will help protect your "back porch" from the weather and it could also be set up as a rain catcher.

ADD-A-COUNTER

One thing there's never enough of on a boat is counter space.

And not just in the galley. Work space for writing letters, building projects, making small repairs and using the sewing machine always is scarce. Sometimes the saloon table gets awfully crowded.

Sabrina had a large counter extension that filled in the space over the forward end of the quarterberth (See Plate 8A). On those rare occasions when we needed the quarterberth for sleeping the extension could accordion-fold against the side of the hull, where it was totally out of the way (See Plate 8B).

You can make a sink cover to gain more counter space in the galley. However, I think that idea is useful only if you have double sinks and only cover one, since virtually every galley operation seems to require using water—hence the sink.

Small shelves that flip up (or down) can be installed in all sorts of places—at the end of a counter (See Plate 9), on a bulkhead, over a berth or settee, over a toilet, on the front of a cabinet door that's seldom opened, on the back of a door that can remain closed when the shelf is being used—even on the face of a shelf (See Plate 10).

Small work surfaces can be made to fit over a partially pulled-out drawer. These often will be of the right height to serve as a typewriter table or a writing desk. *Heron* has one that fits between the forward V-berths, resting on two drawers, that Valarie Pentoney uses for a desk (they also have a chair that does double-duty for guests in the saloon and for Val in the forward cabin). Bruce made an over-drawer shelf to hold the photo enlarger in *Saga*'s workshop/ darkroom.

Saloon tables are often made so they fold up out of the way. The idea sounds good in theory but in live-aboard practice the table is invariably down and in full-time use. It is nice to have

Plate 9 Edon II's *counter extension is constructed of stock shelving materials available at most general hardware stores.*

Plate 10A Heron *has a small but handy shelf hinged to the front of the plate racks in the galley.* (PHOTO BY DICK PENTONEY.)

Plate 10B Heron's *hinged shelf in the "up" position provides mounting space for two sauce pans.* (PHOTO BY DICK PENTONEY.)

Plate 11 *Edson can provide teak cockpit tables for mounting on its steering pedestals.* (PHOTO COURTESY OF THE EDSON CORP.)

a table with leaves so it can be expanded for company yet not intrude on your living space.

At Last's table had a leg at one end, while the other end had a support that fit into a bracket on the bulkhead. The same bracket was fitted to the cabin trunk end in the cockpit, so the table could be carried topside in fine weather. The leg hinged to facilitate moving the table. *Sabrina* also had a cockpit table, designed to fit over her tiller. Boats with pedestal steering (or compass pedestals) generally lend themselves to a flip-up table made to fit the pedestal. Edson even sells ready-made teak cockpit tables for its pedestal units (See Plate 11). Flip-up tables mounted on the aft end of the cabin trunk are especially useful for navigating. (Plate 12 shows a nifty cockpit table aboard a Westsail 32.)

ADD-A-PERSON

We always seem to have boats that don't quite seat enough people. On *Sabrina* Bruce made a very simple seat out of a piece of ½-inch plywood that rested on a pair of cleats: one screwed into a cabinet door and the other into the settee front (See Plate 13). With that, we have had as many as six people for a sit-down dinner. I should note that the cabinet door was able to withstand the weight of the seat and person because it was a snug fit: the bottom edge rested solidly on the cutout in the counter front instead of on the hinges.

Some people (myself included) are fond of sitting on the companionway ladder. So why not go ahead and make a seat for the bottom

Plate 12 *Bob Comstock built this teak cockpit table for use in port; Ruth Comstock macramed the hangers that attach to the boom.*

Plate 13 *Sabrina's extra seat is made of ½-inch plywood.*

step so it will be deep enough to be comfortable? The seat can either be hinged to fold out from the step (See Figure 1), or be a separate piece of wood that slides into place when needed.

You can still buy (if you hunt for them) round, commercially-made, flip-up seats that mount on a bulkhead, or a cabinet front if it's strong enough. The seats are about 12 inches in diameter and don't protrude very much in the stowed position. You could make your own, of course, along the same lines as the flip-up tables. Just be sure the design is sturdy enough to take the weight of an adult.

If the cabin sole is wide enough, you might consider buying a chair. *Heron*'s chair, men-

tioned earlier, is a small wicker chair with arms. Dick says he likes it because it can fall over or bang around while under way and the wicker never leaves a dent or a mark.

Aboard *Saga* we have a folding director's chair. We've always found them quite comfortable and they can be folded to stow in a locker or held against a bulkhead with shock cord. The canvas can be removed for washing; in fact, we have two spare sets of different colors. A folding camp stool would take up even less room, although it wouldn't be nearly as comfortable as a chair with arms and a back.

Powerboats generally have room for a couple of chairs, but a director's chair is still a good choice for occasional extra seating or as a chair that can be carried on deck. Wicker furniture is both lightweight and attractive but its standard finish cannot withstand the marine environment for any length of time—it should not be left on deck. A new craze in patio furniture is chairs and tables made of PVC pipe—a practical choice for a boat, as well.

ADD-A-CARPENTER

I spent most of my childhood wanting to be a carpenter—building models and tree houses and making things with sticks. This upset my mother—little girls aren't supposed to be interested in such things. My father thought it was "cute."

I've never outgrown that building-fixing involvement and I hope I never do. Despite a career as a designer and writer, I still find my greatest pleasure mucking around in the work-

Figure 1 *A folding seat for the companionway ladder, and a folding "counter" as well.*

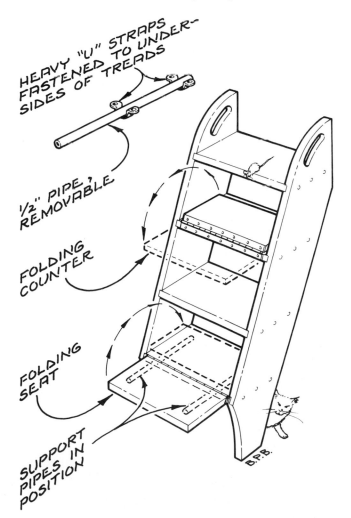

HEAVY "U" STRAPS FASTENED TO UNDER-SIDES OF TREADS

½" PIPE, REMOVABLE

FOLDING COUNTER

FOLDING SEAT

SUPPORT PIPES IN POSITION

shop. It smells good, it feels good and usually something useful comes out of it. Note that I say *usually*.

Once I started building a 36-foot schooner in the family backyard—delusions of grandeur supreme! That project never got past the keel, but something good did come out of it. I managed to build (as a tender for the schooner) an 8-foot rowing/sailing dinghy. Her hull was ³⁄₁₆-inch mahogany planking over ³⁄₄-inch by 1-inch steam-bent oak frames. The hardest skill to learn was that of spiling, but once I figured it out it went pretty easily. I had expected the framing to be the hardest—but it turned out to be the simplest. For a "steam box" I found a section of an old aluminum mast, sealed one end and plugged the other with a piece of wood. Heat was furnished by a two-burner gas stove set on the ground. The pipe was partially filled with water and some rock salt. It took about 45 minutes of boiling for the tiny frames to turn to spaghetti and plop over the molds.

The dinghy was finished bright on the inside, with mahogany seats and transom. The outside was covered with a lightweight canvas and "air-balled" with Thorpes Easy Deck.

Thorpes is a great product—it looks and smells like white glue and is very pleasant stuff to work with. It's water soluble, which makes cleaning up a snap, but is absolutely watertight when it's dried.

Considering my lack of experience, that dinghy turned out rather nicely. Pete Culler, in his book *Skiffs and Schooners*, says, "Experience starts when you begin."

I couldn't agree more. If I had waited until I had "more experience" I wouldn't have had the pleasure of the little dinghy, and our first live-aboard boat, the 36-foot schooner *At Last* that we purchased in 1975, would probably still be pretty bare if I had sat back and left all the carpentry to Bruce. Sure, I made a lot of mistakes. But so what? Most errors can be rectified, even though doing so can be a pain in the neck. Poor Bruce learned to bite his tongue and keep his hands tied behind his back to keep from jumping in and taking over sometimes. But he knew, too, that the only way you learn something is by doing it yourself.

So I would like to offer a few basic hints for those who have the urge to fix up their boats— or even to build one from scratch—but who are feeling timid about jumping in and getting started.

HAMMERS

Now you would think that you'd just grab a hammer and pound away, right? Wrong. I've probably had more advice from more people on the proper way to use a hammer than any other single tool. I knew an old fisherman by the name of Frank Brady out in California who had a saying, "If it can't be fixed with a hammer, it can't be fixed."

I've suspected on occasion that he may be absolutely right. Especially when I've really messed something up and gotten quite frustrated. It's a temptation to grab the hammer and beat the offending work to pieces. I'm sure at least I would feel better.

Where you grab a hammer handle—at the end, at the head or somewhere in the middle —is not as important as how you *swing* it. Hold it however it feels most comfortable and hammer with a steady, rhythmic motion from the elbow. I used to live next door to a house-framing carpenter. Big Joey, all 6 feet, 4 inches and 240 pounds of him, told me the *only* way to swing a hammer was from the shoulder and "really put your back into it." I'm sure that's correct if you're Big Joey and driving 10-penny nails into a 4 by 4. But if you're an average person doing fairly delicate boat work, it's the perfect way to split your work or put big dents in your wood.

So, swing from the elbow and don't try to drive it in with one or two blows. Hold on to the nail with thumb and forefinger for as long as you can—there will be less chance of bending it. Very short nails can be held with needlenose pliers to get them well started.

And, *go slowly.* High-speed carpentry is for the rough-and-ready work so often seen today in house framing. It's appropriate when "time is money" applies. But your work on boats is—or should be—the very best you can do. Think of it as "forever." Much of it will be visible through varnish. The pleasure and pride comes from doing your best *each time,* and watching the finished product *get better.* So don't rush.

If you're using finishing nails, don't drive them all the way home with only the hammer. Drive them to just above the surface, then use a nailset to finish and countersink the head. That way you won't mar the surface of the wood with round impressions from the hammer head.

If you're removing a nail, place a piece of scrap wood behind the claws and pull against it (See Plate 1). This will give you the leverage necessary to remove even a huge nail from a very hard wood like oak. And, again, it will save you from scarring the wood with the hammer.

Pulling big nails out of oak is not a problem most builders will face, of course. The guy who built *At Last* was nail happy. There were 3-inch and 4-inch galvanized nails driven at random into some of the frames and the white oak bilge stringers, for no apparent reason. They all had to be removed and I was surprised at how easily the nails came out using the block of wood as a fulcrum.

If you're nailing near the edge of a plank or anywhere that the nail might split the wood, *always* pre-drill the hole. Use a bit slightly smaller than the size of the nail.

DRILLS AND SCREWS

My biggest problem with drilling is that I can't drill straight. I've come to the conclusion that some people "see straight" and some people

Plate 14 *A piece of scrap wood under the hammer head will add leverage to remove a stubborn nail.*

don't. I don't. I will *swear* that something is absolutely straight until Bruce brings out the square or the level. Then, sure enough, it's crooked. I don't know how to overcome this, so I try to compensate for it. I'll line up the drill and bit until they appear straight, then cock it back and drill. Most of the time it works. I found a $3.98 gadget at the hardware store called a "drill guide." It helps, but can only be used with small bits. For drilling long, straight holes in edge grain, such as joining two pieces of wood together with dowels, I draw a line down the side of the plank, with a square and line up the drill or brace with that.

If you're drilling a hole all the way through a piece of wood, as when making a finger hole in a locker door or bunk-top opening, for example, chances are the wood will splinter and chip when the bit breaks through the other side, especially if you're drilling plywood. To avoid this, put a piece of scrap wood underneath the piece you're drilling and drill *through* the real work and *into* the scrap.

Either kneel down hard over the two pieces or clamp them tightly together so there's no separation between the two planks. If you're using an auger bit in a brace, drill until you feel the point come through and finish drilling from the other side.

You can buy 3-in-1 drill bits for various size screws and these are great time savers. The best ones have an adjustable collar so you can set them for the length of screw and drill, countersink and counterbore—all in one operation (See Plate 2). Otherwise, you have to drill with three different bits for every screw hole. Drill first for the shaft of the screw, to a depth equal to the *entire* length of the screw (plus the counterbore if you're using bungs), or deep enough to putty over the head if you're countersinking. Roundhead or panhead screws

Plate 15 *A three-in-one drill bit will drill, countersink and counterbore all in one operation.*

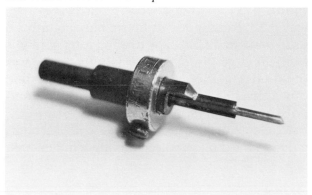

only require two operations—drilling for the shaft and then the shank. The hole for the shaft should be *slightly undersized*. For the shank, the bit should be the same size as the screw for a soft wood such as pine, and *one size larger* for hardwoods like oak. The last hole is drilled to the size of the bung. Wrap a piece of masking tape around the bit so you will drill to the correct depth each time.

Driving screws into very hard wood, like oak, is usually a tough job, even with the proper size hole predrilled. Try dipping the screw threads into a cup of liquid detergent mixed with a little water. Or try using a screwdriver bit in a brace so you can really put your weight behind it.

If you're trying to back out a screw and it's being stubborn, use the screwdriver bit in a brace; or, lean into it, grasp the shank of the screwdriver with a pair of pliers and slowly rock it back and forth until you feel it start to move. Then you can proceed and slowly back it out.

If you do much woodworking at all, eventually you'll own several screwdrivers. It's very important that the screwdriver be a *perfect mate* for the screw. Too small a screwdriver will slip and slide around in the slot and probably strip the head of the screw. If that happens, you'll have a devil of a time driving it the rest of the way in or even backing it out. Too big a screwdriver won't fit the slot properly and, again, you run the risk of stripping the screw. I speak from sad experience on this matter. So don't get hasty and just grab the nearest screwdriver because it happens to be handy. Stop, and go hunt up the proper size.

If you're making a decklight using Plexiglas, or perhaps installing a Plexiglas portlight, *always* drill the hole *larger* than the shank of the screw. Otherwise you run the risk of cracking the plastic. And when you're drilling, take it slow and easy, don't push the drill at all or you'll crack it for sure.

SAWS

There are many different kinds of saws: hand saws, large and small, hole saws, coping saws, hacksaws (for metal), circular saws, sabre saws, scroll saws, to name a few and—if you're lucky —band saws and table saws. We do most of our work with a good small hand saw and a sabre saw, although we own at least one of most of the other kinds.

Ripping lumber (a long straight cut with the grain) is best done on a table saw. If you don't own a table saw or know someone who will let you use his, it can be done with a circular saw or even a sabre saw if that's all you have. Find a straight piece of wood as long as (or longer) than the plank you're cutting. Clamp or nail it securely to your plank and use it as a guide for the saw, carefully measuring the distance from the blade to the edge of the guide on the saw. This trick is so useful for making any kind of long, straight cut (in addition to ripping) with a hand-held power saw that I put the blade-to-guide distance on pieces of tape and stuck them on the bodies of both our sabre and circular saws so I don't have to remeasure each time.

When cross-cutting (sawing *across* the grain) with a hand saw, alternate your stroke from almost vertical to leaning the saw back at a 45-degree angle along the cut line. You'll cut faster and more accurately this way. And make sure the work is well supported while you're sawing—either hold it down with your knee on a bench or saw horses, clamp it to a table, or secure small pieces in a vise. Otherwise your work will wobble around, buckling a hand saw or setting up too much vibration in a power saw.

To cut an opening in a piece of plywood (perhaps you're installing a locker with a ply-wood front, or making an existing top-opening bin into one that is also front-opening) it's eas-iest to drill a large hole somewhere on the cut-out line and start sawing from there. But if you want to save the cutout (perhaps to use it as the door), use your sabre saw (See Plate 3). Tilt the saw forward so the blade is *not* touching the wood and line it up carefully with your cut-out line. Push the ON button. Now tilt the saw back and *slowly* cut through the wood. As soon as the blade is all the way through, seat the saw down flat on its ramp, and continue with your cut. If

you round the corners of the cutout you can do the whole job in one continuous cut. If you want square corners, however, you'll have to repeat this operation four times.

PLANES

A plane is used for smoothing the edges of a board or for cutting a bevel along an edge, as when fitting a shelf or counter top along the hull. Usually the bevel is cut with a saw, but you may have to do some trimming for a perfect fit and this is usually done with the plane.

Always make your cut *with* the grain—going against the grain will cause the blade to dig in and gouge the wood. Don't try to take too deep a cut. Sight along the underside of the plane— the blade should extend *just slightly* through the opening. Hold the plane at a slight angle to your work and make shallow, even cuts. If you're planing in an angle, use a bevel gauge constantly to check your work.

Jack planes are the most commonly used. They measure from 12 inches to 15 inches long

Plate 16 *If done with care, a sabre saw can be used to start a cut without first drilling a hole.*

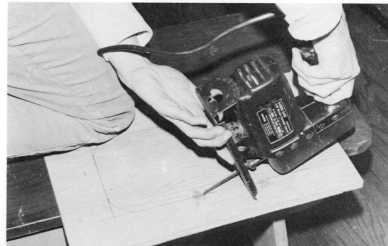

and are held with both hands. A block plane is a smaller version of the jack plane, but it is held with one hand and is used for fine finish work or smoothing edges left rough by the larger jack plane. Large joiner planes can measure anywhere from 18 inches up to 30 inches long. You won't find much use for them unless you're planking a hull or building spars.

Chisels

Chisels are used for removing small sections of wood, like cutting a mortise for a flush hinge or shaving off plugs flush with the surrounding area.

Plate 17 *Trim plugs slowly and gently and never try to shave it flush with one cut.*

I try to avoid using flush hinges whenever I can, since I find cutting a mortise properly is a tedious, painstaking job. Unfortunately, sometimes nothing else will do. First, carefully mark the outline of the hinge with a sharp pencil. Score the edge running parallel with the grain using a knife or an awl. Make your first cuts across the grain at each end, tapping the chisel with a mallet (or hammer) and keeping the bevel side of the chisel towards the area being cut away. This will help prevent the chisel from slipping past the section you want to remove. Now start shaving away the wood inside your cut marks, going with the grain and taking very shallow cuts. Check often with the hinge to be sure you're not going too deep.

When cutting off plugs (used to cover screw heads), never try to remove the plug in one cut (See Plate 4). You're asking for trouble if you do. Plugs should always be inserted with their grain running parallel with the grain of the surrounding wood. Sometimes it's hard to see the grain or the plug may accidently go in a little cockeyed, so I always cut off about half the plug first, to make sure I'm cutting with the grain and to see if it has a tendency to chip in one direction or another. Then I cut it off *almost* flush, tapping the chisel gently with a hammer. This is one job that can't be rushed. To finish it off, I shave the plug carefully, using the chisel without the hammer.

I might add that the chisel must be *very* sharp for this work, but then all cutting tools should be kept sharp. Dull tools are not only hard to work with, but they can be quite dangerous and may ruin the job.

Gauges and Levels

A bevel gauge is a must in every boat carpenter's tool box. You'll use it a 100 times more often than an ordinary carpenter's square. It's simply a tool for transferring an angle or bevel from one surface to another (See Plate 5). Use it for picking up the angle of the hull where it butts against a shelf, berth top or counter top. It can measure the bevel of a bulkhead edge where it touches the hull or the angle of a cab-

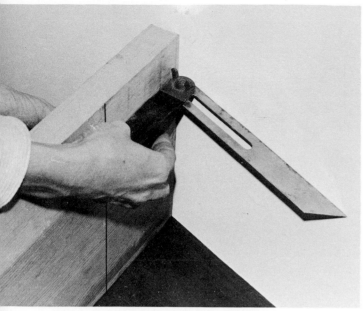

Plate 18 *A bevel gauge is a simple tool used to transfer angles or bevels accurately.*

inet running fore and aft where it joins an athwartships bulkhead.

A level is easy to use ashore, but it can get a bit complicated if the boat is in the water and rarely in perfect trim. To overcome this, place the level on an existing bunk or counter top that you know is level. If the bubble is a little off, wrap one end with masking tape until you get a level reading. Then place it on whatever you're installing. Keep in mind, however, that if your boat is small, you may be changing the trim just by moving around, so try to find a level surface close to where you're working.

Remember, the only way to learn a skill is by *doing* it, and the only way to become really good at it is to keep trying. And everybody, even professionals, make mistakes. So stop sitting there in your armchair dreaming about all those nifty things you'd like to put in your boat. Get off your duff and go to work! You may be surprised at how much fun it is, to say nothing of the pride you'll feel when you can stand back and say, "*I* made that!"

One last word from an old carpenter. Burn it into your mind: "Measure *twice,* cut *once!*"

12

Heating

"Keep it cozy"

SOME TYPE OF heat is necessary on just about every live-aboard boat. About the only exception is a boat that spends all her time in a *true* tropical climate. Even as far south as the Florida Keys (and they're considered tropical) it can get chilly enough on winter evenings after a cold front to make a heater welcome.

HEATING

When considering the economics of heating a boat, keep in mind that the better insulated the hull and deck, the less time you'll spend operating a heater or, for that matter, a fan or air conditioner in the summer. (See Chapter 23 for details about insulation and its installation.)

CALCULATING HEAT REQUIREMENTS

Most heaters are rated by the amount of BTU's they produce. A BTU is a British Thermal Unit, the amount of heat used to raise the temperature of one pound of water by one degree Fahrenheit. A few heaters are rated by watts. To convert watts to BTU, multiply by 3.4. This will make it easier to compare heaters.

The first step in calculating your BTU requirement is to figure the volume of space to be heated. Roughly, measure the cabin (or cabins). Multiply length times height times width to get the volume in cubic feet.

Multiply the volume by a factor of from 10 to 20. Use 10 if you'll always be in warm climates and 20 if you plan to spend winters up north. The answer will be the BTU output you require. It's better to figure on the high side. The heater can always be turned down or off. But if you can't get it high enough, you're really stuck. Let's take an example: a boat with a cabin area that measures, say, 12 feet long by 6 feet high by 9 feet wide is:

$$12 \times 6 \times 9 = 648 \text{ cubic feet}$$

Assume the boat will be south in the winter and north in the summer, but will spend some part of the fall where it's cold (or chilly). So let's use a factor of 15:

$$648 \times 15 = 9,720 \text{ BTUs}$$

If a cabin will be heated only occasionally—a forward stateroom perhaps—or will be closed off on really cold days, use a lower factor.

On a boat with several cabins, figure each

compartment separately if you intend to use a space heater for each one. It will be impossible to *evenly* heat all the cabins from one central heater, unless it's of the forced-air type.

Convection heaters do not produce an even heat. When air is heated, it expands, thus lowering the specific gravity and becoming lighter than the surrounding air. This causes the heated air to rise. This heated air then cools and contracts, raising the specific gravity and causing it to fall again. The result is a convection current, which is primarily vertical. Thus, the overhead will always be warmer than the cabin sole, often to a noticeable degree (See Figure 1).

A fan is a tremendous aid in heat distribu-

tion. Heat will rise and collect overhead while the cabin sole remains cold. A small fan mounted on or near the underside of the cabin top will keep the air circulating—down toward

Figure 1 *The typical convection cycle depends on, and results in, a very uneven distribution of heat. Contrary to most beliefs, convection drafts are very inefficient heat carriers.*

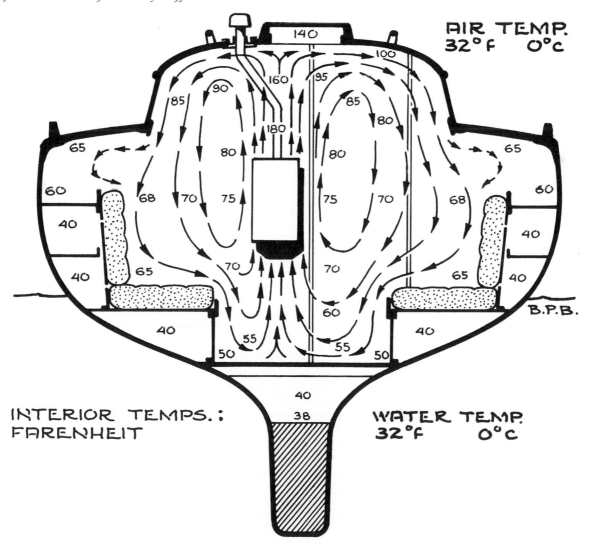

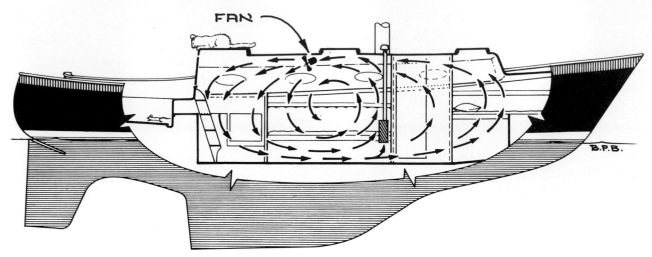

Figure 2 *A high-mounted fan will prevent a buildup of hot air at the cabin top and keep it circulating for more uniform heat distribution.*

your feet, as well as into other staterooms (See Figure 2).

DRY HEAT/WET HEAT

When choosing a heater, condensation is a problem to consider carefully. It happens when the relative humidity reaches 100 percent. (Relative humidity, which is stated as a percentage, is the amount of moisture in the air compared to the total amount that *could* be held by the air at any given temperature.) When the temperature rises, the relative humidity goes down. A *decrease* in temperature means an *increase* in relative humidity (See Figure 3).

A boat can be warm and dry all day, then drip with condensation when cabin trunk and

Figure 3 *Relative humidity decreases with a temperature rise, and increases with a temperature drop.*

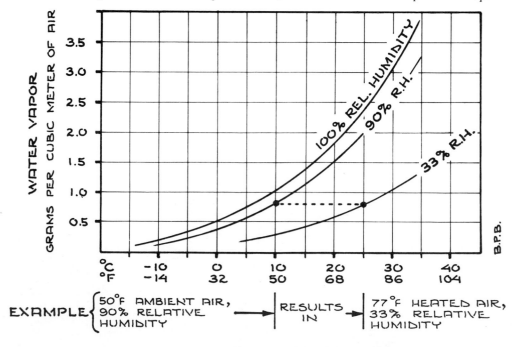

hull cools off at night, even if the *amount* of water in the air (humidity) hasn't changed. The temperature drop has caused the *relative humidity* to climb. At 100 percent relative humidity, water vapor changes into water particles (See Figure 4).

Many factors contribute to the amount of water in the air inside a boat-home: breathing, boiling water, cooking, wet clothes or an open flame. All liquid fuels produce water as a by-product of combustion—generally an amount of water equal to the amount of fuel burned—not much from a kerosene lamp, but a lot from a heater.

A vented heater will carry the moisture outside. An unvented heater will keep water vapor trapped in the air within the cabin. When the vapor touches the cool cabin trunk or bronze porthole rims, the temperature drop will convert it from vapor to condensation almost instantaneously (See Figure 4).

Unvented heaters—such as kerosene or alcohol space heaters, catalytic propane heaters or clay flower pots upended on the stove—can serve to heat, but only as very occasional, very

temporary sources. For frequent or continuous sources of heat, use only a vented heater.

While on the subject of humidity, a very low relative humidity can be just as troublesome as a very high one, particularly on a wood boat. Friends of ours lived aboard their lovely wood schooner through a New England winter. A large, cast-iron coal-burning stove was used for cooking and heating. The arid heat did such a fine job it dried out the deck planking enough so it started leaking. Our friends finally had to keep a large pan of water on the stove to put some moisture back into the air.

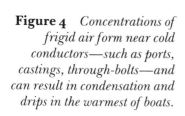

Figure 4 *Concentrations of frigid air form near cold conductors—such as ports, castings, through-bolts—and can result in condensation and drips in the warmest of boats.*

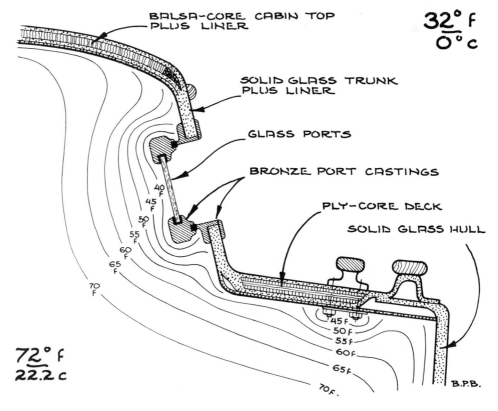

Plate 1 *Catalytic propane heaters, like these Viking units, produce heat by a chemical reaction. They are flameless and produce no carbon monoxide.* (PHOTO COURTESY OF ALLCRAFT CORP.)

LIQUID FUEL HEATERS (UNVENTED)

As a temporary source of heat, an unvented heater does have a distinct advantage. Without the vent, it need not be a permanent installation, so the heater can be moved from cabin to cabin or stored away when not needed.

It is vitally important that these heaters receive an adequate supply of fresh air. I don't think cowl vents alone supply enough. We leave open one or two ports, or partially open a hatch. Theoretically, if complete combustion takes place, poisonous carbon monoxide is not produced; but it's foolish to take a chance. *Don't* leave heaters unattended and *don't* use them at night when everyone is asleep.

The most common fuel used in space heaters is kerosene—like the familiar Aladdin Blue Flame heaters. We used two of them for several years aboard *At Last*. They burn for 16 to 25 hours on a gallon of kerosene, while producing 6,000 to 9,000 BTUs. The kerosene burns with a large circular wick that must be cleaned periodically (just like a lamp wick), and can be adjusted to a high or low flame. The color of the flame is important—a blue flame means it's burning properly, a yellow flame is a sign of trouble.

The Heat Pal is a small heater that can produce up to 7,000 BTUs. Its drawback is that it uses alcohol, an expensive fuel.

A clay flower pot turned upside down on a stove burner makes a good temporary heater on a chilly morning. I've only tried this with a propane stove. I suppose it would work with other fuels, although the flame must be kept very low until the pot heats up or it might crack.

Catalytic propane heaters, like the Viking, are flameless and do not produce carbon monoxide, so there is no need for them to be vented (See Plate 1). They are radiant space heaters, although designed to be bulkhead-mounted, so they're not really portable. Heat is produced by a chemical reaction—the combination of gas (propane or butane) and air with a catalytic agent (platinum). The Viking heaters use a piezo starter so they don't need electricity. The four Viking models will produce from 3,300 to 9,000 BTUs. All have an automatic shutoff device in case of malfunction. If you're already using propane for cooking, a Viking heater makes sense for temporary heat. However, one of the by-products of the chemical reaction is water vapor, so the resulting condensation might be too great to consider this type a full-time heat source.

Another temporary source is oil lamps. While small ones won't produce much heat (except on a hot summer night!), the pressurized kerosene lamps, and the ones that use a mantle, give off a surprising amount of heat—enough to chase an evening chill.

LIQUID FUEL CONVECTION HEATERS (VENTED)

Vented heaters eliminate condensation problems fairly well, but they must be well ventilated since, like the unvented heaters, they draw air for their combustion from the cabin.

Care must be taken in locating these heaters since they are a permanent installation that include an exhaust head (often called a Charley Noble). This is of particular concern on a sailboat where lines may become fouled on it. Or the sails may create strange drafts when the boat's underway.

Pressure kerosene heaters have a burner unit similar to those used in kerosene cookstoves. It's the design and construction of the heater itself, not the burner, that makes them function as a *heater*. Their biggest drawback is that since the fuel is under pressure it must be kept pumped up, just like a kerosene stove. This may become a real bother on a 24-hour basis. These heaters can often be equipped with a flue pipe jacket to provide hot water as well as heat (See Figure 5A).

Among the most popular heaters are the British-made Taylor Para-Fin pressure kerosene heaters, which supply about 7,000 BTUs. These heaters are bulkhead-mounted and quite attractive. They are stainless steel or made of brass and copper. Shipmate makes a stainless steel pressure kerosene heater capable of producing 10,000 BTUs (See Plate 2). It

Plate 2 *Shipmate's pressure kerosene heater will produce up to 10,000 BTUs.* (PHOTO COURTESY OF RICHMOND RING CO., SHIPMATE STOVE DIVISION.)

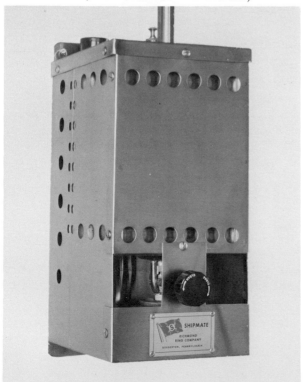

Figure 5A *A typical vented kerosene convection heater with optional hot water system.*

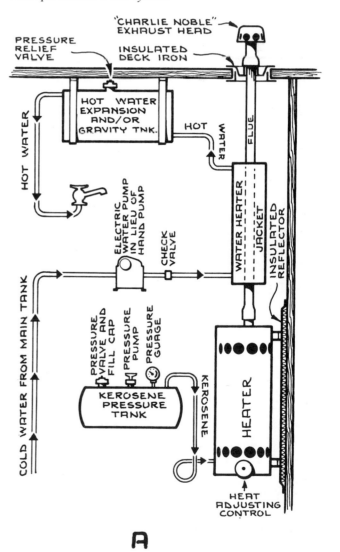

Figure 5B *A typical vented diesel convection heater
with optional hot water systems.*

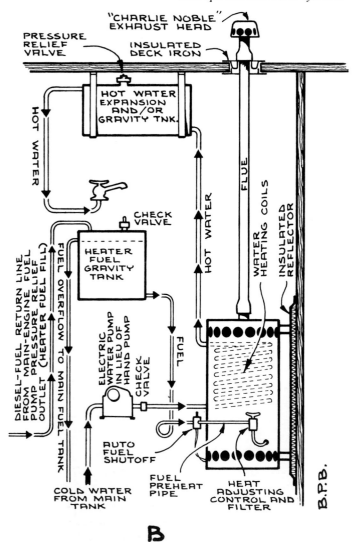

uses a Primus self-cleaning burner and has an integral two-quart pressure tank.

Diesel heaters do not have to be pumped like a pressure kerosene heater. The fuel is supplied either by a gravity tank, by an air pressure system, or by a low-pressure demand fuel pump. With few exceptions, diesel heaters are air-supplied for combustion by natural draft. Several diesel heaters are offered with internal coils for a hot water system (See Figure 5B).

Diesel heaters are a practical solution for a boat that already uses diesel for its engine. Taylor makes two diesel models (See Plate 3). They are both drip-fed and come equipped with a flame-failure cut-off valve. The bulkhead-mounted unit supplies almost 10,000 BTUs. The larger, free-standing one (bolted to the cabin sole) produces 16,000 BTUs.

Other drip-fed diesel heaters are the Hi-Seas Model #100 by Marine Heat Corp. It produces 3,500 to 15,000 BTUs. The Dickinson Marine Products "Chesapeake" heater (See Plate 4), is rated at 2,000 to 8,000 BTUs. Both operate by natural draft and require no electricity.

Drip-fed heaters should be mounted on an *athwartship bulkhead,* so they will keep working

Plate 3A *Taylor's drip-feed diesel heater puts out almost 10,000 BTUs.* (PHOTO COURTESY OF JAY STUART HAFT CO.)

Plate 3B *View of the inner workings of the Taylor drip-feed diesel heater.* (PHOTO COURTESY OF JAY STUART HAFT CO.)

safely at angles up to 40 degrees of heel. Dickinson cautions sailboat owners with heaters having a metering valve feeding fuel into the burner by gravity, that both the valve and the fuel inlet to the burner must be in line with the keel.

Plate 4 *The Chesapeake is a drip-feed diesel heater with an output of 2,000 to 8,000 BTUs.* (PHOTO COURTESY OF DICKINSON MARINE PRODUCTS (US) INC.)

Dickinson's large and powerful free-standing Arctic heater (26 inches high and weighing 39 pounds) comes standard with the valve mounted in front but can be supplied with an in-line back-mount for sailboat installations.

All of these heaters work better by adding a small fan to keep the air circulating. And any heater that is not attached flush to a bulkhead will work better by installing an insulated reflector panel between the heater and the bulkhead. This will reflect heat back into the cabin and protect the bulkhead from overheating.

Diesel heaters require more frequent cleaning than kerosene. Most heaters designed to burn diesel can also burn kerosene, but *don't* try it the other way around.

SOLID FUEL HEATERS

A fireplace is not practical as a continuous source of heat. But few can deny the cozy attraction of a cheery, crackling fire in an open hearth. Among the most beautiful are the Luke Soapstone and the Luke Tile fireplaces. Many other attractive (and smaller) units are on the market. Shipmate builds two, a fairly large free-standing model and a smaller bulkhead-mounted unit.

Most of these marine fireplaces will burn wood, coal, charcoal or pressed logs. One of the really nice things about a solid-fuel fireplace (or heater) is that you can burn up a lot of your trash—paper towels, newspapers, cardboard boxes from pre-packaged foods, grocery bags. Probably half your garbage can be put to use.

Ratelco makes two small fireplaces—the King Cole and the Cole Stove—that are bulkhead mounted and burn charcoal briquets.

Open fireplaces must be installed athwartships on a sailboat. It's an excellent idea to equip them with a door that closes snugly on the firebox.

Shipmate's cast iron Skippy cabin heater (See Plate 5) is quite small (13¼-inches high with a 14-inch by 19-inch top) yet it will hold a coffee pot *and* a small skillet and is equipped with two removable covers.

My own favorites have long been the Pet and Tiny Tot stoves made by Fatsco (See Plate 6). Bruce calls them "funky" and that they are. But they're good little heaters, and people who own them consider them members of the family. Fatsco also produces two larger models called Chummy and Buddy, and is now making cooktops for these models, too.

If you *are* considering a solid-fuel heater or a fireplace, it's important to consider the differences between them. A fireplace that is built-in and is heavily insulated (as it must be to protect its surroundings) will be romantic to snuggle in front of (which is what you'll have to do to stay warm), but useless as a heater for the boat. All the heat will be going right up the flue, just like an open fireplace in a house. They actually draw off more heat than they produce (See Figure 6A).

Plate 5 *Shipmate's cast iron Skippy cabin heater uses solid fuel, although it can be equipped with a natural draft oil burner. It even has a small cooktop!* (PHOTO COURTESY OF RICHMOND RING CO., SHIPMATE STOVE DIVISION.)

Plate 6 *Fatsco's Pet and Tiny Tot are solid-fuel heaters that can be supplied "plain" or with cooktops or heat shields.* (PHOTO COURTESY OF FATSCO.)

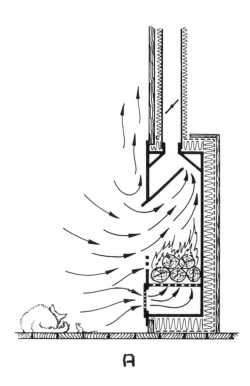

Figure 6A *A built-in fireplace will absorb more cabin heat by internal convection than it can produce through radiation. No heat benefits are derived from the back or sides of the fireplace.*

Figure 6B *The free-standing fireplace, with door closed, radiates and convects from all sides.*

A free-standing (an odd term since all the marine models can be bolted down) heater, stove or fireplace is a better choice. The heat radiates from all sides producing heat. If they are built with double-wall construction (and quite a few are) then convection currents will be enhanced (See Figure 6B).

FORCED-AIR HEATERS

Forced-air heater units are often rejected because their purchase price is high compared to most space heaters and because they require electricity as well as a liquid fuel.

But don't be hasty—in many cases they will be the best choice. To heat a large boat, particularly one with several cabins, a forced-air unit is the only way to get an *even* heat throughout the boat. As noted earlier a fan mounted near a space heater helps to distribute heat, but not very efficiently or evenly—you are using electricity anyway. You can, of course, install a space heater in each cabin. But that will add up to more than the cost of one forced-air unit, so it's a waste of both cabin space *and* fuel.

Forced-air heaters are quite compact and, since combustion occurs in a completely enclosed chamber, they can be mounted in a locker or lazarette, away from living areas. Heat is ducted (the ducting will give warmth to hanging lockers and cabinets that it passes through) and terminates at an unobtrusive register, or grille, in each cabin. Ideally, the grille is located as low as possible, close to the cabin sole.

One of the best features of a forced-air unit is it can draw air for combustion from outside the boat, instead of from the cabin. A warm, dry flow of fresh air is constantly moving throughout the interior. Remember, when cold outside air is raised in temperature, its relative humidity drops drastically (See Figure 3). Another feature I really like about forced-air units is that the fuel, the combustible mixture and the flame are never in contact with the boat's interior atmosphere.

Thermostats are used to control the amount of heat, just like home central heating systems.

The biggest electrical draw takes place when these heaters are started (similar to the high surge drawn by a glow plug when starting a diesel engine). Once the heaters are running, the load varies, depending on the unit, from as low as .5 amps up to about 8 amps for really large units.

Forced-air heaters are available that burn either kerosene (such as the Wallas Thermo- tron heaters that provide from 2,400 to 10,000 BTUs) or diesel (such as the Espar models that produce from 5,800 to 27,000 BTUs). Wallas heaters are manufactured in Sweden, and Espar in West Germany. Both use 12-volt elec- tricity.

The Wallas units are surprisingly quiet. Ker- osene does have advantages over diesel. It's a cleaner fuel and with the Wallas the fuel is not under high pressure, so the units themselves are fairly simple as well as quiet (See Figure 7). They use a stainless steel heat exchanger to separate combustion air and exhaust gas from the heated air. Combustion occurs in a com- pletely enclosed chamber and by-products are exhausted outside the boat. The air actually heated and circulated through the boat can be drawn from inside *or* outside. It is heated by the heat exchanger, and then is blown to var- ious parts of the boat. With the thermostat, the heater can be turned down without being turned completely off, avoiding repeated high-draw surges of electricity. You do have to consider, though, the addition of a kerosene fuel tank (See Figure 8).

Figure 7 *The components and operation of the Wallas Thermotron kerosene forced-air heater.* (COURTESY COOK MARINE PRODUCTS.)

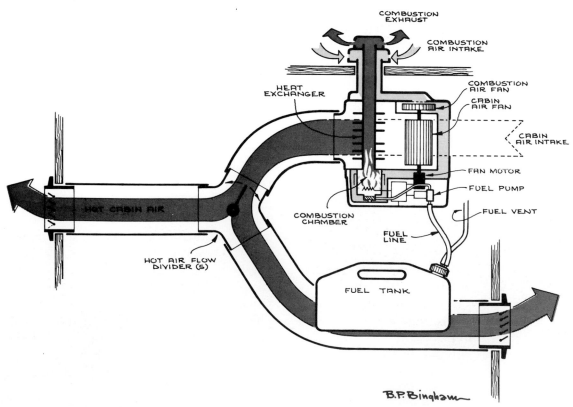

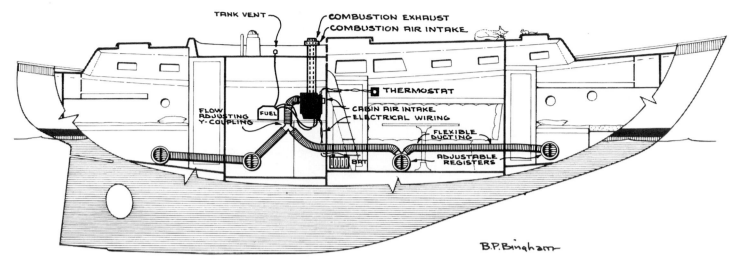

Figure 8   *A typical kerosene forced-air heating installation.*

A heater like the Espar (See Plates 7 and 8) does seem practical on a boat with a diesel engine. The fuel can be drawn directly from the main tank, usually by a top-tank standpipe (See Figure 9). The Espar also uses a heat exchanger system. It transfers the combustion heat to the cabin air, which is then blown throughout the boat. As with the Wallas unit, the cabin air supply can be drawn from inside *or* outside the vessel. The combustible air/fuel mixture is compressed *before* ignition to produce an extremely hot flame, which is exhausted safely outboard. They are noisier than kerosene forced-air heaters, although frankly I have never found the sound objectionable—any more than a house heater or air conditioner (See Figure 10). Espar even makes a hair dryer attachment that can be hooked into one of the register outlets (See Plate 9).

Dickinson makes a central heating system for large yachts called the Marine Comfort Furnace. It's a free-standing stainless steel unit, uses diesel fuel and weighs 81 pounds.

Espar makes a line of gasoline heaters (5,800 to 14,000 BTUs) for boats with gasoline engines. The ignition on the heaters has a continuously firing spark plug and, like the diesel heaters, has ignition and blower over-run sequences to purge the combustion area of any residual fumes.

Plate 7   *Espar's small (5" x 5" x 12") forced-air heater will furnish 6,000 BTUs.* (PHOTO COURTESY OF ESPAR PRODUCTS, INC.)

Plate 8   *This larger hot air heater from Espar (Eberspächer in Europe) will put out 16,000 BTUs.* (PHOTO COURTESY OF ESPAR PRODUCTS, INC.)

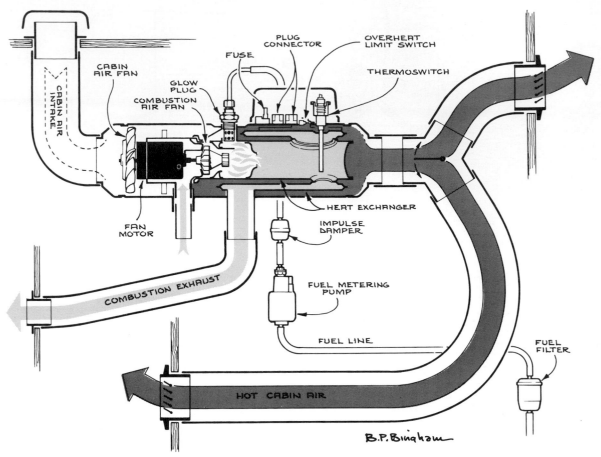

Figure 9 *The components and operation of the Espar (Eberspächer) diesel forced-air heater.* (COURTESY ESPAR PRODUCTS, INC.)

Figure 10 *A typical diesel forced-air heating installation.*

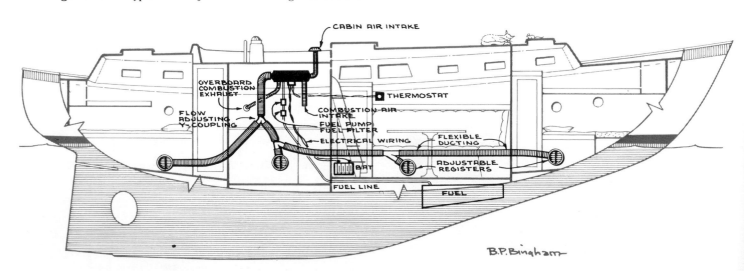

Plate 9 *A great idea for live-aboards is Espar's hair dryer that plugs into its forced-air heating system!* (PHOTO COURTESY OF ESPAR PRODUCTS, INC.)

HOT WATER HEATING SYSTEMS

Hot water heating systems are invariably complicated, expensive and cumbersome and are designed primarily for large yachts. Like the forced-air units, they use both liquid fuel (diesel or kerosene) and electricity in copious amounts. But then they also produce impressive amounts of heat.

Generally, these units heat water in the system to around 190°F, then pump it through flexible heater hoses to convectors in each cabin. Each convector has a radiator and a blower fan that moves air past the radiator where it is heated then sent into the cabin (See Figures 11 and 12).

Some hot water systems use baseboard convectors without blowers or fans.

Figure 11 *The components and operation of a typical circulating water heating system with cabin convectors.*

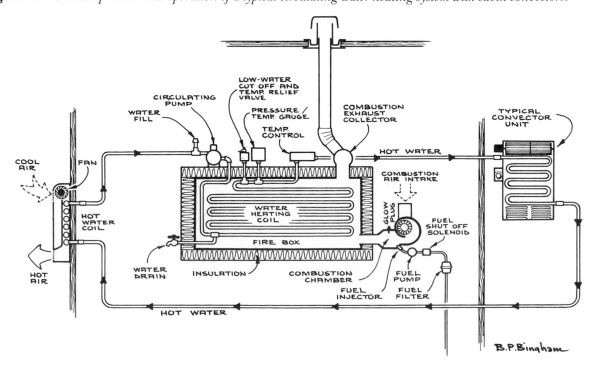

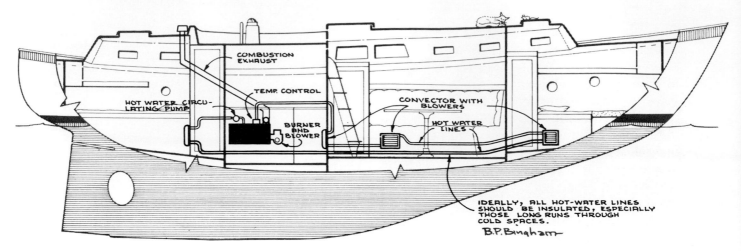

Figure 12 *A typical hot water heating installation.*

Espar has two models—a small unit that will run on 12-volt current and a large unit that requires a 24-volt system and puts out up to 82,000 BTUs.

Some manufacturers, like Neptune Marine Heaters in New York, build hot-water heating systems that will only work with 110-volt power, requiring you to either remain dockside or operate a generator. However, they have units that produce as much as 246,000 BTUs.

Those who spend a considerable time underway with the engine running might consider installing a car or camper heater that makes use of engine cooling water. Even if you're not under way, but run the engine daily for charging batteries or running a refrigerator, that might provide enough heat if you arrange your running time during chilly evening hours.

ELECTRIC HEATERS

If you know you'll be living dockside during cold weather, electric heat makes a lot of sense. It's certainly the cleanest form of heating and the simplest—just plug it in. However, if you're wintering in a northern climate that ices over, you'd better have a backup system in case of a shoreside power failure. Another point to keep in mind is that most marinas "resell" electricity and thus the rates are generally higher to the boatowner than to the homeowner or apartment dweller. Some marinas meter elec-

tricity for each boat, particularly live-aboard boats; others charge a flat monthly rate.

We spent a winter in New York aboard *Sabrina,* using a small Intermatic Heatwave heater that produced about 5,000 BTUs and was barely larger than a shoe box (See Figure 13). It was more than enough for *Sabrina's* tiny cabin. The heater, mounted underneath a companionway step, had a squirrel-cage fan that kept the air circulating to every corner of the boat. Bruce made one change to the heater: he replaced the rather flimsy electrical cord with heavy-gauge wire.

Space heaters that use a fan or blower will be more efficient than the heater-coil or radiant type. An important safety feature to look for is an automatic shutoff device if the heater should tip over.

There are built-in electric heating units

Figure 13 *The Intermatic Heatwave heater produces 5,000 BTUs and uses 110-volt AC current. Small side brackets may be installed with sheet metal screws for mounting under ladder treads, tables or cabinetwork.*

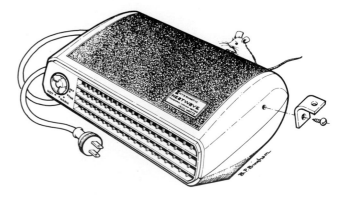

available that you can install as a permanent system, such as the long, narrow, overhead-mounted infrared heaters made by Elecktra Marine and R. V. Systems Co.

Choosing a heating system for your boat is a big decision and not an easy one. It's impossible to recommend one type above all others, since they all provide heat and any particular one may be the right answer—depending on the size of your boat, its layout, the amount of money you have to spend and how and where you are moored. All these considerations must be carefully balanced.

Before you buy any heater, get a copy of the installation booklet (it may cost a dollar or two, but it's worth it), and study it carefully to make sure the heater will not only *fit* in the spot you've chosen, but will operate properly there as well. You may find, for instance, that the height of the flue pipe is critical for proper combustion and that the heater won't operate in your preferred spot without adding an electric fan. Such details are often overlooked in the advertising flyers.

Sabrina had an electric heater and, occasionally, a clay flower pot. Both were ideal solutions for that boat and for the type of cruising we were doing at that time.

At Last had two unvented kerosene heaters. They were purchased on the basis of price alone, a costly mistake. They were dangerous (we almost died one night from carbon monoxide poisoning because we had buttoned up

the boat too tightly) and the condensation they produced throughout the long northern winter can only be described as "grim." Clothing, books, photographs—all sorts of valuables fell victim to mildew caused by the wet heat.

Aboard *Saga*, we installed a forced air heating system. Her interior is not large, but is divided into five separate compartments, so a forced air unit seems the logical choice. If I thought we would be spending considerable time dockside, I would consider buying two or three more electric space heaters like the Intermatic Heatwave (we still have *Sabrina*'s), because they are powerful yet so small they can be tucked away just about anywhere (See Figure 14).

The lessons learned on *At Last* have not been forgotten. Aside from being comfortable in bad weather (which allows *us* to function efficiently), we are protecting what is, for us, a major investment.

Figure 14   *Several small electric space heaters can be placed, or installed, throughout the boat.*

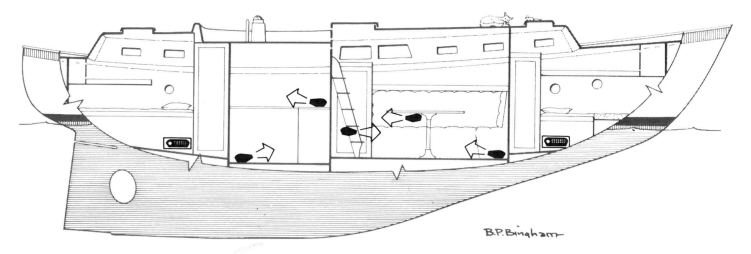

THE COZY CABIN SHOPPING COMPANION

ALADDIN KEROSENE HEATERS, ALADDIN MANTLE
LAMPS
    Faire Harbour Ltd.
    44 Captain Peirce Road
    Scituate, MA 02066

HEAT PAL (ALCOHOL)
    James Bliss Marine
    Route 128 (at Exit 61)
    Dedham, MA 02026

VIKING CATALYTIC HEATERS (PROPANE)
    Allcraft Corp.
    55 Border St.
    West Newton, MA 02165

TAYLOR PARA-FIN HEATERS (KEROSENE AND DIESEL)
    Jay Stuart Haft Co.
    8925 North Tennyson Drive
    Milwaukee, WI 53217

SHIPMATE KEROSENE CABIN HEATER, SKIPPY
STOVES, FIREPLACES
    Richmond Ring Co.
    Shipmate Stove Division
    P.O. Box 375
    Souderton, PA 18964

HI-SEAS DIESEL HEATER
    Marine Heat Corp.
    2431 N.W. Market St.
    Seattle, WA 98107

CHESAPEAKE OIL CABIN HEATER, ARCTIC HEATER,
MARINE COMFORT FURNACE (ALL DIESEL)
    Dickinson Marine Products (US) Inc.
    4241 21st Ave. W.
    Seattle, WA 98199

LUKE FIREPLACES
    Paul E. Luke
    E. Boothbay, ME 04544

RATELCO KING COLE AND COLE STOVE (CHARCOAL)
    Ratelco, Inc.
    1260 Mercer St.
    Seattle, WA 98109

PET AND TINY TOT STOVES (SOLID FUEL)
    Fatsco
    251 North Fair Avenue
    Benton Harbor, MI 49022

WALLAS-THERMOTRON (KEROSENE)
    Cook Marine Products
    P.O. Box 1133
    Stamford, CT 06904

ESPAR HEATERS (DIESEL)
    Espar Products Inc.
    6480 Viscount Road
    Mississauga, Ontario, Canada
    L4V 1H3

NEPTUNE TINY GIANT (HOT WATER SYSTEM)
    Neptune Marine Heaters
    165 Liberty Avenue
    New Rochelle, NY 10805

INTERMATIC HEATWAVE (ELECTRIC HEATER)
    Goldberg's Marine
    202 Market St.
    Philadelphia, PA 19106
    (catalog—$2.00)
    (or try your local general hardware store)

ELEKTRA RADIANT HEATERS
    Elektra Marine & R.V. Systems Co.
    Division of Elektra Systems, Inc.
    4161 Merrick Road
    Massapequa, NY 11758

Cooling

13

"Keep it cool"

IF WE SPENT the hot summer months dockside, I'm sure we'd be shopping for an air conditioner. But we don't, we anchor out. We spent the better part of one summer in Florida, always at anchor, and we really suffered only a few afternoons from the heat and humidity. The majority of the time it was quite tolerable. There was almost always a cooling breeze blowing across the water and through the open ports and hatches.

Saga was rigged with a large awning to keep the sun off her decks and cabin trunks and white curtains to keep the hot sun from blazing in through her large fixed ports. She also had two wind scoops—one in the fore hatch and one aft.

We learned to time our trips ashore and heavy physical work for early morning and late evening. (Countries that observe siesta time know exactly what they are doing.) When we rowed ashore, the increase in temperature would become apparent almost as soon as we stepped out of the dinghy.

On hot, windless days, 12-volt fans will at least keep the air moving (See Plate 1), and they don't use a great deal of electricity (see ventilation chapter). They don't really have much cooling effect, however, unless you stand right in front of them—and even then it's not much.

With 110-volt power available, you can consider using a household-type fan or air conditioner or a built-in model designed specifically for marine use.

There's a wide variety of household fans to choose from. For the smaller areas found in a

Plate 1 *A small 12-volt fan will keep the air moving on a windless day.*

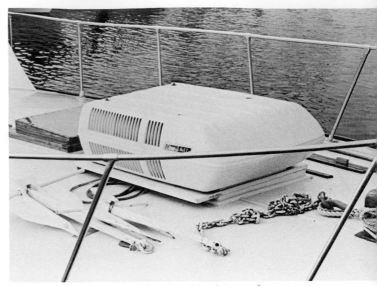

Plate 3 *An RV air conditioner, like this one from Coleman, can be installed in an open hatch.*

boat, look for a fan that's completely protected with grillwork or screening, one with a wide base that will be less likely to topple in a passing wake. The square fans designed to fit in a window are often a good choice, since they can be mounted face down in a hatch (See Plate 2). They come in enough sizes that you can usually find one that fits just right.

I remember my grandmother placing a pan of water in front of a fan so the air would cool as it blew across the water—and it really did make a difference! Of course, that will add to the humidity, which may not be welcome.

Household air conditioners can be adapted for use on a boat. But a few points should be kept in mind. For instance, where to install it? Powerboat owners can usually find a port or window large enough to receive the unit; sailboat owners face a bigger challenge.

Plate 2 *Square window fans often can be mounted face down over a hatch.*

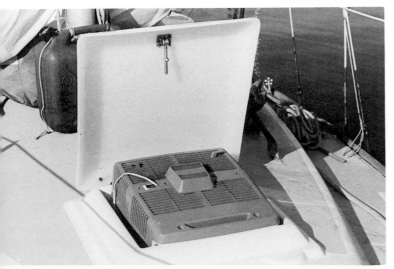

We've seen quite a few installed in the companionway, but that set-up means you must always step over it—not a very convenient arrangement. On the other hand, you don't have to cut any holes in the cabin trunk and that alone might be worth the inconvenience. You sometimes can find units designed for campers or mobile homes that will fit over a hatch (See Plate 3).

If you do cut an opening for an air conditioner, consider how well it will stay in place when underway—particularly when under sail and heeled. Or, when you remove the unit and stow it, how will you plug the hole?

Most household air conditioners must be installed so they are partially exposed to the outdoors so the heat will be expelled *outside* the living area.

Most marine units, on the other hand, expel their heat to the water. This means they can be installed just about anywhere you have the space (See Plate 4). They are invariably expensive and complicated installations, generally requiring adding several through-hull fittings (although sometimes the piping can be connected to existing through-hull fittings). The fans and heat pumps require so much electricity that all marine air conditioners use 110-volt current (220-volt for the large units). I do not know of any models that operate on a 12-volt system.

If you spend a lot of time dockside or have a powerful generator onboard, then a marine unit makes sense. They are built of materials that will hold up in a saltwater environment and are designed to blend in with a yacht interior (See Plate 5). Most household units are cumbersome by comparison.

Most air conditioners can be reversed, and used as heating systems in the winter. L. Gale Noel of Marine Development Corp. (makers of Crusair), says that 90 percent of its units are sold with both cooling and heating configurations. These units will heat effectively in water

Plate 4 *Marine air conditioners expel their heat into the surrounding water and can be installed out of sight, wherever there's room.* (PHOTO COURTESY MARINE DEVELOPMENT CORP.)

Plate 5 *The StowAway from Cruisair is a compact marine air conditioning unit.* (PHOTO COURTESY MARINE DEVELOPMENT CORP.)

temperature down to 40°, so they would obviously not be your choice if you're wintering over, say in New England, where it's likely the water will freeze at least some of the time.

14

The Live-Aboard Galley

"The meal must go on"

ASSUMING YOU HAVE a stove, a sink and an ice box or some sort of refrigeration, it's not likely your eating habits will change much when you move aboard. Food storage and preparation may change a bit, but there's no reason you can't continue to cook and eat the same kinds of food you enjoyed on shore.

The biggest change is that everything will be more compact. With less storage space, you'll probably learn to make fewer pots and pans serve many functions. And using water and fuel efficiently will demand some adjustments. For instance, I use my pressure cooker several times a week; on shore I didn't use it more than twice a year. If I'm cooking, say, a meat loaf, chances are I'll include baked potatoes on the menu since they both require long cooking times.

STOVES

Stoves installed on the boat's fore-and-aft axis should be gimballed, even on powerboats, with a lock (usually a barrel bolt) to secure it dockside and when you open the oven door. I also keep a small (about 2½-pound) lead weight handy to balance the stove when I have a heavy pot or teakettle full of water on a front burner and nothing on the back.

Sabrina's stove arrangement was similar to that found on many small stock boats. It was a two-burner stove with no oven, installed athwartships in the countertop. One of our first projects was to gimbal the stove so we could use it while underway or in a bumpy anchorage. The lead weight for the gimbal mount was installed off-center—it swung in the dead space between the bulkhead and the drawers so as not to infringe on our storage space.

Any number of stove-top ovens are available and I know several cooks who regularly bake in their pressure cookers. On *Sabrina,* I used an Optimus mini-oven that would bake anything but cookies (everything came out shaped like a giant donut). I still use it occasionally for casseroles, either to save fuel or because I don't want to heat up the entire saloon.

Galley stoves need sea rails or fiddles around the top and adjustable clamps to keep pots secure. Be sure the sea rails are cut down in the corners to allow pot handles to project without tipping the pot.

The space around *any* stove should be well

insulated and protected with a metal lining (preferably stainless steel or copper). If the stove is fitted partially under the deck, the underside of the deck should receive the same protection. Be careful, too, about installing curtains over a port above a stove, particularly if you're using alcohol or kerosene that is subject to flare-ups.

Fuel shutoffs should be located off to the side of the stove—you should never have to reach *across* the stove or behind it. And, of course, a fire extinguisher should be within easy reach.

The debate still rages, and probably always will, about what stove fuel is best. My vote is for propane (LPG). We've used it as long as we've been living aboard and I wouldn't have anything else. *Sabrina* arrived with a kerosene stove and we lasted one week before we ripped out the wretched thing and bought a propane stove. Now that I've admitted my bias, let's examine each fuel.

ALCOHOL

Let me relate a horror story about "safe" alcohol (the Coast Guard, by the way, rates alcohol as the safest fuel). We were rafted up one evening with a couple in a lovely old wood sloop. The woman decided to bake biscuits to go with the evening stew, and without realizing it she over-primed the oven. The alcohol leaked out the back of the stove and ran down the side of the hull behind the slotted ceiling.

We were all sitting at the table enjoying dinner before anyone realized the boat was on fire. We had a devil of a time getting the fire out, since we had to remove the table and the cabin sole to get at the flames in the bilge. The primary reason alcohol is considered safe is because an alcohol fire can be put out with water. I don't think we could have pumped water fast enough to put out that fire, so we used a fire extinguisher, instead.

Alcohol is a highly flammable liquid, more so than kerosene. Yet it produces less heat, so food takes longer to cook and you burn more fuel. It's also the most expensive fuel on the

market and it's difficult to find outside the United States. Some people find the smell of burning alcohol objectionable (even sickening). About the only advantage is that some insurance companies will give you a discount for having an alcohol stove.

KEROSENE

Kerosene is loved by seacooks the world over. There were many willing hands around to catch *Sabrina*'s kerosene stove as we started to heave it over the side.

"You have to *understand* it," kerosene proponents keep telling us.

"Then you'll love it!"

Bruce and I must be pretty dense, because we never did understand. Bruce, always the first one up in the morning, boils a pot of water for coffee first thing to fill the thermos and to let the stove chase away the morning chill. I remember, quite vividly, waking up one morning to a cold cabin, no coffee and screams of anguish from Bruce as he underprimed, over-primed and overpumped the tank, resulting in a spew of kerosene on the overhead, followed by much fuming during the long wait for the water to boil. I fared no better. Is that any way to start a day?

In fairness to those who love the Primus stove, I'll grant that kerosene *does* have its advantages. It is hotter than alcohol—although most kerosene burners must be primed with alcohol so you still must carry two fuels. It's *much* cheaper than alcohol, and both the fuel and Primus parts are readily available almost everywhere in the world. But as in buying kerosene for lamps, it is important to use a *very good* grade of kerosene. Judge kerosene by its color. The best, called "range oil" in the United States, is absolutely clear. If it has a yellow tinge it's a lower grade and will burn dirtier, be smellier and clog up the burner jets faster. An inline filter between the tank and the burner is also an excellent idea.

Kerosene is less flammable than alcohol and burns hotter, so food cooks quicker. Most kerosene burners, in fact, can't be turned down low enough to simmer or to cook foods that require low heat, so asbestos flame spreaders must be used. Kerosene, even a high grade, is a dirty fuel. The bottoms and sides of pots and pans turn black and the overhead and surrounding area gets yellow-grimy in a hurry. Kerosene's biggest, and in my opinion, only advantage over propane is that the fumes are not explosive. It will only burn when under pressure or with a wick.

PROPANE

Propane is a pressurized liquid that is contained in a tank and turns into a gas at the regulator only when pressure is released. The gas is heavier than air, so if the flame goes out or the system leaks, the highly explosive gas will sink to the lowest point in the boat—*dangerous!* All LP tanks should be stored on deck with a canvas cover or in an airtight compartment separate from the cabin and with a "drain" that will carry any fumes overboard well above the waterline.

I'm the first to admit that LP is a dangerous fuel. But I've found that people who use it are aware of its inherent dangers and treat it carefully. Propane sold for home use in the U.S. has an additive that gives it a distinct odor. It doesn't smell when it's burning, but you can smell it in its gaseous state.

Some propane stove manufacturers are now installing automatic shutoff valves (thermal couplings) at each burner, which turn off the gas if the flame goes out. You can buy the valves separately to attach to your existing stove or you can buy solenoid valves—such as the Model 580 made by Marinetics—that allow you to shut off the gas electrically, at the tank, by a switch in the galley (See Plate 1). The control panel includes a red light to remind you when the gas is on. There should be a shutoff valve in the galley near the stove, *in addition* to those on the stove and at the tank. Common practice after using the stove is to turn off the gas at the tank, let the gas burn out of the feed line and then turn off the burners.

All fittings and couplings should be checked regularly by covering them with soapy water, then turning on the gas at the tank with the burners shut off. If there is a leak anywhere,

Plate 1 *The yacht* Heron *uses a Marinetics solenoid switch. She also has an engine hour meter wired into the LPG switch to monitor the time of LP use, thus giving an estimate of the remaining quantity.* (PHOTO BY DICK PENTONEY.)

even a tiny pinhole leak, the soap will start to bubble. Several companies make leak detectors or gas sensors that will sound an alarm if fumes collect in the bilge. Special sealants can be used at each connection to ensure they are gas-tight. Polysulfides (like Life Caulk) work well, too.

It's an excellent idea to install a bilge blower. If you have a gasoline engine, you probably already have one. But with a diesel, chances are you don't. Be sure to get a blower designed for bilge service, not just a fan. Bilge blower motors are sealed and because they are spark-proof they can remove explosive gasoline or propane fumes.

You can take some preventive measures for a safe bilge. Periodically discharge one of your CO_2 fire extinguishers (not a dry chemical one!) into the bilge. Since CO_2 is heavier than air, it will displace the air in the bilge and remain there until it's pumped out. Remember, it takes a certain mixture of air with an explosive gas before the blend actually becomes explosive. Besides, it's one way of keeping your fire extinguishers updated.

Now we come to a subject that's a bit touchy. Marine underwriters and safety councils recommend copper tubing for LP installations. I dislike copper tubing on a boat, because the couplings are subject to stress from constant vibration. We use flexible hose purchased at a trailer supply house and made specifically for use with high-pressure gas systems in mobile homes. We've found its flexibility is excellent on a boat. It can be routed around corners without using couplings and a neat loop behind the stove provides the slack that allows the gimbals to work. Clear plastic hose can be slipped over the gas hose to prevent chafe where it passes through bulkheads. Understand, this is not the "accepted" installation method—and your insurance man is liable to have fits about it.

While agreeing that LP gas is dangerous and requires careful handling, I don't believe it's as bad as some of its detractors would have us believe. It's no more dangerous than gasoline engines, battery fumes, or some of the solvents and chemicals sloshing around in your bo'sun's locker or, for that matter, a potential killer like

a reel halyard winch! Use LP judiciously and the advantages are numerous. It burns cleanly and hot, the flame height is adjustable and no priming is necessary. It's just like the stove at home, Mom! It's readily available world-wide, and it's truly inexpensive. We've had a 20-pound tank last as long as six months using a three-burner stove with an oven.

CNG

The newest galley fuel to enter the scene is CNG (Compressed Natural Gas). It is similar to propane in that it burns clean and hot and needs no priming. Whereas LP gas is heavier than air, CNG is *lighter* than air, and will theoretically rise to the overhead and out the hatch if there's a leak. I question whether it would *always* go out the hatch or whether it might collect in a pocket somewhere under the deck or inside a cabinet if a connection came loose. Don't be over-awed by claims of CNG's safety. It's lighter than air, true, but it's still a potentially explosive gas and should be treated with the same care and respect as propane.

CNG is not widely available yet, even in the United States. Unless you live close to a dealer, you must pay for shipping the empty tank back for a refill—on top of the cost of the gas itself.

ELECTRICITY

Electric cooktops that fit over the existing stove are handy for use dockside and will save your galley fuel for use when under way. Electric skillets, toaster ovens, microwave ovens and other appliances also are handy providing you have room to store them. If you want electric cooking as the primary stove, however, keep in mind that away from the dock you must run a generator in order to power it. The filaments in an electric range need so much juice they can only be run on 110-volt circuits. Electric stoves should only be considered as secondary units, except on a large powerboat with a generator that's equipped with a remote start-up switch located in the galley.

Plate 2   *This Vagabond 42 galley has an alcove that's perfect for a microwave oven.*

For boats with generators or boats that spend considerable time dockside, the investment in a microwave oven makes a lot of sense (See Plate 2). Consider that meals can be cooked or foods heated in a fraction of normal cooking times, using scant electricity or requiring the generator to run for only a few minutes instead of several hours.

DIESEL, COAL AND WOOD

Most of these stoves are too large and heavy for the average boat. Diesel stoves are most often seen on workboats in cold northern waters. They do produce considerable heat and a big advantage is that they use the same fuel as the engine. Most of them also use electricity and require a smoke head like coal and wood-burning stoves.

Solid fuel stoves may be a good choice if you spend most of your time in cold climates, since they'll also function as heaters. They produce dry heat (See Chapter 13) that will eliminate condensation problems. I've seen several boats that used a coal stove most of the year and had a portable, liquid-fuel, two-burner cooktop range for summer use.

SINKS AND COUNTERS

Two small sinks are handier than one large one. However, the smallest galley sink should still be large enough to accommodate your dinner plates, large skillets and pans. *Saga* has one massive sink (See Plate 3). We generally use a small dishpan set inside it. On a few occasions we've filled the sink (usually when operating the darkroom) and had the water gain enough momentum from a passing wake to sling itself across the cabin!

Covers for the sink are pretty useless since invariably you need the sink no matter what you're preparing. If you have a double sink, however, you might consider making a cover for one of them.

Counter space is always at a premium in the galley (See Plate 4). Bruce designed and built a

Plate 3 *Saga's one big sink eventually will be replaced with a smaller one. We used acrylics extensively—for the upper shelf over the sink, for spice racks and for a paper towel holder. Jars outboard of the stove are clear plastic with screw-top lids. Tiled bulkheads are light in color yet easy to clean. A large trash can is hidden behind the companionway ladder. We have a pull-out bread board above the drawers and a timer mounted on the cabin side.*

nifty little fold-up table as a counter extension that fits flush against a bulkhead when not in use.

Aboard *Sabrina,* he constructed an accordion-folding galley extension with a narrow shelf at the outboard edge. In use it folded down over the forward end of the quarterberth. In the stowed position, it fit flush against the hull, totally out of the way on those rare occasions when the quarterberth was used for sleeping (See Chapter 12).

Sabrina's icebox top was used as counter space. The problem was that everything had to be moved each time we had to get something out of the box. We hinged the top in two sections (a common feature on larger boats) so we

Plate 4 *The 42-foot trawler* All Hour's *roomy galley includes a large counter extension. Note the dishwasher, ample drawers and cabinets and the row of Yacht Crocks between sink and stove.*

Plate 6 Heron's *bread board was turned into a special drawer for Helen's collection of fine knives. A cutting board was fitted elsewhere in the galley.* (PHOTO BY DICK PENTONEY.)

moved less to get into the box. Plus we lost less cold air when we did open the lid (See Plate 5).

Old-fashioned pull-out bread boards, like grandma used to have, often can be installed just beneath the countertop in the space above drawers or cabinets. They should be notched in the same manner as drawers or have a turn-button to prevent them from sailing across the galley when the boat rolls (See Plates 2 and 6).

A saltwater pump next to the sink is a good addition if you plan on being at sea a lot or are lucky enough to be in an area with clean water. Frankly, I can think of few harbors where I would use the water even for washing dishes, let alone cooking.

GARBAGE

Finding a place for the trash is always a problem in small galleys. I dislike giving up valuable space for anything as mundane as garbage, but it must be reckoned with. On both *At Last* and *Saga* we found a large rectangular plastic trash can fitted nicely behind the companionway steps and was fairly unobtrusive there—but still easy to reach (See Plate 2). In U or L-shaped galleys, the hard-to-reach corner can often be used as a trash bin. Just lift the cover and toss in your garbage, but make sure the opening is large enough to remove a full trash bag. Quite a few boats are now being built with pull-down trash bins. It's a great idea, except that most of them are too small for a normal day's garbage. If they don't hold anything larger than one of the small bathroom-sized

Plate 5 *This ice box offers a choice: a sectioned top-loading unit, or one that's front loading.*

plastic bags, you could easily fill that in half a day.

Powerboats, because of their squarish shape, are more apt to have room under the sink or inside a pantry locker to accommodate a large trash can.

Trash compactors are effective space-savers on boats with the electric power to support them.

STOWAGE

It's amazing how much gear and stores you can cram into what appears to be even the tiniest of galleys. The trick is to use every inch of space, whether by hanging things up, installing nets or carefully compartmentalizing each locker and drawer.

When we gimballed the stove on *Sabrina* it opened up an additional stowage area—the space against the hull, outboard of the stove that was inaccessible with the stove in a fixed position. We installed a bulkhead of ¼-inch plywood with large hand-holes, and used the space for spare coffee and cocoa and bags of onions and potatoes. The dead space behind the sink was also put to use: Bruce cut a large hole in the countertop that just fitted a sizeable thermos jug—our hot water supply (See Plate 7). We filled it with a kettle full of boiling water every morning and it provided hot water for coffee, tea and soup throughout a 24-hour day without having to fire up the stove each time—resulting in tremendous fuel savings.

Bulkheads, cabin sides and the fronts and backs of doors offer a wealth of storage space. Hang cups on hooks (See Plate 8), glasses and

Plate 7   Sabrina's *hot water supply was a large thermos that fit into a cutout just behind the sink.*

Plate 8   Saga's *thermal cups live on hooks over the galley window.*

bottles in special wood or acrylic racks (See Plate 9). Spice racks can be installed near the stove (See Plate 3). We bought a wood rack for *Sabrina* and simply added a brass rod to hold in the bottles. Cup hooks can be used for everything from cooking utensils (See Plate 10) to pot holders and towels. Net bags for fruits and vegetables can be hung in out-of-the-way places such as the underside of a counter.

Aboard the yacht *Heron*, Helen Pentoney had all of her copper-bottomed cookware hung on bulkheads and cabinet fronts. Dick

Plate 9   *Saga's Lexan thermos jug holder is mounted on the side of the companionway ladder, out of the way but an arm's reach of the galley.*

made special brackets for each utensil so it wouldn't bang about underway (See Plate 11).

Compartmentalizing each locker and drawer will keep the contents separated and secure, and allow you to pack more in. We use the plastic divider trays that come in several sizes and can be locked together at the rims. Dish racks can be compartmentalized, or use dowels or shock cord to keep the dishes from sliding around.

A common arrangement on both sail and powerboats is a galley adjacent to the saloon, separated only by the counter. Often soffet cabinets or shelves can be installed along the overhead, giving much additional stowage while still maintaining an open feeling (See Plate 12).

Probably the biggest challenge in galley stowage is keeping foodstuffs *dry*. Glass is undoubtedly the best from the standpoint of being nonporous and nonabsorbent of odors. Unfortunately, it's breakable and therefore often hard to stow. On the Angelman ketch *Gypsy Pride,* Georgina Dillow mounted glass jars over the sink by screwing the lids to the overhead—an arrangement that worked exceedingly well.

Plastic containers are much more common. We find the yacht crocks from Yachting Tableware Co. for salt and brown sugar are excellent. Unfortunately they only come in one small size (See Plate 13).

The plastic containers with vacuum-fitting lids vary in quality and in the effectiveness of the seal. If some product has to be stored for a long time, I run a layer of tape around the top. Screw tops generally give a much better seal. However, square containers use space much more efficiently. Although it's hard to find square containers with screw tops, they *do* exist!

Insert moisture absorbers in all containers. I like the kind that turn from blue to pink as they absorb moisture and can be dried in the oven and reused. A few grains of rice in the salt shaker will keep the salt flowing freely. A whole bay leaf in dry stores will keep away weevils, according to June MacQuarrie of the Alberg sloop, *Impulse.*

Plate 10 Heron's copper tea kettle lives happily on a pair of cup hooks. You also can see the bracket for a SeaSwing stove and above it, the timer mounted on a scrap of perforated metal. (PHOTO BY DICK PENTONEY.)

Plate 11 Heron's mounting brackets for pots and pans are 1/8-inch by 3/4-inch aluminum flat bar. Lids are held securely by sliding them onto the pot handles. The pewter cups slide into a track mounted underneath the shelf. A hinged "gate" keeps them from sliding out. (PHOTO BY DICK PENTONEY.)

Plate 12 Soffet cabinets can increase galley storage space tremendously.

Plate 13 *Yacht Crocks from Yachting Tableware Co.
are excellent storage containers. Made of thermo-
insulated plastic, they are airtight when closed and
feature nonskid rings around the bottom.* (PHOTO
COURTESY OF YACHTING TABLEWARE CO.)

Label all containers, either with a permanent
marker pen, a paper label covered with transparent tape or with a plastic label-maker. This
may sound elementary, but look-alike containers of sugar, flours, Bisquick, etc. can be pretty
confusing. Since I transfer everything from
cardboard containers into plastic or glass ones,
I cut out instructions (such as for hot cereals
and rice) and tape the instructions to the inside
of the lid or wrap them in a Baggie inside the
container.

It's also helpful to divide up the inside of an
ice box or refrigerator, particularly a top-loading unit (front-opening units usually have a
shelf, anyway). Sliding trays increase the usable
space. Placing items in removable plastic containers or Baggies will keep them out of the

water, make them easier to retrieve and help
prevent bits of food from entering the drain or
bilge water where bad odors can form.

ICE BOX/REFRIGERATION

Whether your boat has an ice box or mechanical refrigeration, the most important thing is
that the cooling system be well insulated. Almost all stock boats built today require additional insulation to perform adequately.

Sabrina was built with a large ice box, the
kind that's fine for a weekend sail when all you
do is fill it up with ice and beer and forget it for
the rest of the week. But day-in, day-out, we
found it was actually large for our milk, lettuce,
mayonnaise and fresh meat. We were buying
ice about every four days. We added 2 inches
of urethane foam to the inside of the box and
covered it with white Formica. This reduced
the volume considerably, as well as greatly increasing its insulating qualities. After that a
block of ice lasted for as long as three weeks.

Adler-Barbour produces a comprehensive
guide, called *The Box Book*, which gives detailed
instructions for properly insulating an ice box.
It's available for several dollars from Adler-
Barbour, 43 Lawton Street, New Rochelle, NY
10801.

ICE

Ice is certainly the simplest and cheapest
method of keeping food cold. Its disadvantages, of course, are the need to replenish it
and the tedious task of lugging it aboard. If the
box works extremely well, however, it's not that
much trouble. If your ice lasts two or three
weeks, it's conceivable you could spend more
time servicing a refrigeration unit than transporting ice.

Block ice will last considerably longer than
cubes. It helps, too, if you can keep the box
full. We try only to add items that are already
cold. For instance, we never put warm soft
drink cans into the box. It's more efficient to
chip away a little ice if someone wants a cold
drink.

Make sure the ice box drain has a loop in it

so water can drain without letting cold air escape. If at all possible, don't let icewater drain into the bilge, because everything from decayed lettuce to bacterial scum will end up below the floorboards stinking to high heaven. Try running the hose to a collapsible plastic jug that can be detached and dumped over the side. Or install a small holding tank or jug that can be pumped overboard or into the galley sink drain line. And try to install the drain hose so it's easily removable for frequent cleaning.

HOLD-OVER SYSTEMS

These refrigerator/freezer systems consist of a compressor in the engine room that pumps Freon through cold plates (holding plates) located in the box. The holding plates contain a eutectic solution that "super freezes" at about 0°F. During the freezing process, the liquid Freon absorbs the heat and changes to a gas. The gas goes to a condenser that cools it back into a liquid state—and the cycle starts again. While this is considered the most efficient system (about one hour's running time will keep the box cold for 24 to 48 hours), it's also the most complicated and expensive. These systems are generally only seen on yachts of 40 feet and larger, since the equipment is heavy and requires a good deal of space.

Hold-over systems are available that run directly off the boat's engine (See Plate 14), as DC units (See Plate 15); or as AC units (See Plate 16) that run on shore power or with an auxiliary generator. Grunert's Versimatic (See Plate 17) uses a second alternator mounted on the main engine, so it takes up less space than an engine-driven compressor. The Versimatic is a high-voltage DC system.

Plate 14 *A hold-over system that runs directly off the boat's engine is a common type of on-board refrigeration.* (PHOTO COURTESY OF CROSBY MARINE REFRIGERATION SYSTEMS, INC.)

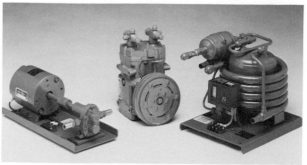

Plate 15 *A 12-volt DC water-cooled refrigeration system.* (PHOTO COURTESY OF CROSBY MARINE REFRIGERATION SYSTEMS, INC.)

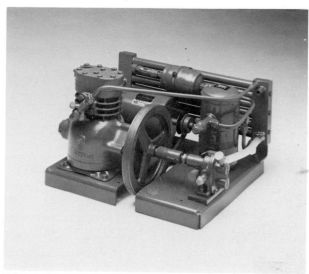

Plate 16 *A 110-volt water-cooled refrigeration unit, requiring either shore power or an onboard generator.* (PHOTO COURTESY OF CROSBY MARINE REFRIGERATION SYSTEMS, INC.)

Plate 17 *Grunert's Versimatic gets power from a second alternator mounted on the main engine.* (PHOTO COURTESY OF THE GRUNERT CO.)

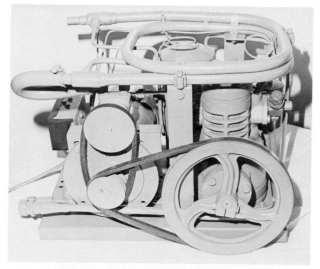

DC Systems (without hold-over plates)

Two types of 12-volt refrigeration systems do not use hold-over plates. They are thermo-electric units like the Unifridge and pre-charged Freon units like Adler-Barbour's TheColdMachine (See Plate 18) and Marvel's Ice Device.

These pre-charged systems operate like a household refrigerator/freezer. They consist of a small pre-charged (Freon) compressor unit that can be mounted as far as 12 to 15 feet away, and an evaporator/freezer mounted inside the box. Lightweight (about 30 pounds), and considerably less expensive than the cold-plate units, they can be used in boxes to a maximum of 9.5 cubic feet.

Power demand can vary widely, depending

Plate 18 *The Cold Machine is a precharged Freon refrigeration unit that runs off a 12-volt battery system.* (PHOTO COURTESY ADLER-BARBOUR MARINE SYSTEMS, INC.)

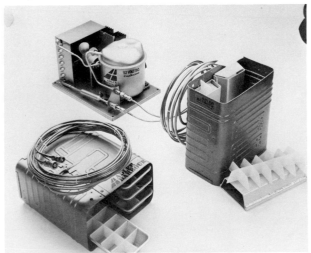

on how well the box is insulated and how high the ambient air temperature is. Under full load, they can draw as much as 5.4 amps per hour. Adler-Barbour recommends, as a minimum, an 85 amp-hour battery for the refrigeration unit (in addition to the engine starting battery).

If you're running the engine to keep batteries charged, figure about an hour and a half daily running (minimum!) to keep up with the unit. In my opinion, these systems really come into their own if you have an efficient wind generator or solar panels to charge the batteries. Daily engine running just to support a refrigerator gets pretty expensive—not just in fuel, but in wear and tear on the engine (See Chapter 15).

Thermo-electric units are even less efficient than Freon systems. However, these solid-state units are also about half the cost, and they are small (shoe-box size) and self-contained. With the air-cooled Unifridge, you cut one hole in the box, install the unit and hook up the wiring.

All of these systems can operate at dockside on 110-volt AC power by passing it through the ship's AC automatic battery charger. Most boxes, particularly top-loading ones, can still use ice. While you're underway and running the engine, or when dockside, then use the refrigeration unit. When you're anchored out or under sail, use ice if it's readily available. There's no rule that says you must use the system 100 percent of the time.

Ready-made refrigerators, or refrigerators with freezers, are available if you have the space to install them. They are generally AC/DC combinations and usually front-opening. Norcold does make some top-loading units. Gas Systems offers three-way refrigerators.

There are also propane and kerosene refrigerators, but these are more suitable to travel trailers than boats. You are dealing with an open flame and they must remain level to operate effectively.

Sources

Adler-Barbour
   43 Lawton Street
   New Rochelle, NY 10801

CROSBY MARINE REFRIGERATION SYSTEMS
204 Second Avenue South
St. Petersburg, FL 33701

GAS SYSTEMS, INC.
5361 Production Drive
Huntington Beach, CA 92649

THE GRUNERT CO.
195 Drum Point Road
Osbornville, NJ 08723

MARINETICS CORP.
1638 Placentia Avenue
Costa Mesa, CA 92627

NORCOLD
1501 Michigan Street
Sidney, OH 45365

MARVEL DIVISION
Dayton-Walther Corp.
P.O. Box 997
Richmond, IN 47374

YACHTING TABLEWARE CO.
1112 East 7th Street
Wilmington, DE 19801

15 Electricity

"More power to you"

THE VAST MAJORITY of boats today have a 12-volt DC (direct current) power system, with power supplied from the ship's batteries. Most of them also have 110-volt AC (alternating current) circuitry for use at dockside or when running a generator. Powerboats are more likely than sailboats to be loaded with equipment that requires AC power.

Make no mistake: we like our luxuries, but try not to be hog-tied by an electrical cord. Considering the steady increase in battery-powered gear, it's becoming easier every day to have convenient gadgets that work off ship's power. Color television, hair dryers, sewing machines and various power hand tools are available in 12-volt models. And there are many tasks, performed electrically ashore, that are really simple to do by hand. We open cans with a good old-fashioned manual can opener, use a stove-top toaster and have a Swedish stove-top waffle iron that makes better-tasting waffles than I ever achieved with an electric one.

About the only AC galley appliance I would consider installing would be a microwave oven. The speed with which they cook makes them extremely energy-efficient. We do carry

around a four-slice toaster. Bruce claims it makes such wonderful toast (as compared to the stove-top one) that it is worth the space it occupies, even though we are rarely at a dock where he can plug it in.

The wiring system on most boats more than a year or two old are often an electrician's nightmare. Indeed, a marine electrician is such a rare bird he should be on the endangered species list. Wiring jobs are too often left to "one of the boys in the yard," who doesn't know any more about electricity than you do. If you're living aboard and doing any kind of cruising, you're better off learning to do at least the simple jobs yourself. Sometimes new boats arrive with a wiring schematic—consider yourself lucky if you have one and even luckier if it actually matches the wiring in the boat!

Otherwise, it's a good idea to make your own. If the boat has elaborate AC and DC systems, with a lot of AC appliances installed, then it's smart to make *two* schematics. Trace each wire from the electrical panel to the outlet, light or appliance. Use colored pencils to color code the schematic drawing.

As you trace each wire, tag it by attaching a piece of tape every few feet and labeling it with a waterproof marker. Or, you can buy numbered tags for this purpose at electronic supply stores. Now is the time to check for worn or frayed wires, corroded connections and wires dangling when they should be securely clipped. Look for anything that could be potential trouble.

AC Systems

Big appliances need big power. It takes a lot of electricity to run electric ranges, ice makers, trash compactors, console color television, air conditioners and other assorted goodies. They are run either dockside or have a separate 110-volt generator to keep them all running when the boat's unplugged. A generator on such boats is a virtual necessity.

If your boat is so equipped, the cost is justified. Generators run on either gasoline or diesel; it makes sense to have one that uses the same fuel as the ship's main engine (See Plate 1).

Plate 1 *Onan's water-cooled diesel generator will produce up to 3,000 watts of 120 volts AC.* (PHOTO COURTESY OF ONAN CORP.)

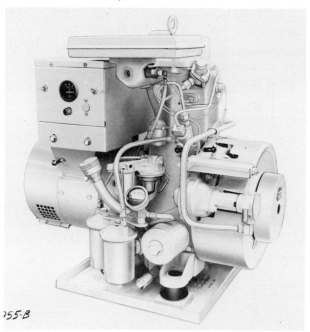

155-B

Most of us, however, lean toward a simpler existence afloat. While I am a firm advocate of having as much equipment as possible running off the ship's 12-volt system, there are times when standard "household" current is awfully handy, even away from the dock. We have quite a few power tools that only run on AC; and a wonderful old, heavy, sewing machine that sews layers of Dacron sail cloth or canvas as though it were cutting butter. The enlarger and timer in our darkroom requires 110-volt current, and Bruce occasionally uses a soldering iron. We don't always want to go dockside just to solder a wire or sew a hatch cover, and such limited use hardly justifies installing an expensive permanently mounted gasoline or diesel generator. Fortunately, there are alternatives.

Portable Generators/Alternators

The terms *generator* and *alternator* are often used (mistakenly) interchangeably.

A general utility *alternator* produces *alternating current* (See Figure 1, Top). This is normal household current and in the United States it is generally 115-volts at 60 Hertz. An alternator can produce direct current (DC) by passing the current through a rectifier. The alternator on your boat's engine is actually producing alternating current, but it converts the electricity (via the rectifier) to direct current that charges your batteries.

A *generator* produces *direct current* (DC) (See Figure 1, Bottom). On the vast majority of pleasure boats this is 12 volts. In order to prothe running watts required. Capacitor motors require even more. The generator must be able to handle this surge, even though it's only for a short time.

Generators small enough to be considered truly portable are all, as far as I know, gasoline-fueled and with integral fuel tanks. They are also air-cooled, precluding enclosed operation. The biggest drawback is undoubtedly the noise they make. Another problem is finding a good place to stow them securely when under way. Another is having to carry gasoline—particularly if your boat is diesel powered. This is less of a problem, of course, if you carry gasoline for a dinghy outboard.

On the plus side, they are economical to run. Compared to a permanent installation, their initial cost is downright inexpensive. Their portability means you can carry them ashore to a beach or to a careening site, or to a repair facility if they break down (instead of paying a mechanic to come to the boat). Since most of them also are capable of producing DC current they serve as a back-up method of charging the ship's batteries.

duce alternating current (AC) the electricity must pass through an inverter. Most portable generators, sold as an AC power source, will include a circuit that bypasses the inverter and can be used to charge 12-volt batteries.

Usually stowed on deck under a waterproof cover, portable generators and alternators produce from around 300 watts to more than 3,000 watts. When deciding what size generator you want, remember to check both the continuous draw *and* the start-up surge of your largest tool or appliance. The start-up surge for induction motors can be two to three times

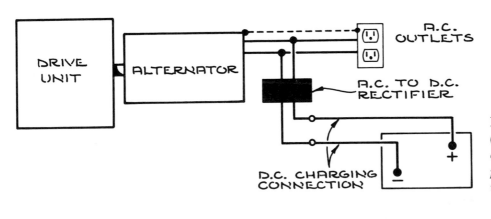

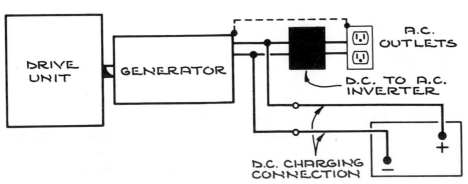

Figure 1 *Both alternators (top) and generators (bottom) can produce AC and DC power, but by different methods.*

Say portable generator to most boating people and the immediate response is Honda. While Honda does produce several quality generators, it is not the *only* manufacturer. Honda's small 500-watt unit seems to be the most popular. It will operate a soldering iron or a sewing machine and it will charge 12-volt batteries, But it won't run most heavy-duty jig saws, ⅜-inch electric drills, belt sanders or AC refrigeration units. Cruising Gear in Miami, Florida, lists the Honda 500W at $390 (1981). The next two larger sizes—1,000-watt and 1,500-watt models are more practical if your use will include rebuilding projects requiring power tools, or if you want to run a small refrigeration unit or a vacuum cleaner. The two larger Hondas, weighing 64 and 75 pounds (compared with 39 pounds for the 500-watt unit), cost about $500 and $660 respectively.

An inbetween size is Clinton Engine's 750-watt generator that weighs 48 pounds. It retails for about $450. While not standard, 12-volt charging capability can be added as an option.

The smallest generator I've seen is the AquaBug (See Plate 2), and it's cute! It only weighs 19 pounds and produces 300 watts of

Plate 2 *The 19-pound AquaBug will produce 300 watts AC.* (PHOTO COURTESY OF AQUABUG INTERNATIONAL, INC.)

AC, or 12 amps of 12-volt DC. The 1981 "introductory price" was $275.

Seven years ago, when we were rebuilding *At Last*—mostly at anchor—we bought a Sears 2,000-watt portable AC alternator. I priced a new 2,000-watt unit recently and it still retails for about $500. Admittedly, it's not "marine." Parts of the housing are mild steel, prone to rust and have to be replaced occasionally. We've changed most of the fastenings to stainless steel—an operation, incidentally, we've performed on quite a few items of marine gear. Still, it's given us thousands of hours of hard use. It has weathered storms—and occasional neglect—and it's still going strong. It will run our variable-speed jig saw, drill, belt sander, router, sewing machine—every tool we own as well as a portable electric space heater. It does have a circuit for charging a 12-volt battery, although we never have used it. Whenever we run the unit, we simply plug into it the ship's 30-amp automatic battery charger.

Our Sears alternator has a Briggs and Stratton engine. We never have had a problem finding a part for it, since Briggs and Stratton makes lawn mowers. Even the most out-of-the-way little village will have a repair shop that carries a supply of Briggs and Stratton parts. Excellent shop and maintenance manuals are available as well.

Another portable alternator equipped with a Briggs and Stratton engine is sold by Heathkit. Its 2,200-watt unit costs in the $500 range and weighs about 110 pounds. The carrying handles make it a bit bulky but with a little ingenuity the handles could be modified so they could be removed for easier storage.

115 volts AC uses 750 watts. Assuming the 75 percent conversion efficiency, 1,000 watts will be required. Next, assume your battery is charged to 13 volts. You will be expending DC current at a rate of 77 amps! Obviously, running the jig saw for any length of time would put a tremendous burden on most boat batteries. These generators are best suited for boats with large battery banks, or for occasional brief spurts—the few minutes a microwave oven is on or a small repair job (drilling a hole with an electric drill usually takes seconds, not minutes).

ENGINE-MOUNTED GENERATORS

These generators are powered by the ship's main engine. Obviously, to run the generator you must run the engine. This may not sound like such a great idea, but if you run the engine frequently, anyway—for a holding plate refrigeration system or just to keep the batteries charged—then it may be the ideal answer.

The Auto-Gen series, by Mercantile Mfg. Co. (See Plate 4), can produce from 2,500 watts up to 5,500 watts and weigh from 102 to 140 pounds. They can be driven directly off the main engine crankshaft and all three models have a magnetic clutch to prevent them from running needlessly. The Auto-Gen models have speed-control pulleys that allow them to maintain an almost-constant 60 cycles, even

Plate 3 *This battery-powered generator from REDI-LINE delivers 1600 watts of "household" current.* (PHOTO COURTESY OF HONEYWELL, INC.)

Honeywell's Redi-Line generators operate on DC battery power, either 12, 24 or 36-volt (See Plate 3). While not truly portable, since they must be located near the batteries, they are compact—the 1,600-watt unit weighs 54 pounds and measures only 6⅝" x 9" x 16¾". To use one at a remote site would require taking a battery ashore as well as the generator. One nice feature is that they can be installed either vertically or horizontally.

When using a battery-operated generator you must keep a watchful eye on battery condition and state of charge. Deep-cycle batteries are recommended. The Redi-Lines are designed to be started and stopped by the on/off switch of the tool or appliance so there is no unnecessary battery drain.

How much battery power do these units draw? Redi-Line's 1,600-watt model, for example, operates at 75 percent efficiency. A 5-amp tool (say a large jig saw), that requires

Plate 4 *The Auto-Gen generators are powered by the boat's main engine.* (PHOTO COURTESY OF MERCANTILE MANUFACTURING CO.)

though the main engine speed fluctuates—an important feature not found in less complicated, less expensive engine-mounted generators.

Infinity Marine in San Diego makes a 3,000-watt generator that delivers 60-cycle AC power at around 1,600 engine rpm. While useable power can be obtained over a range of revolutions, a careful eye must still be kept on the engine speed while the tool or appliance is in use and drawing juice.

Compared to a portable generator, the engine-mounted models are considerably more expensive: The Infinity Marine complete kit, Auto-Gen's 2,500-watt unit and Auto-Gen's 4,000-watt model cost $1,800 and up.

The advantages are that they are permanently mounted in the engine room, present no on-deck stowage problems and they don't require their own separate fuel supply.

Plate 5 *These "power converters" will produce around 115 volts of DC, not AC, electricity.* (PHOTO COURTESY OF GOLDBERGS' MARINE.)

INVERTERS

Inverters are either "dynamic," running off the main engine's alternator, or "static," run off the ship's battery bank.

Large dynamic inverters, such as those made by Dynamote Corp., can produce as much as 6,000 watts. But they require a commensurately large alternator (Dynomote recommends a 130-amp model). Like the engine-mounted generators, a dynamic inverter will work only when the engine is running, although most of them will charge the ship's batteries at the same time. The current produced is 60 Hertz AC.

Dynamote's 3,600-watt model weighs 96 pounds. In 1980 its price, including the installation kit, was about $1,200. However, if you have to purchase a larger engine alternator, that might add anywhere from $300 to $700 to your outlay.

There are inexpensive (as low as $30 to $50) "black boxes" available, such as the "power converter" distributed by Goldberg Marine, that can be wired to your boat's existing 12-volt alternator (See Plate 5). Advertising claims to the contrary, the amount of wattage one of

these units will produce is directly related to the size of your alternator. A 55-amp alternator, for instance, never produces 55 amps. The output rate of an alternator varies with its load. It will not, however, exceed the voltage determined by the voltage regulator. If you have a 55-amp alternator, you should never expect it to produce more than 50 amps under maximum load—to exceed this limit might damage the ship's alternator and wiring. Based on this, you could get 50 amps at 14 volts, producing 700 watts as an absolute maximum. Assuming that the black box is 80 percent efficient, then 560 watts is its true maximum output. At 115 volts, that's only 3.82 amps—enough to run a *very* small drill.

Basically, these black boxes are simply transformers and they don't really generate 60-cycle "household" current the way the larger and more expensive dynamic inverters do. They produce 115 volts (more or less) of *direct current*. Brush-type, or universal motors, can run on either AC or DC, with no adverse effect. (Redi-Line claims that brush-type motors actually run *better* on DC than AC.) While most hand tools have brush-type motors, many household and kitchen appliances have induction motors that require 60-cycle power—*true* alternating current.

Static inverters, using battery power, do not require that you run the engine, although you'd better be sure your batteries are fully charged and capable of handling the load. We have a very small (4" x 4" x 7½") Heathkit inverter (See Plate 6) that produces 175 watts,

Plate 6 *A 175-watt Heathkit inverter powers Saga's darkroom enlarger and timer, as well as the soldering iron.* (PHOTO COURTESY OF HEATH COMPANY.)

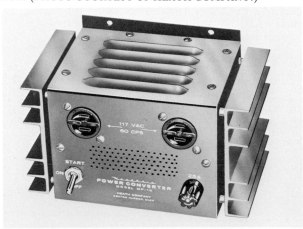

continuous. It operates our darkroom enlarger and timer (its primary function), a soldering iron and the miniature tree lights at Christmas time. The unit cost $55 in 1981.

Radio Shack sells a 300-watt inverter that measures 4½" x 6½" x 7" and costs about $100.

Much larger static inverters are available—some that produce as much as 3,000 watts of continuous 120-volt AC power. The larger units, however, may require more than a 12-volt system. Dynamote's 3,000-watt model must have a 24-volt input as a *minimum*. The largest 12-volt model produces 1,800 watts.

One of the best features, in my opinion, of a static inverter is that they are *silent*. Unlike the noisy portable generator, or the rumble of the main engine, the inverter delivers noiseless "household" power. Of course, unless you're dockside, you eventually do have to make some noise to recharge the batteries (assuming you do that by running the engine). And the drawback to the large inverters may be the size and number of batteries that must be carried to keep pace with the power drain.

DOCKSIDE POWER

If you stay at one marina virtually all the time, you'll buy an electrical cord and install a receptacle to correspond to the dockside power system. Start to travel, however, and the game of "adaptor roulette" begins. *Saga's* equipment includes a 30-amp, 125-volt power inlet (See Plate 7) with a watertight cover mounted in the cabin side and a 50-foot power cord with twist-lock plug and connector (See Plate 8). We've been able to use it "as is" perhaps 10 percent of the time. The rest of the time we've had to buy or borrow adapters of one kind or another or —most often the case—we've plugged a standard household-type extension cord into a dubious-looking dockside receptacle and hoped for the best.

One of *Saga's* most useful little gadgets is a polarity testing device that plugs into any 110-volt outlet. It has three neon lights that glow in a variety of patterns to indicate: open ground, open hot, open neutral, hot/ground reversed

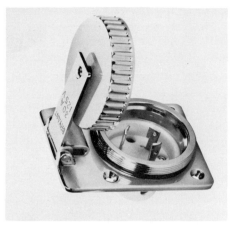

Plate 7 *A 30-amp 125-volt power inlet with a watertight cover is mounted in the hull or cabin side.* (PHOTO COURTESY BRYANT DIVISION OF WESTINGHOUSE.)

Plate 8 *A 50-foot power cord with twist-lock plug and connector.* (PHOTO COURTESY BRYANT DIVISION OF WESTINGHOUSE.)

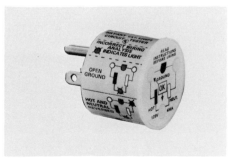

Plate 9 *A circuit tester will indicate faulty circuit polarity.* (PHOTO COURTESY BRYANT DIVISION OF WESTINGHOUSE.)

polarity, hot/neutral reversed polarity, or correct circuit polarity (See Plate 9). Hubbell makes one such gadget that can be built into the ship's electrical panel.

FOREIGN POWER

Few countries outside the United States use 115 volts at 60 Hertz, with voltages covering a wide range. If you plan to cruise outside the United States and the Bahamas, you can buy travel adapters that will convert available electricity to conform to the ship's system. Several companies, such as Radio Shack, make travel adapters. Radio Shack also sells an inexpensive set of four-plug adapters to enable you to plug in the converters to most foreign dockside outlets.

SAFETY CONSIDERATIONS

Regardless of the source of 110-volt power (including dockside plug-in), two items should be standard equipment on any boat with an AC system, an isolation transformer and a ground-fault circuit interrupter (GFCI).

The isolation transformer reduces both the chance of electrical shock and of electrolysis. It prevents a *direct* flow of electricity from the power source (usually on shore) to the on-board circuitry. Instead, power is transferred magnetically. The boat's system is effectively free of ground, with the electricity flowing in a "closed" circuit between the transformer and the outlets.

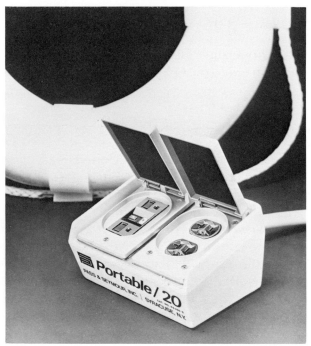

Plate 10 *A portable ground fault circuit interrupter (GFCI) can protect you from lethal electrical shock.* (PHOTO COURTESY OF PASS & SEYMOUR, INC.)

Your best protection from a lethal electrical shock is the GFCI (See Plate 10). GFCI is plugged into the power outlet and your tool or appliance is plugged into the GFCI. If it senses a "fault" as low as 4 or 5 milliamps, it will instantly cut the flow of electricity.

A GFCI should be used, not just aboard your boat, but wherever you're working with power tools—on a dock, in a boatyard—anyplace you are near water or standing on damp ground. Small units can be purchased for under $50— a small price to pay if you value your life.

DC SYSTEMS

Batteries are the heart and soul of any DC system. It pays to invest in good, deep-cycle batteries and to take the time to maintain them in good condition. Batteries sold for automotive use—and most of those labeled "marine"—are not true deep-cycle batteries. They are designed for engine starting, a quick charge from the engine's alternator and then for holding the charge until the next engine start. They are *not* designed for the kind of *continuous,* slow discharge use that live-aboards require.

A deep-cycle battery should be labeled as such and should state the ampere-hour rating. (Car batteries are rated in cold cranking power instead of ampere-hours.) Deep-cycle batteries are heavy: a 135-ampere battery, for instance, will weigh around 100 pounds.

Batteries must be well secured in a dry, ventilated compartment. To avoid damage from battery acid, set them inside a fiberglass or polypropylene box or tray. We keep a gallon jug of distilled water aboard for topping off batteries and a hydrometer to check their specific gravity. A voltmeter tells us at a glance the existing battery charge and the discharge ampmeter shows the amount of power drain whenever something is turned on.

Water that is high in iron content or heavily treated with chlorine is not good for lead-acid batteries. It's best to use only distilled water.

Most master battery switches, with settings for Off, Battery One, Battery Two, and Both, cannot be changed from one setting to another when the engine is running without damaging the alternator. A few companies, such as Marinetics and Sudbury, make switches that *can* be changed while the engine is running. They are more expensive than the other types, but in my opinion they're worth the extra cost—just for safety's sake. Having to replace an alternator because of one accidental flip of a switch could instantly negate any savings.

12-VOLT OUTLETS

DC and AC outlets and plugs should be *totally different* so a tool or appliance never can be accidently plugged into the wrong socket. For the AC system, it's simplest to use standard household outlets. There are several choices for the DC wiring but, whatever type you use, make them uniform throughout the boat.

One solution is to use "cigarette lighter" plugs and receptacles. That, however, makes the appliance cords quite bulky and, I find, very unattractive. It's also an expensive way to wire an entire boat.

Saga is wired below with inexpensive "Jones plugs." These are polarized plugs with matching receptacles, available at any electronics store. Our only objection to them is that a few of the older ones "loosened," so we have to jiggle the plug to make contact.

Another choice is the waterproof, polarized deck plugs, sold as sets at most marine hardware stores. For interior use, you can remove the snap-on outlet cover.

VOLTAGE DROP

Voltage drop is a thief of your battery's power. This loss happens when the electricity must travel a long distance from power source to outlet. It can happen with AC power, too, when you run a long extension cord. Make sure your wiring is adequate or even oversize. That's the best thing you can do for your electrical system.

Voltage drop also occurs if batteries are low. The lower the battery's charge, the faster it will go down. For example, if we have a pump rated at 15 amps and assume a "healthy" battery, charged to 13 volts—that equals 195 watts. If it's a 195-watt pump, then it will *always* draw 195 watts. (We find it helpful to convert the rating of *all* tools and appliances to watts when calculating power requirements and making comparisons.) Now, if the battery is only at 12 volts, then our pump will use 16.25 amps, not 15! If the battery is down to 11 volts, then the pump would need a whopping 17.73 amps, even though it is still drawing 195 watts. More likely, wiring would start to burn if we kept trying to use the pump. So you see, it *is* important to keep batteries healthy and well-charged.

CHARGING BATTERIES

The most common methods of charging batteries are with an AC-powered battery charger or by running the engine and charging through its alternator.

The alternator's charging rate is governed by its voltage regulator. The batteries receive a high charge when the engine is started, then the rate tapers off quickly to a low, steady charge. This often necessitates running the engine for a long time.

On *Saga*, Bruce installed a voltage regulator bypass, with a switch at the electrical panel. While this has greatly reduced our engine running time, we must monitor the charging operation carefully to avoid overcharging the batteries or damaging the circuitry. Some manufacturers, like Motorola, sell by-pass kits for their alternators.

SOLAR PANELS

I believe solar energy has a definite place on the live-aboard boat (See Chapter 17). Pat Rand Rose's *The Solar Boat Book* is filled with ideas on putting the sun to work aboard your boat.

I do not believe, however, that solar panels are a practical way to keep the batteries charged. They can *help*, but they are still too expensive to use as the *only* power source (See Plate 11). One of Free Energy System's 8″ x 28″ x ½″ panels will produce about 20 amp-hours a *week*. (The 1979 retail price was $349.) Most live-aboards use more than 20 amps a *day*.

If you have a powerboat or a houseboat,

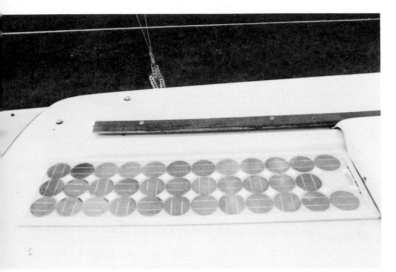

Plate 11 *Solar panels can aid in keeping batteries charged.* (PHOTO COURTESY OF FREE ENERGY SYSTEMS, INC.)

you'll undoubtedly have an easier time finding a suitable place to install an array of solar panels than those of us on sailboats. Canopy decks and wide expanses of seldom-trafficked cabin tops are ideal locations. On sailboats we seem to walk just about everywhere. Sometimes room can be found on the cabin top or atop a hatch. I have seen trimarans with solar panels mounted on the outer hulls. Remember, though, that the further the panels are from the batteries, the greater the voltage drop will be.

Solar panels must be installed with a blocking diode to prevent them from discharging after the sun goes down. Several panels can be wired in parallel to increase the charging amps.

WIND AND TOWING GENERATORS

Wind generators (and alternators) are capable of giving you many more amps for your dollar than solar panels. While windmills have been used ashore for years, they are still in their infancy as on-board sources of power. Fantastic claims are being made by some of the wind generator builders—take all charts and graphs with a grain of salt! Even so, I think they are a more viable choice than solar panels for an extra energy source. I do know a few live-aboards who live simply and use a wind generator as their *only* power source.

Hamilton Ferris sells a direct-drive wind generator that can be equipped with a two-bladed propeller of 30 inches, 36 inches or 48 inches. The 48-inch blade should produce 2.5 amps at 14 knots of wind and about 7 amps at 20 knots. Ham's distributor in southern Florida, John Betus, is constantly tinkering with new blades. His complete unit costs less than $400. John has several mounting methods, including a separate mast and—the most common—a wishbone mount hoisted by the jib halyard into a sailboat's foretriangle.

Wood End Boats' WebCharger ($435 in 1981) is also a two-bladed generator for foretriangle mounting. But it is geared instead of being direct drive. With a 5-foot, 4-inch diameter propeller, it is supposed to produce 3 to 4 amps in winds of 10 to 12 mph.

The Ampair 50 (See Plate 12), is a wind-driven alternator with a top output of about 4 amps. In 20 knots of wind, it should produce 2 to 2.5 amps. It is small—the 14-blade turbine is only 26 inches in diameter. It is designed to be permanently mounted and has been tested in 85-knot winds with no adverse effects. (I saw a two-blade wishbone-mounted generator go berserk in a gale and it was frightening indeed.) Unfortunately, while it is well-made, the Ampair is quite expensive—about $1,000, including shipping from England.

We bought a Hamilton Ferris generator from John Betus and Bruce began experimenting by making different blades with varying degrees of pitch and trying both direct drive and various combinations of gears. He

Plate 12 *The Ampair 50 will produce around 2 to 2.5 amps at 20 knots wind speed.* (PHOTO COURTESY OF AMPAIR PRODUCTS.)

has doubled the generator's output and is still tinkering.

One of the big problems with foretriangle mounting is that it is impossible to eliminate *all* vibration, so we have come to favor solid mounting either on a separate mast or tripod or, on a sailboat, a pulpit mounting. Great care must be taken to mount the generator high enough or far enough outboard so there is no chance of anyone accidently walking or falling into the spinning propeller blades.

Yes, wind generators do make noise. The more vibration you eliminate, the quieter they will be. But I don't object to the sound, finding "natural" electricity rather pleasant compared to running the engine.

The Hamilton Ferris generator can also be used as a towing generator when the boat is underway. At a 6-knot boat speed, it will produce 5 amps (See Plate 13).

Ampair Products also makes a towing alternator—the Aquair 50, that will produce about 3 amps at 6 knots. The Ampair generator also can be converted into a towing rig with a special conversion kit.

ELECTROLYSIS

Electrolysis (actually electrolytic corrosion) occurs when two dissimilar metals touch or are

close underwater—and the less noble metal is eaten away. Protection is most commonly provided by installing sacrificial zinc anodes to the hull and zinc collars around the propeller shaft. (Zinc is one of the least noble metals and is eaten away more quickly than the metal you are trying to protect.)

It's important that all underwater metal fittings and fastenings be as "noble" a metal as possible (i.e., monel, silicon bronze, copper). That's why common household brass gate valves are so vulnerable as through-hull fittings and why I like the new fiber-reinforced plastic seacocks so much. Painting underwater metal fittings helps to insulate them. Zinc anodes, of course, should *not* be painted!

Plate 13 *The Hamilton Ferris towing generator can produce about 5 amps at 6 knots boat speed.* (PHOTO COURTESY HAMILTON FERRIS.)

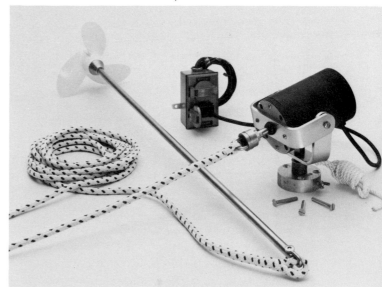

Stray current can also be a cause of electrolysis, particularly when you're dockside. As I mentioned earlier, an isolation transformer is an excellent investment, since it prevents a direct flow of electricity from the dock outlet to the boat's circuitry. Additionally, you'll sometimes see boats at docks with anodes hanging over the side into the water, attached by a wire to a piece of "bonded" metal on the boat. And all boats, other than those of steel or aluminum, should be so bonded.

Bonding connects electrical equipment and metal hardware together, usually with copper wire or tubing, further reducing the chance of electrolysis. Bonding must be done by someone knowledgeable. If your boat is not bonded and you want to tackle the job yourself, I would suggest a careful study of the recommendations offered by the American Boat and Yacht Council (ABYC) and a good book on marine electricity, such as Conrad Miller's *Your Boat's Electrical System*.

SOURCES

AMERICAN HONDA MOTOR CO.
100 W. Alondra Blvd.
Gardena, CA 90247

AMPAIR PRODUCTS
Aston House
Blackheath, Guildford
Surrey GU4 8RD England

AQUABUG INTERNATIONAL, INC.
100 Merrick Road
Rockville Centre, NY 11570

BRYANT
Division of Westinghouse
1421 State Street
Bridgeport, CT 06602

CLINTON ENGINES
Clark & Maple Streets
Maquoketa, IA 52060

DYNAMOTE CORP.
1200 W. Nickerson
Seattle, WA 98119

HAMILTON Y. FERRIS
P.O. Box 1165
Santa Cruz, CA 95061

FREE ENERGY SYSTEMS, INC.
Price and Pine Streets
Holmes, PA 19043

GOLDBERG'S MARINE
202 Market Street
Philadelphia, PA 19106

HEATHKIT
Veritechnology Electronics Corp.
P.O. Box 167
St. Joseph, MI 49085

HONEYWELL, INC.
P.O. Box 106
Rockford, IL 61105

HARVEY HUBBELL, INC.
Bridgeport, CT 06602

INFINITY MARINE
5171 Santa Fe Street
San Diego, CA 92109

MERCANTILE MFG. CO., INC.
P.O. Box 895
Minden, LA 71055

ONAN CORP.
1400 73rd Ave. N.E.
Minneapolis, MN 55432

PASS & SEYMOUR, INC.
P.O. Box 4822
Syracuse, NY 13221

SURFJET CORP.
715 Raymond Avenue
St. Paul, MN 55114

WOOD END BOATS
P.O. Box 139
Provincetown, MA 02657

Television

16

"Soaps Afloat"

"What! You have a television set!"

Like millions of other people, we do indeed watch TV even though we live aboard and cruise as a way of life.

I used to mumble incoherently, "It's nice to . . . ah . . . snuggle up with Johnny Carson every night—heh, heh . . ." and then try to change the subject. Not any more! I've stopped feeling guilty. I watch TV and love it.

Why should I feel guilty? The theory goes, if you move aboard a boat, particularly to go cruising, your primary objectives are (a) a simpler way of life and (b) "getting away from it all." Anything else is considered a sacrilege. But let's try to look at this objectively for a minute.

First, the simpler way of life. To detractors I ask, "Just how simple do you want life to be? Do you do your laundry in a bucket with a washboard or at a laundromat ashore? Do you do without cold beer and mayonnaise or do you have an ice box or mechanical refrigeration? Is your lighting *solely* by kerosene lamps or are they just a backup for your electric lights? Do you have a radio aboard, an RDF, depth sounder, sophisticated electronic equipment? Do you use a calculator when you navigate?"

Some get along without *any* amenities. But they are a rare handful of hardy sailors. I can't help but feel that at least a few of them would have more if they could afford more. Let's face it, we live in an age of electronic marvels and the majority of us have at least a few of these little luxuries on board to make life easier or safer. A television set is just another piece of electronic gear that happens to be used primarily for pleasure, although it does have some practical value.

Next, let's take a closer look at "getting away from it all." If your cruising is limited to weekends and an occasional two-week vacation cruise, it's refreshing to forget the cares of the world for awhile, to escape ringing telephones, nerve-jarring traffic jams, blaring radios—and television.

But if you're away long enough, you'll start to wonder what's going on back in the world—if for no other reason than to feel smug because you're away from it. So what do you do? You turn on the radio and spin the dial for a news station. So do we—but we get to look at a picture, too.

Just because we have a television set doesn't mean we spend all day watching soap operas and game shows, any more than we did when we lived ashore. And, we don't just watch the news, we watch other programs—just for entertainment.

Look at it this way—part of the reason for living aboard and going cruising is for *enjoyment*. If you really enjoy certain TV programs, why give them up if you don't have to? All of your time while cruising is *not* spent rising to the challenge of the sea, it's *not* spent sailing rail-down, it's *not* spent exploring ashore. Many quiet evenings are spent aboard, without company to entertain, just time to yourself—to relax, watch a sunset, look at the stars, read a book or . . . watch television.

For relaxation, sometimes I read a book, sometimes I go for a row and other times I watch television. I like having the choice.

Occasionally those who pooh-pooh television have been known to do a quick about-face when they realize something special is about to be aired. We were at the Newport Boat Show during the telecast of the Mohammed Ali-Leon Spinks fight. We were the only people around with an operating television set. People started dropping by during the day. "Oh, I heard you had a TV set. Uh, did you know the big fight's on tonight?"

We wound up with eight cheering live-aboards crowded below in *Sabrina*'s tiny cabin with countless others stopping on the dock wanting to know how the fight was progressing. Had it occurred to me, I would have sold "porthole passes" and turned it into a profitable evening.

We have met the odd couple (no pun intended) who have looked longingly at our TV set and said they really did miss such-and-such

program. We try to oblige when we can, and invite them over for an evening of boat talk and coffee—with a half-hour break for their favorite show.

Once in a while this idea doesn't work out, of course.

We were anchored in the harbor of Hyannis, Massachusetts, and had invited a friend from another boat to come over and watch a movie we all wanted to see. The TV reception in Hyannis was none too good, so Bruce and I spent the better part of an hour setting and resetting our anchors, adjusting the antenna and changing the position of the boat in an attempt to pick up the station and hold it. Finally, the big moment arrived and we all settled down with high hopes and a jug of wine.

First, a news break; then the commercials; finally, show time! At that moment, a lady in the marina decided to call a friend on her ship-to-shore—wheezes, static, fuzzy picture and, "This is Black Bird . . . this is Black Bird . . ." The jug of wine saved the day. Who wanted to watch a dumb movie anyway! And so, back to sea stories again.

Entertainment aside, television does have a practical side. I think NOAA weather reports often are a joke. Making a decision to get underway based purely on a report from NOAA of "southerly winds at 10-15 knots," is a pretty good way of finding yourself sailing into the teeth of a howling nor'easter. We usually try to watch the evening news and weather on a local TV channel. Not that local TV weather forecasters are much better—some are and some aren't. What we like to see are the weather maps and satellite pictures showing fronts and systems all across the country.

When we were sailing north from Florida along the Intracoastal Waterway we would watch the weather forecasts each evening after we had anchored. A cold front was approaching, but appeared to be stalled. We knew we could look forward to several days of southerly winds. At that time we only wanted to reach Hilton Head, South Carolina, where we planned to spend several weeks. Knowing that a good southerly was pretty well assured we were able to take our time. By the time the cold front arrived, bringing driving rain and 35-knot winds, we were snug at anchor in protected Palmetto Bay at Hilton Head.

Being able to look at weather maps and satellite pictures can give you a good handle on long-range weather forecasts. It can be a valuable tool in planning a cruise. NOAA weather and local radio stations give you, *at best,* a 24-hour forecast.

Local news programs can give you a fascinating insight into the attitudes, politics and problems of local townspeople. Radio stations generally devote five minutes to news, television stations a half hour to an hour. You may not really care that the hot-dog vender at the baseball park sings his wares in a booming baritone and makes up limericks to boot or that the major topic to be discussed at an upcoming city council meeting is whether or not the downtown traffic lights should be synchronized. But these topics often provide an interesting perspective on the lifestyles of the local people. And you are cruising through or stopping at small port towns to pick up at least *some* of the local color, aren't you? Even the local commercials are fun—in the South heavy on snuff and chewing tobacco. The big sellers in Nassau, Bahamas, are rice and 7-Up.

Yes, Nassau. The Bahamians have one television station, and are *very* proud of it. I saw a *TV Guide* in a grocery store and asked the clerk "Is this for Miami stations?"

"No, *we* have our own TV station," she told me disdainfully, as if I'd asked if everyone in the Bahamas used outdoor plumbing. Bruce's brother spent some time with us in the Bahamas. He likes to "get away from it all" and was more than a little dismayed to find virtually every quaint little pastel house in sleepy Spanish Wells sporting a huge TV antenna! Civilization is encroaching on paradise everywhere and we might as well learn to roll with it. Besides, Bahamian television was just downright fun. Dorothy Panzer, the charming "weath-wa girl," is an indelible memory. And some of the British series, beamed by satellite, were riotously funny.

Don't underestimate the value of television in a non-English speaking foreign country,

either. Many people have found it indispensible in learning a foreign language, as well as discovering the pronunciation of different geographical names. We met a Japanese couple who were using television to help them learn English. Their six-year-old son was becoming quite proficient.

POWER DRAW

"Sure," I can hear some saying, "but you can get all that on the radio." Not quite! On shortwave, perhaps, but most AM and FM stations ar predominantly music. And, of course, you don't get maps and pictures, which can be invaluable in understanding a topic. Finally, our television set puts surprisingly little drain on the boat's power supply.

We had a small black-and-white Sony with a 12-volt converter so it ran directly off the ship's batteries. It drew about 1.5 amps—less than a standard incandescent bunk light. *Saga*'s Sony 12-volt color TV uses slightly more. Many of these small sets are available with their own battery packs, but after about four to six hours viewing time the batteries must be recharged. It seems more practical to buy the converter and hook up the TV with the rest of the boat's electrical system. The television also does double duty as a voltmeter. When Johnny Carson appears to be shrinking, I know it's time to charge the batteries. Actually, the TV is a *more* sensitive indicator than the boat's voltmeter—unless you have a voltmeter with an extremely expanded scale.

ANTENNAS

Keeping a channel tuned in can pose some problems when the boat is anchored rather than tied to a dock. Unless you have an omni-directional antenna, the set will have to be adjusted every time the boat swings. We have occasionally put out a stern anchor to keep the boat in a set position if there was a program we particularly wanted to see. Usually, we just reach over and push the antenna to the other side.

On *Sabrina*, we got fairly good reception with just the television's stock antennas, both on VHF and UHF channels. Sometimes a piece of tin foil stuck on the end of the antenna helped reception, too. Keep in mind that the rigging of a sailboat actually bends and deflects the in-

coming signal so the heading of the boat is as important as the antenna in determining the quality of the reception.

It is somewhat harder to tune *Saga*'s color set for good reception. Bruce made an omni-directional antenna that we've mounted permanently at the masthead (See Figure 1 and Plate 1) that does an excellent job. An omni-directional antenna can also be mounted on a pigstick and hoisted above the masthead for an extended range and possibly overcome much of the wave-defelction problem by getting it above the rigging.

While we've always made our own antennas (at a nominal cost for materials), there are several available commercially (See Plates 2 and 3). All the ones we've priced have been in excess of $100. One type, made by RCA and sold by many television and appliance stores, is a disk mounted topside that can be turned in any direction by remote controls located below. But it does require electricity to operate.

Aquadynamics, Inc. makes omni-directional antennas: three models that require electricity and three that do not. They are disks with 10 antenna rods inserted around the perimeter, making their overall diameter from 42 inches to 54 inches, depending on the model. A powerboat could accommodate one of these antennas more easily than a sailboat.

Figure 1 *Bruce made this omni-directional TV antenna for* Saga, *and it works extremely well.*

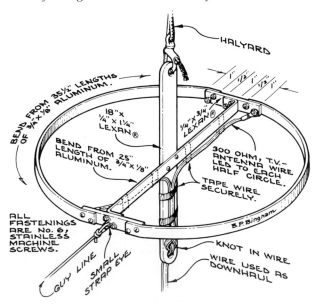

Plate 1 *A homemade omni-directional antenna mounted from a sailboat's spreader.*

Plate 2 *This RCA omni-directional disk antenna is turned by remote controls located below.*

Our first television set survived three years of *At Last*'s leaky decks before it succumbed. The TV repairman told me he would normally have offered at least five dollars and used the set for spare parts. But in that set not even the

Plate 3 *Winegard's marine TV antenna operates on 12-volt power.*

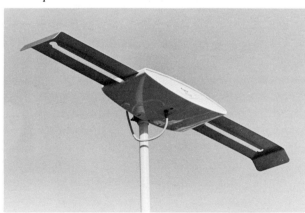

knobs were worth saving. Obviously, a television requires the same care you would give any piece of sophisticated electronic gear. Primarily, keep it dry and stow it where it won't get knocked around. Ours sits on a fiddled shelf, held securely against a bulkhead with shockcord when we're under way.

Radio/stereo cassettes are more "acceptable" in the minds of many people. Ours is on much of the day. If we can't find a good classical music station, we turn to our tape collection. We have more than a hundred cassette tapes and add more whenever we can. We have learned one lesson the hard way: it just does not pay to buy *cheap* tapes. They stretch, distort and do not hold up in the marine environment. Buy quality Mylar tapes and store them in a dry place. If they are inside a box or a cabinet, include bags of silica gel.

SOURCES

AQUADYNAMICS INC. (TV ANTENNA)
    168 Rockland Avenue
    Woonsocket, RI 02895

WINEGARD CO. (TV ANTENNA)
    3000 Kirkwood Street
    Burlington, IA 52601

17

Plumbing Systems

"Think a head"

WHILE REPLENISHING THE water in your tanks is of paramount importance to ocean voyagers, it's also becoming increasingly important—and difficult—for coastal cruisers and stay-in-one-place live-aboards. You may anchor out a great deal where there is no tap to turn on, or find yourself in an area where local water is tainted, brackish or simply distasteful. As we humans continue to pollute our environment, water shortages and water rationing are becoming more and more frequent occurrences ashore.

There are several methods of catching rainwater. On both *Sabrina* and *Saga* we rigged our sun awning with a plastic through-hull in the center attached to a length of hose. This provides a large surface area to catch water, but it does have some disadvantages. Rain is frequently accompanied by wind that can blow off the rain, or flip the cover before water has time to collect. A partial solution is to rig the awning as tightly as possible, but this puts a strain on the fabric (See Figure 1). The awning creates enough windage so that it must be taken down during high winds—anything higher than 30 knots.

A small trough of water-repellent canvas can be made with a through-hull fitting and with grommets or Dot fasteners placed all around the edges. This cloth can be lashed under the boom (on a sailboat) or along a side deck between the lifeline stanchions and the handrails. If it's fitted with dowels to hold it open at the top, it can hang from a canopy deck support on a powerboat (See Figure 2). It could even be attached to the lower edge of a tilted awning.

An excellent permanent water collector has been described by Eric Hiscock, in *Cruising World* magazine. He converted his cabin top to a catchment by installing 1-inch by ¾-inch wood ledges around the perimeter. At the aft lower corners he installed a short length of pipe. During rainstorms hose is inserted in the pipe and led to the water tanks. This system could be used on both sail and powerboats. Its great advantage is that it is not affected by wind and could be used even in gale-force storms (See Figure 3). Another idea is to plug the scuppers and use the entire cabin top and deck as a catchment.

With any system, let the first few minutes of rain cleanse the canvas or cabin top of salt and dirt before collecting. Even then the water won't be "pure," so it's good to add water puri-

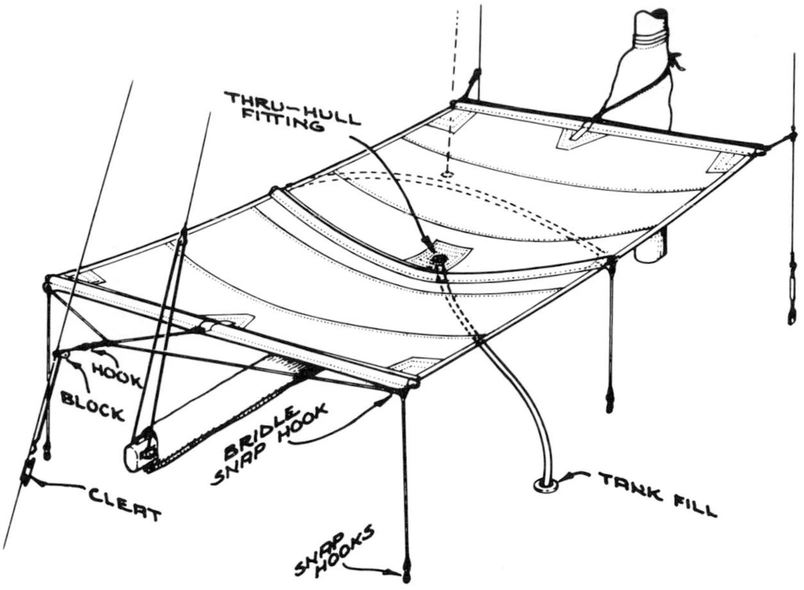

Figure 1 *Most sun awnings can do double-duty as rain catchers. Raise the corners so water will funnel towards the center.*

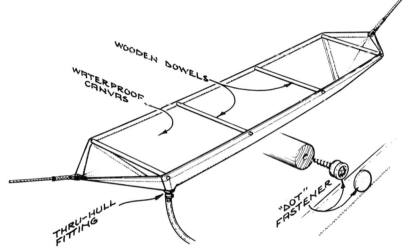

Figure 2 *A narrow trough for catching water can be lashed or (as shown here) snapped into a variety of positions around the boat.*

Figure 3 *Adding wood ledges and pieces of pipe can turn the entire cabin top into a water catchment.*

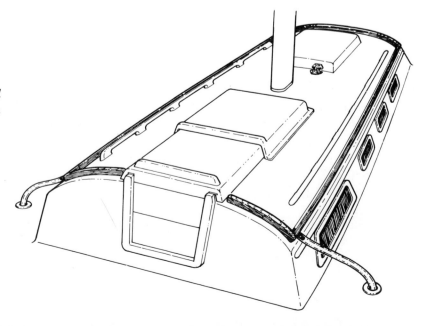

fication tablets or Clorox to the tank. I add Clorox at the rate of 10 drops per gallon (60 drops = 1 teaspoon). Remember that each droplet of rainwater forms around a nucleus. These nuclei can be air-borne dust particles, sea salt, bacteria or any form of solid air pollution. A lot of them are harmless, of course, but you have no way of knowing. The closer you are to a city or industrial area, the more polluted the rain is likely to be.

It's a good idea to add a filter between the water fill and the tank to remove most of these particles. It will also help keep corrosive elements out of the tank, especially if you have metal tanks (See Figure 4). A piece of crumpled netting or a Tuffy pad in the fill pipe will strain out large pieces of debris.

Another way to obtain fresh water is to install an on-board water desalinator. Most of these

work on the principle of reverse osmosis, pumping sea water through a membrane that separates fresh water from brine. While they can produce anywhere from 100 to 4,000 gallons a day, their power requirements, size and cost generally limit them to the largest of yachts. Sweet Water, Allied Water Corp.'s smallest reverse-osmosis watermaker, for example, weighs 90 pounds, measures 26″ x 16″ x 16″, runs on AC power and will produce 100 gallons a day. In 1981 it listed for $3,500. Galley Maid Marine Products, Inc., makes a line of diesel-powered reverse-osmosis desalinators. Its smallest model produces 350 gallons a day and lists for about $8,000.

While these figures sound staggering to most of us (Bruce and I use about 100 gallons a month without being unduly careful, although we do our laundry ashore), they are a giant step forward in self-sufficiency.

ROUTING SYSTEMS

MANUAL

A manual pump (See Plate 1)—either hand or foot-operated—is undoubtedly the simplest and least expensive way of moving water from tank to faucet. My own preference is for a foot pump so that both hands remain free (See Plate 2). Care must be taken in locating a foot

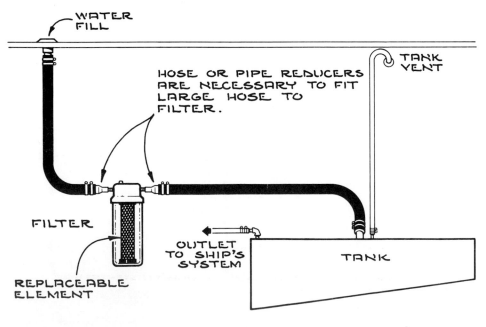

Figure 4 *A filter between deck fill and tank will remove bacteria as well as solid and corrosive elements before water reaches the tank.*

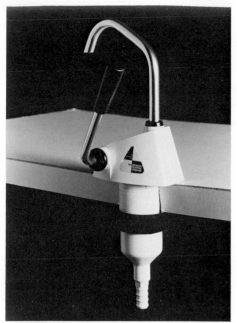

Plate 1 *A manual pump, like Flipper from Whale Pumps, is one of the simplest ways of routing fresh water.* (PHOTO COURTESY OF IMTRA CORP.)

Plate 2 *A manual foot-operated pump allows both hands to remain free. The pump can be located inside a cabinet, with only the pedal exposed.* (PHOTO COURTESY OF IMTRA CORP.)

pump so no one trips over it or accidently steps on it. Hand pumps should be installed with enough space around them to allow for a full stroke without rapping knuckles (See Figure 5).

Boats with pressure water systems should *still* have a manual system installed as a backup in case the pressure system fails and as a water-saving device on long passages.

Figure 5 *A manual pump at each outlet, either hand or foot operated, is the simplest onboard fresh water system.*

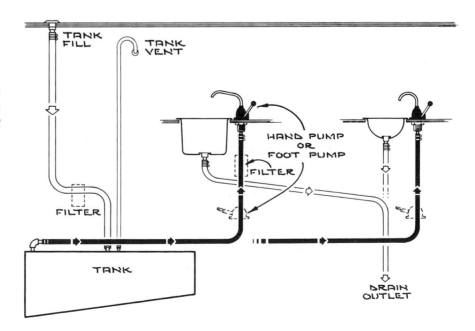

Gravity Pressure Systems

A gravity system is a lot like a pressure water system—without requiring electricity. Instead of a hand or foot pump, you install household-type faucets. For a gravity system to work, the tank must, of course, be located higher than the outlets. And remember that the higher you can place the tank, the more pressure you will have (See Figure 6).

On *At Last,* we built a five-gallon gravity tank that fit unobtrusively inside a deck box at the forward end of the cabin trunk. Once a day, we would manually pump water from the main tank below up into the gravity tank, an operation that only took a minute. Then we'd have our "pressure" water for the day. Bruce painted the tank black so when we wanted to

shower we could remove the tank from the deck box and expose it to the sun. Ideally, of course, we would have had a separate tank for hot water.

Electric Pressure Systems

Electric pressure systems are the most convenient to use and the most complicated to maintain. But they don't waste as much water as some claim (See Plate 3). The water flow can be regulated to a mere trickle if you wish. Anyone who's ever tried to wash and rinse both hands under a hand pump knows how difficult and wasteful *that* can be.

An electric pump can be used with a hand or foot switch located near each faucet. A flick of the switch will activate the pump. A drawback is that unless you install a pressure relief switch (not just an on/off switch) it's very likely you could mistakenly turn on the switch and burst the system (See Figure 7A). A pressure relief switch (sometimes called a "demand" switch) *is* a must, and these switches can be installed in virtually every pressurized system. The pressure relief switch on a demand pump senses water pressure whenever a faucet is turned on (See Figures 7B and 7C). Another alternative is to install a separate pump at each outlet (See Figure 7D).

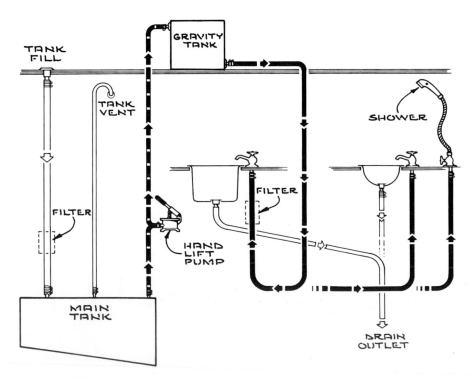

Figure 6 *A typical gravity installation, with the gravity tank* higher *than any of the outlets it serves. The higher the tank, the greater the pressure.*

Plate 3 *This PAR automatic water system pump will provide pressure water to several outlets.* (PHOTO COURTESY ITT JABSCO PRODUCTS.)

Figure 7 *Four methods of electric pressurization.*

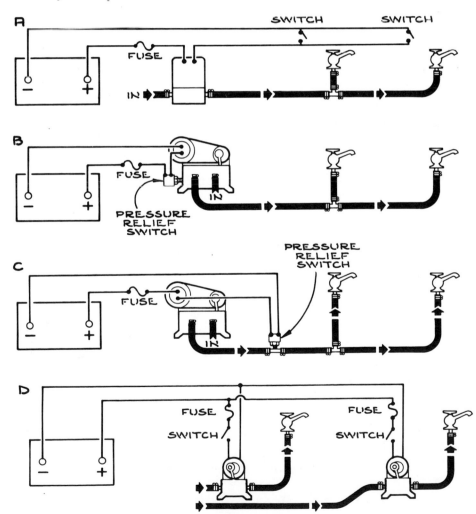

Plate 4 *A PAR Pumpgard In-Line strainer will prevent debris from clogging a pump.* (PHOTO COURTESY ITT JABSCO PRODUCTS.)

A strainer, such as Jabsco Products' PAR Pumpgard InLine Strainer (See Plate 4), installed between the water tank and the pump, does not filter water adequately for drinking but does prevent any particles from clogging the pump (See Figure 8).

An accumulator tank is sometimes installed between the pump and the outlets (See Plate 5). Such a small tank is prefilled by the pump so you can draw off small amounts of water without the pump switching on. This prevents pulsations as the water is pumped and allows for a smoother flow. Pulsations are really only noticeable when the water is running for a lengthy time—when taking a shower, for instance. Pulsations are caused by reciprocating diaphragm pumps, not by rotary pumps (See Figure 8).

DOCKSIDE

If you'll be dockside for any length of time, you may want to install a water intake so that shore water can be pumped directly into the boat's system, through a garden hose. Keep in mind that most onboard systems can only withstand pressure of between 20 and 35 psi. Shore pressure can be much higher and it's not always regulated at dockside outlets. Too high pressure can burst water lines within the boat or blow off connections even when they are well clamped. It can fracture water heater tanks and even burst your water tank if the vent is clogged.

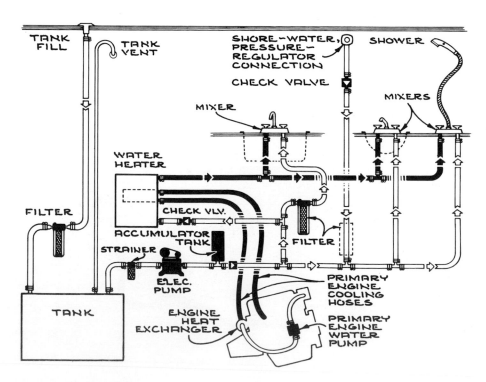

Figure 8 *A typical onboard fresh water pressure system, including hot water and shore pressure.*

Plate 5 *An accumulator tank reduces
pulsations and sometimes allows you to
draw small amounts of water without
cycling.* (PHOTO COURTESY ITT JABSCO
PRODUCTS.)

Water inlet fittings can be purchased with
built-in pressure regulators (See Plate 6). Or,
you can buy an in-line regulator that's usually
installed on the spigot at the dock (See Plate 7).
Two check valves should be installed, one at
the hull inlet, so the hose can be disconnected

easily by eliminating back pressure at the inlet,
and one at the pump outlet to keep the shore
water from traveling back through the pump
and overflowing the ship's water tank (See Figure 8).

WATER HEATERS

Electric hot water heaters use AC current and
are designed to run on dock power or with an
on-board generator. The heating elements in
these heaters use so much power that a 12-volt
DC system would be impractical. Most of them
can, however, be provided with a heat exchanger that will use engine cooling water to heat
the water in the tank when the engine is running (See Plate 8).

Saga has a seven-gallon AC/heat-exchanger
water heater. Dockside, of course, we always

Plate 6 *This fresh water inlet, mounted in hull or cabin
side, will let you hook up a water hose dockside while
regulating the pressure to prevent damage to the boat's
system.* (PHOTO COURTESY OF ITT JABSCO PRODUCTS.)

Plate 7 *A pressure regulator can be installed between
the dock spigot and the hose leading to the boat.* (PHOTO
COURTESY OF ITT JABSCO PRODUCTS.)

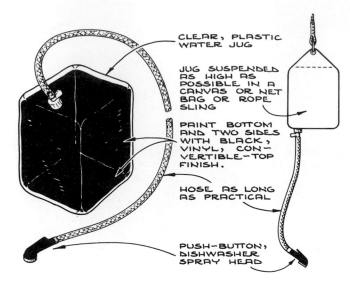

Labels in figure:
CLEAR, PLASTIC WATER JUG

JUG SUSPENDED AS HIGH AS POSSIBLE IN A CANVAS OR NET BAG OR ROPE SLING

PAINT BOTTOM AND TWO SIDES WITH BLACK, VINYL, CONVERTIBLE-TOP FINISH.

HOSE AS LONG AS PRACTICAL

PUSH-BUTTON, DISHWASHER SPRAY HEAD

Figure 9 *A simple homemade solar-heated gravity system.*

have hot water. Underway or at anchor, an hour of engine running will provide us with several days' worth of hot water. Adding additional insulation around the heater will extend that time even longer (See Figure 8).

A viable alternative is a solar hot water heater. Pat Rand Rose, in *The Solar Boat Book*, gives directions for making a number of different solar heaters, ranging from one as simple as coils of dark-colored garden hose to one that uses a heat exchanger with antifreeze in it.

One point to consider when building a solar heater is that some means of insulating the sun-heated water must be provided to keep it from cooling off when the sun goes down. It must

either go into a storage tank or the container must be wrapped in insulating material to hold the heat in through the night.

A number of simple solar showers are available and, of course, these don't have to be confined to that use. The water can be fed into the ship's hot water system for general use.

One of the simplest heaters is to purchase a five-gallon clear water jug and paint the sides and bottom with black vinyl paint (See Figure 9).

Small "instant" water heaters that run on propane or CNG provide another choice for those using either fuel for cooking. Usually bulkhead-mounted, they do heat water almost instantly and use very little fuel. They have no pilot light, like a household gas heater. They are simply turned on manually whenever you want hot water and turned off again just as quickly. Our friends on *Endymion* have been using a Nymph gas-fired heater (made in England) since they moved aboard. They swear it's the handiest piece of gear on the boat.

Plate 8 *Most hot water heaters, like this 7-gallon unit, can use either electricity or engine cooling water.* (PHOTO COURTESY OF AMERICAN APPLIANCE MFG. CORP., MORFLO INDUSTRIES, INC.)

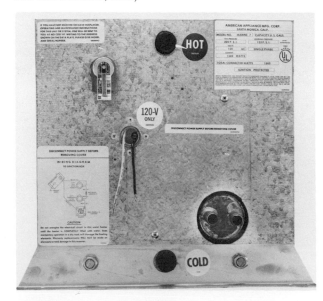

SHOWERS

We used a portable SunShower aboard *Sabrina* (See Plate 9). While it was certainly adequate (and simple!), I still felt that it was a form of

Plate 9 *We used a SunShower, similar to this one, aboard* Sabrina *for several years. With care, we could each get a shower and shampoo from one fill.* (PHOTO COURTESY OF BASIC DESIGNS, INC.)

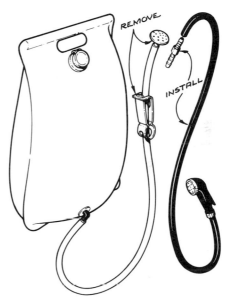

Figure 10 *Adding a kitchen dishwasher nozzle to a portable shower conserves water and makes the shower more convenient. The longer hose allows a greater hoist for increased pressure and mobility of the shower head.*

Plate 10 *A telephone showerhead can be hand-held or placed in a bulkhead-mounted bracket.*

"camping out." We put a larger hose on it so we could hoist it high in the rigging (for greater pressure) and run the hose to *inside* the cabin. Bruce also switched its clip-type shower head to the kitchen dishwasher type, so the on-off mechanism was right in your hand (See Figure 10).

A pressurized garden sprayer can be used for a portable shower. Paint it black and it's a solar shower.

Saga has a pressure water system, a hot water heater and a shower in the head compartment —all the comforts of home. Her telephone shower, with an on/off push button on the shower head, can either be hand-held or placed in a bulkhead-mounted bracket (See Plate 10). The push-button feature allows us to conserve water without having to readjust the hot/cold mix each time the shower is turned off and on again (See Figure 8).

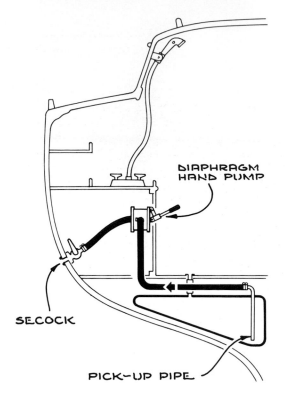

Figure 11 *The shower sump can be emptied manually using a diaphragm hand pump.*

It is not necessary to wipe down an entire head compartment after each shower. On *Saga* we rigged two shower curtains that completely protect the sink, counter, toilet and all cabinets and doors. We used standard household shower curtain *liners,* since they are light and can be tied off unobtrusively against a bulkhead when not in use. I cut them to length and Bruce made small curtain hooks from short lengths of brass rod.

The shower can drain directly into the bilge or into a separate sump tank to be pumped directly overboard. I prefer the sump tank. Shower water contains hair, dirt and bacteria that turn a bilge into a foul-smelling mess. It soon becomes a constant chore to keep the bilge clean and sweet-smelling. The shower sump can be pumped by hand (See Figure 11), by an electric pump using a manual on/off switch (See Figure 12A), or by an electric pump activated by a float switch (See Figure 12B).

Hair will certainly clog your pump, so get a kitchen Tuffy pad, cut it to fit and stuff it in the shower drain as a hair filter.

Figure 12 *The shower sump can be emptied by an electric pump, using a manual on/off switch (A) or an automatic float switch (B).*

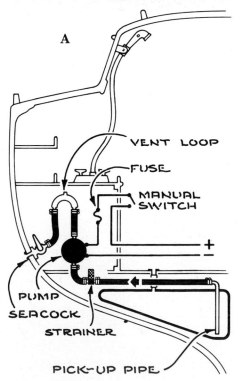

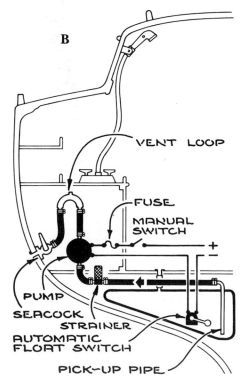

Water Filters

I never gave much thought to water filters until we started cruising in the southeastern United States—where the water often contains so much sulphur that both taste and smell make it unpalatable. *Saga*'s charcoal filter, installed at the tank outlet, removes bad tastes and odors. The filter cartridges must be replaced as soon as they *start* to appear dirty, because charcoal can become a breeding ground for bacteria. The advantage to these units is that they're easy and cheap to install. The replacement cartridges are inexpensive and not difficult to locate since most cartridges are interchangeable.

More sophisticated systems are available that will filter out harmful bacteria as well as bad taste—something to consider if you're planning a foreign cruise. We have taken on questionable water as close to the U.S. as the Bahamas.

There are several "bacteriostatic" water filters, such as Astro-Pure's Fail Safe System, that will remove solids down to 5 microns in size (a red blood cell is 7 microns long), and eliminate coliform bacteria (cause of cholera, typhoid and dysentery). These systems, however, are designed to work with water that has been pretreated with chlorine—the predominant purification technique in most of the world.

Astro-Pure's RV unit costs about $100 and will filter a minimum of 1,000 gallons before it needs replacement.

An even more sophisticated system is the Seagull IV water purification device made by General Ecology (See Plate 11). It's one of the few units that does *not* require pretreated water and will purify even massively polluted water. It employs both micro-filtration (down to 0.4 microns to remove disease-causing bacteria) and activated carbon that removes bad taste, odors and chemical contaminants like pesticides and methyl mercury. The small units cost about $270, with replacement cartridges (rated at 1,000 gallons) costing about $37.

Don't be misled by the 1,000-gallon figure. These units can be installed with a separate

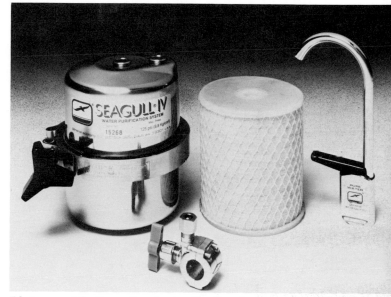

Plate 11 *The Seagull water purification device employs micro-filtration and activated carbon and will purify even massively polluted water.* (PHOTO COURTESY OF GENERAL ECOLOGY, INC.)

spigot so only water for consumption is filtered. You don't have to waste purified water for showers, laundry and dishwashing (See Figure 8).

Saltwater Systems

I've already mentioned the advantages of having a saltwater pump in the galley for washing dishes, and occasionally for cooking. Some live-aboards like a saltwater outlet in the head as well—for washing and showering, followed by a fresh water rinse. It is a way of conserving used for bathing as well as washing hair. Some liquid detergents (like Joy) work well, too.

Saltwater can be plumbed aboard and pressurized for uses such as washing down decks and cleaning ground tackle. You can pressurize a saltwater system through *any* type of pressure pump (See Figure 13). A saltwater system need not involve installing a separate through-hull fitting. Simply install a T in the engine cooling intake hose. (This diverted saltwater line can also be used for other unpressurized purposes.) For hot water, divert the raw cooling water just before it's injected into the exhaust system, or *just after* the raw water pump intake for cold water (See Figure 14). However, using raw engine cooling water should be a controlled flow so as not to run the

water. But I personally would find it unpleasant unless there is some method of heating the shower water first and, of course, special saltwater soap is used. We've found that most shampoos lather well in saltwater and can be

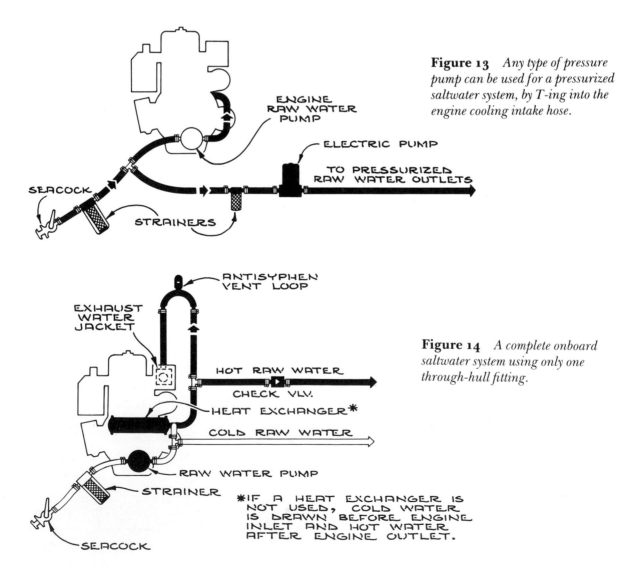

Figure 13 *Any type of pressure pump can be used for a pressurized saltwater system, by T-ing into the engine cooling intake hose.*

ENGINE
RAW WATER
PUMP

ELECTRIC PUMP

TO PRESSURIZED
RAW WATER OUTLETS

SEACOCK

STRAINERS

Figure 14 *A complete onboard saltwater system using only one through-hull fitting.*

ANTISYPHEN
VENT LOOP

EXHAUST
WATER
JACKET

HOT RAW WATER

CHECK VLV.

HEAT EXCHANGER*

COLD RAW WATER

RAW WATER PUMP

STRAINER

*IF A HEAT EXCHANGER IS
NOT USED, COLD WATER
IS DRAWN BEFORE ENGINE
INLET AND HOT WATER
AFTER ENGINE OUTLET.

SEACOCK

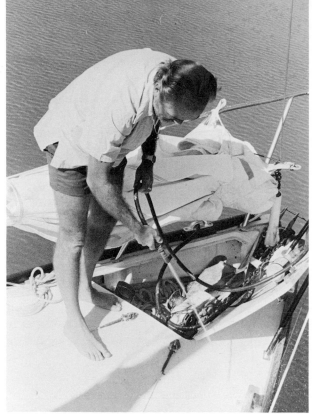

Plate 12 *George Cranston demonstrates his pressure saltwater washdown system aboard* Endymion II.

engine dry. The water should very definitely be strained before it goes through the pump. After the strainer, the line can be run to the pump, then to a shower, the deck, or wherever. If it's used for deck washing, the pump must have a high-lift capacity. Because there is never a chance of running out of saltwater, any type of pump can be used. Be sure that an antisiphon device is installed in the system. A simple in-line check valve is ideal.

A direct-flow spigot can also be installed. Just T into the raw water engine intake and run directly to a spigot; but remember that the spigot and its lines must remain *below* the waterline.

George Cranston put together an inexpensive saltwater washdown system for *Endymion* (See Plate 12). He installed a 12-volt pressure pump (impeller type) in *Endymion*'s foredeck anchor well. From a local hardware store, he purchased a hose kit for an automatic washing machine, consisting of two lengths of hose and a strainer. One piece of hose, attached to the pump inlet, is thrown over the side with the strainer attached, weighted with two lead fish-

ing sinkers to hold the hose end under water. The other length of hose is attached to the pump outlet. It's a simple and efficient arrangement, involving no routing or T-ing of hoses. When not in use the hoses are coiled up and stowed out of sight in the anchor well.

BILGE PUMPS

I've been on boats that had only one or two bilge pumps—both electric. I believe this is a grave mistake. At least one large-capacity manual bilge pump should be on every live-aboard boat. My preference is for a diaphragm pump (See Plate 13). They are simple in construction, easy to maintain and are capable of passing small bits of debris without clogging.

Plate 13 *A diaphragm pump, like this Whale Gusher, can pass bits of debris without clogging.* (PHOTO COURTESY OF IMTRA CORPORATION.)

Plate 14 *Submersible bilge pumps generally have motors that are hermetically sealed.* (PHOTO COURTESY RULE INDUSTRIES, INC.)

Saga came equipped with a bronze Edson lever-action diaphragm pump, capable of pumping almost a gallon a stroke (five gallons in two minutes). We consider this marvelous but massive piece of equipment as THE emergency bilge pump and added a smaller Guzzler diaphragm hand pump—about 12 gallons a minute—for more frequent use. In additiion, *Saga* has a PAR electric bilge pump, capable of pumping eight gallons a minute. It, too, is a diaphragm type, so it can run dry without being damaged.

Having read and heard all too many stories about the siphoning action of automatic bilge pumps I refuse to leave my boats with the switch turned on to automatic to pump the bilge. Siphoning action, however, can be prevented by installing a vent loop (sometimes called an antisiphon loop or an antisiphon device), or a check valve.

Submersible electric bilge pumps (See Plate 14), are generally much less expensive than nonsubmersible ones and, because of the environment in which they work, they also are shorter-lived. The motors are hermetically sealed, so instead of buying replacement parts, you usually buy a whole new pump. While most of them can be run dry, they will last longer if you avoid letting that happen.

For pumping huge volumes of water in an emergency, a belt-driven clutch pump can be run off the ship's engine (See Plate 15). The clutch can be either a hand lever or electric. A vacuum switch can be added to disengage the clutch automatically and prevent the pump from running dry. This is a good idea because these pumps generally have a flexible impeller that depends on the flow of water for its lubrication. If the pump runs dry it will destroy the impeller in a few seconds.

An emergency bilge pump can be rigged by using the engine's raw water pump, diverting the pump suction from the seacock to the bilge with a Y gate valve. Care must be taken to switch the Y gate back to the seacock position as soon as the bilge is dry (See Figure 15).

Plate 15 *A clutch-driven pump, run off the ship's engine, will pump huge volumes of water in an emergency.* (PHOTO COURTESY ITT JABSCO PRODUCTS.)

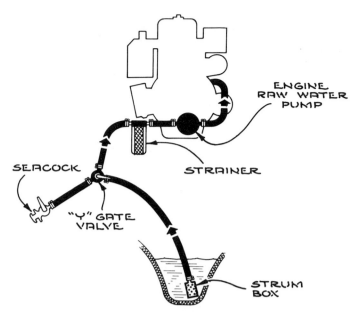

Figure 15 *A pressurized saltwater system using the engine raw water pump. Hot or cold water can be drawn.*

HEADS

Although the U.S. government has regulations governing marine sanitation devices, the Coast Guard admits that right now it's making no special effort to enforce them. Manufacturers, nonetheless, are in high gear cranking out cer-

Plate 16 *A Y gate valve installed in the plumbing system can divert sewage into a holding tank, treatment unit or directly overboard.* (PHOTO COURTESY OF ITT JABSCO PRODUCTS.)

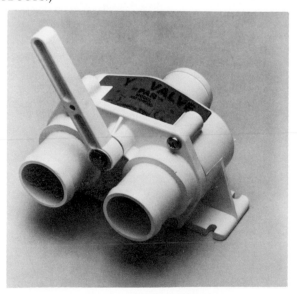

tified equipment. My guess is that the big sellers are Y gate valves (See Plate 16).

PORTABLE TOILETS

We've heard a lot of bantering about Herreshoff's cedar bucket. Don't laugh too hard: we used a plastic bucket on *Sabrina* and it was a simple and efficient solution. *At Last* had a galvanized bucket that fit under a hinged step; it even had a wood seat. That served us well for almost a year until the head compartment was completed and a marine toilet installed.

Portable toilets, including buckets, are not considered "installed devices" under the law, and are therefore not subject to regulation. So, while we can say that a bucket is perfectly legal, that's only true if you don't empty it over the side. If you do you are breaking the law.

Portable toilets are generally unsatisfactory on a live-aboard boat. They are heavy and cumbersome to lug ashore for emptying and the small size of the holding tank (usually three or four gallons) means you'll be lugging it ashore pretty often. Quite a few marinas will not allow you to empty them in their facilities, claiming that it places a burden on their already overworked, outdated plumbing and that it frequently creates one hell of a mess. Several states around the Great Lakes do not allow portable toilets at all, on the assumption that most people would take the easy route and empty the tank over the side in the dark of night. This leaves us with two basic choices for a live-aboard boat: a treated flow-through system (Type I and II devices) and/or a holding tank (Type III device).

HOLDING TANKS

I believe the easiest way to comply with the law is to install a holding tank, along with a Y gate valve so sewage can be pumped directly overboard (outside the three-mile limit of U.S. waters) or into the holding tank (See Figure 16). There are a wide variety of sizes and shapes of holding tanks available. Quite a few have monitoring devices to indicate when the tank is full. If you don't have the space for a rigid tank, a flexible holding tank probably will fit into an odd-shaped space. While these tanks are heavily constructed (usually of nylon and a synthetic neoprene rubber) they should be installed so they will not slide or abrade. *Sabrina*

had a flexible water tank and we lined the fiberglass hull with a thin layer of foam to protect the tank. Flexible tanks also are a good choice if you only wish to comply but have no intention of ever using the tank—the flexible ones take up almost *no* room when they're empty (See Plate 17).

If you do use the holding tank, there are a few points to remember. Methane gas will be produced by the sewage. The Coast Guard assures us, "There has not been a single safety problem with methane gas." You can believe that or not. In any case, the tank must be vented overboard. Make certain the vent does not become clogged. Also use a holding tank deodorant that contains a bacteria inhibitor (an oxidizing agent like a biocide or hydrogen peroxide). All the hoses, *including the vent line,* should be a heavy reinforced type, designed specifically for this use. Lighter hoses or PVC tubing possibly could allow gas fumes to get into the boat interior.

Another consideration is how you're going to empty the holding tank. This generally is done through a deck fitting. The assumption is that the tank is pumped out at a dockside facility—but that's not always practical or possible. The wisest course is to be able to pump it out

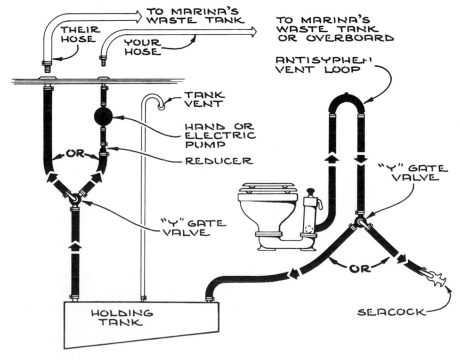

Figure 16 *A most flexible holding tank installation.*

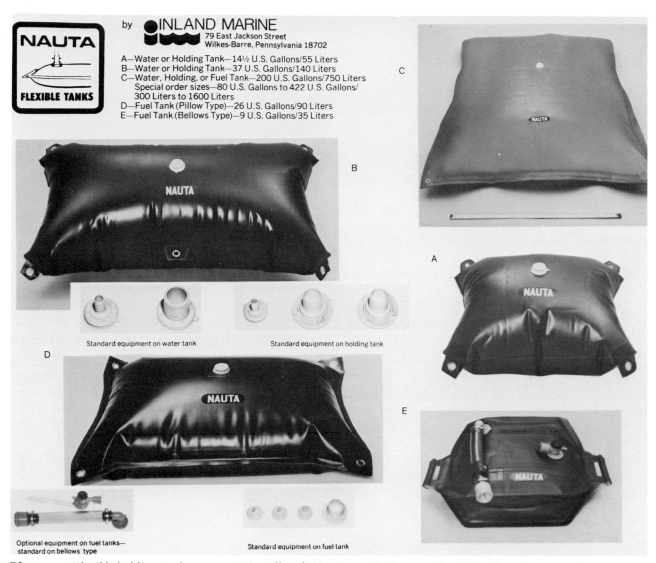

by **◉INLAND MARINE**
79 East Jackson Street
Wilkes-Barre, Pennsylvania 18702

A—Water or Holding Tank—14½ U.S. Gallons/55 Liters
B—Water or Holding Tank—37 U.S. Gallons/140 Liters
C—Water, Holding, or Fuel Tank—200 U.S. Gallons/750 Liters
    Special order sizes—80 U.S. Gallons to 422 U.S. Gallons/
    300 Liters to 1600 Liters
D—Fuel Tank (Pillow Type)—26 U.S. Gallons/90 Liters
E—Fuel Tank (Bellows Type)—9 U.S. Gallons/35 Liters

Standard equipment on water tank

Standard equipment on holding tank

Optional equipment on fuel tanks—
standard on bellows type

Standard equipment on fuel tank

Plate 17 *Flexible holding tanks are easy to install and take up very little room when empty.* (PHOTO COURTESY OF IMTRA CORP.)

yourself. PAR makes a dual deck fitting that has a standard 1½-inch connection for dockside pumpout and a ¾-inch connection for do-it-yourself pumpout.

On-board pump-out can be accomplished by a hand pump (use the diaphragm type) or by an electric pump. There are macerator pumps available for this that run on DC power for on-board use or AC electricity for dockside. Another alternative is to route all discharge into the holding tank and then to a Y gate valve, leading either to a macerator pump and out of the boat, either through-hull fitting below the waterline or to a deck fitting for dockside pumpout (See Figure 16).

FLOW-THROUGH SYSTEMS

Flow-through systems are basically sewage treatment plants on an individual scale. Most commonly, the waste is first macerated into very small particles, then treated with a biocide (usually chlorine), and them pumped overboard.

While the treatment systems are often separate units that can be connected to either a manual or an electric toilet, the treatment units themselves, as far as I know, all require electricity to operate. Since some areas prohibit discharge, holding tanks are frequently installed as an alternative to flow-through systems.

able amounts of electricity (as much as 1.5 ampere hours per flush). They also are complicated, so comprehensive repair kits should be carried on board as well as a good supply of any necessary chemicals.

Most of the systems require that you add chlorine tablets or other chemicals on a regular basis. One of the few that doesn't is Raritan's Lectra/San system (See Plate 18). It manufactures its own disinfectant (hypochlorous acid) by electrolyzing the saltwater used for flushing. If you keep your boat in fresh water, of course, you would have to add salt.

Flow-through systems are generally the most expensive and some of them do use consider-

THROUGH-HULL FITTINGS

All through-hull openings near or below the waterline should be fitted with marine seacocks. I have seen boats equipped with brass gate valves—an invitation to trouble. Seacocks can either be bronze or a glass-reinforced nylon—like the Zytel seacocks imported by R. C. Marine Corp. of Redondo Beach, California.

The fewer through-hull fittings a boat has, the better. We eliminated two of *Saga's* the first time we had her hauled by routing the galley sink drain and the head sink drain into the salt water intake for the toilet. The old holes were

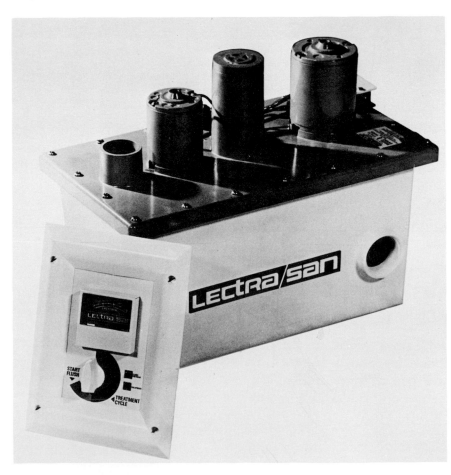

Plate 18 *Raritan's Lectra/San is a flow-through treatment system that makes its own disinfectant and does not require adding chemicals.* (PHOTO COURTESY OF RARITAN ENGINEERING CO.)

then plugged and glassed over. If you have more than one bilge pump, they can be routed to the same through-hull aperture, but they should go through a Y gate to prevent any back pressure into the unused pump.

SOURCES

ALLIED WATER CORP.
Marland Environmental Systems, Inc.
P.O. Box 9
Walworth, WI 53184

AMERICAN APPLIANCE MFG. CORP.
Mor-Flo Industries, Inc.
18450 South Miles Road
Cleveland, OH 44128

ASTRO-PURE, INC.
4900 N.W. 15th Street
Margate, FL 33063

BASIC DESIGNS, INC.
Box 479—Star Route
Muir Beach, CA 94965

GALLEY MAID MARINE PRODUCTS, INC.
P.O. Box 10417
Riviera Beach, FL 33404

GENERAL ECOLOGY, INC.
P.O. Box 320
Paoli, PA 19301

IMTRA CORP.
151 Mystic Avenue
Medford, MA 02155

ITT JABSCO PRODUCTS
1485 Dale Way
Costa Mesa, CA 92626

R.C. MARINE CORP.
P.O. Box 7000-38
Redondo Beach, CA 90277

RARITAN ENGINEERING CO.
1025 North High Street
Millville, NJ 08332

RULE INDUSTRIES, INC.
Cape Ann Industrial Park
Gloucester, MA 01930

SEAGULL MARINE
1851 McGaw Avenue
Irvine, CA 92714

18

Children Aboard

"Growing up before the mast"

SINCE I'M NOT a parent, I had to rely heavily on the observations and knowledge of live-aboards who raised their children on the water. I owe a debt of gratitude to Devin's parents— Jack and Pat Tyler (See Plate 1) and to Michal's folks—Chuck and Laurie Paul—who willingly shared their wealth of experience with me.

While we have met live-aboard children of all ages, the general consensus among their parents seems to be that *babies* are the easiest to care for. Babies just eat and sleep, and appear especially to love sleeping in a gently bobbing

Plate 1 *Pat and Jack Tyler, with 4-year-old son Devin, aboard their Flicka sloop* Felicity.

boat. As soon as they start to crawl and climb and discover the fun of watching things go "Kerplunk!" over the side, they can become a real handful. The "terrible twos," it seems, are just as terrible afloat as ashore.

I admire people who take their small children and go cruising. I remember one rainy day when I had taken our golden Labrador, Natasha, ashore for a walk. We were heading back to the dinghy, playing "chase the stick," when I saw a father from a neighboring boat trudging down the path with his two small sons —ages about two and four—all of them bundled in yellow slickers. I thought how fortunate I was to have no greater responsibility than a playful puppy.

As they passed us by, he looked at me with a sympathetic smile and said, "Boy! It must be an awful lot of trouble to have to walk a dog every day!" *I* was having no trouble and apparently neither was he.

Actually, I can't think of any boat kid we've met who didn't seem to thrive on the lifestyle. But we have met parents who worried about whether they were being fair to their kids. They were afraid their children would be deprived of a "normal" upbringing—lacking interaction with peers and everyday dealings with the "real" world. The amount of worry varies with the age of the child and certainly the problems in each age group are vastly different.

INFANTS

One of the first priorities is a secure bunk, a place where the child can sleep snugly (particularly when the boat's under way). You want to be able to bed them down and then go about your business without worrying about them rolling out and getting hurt if the boat pitches or heels. We've seen babies placed in padded cardboard boxes and in blanket-lined hammocks. Chuck and Laurie Paul strung netting across the forepeak and padded that portion of the hull, turning the entire area into a totally secure playpen for their daughter.

An ongoing problem, especially if you're cruising or on a mooring, is dealing with diapers. We know some who make frequent trips to the laundromat, others who use only disposable diapers (and make frequent trips to the trash bin). Diapers can be washed in saltwater, but they have to be thoroughly rinsed with fresh water before drying. This can put quite a burden on your fresh water supply, even on a

big boat. Pat Tyler says that disposable diapers can cause a rash in warm weather and she found it easiest simply to let Devin go without when they were cruising.

TODDLERS

As soon as children start to get around under their own steam, the problems magnify *and* multiply. Sailboats with very small children are generally easy to spot because of the netting strung around the life lines. Powerboats often have high enough bulwarks to make netting unnecessary. Netting, if properly installed, gives great peace of mind since it allows the little ones to play topside and prevents them from falling overboard (See Plate 2). It also can

Plate 2 *Netting will help keep baby and toys safely onboard.*

catch various pieces of boat gear that might get tossed around. Laurie told me, however, that it didn't take Michal very long to start climbing up (and over) the netting, so vigilance was still required, netting or no netting.

Toys should be the type that float. You can sometimes stuff pieces of foam into a plastic toy to make it buoyant. Steel toys and ones with wind-up motors don't last long on the water. Provide accessible storage for toys and games. Net or cloth bags hanging by the child's berth work well.

The sooner your child learns to swim, the better off he'll be. They can start quite young. Devin started at six months with YMCA lessons. I've heard of programs that "drown-proof" tiny babies. They learn to jump in, hold their breath and kick to the surface, then to float calmly and not be afraid when water swooshes across their faces.

It's always a good idea to keep a ladder over the side, even when the boat is dockside. Docks are usually high enough to give even adults trouble getting out of the water if they go overboard.

I gather that this very young, but very mobile, stage can be the most trying time for parents. While hazards exist in houses, they are greater aboard a boat. The small, confined areas of a boat will present many more edges and corners for kids to fall against, and it's much easier for them to climb up and around and into trouble. A kitchen stove on shore may be totally inaccessible, for instance, but on a boat it may be within easy reach of a quarter-berth or settee. "Child-proofing" a boat is necessary, although a difficult and time-consuming, task. Mike Saunders, in an article in *Sail* magazine, suggests crawling through the boat with head at child level in order to determine what dangers actually exist for him. It sounds like an excellent idea.

While a life jacket or a harness and life line may be too much on shore, they should be used under way when the child is on deck. Our friends Ray and Hilary Groves often kept their small daughter Carolyn in a harness with a life line cut to a length that would allow her freedom of movement in the cockpit and on the seats, but did not allow her to reach the edge of the deck.

SCHOOL-AGE CHILDREN

Despite the difficulties with preschool children, it's when children reach school age that parents seem most prone to move back ashore, or at least stop cruising and live dockside. Some are intimidated by the prospect of becoming teachers, even though the correspondence schools are excellent. The Calvert School (Tuscany Rd., Baltimore, Maryland, 21210), provides "home study" courses that cover kindergarten through the eighth grade.

Parents may, indeed, be the best teachers their offspring can have. They certainly care the most about the child's education, and within the stimulating, ever-changing world of shipboard life, they can provide a level of personal attention, consistant discipline and variety of lessons the child could never receive ashore. The whole environment provides a unique and, in my opinion, very special, education. Even on *Saga*, some of our most-used volumes are the reference books on birds, trees, plants, wildlife and sea life. The weather —so important to mariners—provides a never-ending subject for additional knowledge.

Pat Tyler is a teacher by profession, and she offers some advice to parent-teachers: "Our own egos are so interwoven with our expectations of our children that allowing 'our' child to stumble, fail or be less than perfect is often quite difficult." Jack adds that despite the advantages of a parent becoming the child's teacher, there is one disadvantage: the parent must wear several different hats and is forced to deal directly with the child continuously—with no "breaks" for either of them that school normally allows.

What *is* lacking, and what many parents feel is vital, is their child's interaction with his peers. When you're cruising, other boats with school-age children are few and far between. Finding another couple with a child the same age as yours is a rare occurrence (and usually a lucky one). We have noticed, however, that boats with children on board gravitate towards each other—we often see two or three grouped together with much visiting back and forth and trading-off of watching the kids to give each set of parents some time off.

The cruising child will meet many people, from an incredible variety of backgrounds and lifestyles. But they will almost always be *adults*. He or she will miss out on Little League, scouting, all those organized activities that involve groups of children.

This is not to say he or she will become a social misfit! The cruising kids we have met have *all* seemed happy, outgoing, well-behaved and well-adjusted. In fact, we tend to like them better than the kids we know who lead lives on shore. I'm very conscious as I write this that I am *not* a parent. These happy well-adjusted kids that I like so well are obviously ones who have adjusted to living in an adult world, and maybe that's why I like them. Perhaps they would be more "normal" if they were less well-mannered and more child-like. Only you as a parent can decide what is best for your child.

If you want to go cruising and he wants to play baseball, I don't envy you your decision. If you decide he needs his peers, it should not mean, of course, that you must move ashore. You could live dockside and cruise during holidays and vacations.

PRIVACY

Everyone needs a little space to call his own and children need it every bit as much as adults (See

Plate 3). They might have to share a stateroom with a brother or sister, but they should definitely be able to close a door and get away by themselves. And you, of course, should be able to get away from *them* sometimes.

A tri-cabin layout can be an ideal solution. Forward V-berths for the kids, an aft cabin for the parents and "family" space in between.

Plate 3 *This forepeak with upper and lower berths would make a nice stateroom for one or two live-aboard kids.*

Devin had his own "room" on *Felicity* (See Plate 4). The quarterberth was his, with nets for his toys, an opening port and a curtain he (or his parents) could close. Jack and Pat instituted a "quiet time" each day—time for reading, napping, writing, playing quietly, for any peaceful pursuit, but no *talking* allowed. They also took turns taking Devin on shopping trips, leaving the other parent some time to be alone.

Children who live on boats *do* appear to be better behaved. I don't think it's just because they live primarily with adults. Instead, I think the close confines of a boat teach everyone, but most particularly children, the importance of courtesy and consideration for others. A boat is simply too small for temper tantrums, yelling and slamming of doors. If a child on shore doesn't do as he's told, the consequences are usually minimal. If he doesn't behave on a boat, the results can be extremely dangerous. He quickly learns that if he's told to sit down or to get off the bowsprit, he had better do it and do it *instantly*.

Boat living is a healthy way of life and children seem to take to it naturally. They are outdoors a great deal, swimming, rowing, beachcombing, in a healthy, natural environment.

Plate 4   *Only 20 feet on deck,* Felicity *is a comfortable home for the Tylers. Devin even has his own room.*

Plate 5 *Zorana Jordon's parents gave her the dinghy as her responsibility. She rows it around the anchorage like shore kids ride their bikes around the neighborhood.*

Dinghies and kids go together like cake and ice cream (See Plate 5). The dinghy, besides being just downright fun, can be a wonderful trainer for learning basic sailing, rowing skills and seamanship. And it can be a perfect baby-sitter when Mom and Dad need some time alone.

Live-aboard kids seem to develop a keen sense of responsibility, particularly when they are assigned specific tasks to do around the boat. Boat jobs are generally more fun than shore jobs simply because they *are* on a boat. The reason they need regular doing is readily apparent to the kids, so there is more satisfaction gained by doing them.

I believe boating families are more closely knit, more caring and more sharing than those on shore—possibly because the parents have more time to be with their children. Jack Tyler says I'm dealing with a biased sample—that a family has to *start off* being pretty comfortable with one another just to *want* to isolate themselves on a boat together. It's a valid point.

Dick and Helen Pentoney told us that when they moved aboard and started cruising they became aware of a tremendous sense of "family teamwork," more so than they ever experienced on shore, though they always had been a close family. On *Heron,* they are all pulling together towards the same goal. They look out for each other and are more sharing of one another's feelings, fears and hopes.

Live-aboard families cruise together, shop together, walk and *talk* together. They share problems, frustrations and pleasures. If you think that living aboard would allow you more time together as a family unit, that alone might motivate the move aboard.

19

Pets at Sea

"The dog watch"

FROM A PURELY practical point of view, the disadvantages of having an animal aboard are pretty overwhelming—shedding hair, fleas, the *smell* of a wet animal, the ubiquitous daily dog walks and the mess of a kitty litter box. All problems seem compounded by the confined areas of a boat.

Yet I don't know of any pet owner who is purely practical. Natasha, our golden Labrador, adds so much joy to our lives that the disadvantages seem minor by comparison (See Plate 1). So, if we assume that you're willing to go through fire to take your furry friend with you, then the first question must be: what is *he* willing to go through to be with *you*?

THE POTTY PROBLEM

Most dogs are adaptable and want nothing more than to please their owners (See Plate 2). But this wanting to please can work against you when it's time for a walk and there's no land in sight. I believe it's the hardest obstacle to overcome. Your dog is housebroken, the boat becomes home and now you must convince him that something that's been a "no-no" all his life is suddenly "OK". It's not easy!

We anchored once for three days at the northern end of the Alligator River/Puengo Cut Canal in the ICW, waiting for a gale to blow itself out so we could continue. Natasha could see land and wanted to go ashore. There were plenty of trees all right, but sadly no land —it was swamp country. For the first day and into the night, when we'd say, "Do you want to go for a walk?" she'd leap into the cockpit and wait for us to bring the dinghy alongside. Instead, we'd drop in the cribboards and shout from below, "OK! OK! Go for a walk!" Finally, late that night, she gave up on a dinghy trip. I think we were as relieved as she was! We smothered her with love and rewarded her with cookies. We haven't had a problem since then, but we make a point of taking her ashore for a minimum of twice a day, rain or shine, unless it's absolutely impossible.

We try to keep her on a fairly regular schedule and she does not make unreasonable demands. We met a couple who rowed their dog ashore whenever *he* wanted to go several times a day *and* night, always. They planned their entire cruise around their dog and thus his habits eliminated any possibility of an overnight or offshore passage. This wasn't the

Plate 1 *The author gets a helping paw from Natasha. The "habitat" on the port shelf is home to Sherman Hoyt and Charlie Barr, a pair of field mice.*

dog's fault. The people were just too lazy to bother training him.

Be fair to your dog. Take him on a few short cruises at first to see how he adjusts and anchor where you *can* get him ashore without too much trouble. Check with your vet about laxatives for the dog—chances are that once he discovers he gets rewarded and praised for using the deck, he'll be fine. On rare occasions you'll find your dog really can't adjust to a boat, so the only humane thing to do is to find him a new family ashore.

All this points up the advantage of cats—they don't have to be walked. Your only concern is to find a secure place for the litter box (usually in the head) and to keep it clean and odor-free. Some people scoop sand from the beach, or shred up old newspapers. But many still prefer the commercial kitty litter since often it has a deodorant additive and it's less messy than beach sand.

TRAINING

A live-aboard dog must be well-mannered and *very* well-trained. An unruly dog may be cute

in your backyard but he won't endear you to marina owners if he tears through the trash cans, digs up flower beds and terrorizes the boatyard cat and he won't endear you to fellow yachtsmen in a peaceful anchorage if he's con-

Plate 2 *Sabrina loved her daily rows from the schooner into the beach.*

stantly yapping and starts howling when you row off and leave him.

One advantage to a small dog is that you can carry him in your arms until you find a place to put him down and let him run. A large dog should be on a leash, of course. But without a leash he still should heel and respond instantly to your commands. Going cruising, you're taking him into new and constantly-changing surroundings. You need to know that you can keep him under control in all circumstances. Training takes time and hard work, but it's worth it.

Natasha knows some interesting commands besides "heel," "sit," "stay," "down" and "come." She also knows "go below" and "get in your bunk." When things are happening fast on deck or the weather is rough, we don't want her underfoot in the cockpit. Remember that dogs sense the mood of the people around them. A calm skipper generally means a calm and happy pet. Start yelling, getting uptight and sending the crew into a frenzy and watch the dog go berserk too! We find that Natasha actually has a soothing effect on us. When things start to get out of hand we send her below and take a minute to reassure her that all is well—those extra moments help us remain calm, too.

Let's not forget that almost any dog can be trained to be a watchdog and still remain a loving family pet. It's instinctive for them to protect their territory. They needn't be trained to attack, just to bark if someone comes alongside at night to awaken you to possible danger or to scare away an intruder.

Cats may not have to be trained, but they should be *contained.* Not everyone in a marina will appreciate your cat coming aboard uninvited, particularly if he decides to sharpen his claws on the settee cushions! Get a scratching post and encourage him to use that instead of your cushions and topside canvas-work.

PET CARE

Find a place on the boat that will be your pet's permanent bunk, somewhere out of the way. On *Sabrina,* we tried to give Natasha the quarterberth, but she would have none of it, choosing instead the small space under the V-berth insert. But that worked out perfectly. She was enclosed by three sides and the top and was absolutely secure in any kind of sea and at any angle of heel. She was low in the boat where the motion was the least severe. I've seen her slide, blankets and all, part way up the side of the bunk and look totally unperturbed.

One problem that's always present is fleas. Be sure the flea collar you buy is the kind that works even when it's wet. I've seen a few that were supposed to be removed if the animal went swimming or was given a bath. We keep a supply of flea powder and frequently dust Natasha's blankets. We use flea shampoo and a special shampoo (actually a dip) to use if she gets ticks.

Keeping your pet's nails trimmed will help protect brightwork topside, teak decks and natural cabin soles.

Boat dogs (more than cats) seem more prone towards dry, itchy skin from too much swimming in saltwater. Long-haired dogs, particularly, may suffer from salt sores. We've found Sulfadine works well to cure them, although it's awful, smelly stuff. An oil-based vitamin supplement is a good preventive measure.

Another problem always present is hair. Dog or cat hairs can foul up bilge pumps, clog drains and find their way into virtually every little corner. There's no way to eliminate the problem, only to minimize it as best you can. The area of a boat is so much smaller than a house that you may be surprised at how troublesome this can become. The strumbox filter on a bilge pump is only designed to keep large particles out of the pump. We feel that an additional in-line filter (such as the Par pump guard) is an absolute must. Be sure to get one that's easily cleaned. Brushing your dog daily helps. Routine cleaning and sweeping must be done more frequently. We find our carpet needs to be vacuumed once a day. We have a 12-volt Black & Decker vacuum cleaner, the kind sold in automotive stores. In this respect, a poodle is an ideal boat dog, since they don't shed.

When you're cruising, it's a good idea to carry as large a supply of your pet's regular food as possible. Large supermarkets can be few and far between and you may have trouble finding a particular brand. Avoid kibble (dry food) unless you have a really safe, dry place to stow the bags. Even then, double-bag it in plastic bags and include packets of silica gel to absorb any moisture.

It's a good idea to have your pet neutered if she (or he) isn't already. What you don't need on a cruise is a boat full of puppies or kittens or an animal in heat, for that matter. Most people don't object to having a female pet spayed, but balk at the suggestion of having a male neutered. It does *not* turn a tough "he-man" watchdog into a quivering mass of jelly, afraid of his own shadow. It does make a male dog or cat less likely to go off wandering and less likely to get into scrapes with other males.

Losing the family pet in a strange town is a concern. If he's wearing an ID tag with a Jamestown, Rhode Island, address and you're in Miami, Florida, the tag won't be much help. We met a live-aboard couple in South Carolina (they were from Michigan). Their Irish Setter had a tag that gave the boat's name and stated simply, "in the harbor." Rory did go off exploring once and the lady who found him took him to the local marina, where he was reunited with Anne and Brendon. We thought it was an excellent idea—Natasha's tag now says, "aboard the yacht *Saga,* in the harbor," along with our names.

Besides the I.D. tag, he should have a tag showing that his rabies shots are up to date. The dog's rabies and distemper certificates should be kept with the ship's papers.

If you're heading south for the first time with a dog aboard, talk to your vet about heartworm medication. Heartworm is an insidious, often fatal disease. It used to be confined primarily in the southeast, but cases are starting to show up everywhere during the warm months. (The disease is carried by mosquitoes.) When Natasha joined us in South Carolina she arrived with a jar of heartworm preventive tablets and she's been taking them ever since.

It's a good idea to visit your vet before you cruise, anyway, particularly if you're going to remote areas. Your vet can help you assemble a first aid kit for your pet, recommend medications to carry and give advice on when and how to use them.

PET OVERBOARD!

Keeping Natasha from going overboard is probably my biggest worry. I admit I'm almost paranoid about it, since we once lost our black Labrador, Sabrina, overboard 150 miles from shore and in huge seas. We got her back safely but it was a frightening experience that I've never fully recovered from. In this instance, the scale tips in favor of a large dog. Sabrina was an 80-pound lab, with the strength to keep swimming while we brought our engineless schooner around and effected a rescue. A small dog would have been harder to spot and possibly not strong enough to keep afloat in those seas. Also, the Labrador breed is one that's noted for its swimming ability and endurance. *She* thought the whole affair was a lark, but Bruce and I were left shaken and scared.

A live-aboard dog should be a good swimmer, of course. But I've known a few who liked the water so well they would leap overboard whenever they felt like it to take a little dip. That's fine unless you're under way and no one hears the splash or sees him take the plunge. He must be taught to stay aboard unless he has your permission to swim.

There are life jackets made especially for dogs. But even with a life jacket, give some thought as to how you would get the dog back aboard if he does go over the side. This problem increases in direct proportion to the weight of the dog and the height of the freeboard. We rescued Sabrina by getting her into the dinghy. Then she scrambled from the dinghy seat to the boat's deck. Our Trinka dinghy is stable enough to allow such a maneuver, even in rough seas, and we were towing the dinghy so it was ready for action.

Small dogs and cats can be scooped up with a large fish net, but make sure it's sturdy enough. Larger dogs are better off wearing a harness instead of a collar. I've seen ones made of heavy webbing, like the "Pet Safety Harness" from June Enterprises (See Plate 3). These can have a heavy strap or a large ring on top so the dog can be grabbed with a boat hook. The only way you can get a line attached to him is to don your own life jacket and safety line and go in the water with him.

A platform-type boarding ladder can aid in retrieval, assuming the boat is large enough to warrant carrying one. *Saga* has fairly high freeboard so we built a single platform step for Natasha so she could jump in and out of the dinghy by herself. The step measures 11½

inches by 20½ inches and is hinged to fit flush against the hull when not in use. Netting strung around the life lines may be a little unsightly in appearance, but they ease the dog-overboard worries.

Bruce's brother leaves a length of heavy line hanging over the side so if his cat falls in she can climb back aboard. I knew a sailor in California who spent considerable time throwing his Siamese cat into the water and teaching her to climb aboard via the bobstay chain.

If you're going to leave a dog on a leash while he's aboard, make very sure it's short enough he can't slip over the side and hang himself. A collar should be loose enough so it will slip over his head if he gets it caught on something. Bruce once lived on a schooner in Ft. Lauderdale with another fellow, who owned two German shepherds. The dogs would frequently leap over the side, swim ashore, then swim back to the boat and climb up the accommodation ladder. When alone on the boat they were usually put on a leash. One day he and Bob were walking across the bridge to the cove where the boat was anchored, when they heard a dog yelping. One of the shepherds had jumped overboard and was hanging just below the

Plate 3 *This sturdy harness will make it easier to get your pet back aboard. The harnesses are custom made for each dog for a good fit.* (PHOTO COURTESY OF JUNE ENTERPRISES.)

sheer, choking to death on an aptly named choke-chain collar. Bruce ran for the dinghy and Bob jumped off the bridge to swim to the boat. They saved the dog, and it was the last time they used that type of collar. From then on, the dogs were either left below or on a short length of line that restricted them to the cockpit.

OTHER FURRY FRIENDS

Dogs and cats aren't the only types of pets, of course. Hamsters, gerbils or mice all make sweet, friendly little pets. They are clean, don't eat or drink much and their cages don't require a lot of space. Our tiny grey field mice, Sherman Hoyt and Charlie Barr, have been with us for over two years and they have the best sea legs of anyone aboard.

Birds too, are good pets, provided you can find a suitable place for the cage. Take care to choose a hardy, adaptable breed. Some types of birds are highly susceptible to drafts, changes in temperature, etc.

GOING FOREIGN

A long-distance cruise, crossing oceans and visiting foreign countries, brings forth new considerations, such as how to exercise the animal, particularly a dog, if you're at sea for days or weeks on end. Some dogs *do* need a great deal of exercise. Others can have acres to run in and will spend all day lying on the back porch. It's been my impression that most boat dogs get plenty of exercise, more than most shore people would believe. They certainly live in a healthier environment than a city dog who's confined to an apartment all day.

The bigger question on long cruises is the reception you're going to receive at the foreign port. Some countries require only a valid rabies certificate, some will quarantine the animal on arrival and some will not allow you to land at all. Check the regulations of every country you plan to visit or even *might* visit *before* you set sail. You may be faced with some hard choices. Only you can decide if you and your pet will be able to survive a lengthy quarantine. Also, is the boat big enough to allow him sufficient exercise and freedom of movement and is he calm and well disciplined enough to accept the rough parts of any long passage and still come up wagging his tail (or purring).

Despite all the problems inherent in having a pet aboard, I have to point out that every boat dog or cat I've met seemed to be trim, fit and happy with his way of life. Natasha loves living aboard. She'll sit for hours facing the wind, ears awing, sniffing the air, soaking up sunshine and watching for sea birds or porpoises. After we've been ashore for awhile, she's the first one back in the dinghy and ready for the row home.

SOURCES

JUNE ENTERPRISES
222 St. Charles Street
Victoria B.C. Canada
V8S 3M7

20

Boat Plants

"The greening of a yacht"

HOUSE PLANTS ARE one of the nicest ways to add a touch of hominess to your boat. Notice I didn't say the easiest! Before moving aboard, my house on shore was a jungle, overflowing with every imaginable variety of plant. It wasn't until I started growing plants aboard that I experienced some smashing failures.

There are several reasons why it's harder to keep plants healthy afloat than ashore. For one thing, their environment is constantly changing. A house usually has central heating *and,* frequently, air conditioning. So the temperature remains fairly constant. A boat is heated sporadically, so both temperature and humidity fluctuate to a greater degree. Ample natural lighting is often elusive—there's no such thing as a "sunny southern window." Shelves are too often tucked under decks and in constant shadows. Most plants do not like drafts, and what you consider a *nice* flow of air in a boat will frequently be a draft to a plant. Plants do like *clean* air. I'm not suggesting your boat (or mine) is dirty, but the small spaces and low overhead can concentrate fumes in the cabin that you may not notice but will soon have your poor plant choking and gagging. Among the culprits arc fumes from cooking stoves, space heaters and cigarettes.

TYPES OF PLANTS

I believe the requirement for a successful boat plant is that it be hardy, easy to grow, and one that likes shade or indirect lighting. Both philodendrons and scheffleras fall into this category and are beautiful plants. But they tend to be on the large side and you may not have room for them. Among other plants that I've found easy to care for are baby's tears **(Soleirolia soleirolii);** piggybacks **(Tolmiea menziesii);** creeping Charlies **(Pilea nummularifolia);** and quite a number of succulents.

I've seen several boats that carry aloe plants **(Aloe barbadensis),** not just for their appearance but because the liquid from a cut aloe leaf is an excellent remedy for burns.

Another practical idea is to grow some of your own herbs in small pots in the galley. I've often thought that a small terrarium would work well on a boat, although I've never seen it done. The plants would live in their own humid environment, protected from drafts and fumes. As a general rule, keep in mind that flowering plants are usually harder to care for and require more light than foliage plants.

PLANT CARE

Even plants that do best in shade require a *certain* amount of light. If your plant starts getting "lanky," if deep, rich green leaves begin to fade, or if variegated leaves turn to a single shade, it's a good indication that the plant isn't getting enough light and should be moved to a

Figure 1 *I think wicker baskets are ideal containers. Attractive and lightweight, they are simple to secure and allow the plant to be rotated or removed. A flower pot and saucer can be placed inside the basket.*

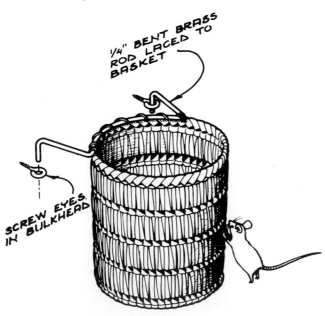

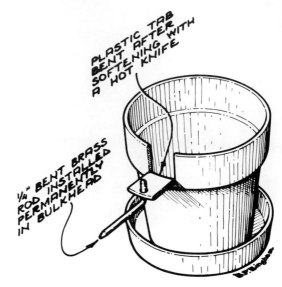

Figure 2 *An acrylic holder keeps a plant secure underway. You can make your own or shop around for one designed to hold an air horn or a liquor bottle. Small pots of herbs could be placed in a rack designed for drinking glasses.*

different spot. A plant in a corner or close to a bulkhead will benefit from being turned occasionally so all sides receive ample light—otherwise you're likely to end up with a very lopsided plant.

Whenever we're in port I put the plants outside on a nice day and they seem to thrive in the light and fresh air. However, few house plants like hot, direct sunlight so they should be placed in the lee of the cabin trunk or under an awning. Don't make the mistake I did once of setting a plant inside the dodger. The intensified light and heat shriveled the poor thing before I realized what was happening.

Saga has a couple of translucent deck lights over shelves that are ideal for plants, where they receive ample diffused lighting. A *clear* deck light creates a hot, strong light that would probably be too much for most indoor plants. A shelf in front of an opening port might seem ideal, allowing both light and fresh air. But be careful that a draft isn't created when the port is open.

Watering plants on a boat is no different than on shore—the amount and how often depends on the type of plant. I have found, however, that the leaves seem to need cleaning

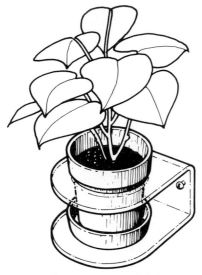

Figure 3 *This arrangement works!* Saga *was on her ear for a while in a gale and the pot stayed in place at a 35-degree heel.*

more often. Frequent misting helps, too, with the exception of fuzzy plants (like a piggyback) that should be cleaned with a soft brush.

For feeding, I've had good luck using plant spikes that are simply inserted in the soil.

Plants are alive and growing, and may eventually outgrow their allotted space. Pinching or cutting back new growth at the top will help them stay short and grow bushier instead. When they do need to be repotted (when you see roots growing out of the holes in the bottom of the pot the plant is getting root-bound) and you can't go to a bigger pot, you may be able to divide the plant and return part of it to the old pot with new soil. Or you may want to take some cuttings and start over, giving the big plant to someone on shore. When my creeping Charlie starts to devour the RDF, it will have to go!

I'm not going into a great deal on the care of specific plants, since it varies so greatly with each one. And there are certainly many more varieties of suitable house plants than the few I've mentioned. There are several paperback books that cover the exact requirements of each species and I recommend getting one. My habit on shore of buying a plant just because I liked it has had to change. Now I find out what it is and then check my book to see if it can survive living afloat.

KEEPING PLANTS SECURE

Perhaps the biggest challenge of growing plants aboard is keeping them upright under way. A tipped-over pot spilling dirt all over the place takes some of the fun out of horticulture afloat! At first I put them in the sink, but that got to be a hassle. They were in the way or they would still tip over, and it was just one more thing to remember to do before getting under way (See Figures 1 through 4).

I like to use a pot within a pot: a flower pot with drainage holes and accompanying saucer

Figure 4 *A gimballed drinking glass or cup holder is an excellent method for suspending small plants and being able to move them around at will.*

Plate 1 *Valarie's garden aboard* Heron. *Teak trivets were sawn in half, cut to fit the flower pots, then relashed with small stuff.* (PHOTO BY DICK PENTONEY.)

for planting, with both set inside another container *without* drainage holes. The container can be well-secured and the plant can still be turned or removed for watering or be set outside. The outside container will catch and hold any spills. Most plants like to be watered before the soil dries out completely. Moist soil is less likely to spill when the boat rolls, so don't let it get dry and crumbly. It helps to keep the top of the soil an inch or so below the rim of the pot when you're planting.

I particularly like wicker baskets for the outside container. They are lightweight, unbreakable, easy to secure and the natural "earth" color complements both the green foliage and the wood tones of most yacht interiors. Clay pots, for all their good points, are unfortunately both heavy and easily broken. While I would prefer clay, I stick to plastic ones.

You may be lucky and find a place on a shelf where the plant can be wedged securely or perhaps held in place with shock cord or light line. This will be easier to arrange if the container is cylindrical or square instead of the more common, tapered flower pot.

Hanging plants are lovely to look at. But consider the prospect of being bonked on the head by a swinging flower pot when the boat lurches. Better to secure the container firmly to a bulkhead or let the plant creep over the edge of a shelf. One idea for a very small (3-inch or 4-inch) pot would be to place it in a lamp gimbal or in a gimballed drinking glass holder.

Mail

21

"Keep in touch"

"HELLO, SALLY? WE'VE been waiting *three weeks* . . . didn't you send our mail?"

"Oh! Gee. I forgot all about it. Little Timmy got the measles and Jim's car broke down and I've been driving him to work and I had to make the sandwiches for the bridge club . . . so how's the cruise? Must be nice, huh? No worries, just lazin' around those fancy marinas. . . !"

There have been times, over the past seven years, when I could have crawled through a telephone line and cheerfully throttled a good friend. Mayhem, however, is a good way to *lose* a friend, and it's no way to ensure that your mail will arrive when and where you want it.

Receiving mail is a universal concern of cruising people and from the complaints I've heard—I could almost call it a universal problem. As with any number of "ordinary" facts of life I used to take for granted (like electricity and fresh water), mail has taken on an importance it seldom had on shore. Our mail is a vital link with family and friends left far behind. It's often our way of keeping tabs on other cruising folk we've met along the way. And, in our case,

it's how we receive the earnings that allow us to keep cruising.

Once you decide to go cruising for a lengthy period of time (most live-aboards do, eventually), proper mail arrangements MUST be made. The first requirement is an address. It could be the address of the person who's handling the forwarding. Cross your fingers that they don't move.

Many of us keep a post office box—this means someone must physically go to the post office periodically and pick up your mail. If your forwarder goes to the post office regularly for his own mail, this should work out. If they must make special trips just for you—look out! He could grow tired of the inconvenience quickly.

Deciding *where* your mail is delivered is inevitably easier than choosing someone reliable to handle it for you. Who is this magical person? The key word here is *reliable*—along with stable, trustworthy, dependable, intelligent, able to both make decisions and follow directions. You need someone who realizes the importance of sending mail precisely when you tell them to—not two days or two weeks later. My ideal candidate is a person with a house in the suburbs, a new car and a job that doesn't require traveling—someone firmly anchored to the shore. Forget about your boating friends, who are as likely as you are to chuck it all.

Friends may do if you only go on short cruises, lasting at most only a few months. But if you'll be away for an extended time, a year or longer, then problems are likely to develop. They may start out thinking it's going to be fun and the perfect way of making sure you don't lose touch with them. The truth is it doesn't *sound* like much work. All they have to do is gather the mail, put it in a large envelope and send it as soon as they receive instructions. Nothing to it!

Now try it this way. They must go to the post office every few days to check the box, figure out where to keep the mail so it doesn't get lost and the dog doesn't chew it up, repack it in large envelopes (and remember to buy more when they run out) and mail *immediately* upon instruction (it means another trip to the post office since the package must be weighed, charges calculated and postage paid—and it's pouring rain and they have a rotten cold and you forgot to send them more postage money).

The "fun" job can soon become tedious, another responsibility in what may already be a hectic life. If they do start making mistakes or neglecting to send mail on time, you really can't yell and stamp your feet, demanding that they "shape up." That's a quick way to end a friendship. Remember, they're doing *you* a favor.

I've noticed that cruising people who are using family members to handle mail experience far fewer difficulties than those who use friends. I'm not sure why, unless it's because families *do* feel a greater sense of responsibility towards each other.

After trying it several ways, I'm convinced the best way to ensure correct handling of your mail is to hire a professional. Since we signed with a mail forwarding service our mail arrives promptly and addressed correctly. We receive a notice when our postage reserve is getting low. And I hardly think about the problem any more. We do say, every once in a while, "Why didn't we do this years ago!"

When you are paying someone to perform a service, then you are entitled to insist that they do it right; it's a business relationship, not a friend doing you a favor.

We've discovered that our forwarding service, MCCA, Inc. in Estes Park, Colorado, is actually less expensive than having friends do the work. This is primarily because MCCA maintains a toll-free phone number that we can call as long as we're in the United States. We prefer telephoning if at all possible, since it virtually cuts in half the turn-around time for receiving mail. When we called our friends we never kept the conversation short, so our phone bill each month was frightfully high.

MCCA also allows us to use their address for the delivery of packages by United Parcel Service (UPS). They will then hold the packages until we make arrangements with them for shipping. This may not sound terribly important, but consider that many companies ship UPS automatically, and you never know if they are shipping promptly, back-ordering or taking forever. We can continue cruising until MCCA receives the package.

We received information from a half-dozen forwarding services (I wrote to several with classified ads in the boating magazines). Their rates were all comparable. We settled on MCCA primarily because of the toll-free number. They have proved to be completely reliable and efficient. It cost us $45 to join. That covered a $30 annual fee plus a $15 postage deposit.

One company appeared to handle primarily

travelers in motor homes and trailers. They would only ship mail twice a week. That might work for land travelers who can keep to a schedule, but I reasoned that, given the vagaries of wind and weather, it wasn't a solution for cruising people. Depending on when they receive a "send-mail" card, it could add as much as four days to the time it takes the mail to reach you. Look for a service that seems to understand the unique problems of travel by boat.

One friend now cruising in Europe is a retired college professor. He rehired his secretary, on a part-time basis, to continue handling his mail and keep track of his paperwork. She enjoys the work and the extra income and he reports that after six years the arrangement is still working well.

An alternative to a mail-forwarding service might be a secretarial service in your home town. This could be a good choice if you don't want to give up your local post office box as an address. Secretarial services, however, may not understand the importance of sending mail. Make sure they understand that when you tell them to send it, they'll do it *at once* and not let your order sit in an in-basket for a week. Their rates will vary widely, so it pays to shop around. We talked with one couple recently who are using a $15-a-month secretarial service just for handling their mail.

While mail-forwarding services offer little else (some do have a phone message service), a secretarial service can usually handle all sorts of tasks for you, such as paying bills, collecting and depositing checks, getting film developed or sending a bouquet of flowers to your great-aunt on her birthday.

There are a number of things you can do to ensure your mail will reach you as quickly as possible. If your forwarding agent is a friend or a family member, ease the burden as much as possible. Purchase a large inventory of different-size envelopes—as many as you think they'll need and then a few more. Include several padded envelopes for items that might need protection. Then, write in their return address, or—a nice gesture—have a rubber stamp made with their name and address. Give

them as large a postage deposit as you can afford. Chances are, you have offered to pay them for helping out and they have refused. If they won't take money, then send presents. They'll love getting treasures (however small) from far-away ports. And it will be a frequent reminder that you are thinking of them and appreciate greatly the work they're doing.

Unless you're prepared to wait a very long time, have mail sent "first class" or "priority" in the United States and air mail to a foreign country.

If you are having mail sent ahead to a marina or a port captain, the envelope should show your name, the name of your boat, *and,* in a lower corner, "Hold for Arrival". American post offices will hold general delivery mail for 10 to 15 days (it varies from town to town). If the envelope says, "Hold for Arrival," it is possible, but not likely, that they will hold it past the prescribed time.

Envelopes and packages mailed at the same time, from the same place, will not always arrive at the same time. Instruct your agent, if they are sending more than one item at once, to mark each one "#1 of 3", "#2 of 3", etc. Last year we picked up a packet of mail in Charleston, South Carolina, and sailed on our way. A second package arrived a few days later (marked "Hold for Arrival") and the marina in Charleston held it for three months before someone remembered we'd already been there.

Try to do as much weeding out and sorting of junk mail as you can *before* you leave. If you want an agent to do it for you, be very specific —your definition of "junk" mail may vary widely from theirs. Have your name removed from as many mailing lists as possible. You may want to receive an electronics catalog wherever you are in the world. But do you really need that seed catalog now that you've left the farm?

As long as you're in the United States, it's cheaper to buy magazines off the newsstands than to have them forwarded, particularly with first class postage. Cancel your subscriptions or tell your agent to keep and enjoy them.

You will find that there are a few people who will have trouble dealing with your new "middleman." My father and Bruce's attorney both fall into this category. "Just write and tell me what your next port will be," they say, "and then I can write you *direct!*" Don't fall into this trap. Lovingly (or politely, depending on who you're dealing with), but firmly, explain that the middleman is the fastest and surest way to reach you. Otherwise, you'll find yourself making extra trips to the post office or hanging around a port when you would rather leave, waiting and wondering whether or not that "special" letter was really mailed.

The following is a list of mail forwarding services. I'm sure there are some that I have overlooked, but this is a good sampling. The ones marked with an asterisk advertise in boating publications.

AIMS
  Box 1329
  Ontario, CA 91761

*Bellevue Avenue Executive Mailboxes
  38 Bellevue Avenue
  Newport, RI 02840
  (401) 849-2200

*Home Base
  P.O. Box 226
  Long Beach, NY 11561

*The Mail Bag
  P.O. Box 6592
  Anaheim, CA 92306

*MCCA, Inc.
  P.O. Box 2870
  Estes Park, CO 80517
  (800) 525-5304

*NATO
  Box 1418
  Sarasota, FL 33578

TOMA
  Box 2010
  Sparks, NV 39431

TRA
  710 W. Main
  Arlington, TX 76013
  (817) 261-6072

Urban Mail Box Service
  111 E. Second St.
  Perrysburg, OH 43551

*Yacht Services
  Box 147
  West Mystic, CT 06388
  (203) 536-3864

Land Transportation

"The options to autos"

MUCH OF THE American way of life is centered around, influenced by and dependent upon the automobile.

One of the great joys of many new live-aboards is discovering that a whole world of alternative means of getting there is available, including your own two feet! Those who stay marina-bound and keep full-time shore jobs may take longer to make these discoveries. But those of us who push away from the dock to go cruising learn pretty fast.

BICYCLES

We managed for a long time without bicycles —mostly because *Sabrina* was so small that we really couldn't figure out where to keep them short of sleeping with them. And now that we *do* have bikes we can't imagine how we ever got along without them. It has increased the scope of our travel ashore tremendously and we have discovered that bicycling is just plain *fun*.

It *is* a pain in the neck lifting them from deck to dinghy and from dinghy to shore. But that's just a few minutes of bother and well worth the

effort. The lifting and transporting does point up the value of a lightweight bike *and* a folding one. Ours are neither and when they die of rust and old age they'll be replaced with folding bicycles (See Plates 1 through 6).

One of the best features of a folding bicycle, obviously, is that it can be stowed more easily than a standard bike. Chances are good it can be stowed below, out of the weather. Topside, a canvas (not plastic) cover will offer some protection and will also help "smooth out" the whole assembly so you're less likely to snag a handlebar or smear grease from the chain all over your slacks. Our non-folding bikes are kept lashed to the life lines, as far aft as we can get them. It's the parts that stick out that make them so unwieldy. You can reduce the thickness considerably by removing the handlebars, the pedals and the seat. This will reduce most bikes to about six inches wide, and at the same time eliminate most of what you snag on and trip over.

I'm convinced that expensive 10-speed racers are not worth their cost aboard a boat. They are just as prone to rust as the cheaper models and, ashore, more of an invitation to theft. A

275

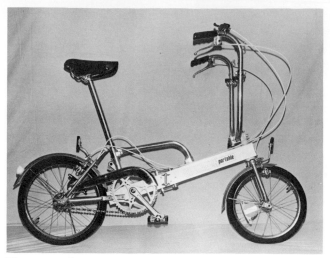

Plate 1 *The 3-speed Bickerton portable bicycle weighs 23 pounds and is constructed almost entirely of aluminum.* (PHOTO COURTESY BICKERTON BICYCLES (USA) INC.)

Plate 4 *The Workman folding bicycle is available as single speed or 3-speed. It weighs 35 pounds.* (PHOTO COURTESY JIM MINCHER, TWO WHEELER DEALER.)

Plate 2 *The Bickerton folds compactly in less than a minute.* (PHOTO COURTESY JIM MINCHER, TWO WHEELER DEALER.)

Plate 5 *The Workman folds up to measure 34" x 30" x 10".* (PHOTO COURTESY JIM MINCHER, TWO WHEELER DEALER.)

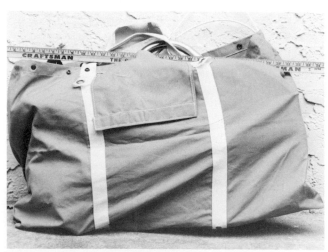

Plate 3 *The Bickerton stores in a canvas bag measuring 30" x 20" x 10".* (PHOTO COURTESY JIM MINCHER, TWO WHEELER DEALER.)

Plate 6 *A Stuyvesant bicycle can be either single or 3-speed. It weighs 34 pounds and can be folded in half.* (PHOTO COURTESY STUYVESANT BICYCLE DISTRIBUTORS.)

Plate 7 *Each of our bikes can carry, in folding baskets,
two chuck-full grocery bags.*

good chain or wire cable, preferably vinyl-covered with a padlock, is a must.

Bikes, especially those left topside, do require care to prolong their useful lives. One of the first things you can do is to change as many nuts and bolts as possible to stainless steel. Even the control cables on three-speed and 10-speed bikes can be changed to stainless steel. Remember that cables encased in conduit must be kept oiled.

Keep the bike oiled and greased. For this the waterproof water pump grease is great. The operation of a bike depends on the smoothness of the chain. Take the bike ashore periodically and scrub the chain with a toothbrush, using a lubricant like WD40 or CRC.

My bike has a wicker basket on the handlebars, and both bikes have metal rear carriers and a pair of folding metal baskets. When open, each basket measures 7¼" x 12¾" x 8½" deep, and will hold a standard grocery bag (See Plate 7). To close them, the bottom raises up, the ends fold in half inward and the entire basket fits flush against the rear of the bike (See Plate 8).

We saw a man's bike in a marina parking lot that was fitted with a triangular canvas bag attached to the bike's crossbar, inside the tubular framework. You can buy two-wheeled bike trailers or carts that tow along behind the bike and are great for carrying a big load of gear. Most of them will fold fairly flat for stowage.

For traveling long distances or in mountainous country (or just because you're lazy!), you can add a small motor to your bike. The gas motors will get up to 200 mpg and weigh from 7 to 11 pounds.

Bumble-Bike's 1.3-hp. motor attaches to the rear fork of just about any bike and will go up to 35 mph (See Plate 9).

Bike Bugs' 1.2-hp. motor mounts on the *front* fork, instead of the rear, and will go up to 24 mph. Both motors are started by pedaling

Plate 8 *The wire baskets collapse to fit flush against the rear of the bike.*

Plate 10 *The folding Di Blasi moped weighs only 72 pounds.* (PHOTO COURTESY JAMES C. MOONEY FOR PED-MO INTERNATIONAL, INC.)

Plate 9 *Bumble-Bike's 1.3-hp motor will let you travel at up to 35 mph. It attaches to the rear of the bicycle.* (PHOTO COURTESY OF BUMBLE-BIKE.)

up to a certain rpm (usually 5 to 10 mph) and then engaging the motor.

Most towns do not require special licenses or permits for a motorized bike. If they do, it's a simple matter to remove the engine. Having the engine on the bike does not interfere with normal pedaling and the added weight is scarcely noticeable.

MOPEDS AND MOTORCYCLES

Mopeds and motorcycles designed for "street use" generally have to be licensed (which might also mean insured), and in most areas you are required to wear a helmet. The license could be a hassle if you are cruising and on the move a lot.

The biggest disadvantage, even with a moped, is the weight. Even the small DiBlasi

Plate 11 *The Di Blasi moped folds to an amazingly compact package.* ((PHOTO COURTESY JAMES C. MOONEY FOR PED-MO INTERNATIONAL, INC.)

Plate 12 *The Di Blasi moped stores neatly in its own carrying case.* (PHOTO COURTESY JAMES C. MOONEY FOR PED-MO INTERNATIONAL, INC.)

weighs 72 pounds—no small job to swing off the boat and into a dinghy. The DiBlasi is one of the few *folding* mopeds (See Plates 10 through 12).

Another disadvantage is that, unlike a motorized bicycle, it is not easy to pedal a moped. You can do it, but it's *work*.

If you are staying at a marina, however, where you can leave the bike ashore most of the time, you might find a moped a viable alternative to a car. We have friends who work at shore jobs for six months to a year at a time, then cruise for a year or so. While living dockside and working ashore, they each buy a small motorcycle. When they leave for the cruise, they sell the cycles.

CARS

All right, I'll admit it. Sometimes it *is* nice to have a car—like when it's raining and you must go somewhere. Occasionally, someone is nice enough to lend us their car, but after a few traffic snarls we remember again why we like our bikes so much! Even if you're working and consider a car a necessity, it is still a major expense—licenses, insurance, repairs and, of course, fuel.

When you're cruising, a car may be more trouble than it's worth. You travel from one port to another by boat, then someone must return to pick up the car and drive it to the new area. If you anchor out, it's not always easy to find a place to park. Marinas usually frown (justifiably) on people who use their parking lots but don't pay for dockage. And some municipalities will ticket transient cars left parked for too long in one spot.

Large power yachts sometimes deckload a compact car. And one of my favorite ideas was on a 40-foot powerboat, Pete Smyth's *Great Expectations*. Her whole stern opened out, forming a ramp so Pete could drive a Volkswagon right into the aft end of the saloon.

One alternative, if you feel you need a car occasionally, is to rent one. This gives you the pleasure of using one without the attendant headaches of actually owning it.

Some marinas have "courtesy" cars that transients can use. Whenever we've stayed at a marina, even just overnight, there's usually someone who offers us a ride to the store or post office. Whenever we do borrow a car, we always top up the gas tank for the owner.

Restaurants in waterfront areas will often send a car to marinas to pick up customers. A quick phone call will tell you if they offer this service. And grocery store managers will sometimes give you a ride back to the boat if you've just completed a "major shop" and spent quite a bit of money at their store.

TAXIS

Taxis are pretty expensive on a regular basis. However, an occasional cab is quite inexpensive compared to owning a car! Before we bought the bikes, we would sometimes walk quite a distance to a town or shopping center, do all of our shopping, then call a taxi for the return trip, especially if we were tired *and* loaded down with packages.

BUSES

The larger the town, the more likely they will have a bus system. In cities, especially, you can usually get just about anywhere you want to go by bus. Remember, however, if you are filling an LP tank, you will *not* be allowed to carry it on a bus.

I know several cruising people who get on a bus in a new town and ride the entire bus route, just to sight-see! It's a good way to spot a handy market or a restaurant for a treat ashore.

Many small and medium-sized towns are

280

The
Complete
Live-Aboard
Book

WALKING

Let's not neglect that most basic mode of travel —walking. It's good for you, as you know—for some *better* than jogging—and most people find they enjoy it as long as their shoes are comfortable and they don't overdo it.

The biggest boon for anyone who walks to the store is a collapsible shopping cart. We're on our third cart (they do rust, eventually) since moving aboard. It will carry several bags of groceries, several loads of laundry or the LP tank. It folds almost flat for storage—only the wheels stick out. On *Sabrina*, the cart stowed in the quarterberth. On *At Last*, it was lashed to the underside of the deck over the quarterberth. On *Saga*, it lives on two hooks on the

buying "mini buses" that run pretty much between shopping centers. These are generally intended to help the town's senior citizens get around, but if one stops near the waterfront, it can be a real asset for boat people.

Figure 1 *A folding scooter that could accommodate bicycle baskets, but would occupy a lot less room.*

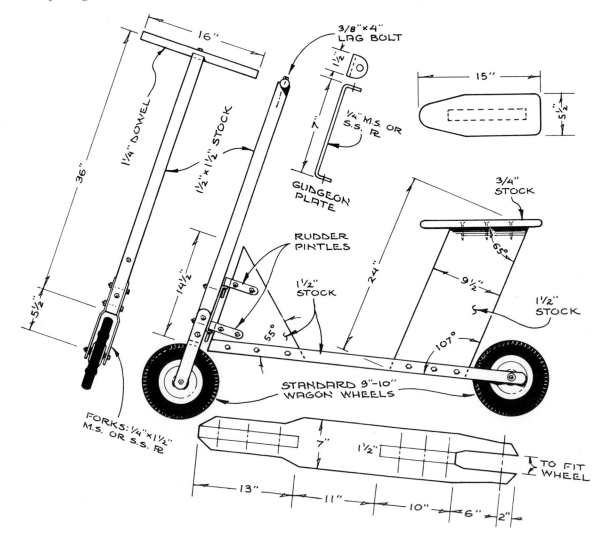

inside of the engine access panel. They are worth making room for.

SOME ESOTERIC LOCOMOTION

Hitchhiking is not everyone's cup of tea, and it *can* be dangerous, so I don't recommend it. However, I have on occasion stuck out my thumb and gotten a ride. The most notable time was at Hilton Head Island, South Carolina, that lovely community for wealthy retirees. It's the only place where anyone over the age of 50 has given me a lift and the only place where I have gotten rides in a Mercedes and a Bentley. If you hitchhike, pick your spot with care.

If you are the athletic type, you might consider roller skates. They are not bulky, would be easy to stow and easy to carry on and off the boat. You would have to have good balance, of course, to roll along with bags of groceries or the laundry. With roller skates, you could perhaps pull the shopping cart with you.

With the recent craze for roller skating, skaters are getting to be a fairly common sight in most towns. I remember during the transportation strike in New York City, stores couldn't keep them in stock. When Bruce first suggested roller skates a few years ago, we both laughed. Now I can consider them more seriously. Most shops won't let you come in wearing skates, so you'd have to take them off and shop with shoes on and the skates slung over your shoulder.

Remember when you were a child and had a scooter? Well, that's not such a bad idea for a boat, especially for the more sedate who can't get excited about roller skating. It would take up some room, of course, but a lot less than a bicycle. With a basket attached, it could be quite practical. Bruce designed a nifty little folding scooter (See Figure 1). Now I'm just waiting for him to build it.

SOURCES

BICKERTON BICYCLES (USA) INC.
9-11 Kings Highway, East
Haddonfield, NJ 08033

BUMBLE-BIKE
P.O. Box 1116
Havana, FL 32333

BIKE BUGS, INC.
P.O. Box 681
Bedford, IN 47421

JIM MINCHER
Two Wheeler Dealer Inc.
4406 Wrightsville Avenue
Wilmington, NC 28403

PED-MO INTERNATIONAL, INC.
Box 784
Lake Ronkonkoma, NY 11779

STUYVESANT BICYCLE DISTRIBUTORS
349 West 14th Street
New York, NY 10014

23

Wintering Up North

"*Keeping the ice palace comfortable*"

FOR MOST OF US, living aboard is synonymous with following the sun. If we're not off cruising to warm and distant foreign ports, it's assumed that we at least go north in the summer to keep cool and south in the winter to stay warm. Well, it ain't necessarily so! A surprising number of us winter north, with varying degrees of success. Bruce and I have wintered over twice, both times in the New York area.

The first year was aboard *At Last*. It happened quite by accident—we were *trying* to get south, stopped to work for "a few weeks" and were iced in before we could say "Jack Frost" (See Plate 1).

The second time was aboard *Sabrina*. That was a planned layover, again for business reasons. Since it *was* planned, we spent considerable time in preparing for the cold weather and were actually more comfortable on *Sabrina* than we had been on *At Last*, even though *Sabrina* was a smaller boat.

There's much that can be done to ensure a pleasant winter afloat and if it sounds like an awful lot of work, consider that much of it (like adding insulation) will also keep the boat *cooler* in the summer. So your labor is paying dividends year-round.

DOCKAGE

Let's assume you are thinking about wintering over in an area where the water is likely to freeze. Forget about anchoring out. I suppose it could be done, but what a miserable existence! You'd be dealing with the prospect of rowing ashore in freezing cold (assuming you could *get* ashore), maneuvering in ice, securing the boat in winter gales and running the chance of ice damaging the boat or cutting through the anchor rode.

We met one couple who were going to live aboard their hauled-out trimaran in the boatyard. They wisely decided to leave the boat in the water. Keeping the interior warm, even with insulation, while the entire hull is exposed to howling winter gales would have been horrendously difficult. I can't say that water is really an "insulator," but it will never get colder than 28 degrees, the freezing point of saltwater. That's often *much* warmer than the frigid winter air that swirls through a boatyard, so even on the coldest nights at least the underbody is *relatively* warmer. Navigating slippery ladder rungs is not too appealing, either. Besides, most boatyards, while fun places in

spring and summer, are generally dreary and depressing in the winter.

At Last was tied to a pier at a yacht club. The floating docks were removed to protect them from ice damage, leaving us with the problem of getting ashore with a nine-foot tidal range. Luckily, after a few weeks the ice grew thick enough that we could cross it to the shore at low tide. It was still slippery, but better than the ladder.

Sabrina was in a marina with floating docks, simplifying life immensely. The marina also had

Plate 1 At Last *was iced in before we even had time to remove the sails.*

a circulating system to keep ice from forming under the boat. They said it was to protect their pilings, but of course it protected the boats at the same time.

Preventing ice damage is a major concern of anyone wintering north. A marina, with jetties or bulkheads that keep the boats in relatively calm water, and one with a bubbler or a circulating system to keep ice from forming in the first place, is undoubtedly your best bet. Marinas located near sewer outfalls may sound grim, but they can have advantages. Several marinas on Long Island did not need a bubbler system because the sewer outfall kept the water circulating and raised the temperature just enough to prevent freezing.

You can purchase a bubbler or a circulator system and install it around the boat yourself. They are expensive, but worth considering if you plan to winter up north for several winters. Just be sure the marina will allow you to use the additional electricity. They may charge extra for it.

These systems move *deep* water (which is always warmer than surface water in the winter)

up around the hull. This constant flow of relatively warm water prevents freezing.

Bubblers work by forcing air through pipes or hose beneath the boat. As the air bubbles rise to the surface, they circulate warm water in the process (See Figure 1). Circulators usually consist of a small propeller that is suspended beneath the boat and keeps the subsurface water in motion (See Figure 2).

A bubbler or a circulator is not absolutely necessary, of course. *At Last* was iced in all winter and sustained no damage until the floes broke up in the spring and started moving out

Figure 1 *Bubblers work by forcing air through pipes or hose beneath the boat. Air bubbles rise to the surface, circulating warm water.*

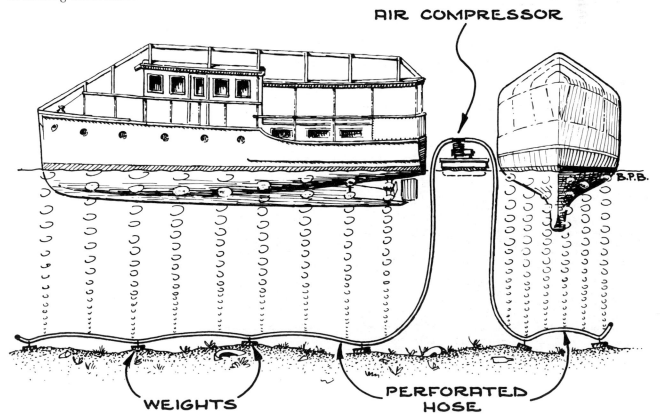

AIR COMPRESSOR

B.P.B.

WEIGHTS

PERFORATED HOSE

into Long Island Sound (See Plate 2). Even then the damage was minimal. Keep in mind that it's *moving* ice that causes the harm. Don't tie to a dock or pier that's subject to swift currents or exposed to winds that can cause a sea to build up.

Donald Street suggested to us—after the ice had formed, unfortunately—that we could have nailed a "skirt" of plywood strips around *At Last*'s waterline to take the brunt of the moving ice, leaving only small nail holes to be filled in at the spring haulout (See Figure 3).

When looking for a marina, carefully check the condition of the docks and pilings. If they're half-rotted away or just plain rickety, they may not withstand the onslaught of winter. We have heard of several boats sustaining considerable damage when pilings broke and fell onto the boats tied to them.

Willie Glenn, one of our neighbors in the marina, told us that before the circulators were installed they would wait until ice formed, then chop a clear space around each piling and pour oil into the opening. It would keep ice from reforming and protect the pilings. Of course, pouring oil into the water is now illegal.

Since most marinas charge by the foot, (you won't be going sailing) consider "shortening" the boat. You may be able to remove a bowsprit, a boomkin, an overhanging boom or an outboard rudder to save yourself quite a few dollars. We removed *Sabrina*'s rudder, primarily because we were tied stern-to and it made getting on and off the boat easier. The savings paid for the winter's electricity!

Check out the proximity of the marina to

Figure 2 *Circulators are generally small propellers suspended beneath the boat that keep the subsurface water in motion.*

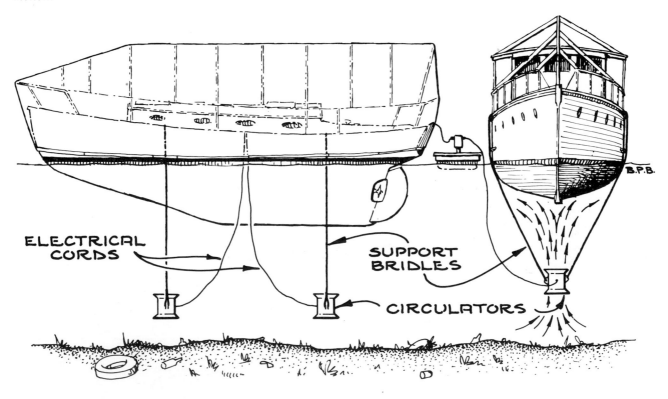

ELECTRICAL CORDS

SUPPORT BRIDLES

CIRCULATORS

B.P.B.

Plate 2 *At Last sustained no damage until the ice floes started breaking up in the spring.*

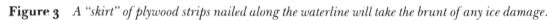

Figure 3 *A "skirt" of plywood strips nailed along the waterline will take the brunt of any ice damage.*

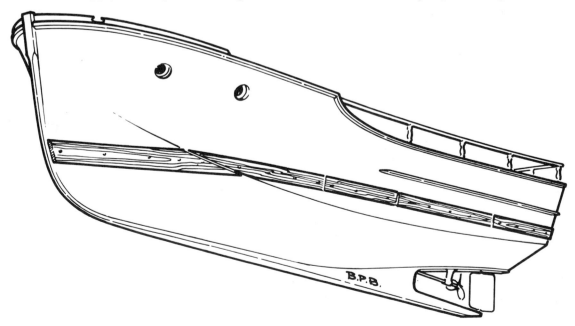

B.P.B.

stores and services. It's fine to go for long walks or bike rides in good weather, but it's not so appealing when it's 10 degrees and snowing. We were lucky that *Sabrina*'s dock was just a short walk to town and the train station that took us into New York City. Otherwise, I'm sure we would have seriously considered buying a car of some sort.

If you do have a car, remember that not all marinas or boatyards keep their parking areas cleared of snow. Many of them are located at the ends of little-used roads that would be one of the last to get cleared by city or county snow-removal equipment.

SECURING THE BOAT

Dock lines will receive more abuse through one northern winter than in several average sum-

mers. Most people use a much heavier line than normal or double up on the existing lines. And, chafing gear is essential. Once a dock line freezes it will wear faster and it will abrade anything it touches.

We found that ice built up on the lines quite rapidly, increasing the diameter by several inches. A weekly task was to go around the boat with a small hammer, knocking loose all the accumulated ice.

To help relieve the surging strains imposed by winter winds, it's an excellent idea to rig all dock lines with snubbers. You can purchase ones that are commercially made, like Line-Masters from Elvström, that are constructed of a very stretchy rubber. The line is spiraled around the snubber, which then acts as a shock absorber. These do an excellent job. Or, you can make your own. Bruce made a set for *Sabrina* using four strands of heavy 5/16-inch shock cord, seized to bronze snap hooks at each end. (Stainless steel carabiners also could be used.) Each snubber measured about 4½ feet in length and hooked into figure-of-eight eyes tied in the dock lines, leaving a length of slack line between the eyes (See Figure 4).

Boats that are side-tied would benefit by setting out an anchor to hold the boat off the dock in a winter storm. We used one for *At Last* (until both she and the anchor were frozen in solid!) that was about in line with her midships station

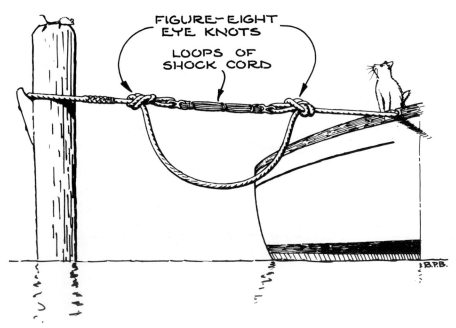

FIGURE-EIGHT EYE KNOTS

LOOPS OF SHOCK CORD

Figure 4 *Snubbers on all dock lines will help relieve the strains imposed by strong winter winds.*

and rigged with a bridle arrangement so we could make adjustments from either bow or stern. A 40-knot gale would have pinned her to the dock (and I've seen fenders burst under such circumstances) but the anchor held her clear (See Figure 5).

Every piece of deck gear that's not needed through the winter and that can be removed, *should* be removed. This is particularly true of anything that could be damaged by moisture or freezing temperatures. Remove the compass and all electronic gear that is installed in the end of the cabin trunk. If the face of the instrument is outside (where it's freezing) and the body of the instrument is inside (where it may be 70 or 80 degrees), you're likely to have problems with condensation and corrosion. Remove the instruments very carefully, being sure to mark all the wires so you can reinstall them correctly in the spring. Then stuff the

Figure 5   *An anchor rigged with an adjustable bridle will hold the boat away from the dock during a storm.*

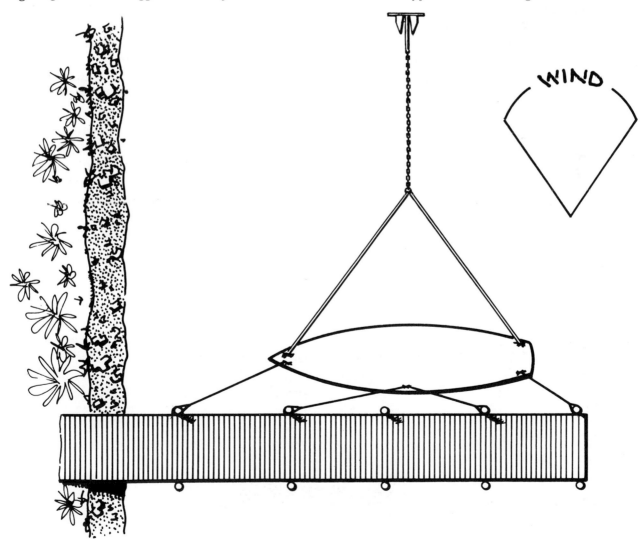

empty cavities with chunks of foam or even old rags or towels and waterproof tape (duct tape works well for this). We made the mistake of not removing *Sabrina*'s clinometer. The liquid (we thought it was colored alcohol, but now assume it was water) froze and broke the instrument.

Remove all the sails. A perfect winter project is to overhaul each one, checking for tears, loose stitching or signs of chafe and then giving them a thorough cleaning. If the rig is left in, make sure that every halyard is tied off securely so it doesn't touch the mast. Better yet, remove halyards, too. Rigs with internal halyards can run light messengers in place of the halyards to make re-reaving them in the spring an easier task.

Halyards (and sails, too) that are the slightest bit damp will become extremely brittle when they freeze. The ice will cut the fibers, even dacron, weakening and reducing the life of the line or sail.

If at all possible, keep your dinghy in service. It will be invaluable for getting around the boat, checking lines and pilings and chipping ice. The best way to stow it is upside-down, so water doesn't collect in it and freeze. Stow it on the dock, where it's easy to launch, not on the cabin top or on the foredeck under a cover.

COVERING THE BOAT

A boat cover will add immeasurably to your comfort aboard. We did not have one on the schooner and while the snow did act as an insulator, a cover would have been much better. Aside from the protection it gives, a major ben-

efit is being able to step aboard, shake off the snow, remove wet jackets and boots and leave them in the cockpit before going below.

The cover can be an elaborate, framed and fitted affair, with windows and zippered closures or as simple as tarps stretched across a framework (See Figure 6). It can be canvas, acrylic, a vinyl-coated fabric, one that's fiberglass reinforced or clear plastic. A dark-colored fabric will absorb heat, but it will also make everything gloomy beneath it unless the cover has windows to let in some light (See Figure 6). *Sabrina*'s cover was made of 6-mil clear polypropylene. It was like living in a little greenhouse. We took a lot of teasing about "growing tomatoes," but it turned the cockpit into another stateroom. On sunny days (and it was sunny more often than not), with the temperature below freezing, it would climb to 70 or 80 degrees under the cover and we could turn off the heater until dusk.

The type of material you choose for a cover should be decided by how often you plan to winter up north. We knew we would only be spending one winter on *Sabrina*. The clear polypropylene did an outstanding job and it was quite inexpensive. However, the sunlight and the freezing were slowly turning it brittle. Small tears were appearing by the end of winter, which we repaired with duct tape as they occurred. The 6-mil thickness was adequate for one season, but heavier material would obviously have been better. If we were going to spend several winters north, I would make a heavy canvas cover with large windows.

The framework for the cover can be of wood, aluminum tubing or even PVC pipe. If the boat remains rigged, the boom can be used as a ridge pole, I've seen some clever arrangements using the life line stanchions as base supports for the framework, with aluminum tubing sliding down over the stanchions or into the stanchion sockets (See Figure 7).

Whatever the framework is made of, the secret to a cover that will stay put in high winds is getting it to fit as tightly as possible—and I mean *drum-tight*. If it's loose, and the wind can get beneath it, or between the cover and the framework and make it billow or flap, it's likely

Figure 6 *Windows in the winter cover will brighten dark, dreary days immensely.*

Figure 7 *Life line stanchions can be used as base supports for the cover's aluminum tubing framework.*

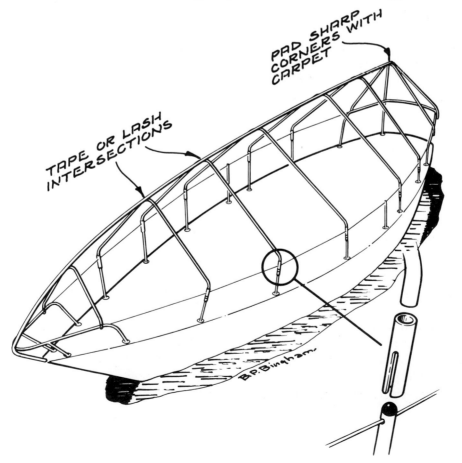

PAD SHARP CORNERS WITH CARPET

TAPE OR LASH INTERSECTIONS

it soon will get carried away altogether—perhaps even taking the framework along with it. If there is a corner that can flap, it can flog itself into shreds and start a rip in the whole cover in a surprisingly short time.

The task of securing it will be infinitely easier if you choose a *calm* day to do the work, and you'll want a helper to stretch the cover tightly while you're securing it.

If you are stapling or nailing a cover to a wooden framework, use a wooden batten to "sandwich" the cover between the batten and the frame and drive your nails through the batten. This will help prevent the cover from tearing at the nail holes (See Figure 8).

All openings in a cover (holes for lines to cleats, fenders, etc.) should be heavily reinforced. This can be fabric tablings, the covering material doubled over several times or the cover sandwiched between layers of reinforcing tape.

Canvas covers sometimes are tied to the framework from the inside, and sometimes secured only along the bottom edge of the cover. Keeping the bottom edge down is usually done by weights of some sort (usually sewn into pockets), or plastic jugs filled with sand and hung with lines tied into the cover's grommets. It takes a lot of sand-filled jugs to hold down a cover. We've seen strong winds lift the jugs and then slam them hard into the side of the boat. If you make the lines long enough for the jugs to hang in the water, remember that their effective weight is then reduced by about a half.

Several boats near us ran lines *beneath* the boat to hold the cover in place, then used intermediate weights to help it stay put. We taped *Sabrina*'s plastic cover directly to the hull, again

using duct tape. The sticky tape residue was removed from the gel coat in the spring by using naptha (lighter fluid).

Any cover will need a door so you can get in and out easily. But you'll want to be able to close it up tightly from inside or outside. It's probably the most vulnerable part of the cover. A zippered closure, using a heavy zipper that can be worked from either side, is the best solution, but this can be a complicated and time-consuming installation. Snaps or Velcro can also be used. Or it could just be a reinforced slit in the canvas with line rove through a row of grommets (like lacing up a boot).

No matter how tightly you stretch the cover, there's bound to be some movement. Any place it touches the boat it will chafe, so take measures to protect both the cover and your brightwork or you'll face a major refinishing job in the spring. Wrap all sharp or protruding fittings, like stanchion tops, turnbuckles, winches, cleats—anything that touches the cover. Wrap the docklines where they pass through the cover. It's a good idea, too, to pad the ridge pole *and* the toe rail or bulwark cap. You can use towels, rags, pieces of foam or synthetic batting from a local fabric store (the stuff used in making quilts).

It's not a bad idea to put ventilators in the cover to ensure circulation of fresh air. Snap-

Figure 8 *You can "sandwich" the cover between a wood batten and a wood framework to help keep the cover from tearing at the nail holes.*

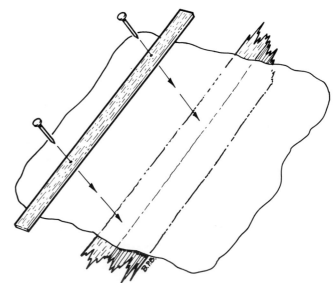

in ventilators, like those from Airlette, are both inexpensive and easy to install. They're designed specifically for use with canvas or plastic covers and tarps.

Adequate ventilation is of critical importance if you are using a heater that has a smoke head. Install vents at the peak of the cover so fumes can exhaust *outside* and make sure there is a continuous flow of fresh air. Check for fire hazards, such as the cover being too close to the Charley Noble. I consider it best to pipe the exhaust *outside* the cover.

Plumbing

To keep pipes from freezing and bursting, marinas often shut off the fresh water to the docks. If their offices or shops remain open year-round you may be able to get water from inside a building. If you're lucky you may even find that a few hoses coupled together will reach your boat. Otherwise, you'll have to locate a source of fresh water and carry it back to the boat in jugs. We found that our folding shopping cart was invaluable for these expeditions.

Both *At Last* and *Sabrina* were kept warm enough below so we never experienced a problem with water freezing in tanks or lines. If you think they *might* freeze, however, you can cover the tank or line the hull next to the tank with foam, carpeting or "space-blanket" material. Hoses and piping can be wrapped as well.

Plumbing for the head should receive the same treatment. Boat through-hull fittings are generally located far enough below the waterline not to become blocked by ice forming around the boat. If you normally use a holding tank, consider whether or not a pump-out station will be open year-round. And—equally as important—whether or not you will be able to get *to* the station. Chances are, if you've installed a cover, you'll be immobile. Then, it may be possible to find a septic tank service ashore that will send a pump-out truck to the marina.

Generally, marinas that allow live-aboards have heated heads (and showers) that can be used. If not, you may have to install a portable

toilet unit for the winter and make arrangements somewhere ashore for emptying it.

If the boat has two heads, you may want to close one off for the winter. It can be drained or protected with antifreeze. And while you're at it, pour a little into the bilge to keep bilge water from freezing. This also will protect the bilge pumps. Antifreeze will not harm pump or toilet parts.

Any piping that will not be used (such as cockpit drains) should be drained or protected with antifreeze.

If you decide to shut down a water tank, however, *don't* use antifreeze. Our friend Willie Glenn gave us a great tip for this. Since a water tank can never be completely drained, pour in a bottle of vodka—or the booze of your choice. It will protect the tank and hoses from freezing and add a little zip to the water supply in the spring.

A hot water heater located in a cold compartment should be insulated, along with the piping. You can buy a special insulation tape made for wrapping pipes. "Insulite," a flexible insulation material, works well, too.

Electricity

If you're living dockside and paying for electricity, you may as well use it. Be sure the extension cord running from the junction box on the dock to the boat is heavy enough to carry the load, particularly if you're using an electric heater. Check the draw (and the start-up surge) of each appliance. We discovered that we had to unplug the heater whenever we wanted to make toast.

The connectors to the boat and to the junction box should be protected with a watertight cover or covering. The plug to the boat usually has a threaded sealing cap, but be sure there's a weatherproof cover on the junction box connection as well. Or, slip a plastic trash can liner (or an old canvas duffle) over the junction box to keep snow and rain off the connections. Tie up the electrical cord at several points to make sure it does not hang in the water.

Don't depend solely on electricity for heating the boat. The possibility of a power outage during a winter storm is very real. And the marina may not be high on the priority list of who gets power restored first. Plan on some type of backup heat for emergencies, even if it's just a kerosene or alcohol space heater with a spare jerry jug of fuel.

A good reason for *not* winterizing the engine is so you'll have a means of keeping the batteries charged and 12-volt systems running if there's a power failure on the docks (I'm assuming you're using a battery charger and that 110-volt current is available).

Cold batteries lose their storage capacity drastically. Keep them warm, even if it means moving them to a different place. A good automatic battery charger will keep them topped up.

If the engine will be used occasionally, change to a lighter weight engine oil (check your owner's manual for the manufacturer's recommendations). An electric dip stick is an excellent idea. It warms the engine oil, making it easy to start.

A word of warning: make very sure the running engine will not be exhausted *inside* the boat cover.

KEEP OUT THE COLD

Condensation is one of the major problems faced by winterbound live-aboards. Even if the boat is kept toasty warm, you may find dampness, mildew and even frost inside lockers and cabinets. One of the most effective and permanent ways of dealing with it is by installing insulation. On *Sabrina,* we removed the wood ceiling and installed 1½-inch urethane foam planks against the hull, then replaced the ceiling. The decks received ¾ inches of foam. It did the job: condensation ceased, the dripping stopped, *Sabrina* stayed dry and we kept the heater running less to keep her at the *same* temperature as before.

The best foam for insulation is a urethane foam. It's available in rigid sheets, generally 2 feet by 8 feet, and from ½-inch up to 4 inches thick. It is a closed-cell foam that cuts easily and cleanly, leaving a fine powdery residue. Don't confuse it with Styrofoam, which is *not* of closed-cell construction, is messy to work with (when you cut it there will be hundreds of tiny white balls), and is about half as effective as urethane. One way to tell is that urethanes are usually colored (most of what we've bought has been blue), while Styrofoam is white.

Freon-expanded urethane foam (the top of the line) can most easily be located through refrigeration companies that specialize in building commercial ice boxes and refrigerator trucks. Urethane foams can *sometimes* be found at lumber yards or building supply stores, although it may take some calling around. Many places will try to sell you Styrofoam; don't accept it.

Insulite is also good, with the advantage of being flexible. However, in several areas of tight curves we cut rigid urethane into narrow pieces and literally strip-planked the inside of the hull.

Other materials, such as foam-backed vinyl and cork, may have a more finished appearance but are much less effective insulators. Foam can be covered, of course, with wood, vinyls or Formica, or simply painted if it's in a little-used area. But it *will* dent.

I should mention that insulation can be applied to fiberglass, steel or aluminum hulls, but not to a wood hull. Luckily, wood in itself is a fairly good insulator. Ceiling attached to the framing, with space for ventilation, is generally all that's required on wood boats.

Since insulation should be installed against a *dry* surface, the earlier in the fall that you install it, the better. Don't wait until freezing temperatures set in and condensation is already a problem or you may never get the hull really dry, particularly inside lockers and bins.

There are several ways to install foam (or cork) insulation. It can be glued directly to the hull. On *Sabrina,* we used an adhesive made for installing home paneling. If you're not sure about an adhesive, test a small area first. This is a permanent installation and you would not want to do it anywhere that you might have to get at fastenings. If the foam can be wedged tightly in place, you may be able to hold it there with the ceiling strakes and not even need an adhesive.

Battens work well for under-the-deck installation. We used varnished wood battens in all open areas that were "visible" and they added a nice touch to the interior. Measure carefully for the length of the screws (use stainless steel sheet metal screws). They're not holding up anything terribly heavy, so they don't have to be very thick. The deck thickness should be measured and the drill bit marked with masking tape to limit the depth of the hole. Neither the pilot hole nor the screw should penetrate more than three-quarters of the deck thickness. When installing the screw, if it resists turning when near its total depth it may be in contact with the outside layer of fiberglass (assuming a cored deck). Continuing to force the screw will damage the outer fiberglass and the outside gel coat, so back out the screw and try a slightly shorter one, or nip off the end of the screw with a pair of cutters.

In places that don't show, like the inside of a hanging locker, you can eliminate the battens and just use screws with large washers or finishing washers.

A flexible insulation (like the foam-backed vinyl or Insulite) can be held in place using snaps or Velcro if you want to be able to remove it. Such fastenings will not work on rigid foam—it would most likely tear away from the foam when you started to tug at it.

Lay carpet on the cabin sole if you haven't already. Since heat rises the sole will always be the coldest part of the boat and carpeting will make considerable difference. It's added insulation and it just plain feels good under bare feet. Scraps of carpeting also can be used as temporary insulation around water tanks, battery boxes and as added protection for anything stowed in the bilge. A piece of carpet on the dock and in the cockpit will keep snow and slush outside, where it belongs.

Close off and seal any part of the boat you won't be using during the winter. Be sure, of course, that anything stowed there won't be harmed by cold or moisture. As an example, there was no need to go into *Sabrina*'s chain locker while we were dockside. But it was an area that would absorb heat from the rest of the boat. We cut a piece of 3-inch foam to fit the opening and sealed it in place with duct tape. Other areas that might be closed off include a quarterberth, the lazarette or even an extra gear or hanging locker.

Ports and decklights are probably most susceptible to condensation. Trying to insulate them would turn the interior into a dungeon (although they could be covered only at night to retain heat). It will help a great deal to tape on a layer of clear vinyl or clear plastic to the outside frame, leaving an air space between the port and the plastic.

Regardless of the type of heating system you are using, it is important the heat be distributed throughout the boat. The addition of a small fan could be a tremendous aid in circulating warm air. This may be a good time to consider replacing solid berth fronts and cabinet doors with caning or perforated Masonite, or making cutouts for ventilation (See Chapter 8). Sometimes just a bare light bulb left burning in a locker is enough to keep the contents warm and dry.

One idea we adopted that turned out to be an absolute delight was making up flannel bunk sheets. You can usually purchase them by mail order (try L. L. Bean in Maine), or buy flannel by the yard and make a set of fitted sheets.

There is one disadvantage to living aboard through a winter that must be considered. You simply cannot lock up the boat and go away for very long. Any heater with an open flame should not be left unattended and most marine heaters do require some type of constant tending. Many marinas have strict rules about leaving a boat with a heater running, particularly an electric one.

You couldn't go off for, say, a weekend of skiing without either winterizing all the systems (draining the water tank, adding antifreeze to head and engine, etc.), or finding someone reliable to "boat-sit" for you.

Boat owners who don't live aboard, on the other hand, will undoubtedly discover the advantage of having *you* in the marina 24 hours a day. Many of our neighbors gave us keys to their boats and phone numbers where they could be reached. We kept an eye on all the boats, particularly during storms, occasionally retying dock lines or adding fenders.

Wintering up north requires a vast amount of preparation, followed by constant vigilance through the long cold months. Yet, like every aspect of boating, it has its own special rewards. You may discover a new winter sport, like ice skating or, as we did, ice boating—experiencing the indescribable thrill of screaming across a frozen bay at 60 miles an hour. There were quieter joys, too: long walks in the white wonderland of the state park near our marina, the marvel of studying the intricate varieties of snowflakes blanketing *Sabrina*'s plastic cover, the extra time Mother Nature seemed to have handed us by virtue of our enforced hibernation. Wintering north does not, and should not, have to be an endurance contest. It can be a gratifying and fulfilling experience—a satisfying variation in your cruising lifestyle.

SOURCES

LINE-MASTERS MOORING SNUBBER:
Elvström-USA
725 Boston Post Rd.
Box 446
Guilford, CT 06437

AIRLETTE SNAP-IN VENTS:
Airlette Manufacturing Corp.
P.O. Box 3494
Lantana, FL 33462

IF YOU CAN'T FIND URETHANE FOAM LOCALLY, WRITE:
Adler-Barbour
Marine Systems, Inc.
43 Lawton Street
New Rochelle, NY 10801

FLANNEL SHEETS:
Garnet Hill
Box 262
Franconia, NH 03580
or
L. L. Bean
Freeport, ME 04033

DE-ICING EQUIPMENT:
Hinde Engineering Co.
P.O. Box 188
Highland Park, IL 60035

Unarco-Rohn
P.O. Box 2000
Peoria, IL 61656

The Power House, Inc.
2682 W. Patapsco Ave.
Baltimore, MD 21230

The Real World

24

"There's no free lunch"

I'M NOT SURE when it happened, or even when I started noticing it. But the longer I live on a boat the more estranged I feel from the world "out there." Even dockside I can feel it: the waterfront is *my* world and anywhere farther away than a few miles inland seems to lack reality.

Whether this is good or bad, I can't say. What's odd about it is this: the world inland is friendly, receptive and fascinated by our strange and transient lifestyle. The closer we get to the water, to "home," the higher are the chances that we will meet anger, resentment—sometimes even open hostility.

PAYING YOUR DUES

Off and on over the past five years we have anchored in a quiet, protected harbor near Miami, Florida. The first time we were there, we made friends with a woman who lived on shore in a lovely home overlooking the water. She offered us a place to tie up our dinghy, the use of her telephone and even her car. Mary couldn't have been nicer or made us feel more welcome. Each year the friendship deepened. We came to know her family and they enjoyed stories of our travels.

We had quite a shock in 1981 when we sailed in and anchored. The usually half-empty harbor was crowded with boats. These weren't the well-found cruising boats that used to gather there, they were run-down and dirty, with garbage littering the decks and in desperate need of paint—boats that were, in a word, eyesores.

Bruce and I rowed in to visit Mary. She was as cordial as ever, but we could sense that something was bothering her. We had to press her before she would tell us what was wrong.

"It's *them,* the people on those boats! Most of them have been here for quite awhile and they look like they're here to stay. They park their run-down cars along the street right outside my front door. The leave *their* garbage on *my* sidewalk assuming it will be picked up. They anchor 50 feet in front of my windows and run around in the nude. Last week, one guy sat in his cockpit using a bucket, then dumped it over the side, *in front of my window!*"

Then she added, "We pay *very* high taxes for the privilege of owning property here, for being able to live on the shore with a view of the harbor. So, we're forming a homeowner's association to see what we can do about keeping those people out."

And there you have it. Any ordinances designed to keep "those people" out will have the

297

effect of keeping *all* of us out. You may feel they have every right to be there. Perhaps at this point they do, legally. But certainly Mary and her neighbors have their rights, too. Legality aside, I don't believe our rights extend any further than our transoms (and in the case of the man with the bucket, not even that far). In five years, no one in that harbor had objected to our anchoring there, even if we stayed for awhile. It was only when boat people became obnoxious, when they began to abuse the hospitality and good will of those on shore, that trouble started. And thus another nice harbor is lost (See Plate 1).

Sometimes "those people" are referred to as "hippies" and sometimes, increasingly, as "live-aboards." When you become a live-aboard, particularly one who anchors out more often than living dockside, you will have that "hippie" stigma to overcome. As the number of live-aboards increases, we all become more visible and, therefore, more of a "problem." Among the problems are that we are polluting the water, we are putting our kids in local schools and not paying school taxes, we are simply *not paying* taxes, that we are in essence getting a "free ride" from society, while the people on shore pick up the tab.

I don't believe this is true. Most of us do pay taxes, both directly and indirectly. Some of us work and some of us are retired. We all give up quite a few luxuries that people ashore consider necessities, in order to maintain our lifestyle.

Often the resentment stems from jealousy. A lot of people would like to do what we are doing but for some reason believe they *can't* do it, that they are trapped on their own treadmill. To see us on our boats, to all outward appearances having a wonderful time without a care in the world, sunbathing on our foredecks while *they* trudge off to work every day, is bound to cause some bad feelings, particularly if we rub their noses in it by taking advantage of *their* community.

Whether these attitudes are right or wrong

Plate 1 *Tranquil, protected harbors like this one are becoming fewer and farther between.*

is really beside the point. The point is that they exist. Legislatures and town councils are influenced by them and the results affect us, sometimes drastically. Laws are passed banning anchoring, living aboard or staying overnight for more than a weekend. Luckily these laws are seldom enforced and many cruising people don't know they exist. They exist primarily to keep out "undesirables," to give police or local citizens the option of enforcement if they choose.

A few groups have been formed to fight some of the grosser injustices and some of them have been highly successful. The Florida Boater's Association, for instance, managed to stop the live-aboard tax passed by the state of Florida.

Most live-aboards, however (Bruce and me included), are not joiners by nature. We are individualistic, almost loners. We like "doing our own thing" and letting others do theirs. The last thing most of us want to do is fight city hall. We would rather just up-anchor and leave.

Still, the problems ashore must be dealt with. We can't keep upping-anchor forever, because eventually all the "next" anchorages will be gone. If we don't want to join a cause, wave flags, write our congressman (with no permanent residence many of us don't really *have* a congressman), what can we do to improve our image and still keep that all-important low profile? Plenty, actually.

A big step is paying your way. Even if you don't stay at a marina, chances are you will be anchoring near one. People from anchored boats taking advantage of marina facilities is probably the biggest complaint of marina owners/operators along the waterfront. The instant your hook goes down, go to the marina office and **insist** they take your money. Offer to pay for dinghy dockage, for the privilege of dropping your garbage in their bins, for filling up your water jugs. If the marina is small and off the beaten track, chances are they'll refuse your money. But it doesn't hurt to press the point. A lot of marina owners feel that their shower and laundry facilities are inadequate for their dockage-buying customers. Don't be surprised at a flat no (regardless of money offered) when you ask to use those particular services.

When you are paying for dockage, attitudes do change. Marinas that allow live-aboards generally have live-aboard "communities" that are fun places to be a part of. And the nicer ones, the ones that bring the fewest complaints from shore, are the ones with uncluttered docks and uncluttered boats. Remember, the weekend sailors around you are paying for dockage *and* a house or apartment on shore. If they have to pick through live-aboard litter to get to their weekend retreats the resentment will surface just as quickly as it does against boats anchored out beyond the docks.

Anchored boats generate the greatest animosity. They are most visibly "getting away with something." Sailboats engender bad feelings quicker than powerboats and multihulls—particularly trimarans—quicker than monohulls. When anchored, it's doubly important to keep a low profile, especially in a residential harbor. Three weeks' worth of laundry strung in the rigging, generators running and power tools being used late at night, loud music, loud voices, landing a dinghy on private property—none of this will endear you to the community. Do you really want a police boat snooping around, asking questions and hinting that perhaps you should think about moving on? I doubt it.

A little respect for the privacy and feelings of those ashore can go a long way towards avoiding confrontations.

A lot of the accusations hurled at live-aboards are unjust, unfounded and sometimes downright stupid. I happen to believe that most of us *do* contribute to society and often in a more positive manner than those ashore who are so quick to point fingers at our "pollution" and our "living off the fat of the land."

When you're living dockside, property tax is included in your slip fees just as it's included in apartment rent ashore. It's paying a tax indirectly, but it's paying the tax just as surely. Anchored or under way, we are still consumers and paying sales tax on everything we buy.

I believe we control our pollution (sewage) as well as or better than shore people. Certainly we're more acutely aware of the problems. How many people ashore flush a toilet and ever consider where it's *really* going? Too often it goes in a direct line to the nearest body of water—a direct line to where *I* live. And, since a lot of us have turned to walking and biking instead of driving cars, our contribution to air pollution is practically nil.

If there is any one group of people around who is a living example of how to conserve our natural resources, it is live-aboards. Since we must *work* to keep our water tanks filled, we learn to use it sparingly. I would say if a live-aboard used three gallons a day he would be living extravagantly. I remember a few years ago when there was a water shortage in New Jersey and people were asked to limit their consumption of water to *50* gallons a day. I find that figure staggering.

Most of us can generate our own power. If we plug in dockside we are still using a fraction of the wattage consumed by homeowners. We are in the forefront of the movement that is experimenting with alternative energy sources —harnessing the wind, the water, the sun, for natural forms of power.

Since we take pride in our independence and our self-sufficiency, we use fewer of the services available on shore and are *less* of a public burden. We are less likely than a homeowner or apartment dweller to use the services of police, fire department or ambulance/rescue personnel. Aside from the "hippies," I don't know of a single live-aboard/cruiser who is drawing welfare or food stamps; who is not, in fact, paying his or her own way.

If anything, shore people could learn a lot from *us* and from our "strange and transient" lifestyle. I believe *we* are the wave of the future, the coming age, the new renaissance.

BUYING MARINE QUALITY

Another problem for the live-aboard, operating as he does in the real world, is his role as a consumer.

Time was when I did all my boat shopping at a marine hardware store because "marine" implied top of the line, the very best quality one could buy. I've learned a few things since then, and try not to buy marine unless I have no other choice. For many smaller items, such as sandpaper, paint brushes or flashlights, you're invariably better off in a general hardware store, auto parts store or discount house.

I don't think I'm being cheap. I know the yachting market is relatively small compared to mass-market household items. Anything produced specifically for a boat is bound to cost more, since it really isn't mass-produced. But if I'm going to pay a premium price for *any* item, I expect premium quality! More often than not, it's not what I get when I buy marine.

THE LIGHT GREMLIN

My biggest bugaboo is flashlights. I would hate to add up how much money Bruce and I have spent buying a "really good flashlight," marine quality, of course, at $10 to $15 a shot. Each one was encased in rubber so it would float, was shockproof, rustproof and weatherproof—whatever that means. Not one of them has ever worked right after the second use. Well, one still works if you rap it a few times. But the $3.95 flashlight Bruce bought at an auto store has worked like a charm for more than a year now. It's encased in rubber and has been left out overnight in the cockpit often enough that I actually consider it "weatherproof."

The first man-overboard light we bought was the most expensive one on the market and considered the best. I didn't object to the price—after all, my life might depend on it someday. Man-overboard lights are designed to hang upside down until they're needed. Once flipped over, they automatically emit a flashing strobe light while floating in the water. There's no switch—the only way to turn them off is to up-end them again.

Ours, however, became possessed by the light gremlin. It was hanging on the rail—looking innocent—when suddenly it started flashing. No amount of turning, twisting or shaking could turn it off. It finally stopped flashing of its own accord—never to flash again. We wrote the manufacturer, but the light was past warranty—tough luck! The second light we bought was one step down in price and so far is behaving itself. My only complaint is, couldn't a $60 light have been designed to float without requiring a tacky Styrofoam ring around its middle to keep it right-side up? The ring slides off easily and I have visions of someone (me, maybe) going down for the third time accompanied by a flashing, ringless, overboard light.

Our schooner *At Last* had four brass kerosene lamps. They were very pretty. They were also pretty useless. Each one had a ½-inch wick. The "big one" held more kerosene, but its wick was still only half an inch. They didn't give off enough light for either of us to read by, and no matter how carefully we trimmed the wick, they always produced more soot than light. This was due in part to the chimney being so short—the higher the chimney, the better they burn. We solved the problem by buying two kerosene lamps from a local hardware store, at $5 each. They had tall chimneys and 1-inch wicks and never failed to produce a bright, clean light. Their brass-plated steel burner units rust after a year or so, but are easily replaced for about $1.

Considering all my "fun" experiences with marine lights, I was less than overjoyed when Bruce decided to spend another $60 for a trilight for *Sabrina*. I agreed that a trilight was a good idea—only one bulb doing the job of three. It's just that I had learned to respect the light gremlin. The big day arrived. Bruce lifted the light gently from its packing. My faith in mankind was restored. Here was a piece of hardware worthy of the title "marine quality." This was no ordinary light, this was a work of art. We finally had bought something that was worth the price. The German-made trilight was beautifully tooled, with a brushed stainless steel finish and carefully engineered—easy to get to the bulb, but impossible for moisture to creep in. Best of all, it *worked!*

Before I turn off the lights here, I have to mention our compass. It's a fine compass (after we fixed the bubble it belched when it was only two weeks old) and we are careful to carry spare bulbs for it. When the light burned out, Bruce grabbed a new bulb and started to replace the old one. But what's this? Clever manufacturers—they had *soldered* the wires directly to the light bulb; there was no socket. And to replace the bulb we had to solder it back again. We do have a soldering iron, but the cord isn't long enough to reach the socket back on shore. Ah, well, Bruce handed me a flashlight so I could check the course occasionally. Oh, that flashlight! *Rap, rap.* There. Now it works.

Maybe you're lucky and have never met the light gremlin. But I don't know of a single boat owner who's avoided battle with the sly little rust gremlin. I don't pretend to be an expert on metals, but I do know that ferrous metal rusts and stainless steel, aluminum, brass and bronze supposedly don't. So why is our stainless steel stove showing spots of rust?

And the beautiful, special bronze castings on Bruce's brother's catboat—stemhead fitting, cleats, even the winch drums—all are streaked with rust. One sailmaker we know told us he was using new stainless jib hanks until his customers started complaining about rust stains on their sails.

Conclusion—you can't tell by *looking* at a new piece of hardware whether it has ferrous metal in it or not. But there is an easy way to find out. Steel is magnetic. Buy a small magnet and *always* take it with you when shopping. It's your best insurance against buying poor quality. Or, take the suspicious fitting over to the store's compass display and see if it makes the compass go berserk. Aha! Maybe that's why some stores keep the compasses locked up in glass cases!

Watch out for hidden parts that might be steel. I've seen all-brass door latches with *steel* springs, all-brass hinges with *steel* pins and brass locks with *steel* inner-workings that seized up after a few weeks' exposure to salt air. Our stainless steel deck chain pipe had a steel hook that rusted through and fell off. The seat of our "top-quality" marine head is attached with bright steel (now rusting) bolts. Then our marine-grade and (naturally) expensive electrical breaker switches were constructed entirely of bright steel and froze in position, one by one. We replaced them with switches from a non-marine electronics shop and they're still switching after three years on the boat.

While aluminum doesn't rust, it *will* corrode. I try to keep a good coat of wax on everything that's aluminum. What it never occurred to me to wax, however, were the zippers on our fancy Coast Guard inspected and approved life jackets. I just assumed they were nylon. They're only about a year old. I pulled one out the

other day to see how it felt—you never know when you might need one in a hurry. I started zipping it up and all the little teeth crumbled on impact and floated silently to the deck. Just what I need for emergencies—a toothless life jacket.

One metal (if you can call it that) to stay away from is chrome-plated, die-cast Zamack. I don't know what Zamack is, but I suspect it's pot metal. I bought a pair of oarlocks for the dinghy made of die-cast Zamack. In that case I *was* being cheap—what did I expect for $5? They broke on the first hard stroke of the oars. An inspection showed air bubbles in the castings—not in one of them, but in both. It's true you get what you pay for and I should have known better, but I still take issue with any manufacturer who dares to produce such garbage and then push it off as marine quality.

There are so many different plastics and vinyls on the market today that it's almost impossible to keep track of them—unless you're a chemist. There's PVC (polyvinyl chloride), PVA (polyvinyl acetate), ABS, Celcon and Cycolac—to name a few—and of course just plain "molded plastic" or "tough, durable vinyl."

Two of our tough "durable" bumpers opened up like bananas at the first kiss of the dock. We installed a plastic inspection port in a tank using a polysulfide bedding compound that turned the plastic brittle. We bought brightly colored heavy plastic mugs to liven up the galley. The first time I poured hot coffee into them they emitted strange crackling sounds. I looked down to see the coffee seeping out and dripping onto the cabin sole. The whole batch of insulated cups had each sprung a leak between the layers. On the other hand, we have plastic screw-top canisters we bought at the grocery store that are in their third year of service and have never crazed or turned brittle and keep their contents crisp and dry.

There must be a gremlin out there somewhere who designed stove-top toasters. Toaster #1 was purchased at a grocery store—why pay $5 or $6 for a "marine" toaster (we reasoned) when you can get the same thing for $1.98 in a grocery store? Because the $1.98 toaster is not stainless steel, that's why, and rusty toast is really awful.

Toaster #2 was a stainless steel model, a square-based pyramid toaster that would rarely hold the toast on, and burned it when it did.

Toaster #3 was a stainless steel flip-up, fold-down toaster that *held* the toast—but wouldn't toast it.

In desperation Bruce drilled at least 20 more holes in the bottom of #3 and now it works pretty well—as long as we remember to put a piece of toast on the top of it so the heat is deflected to all the pieces of bread, instead of escaping through the open top.

One morning we finished our toast and went off to a chandlery to buy some shackles for *Sabrina*. Wandering into a back room, we started rummaging through chandler Jim's "grab bag" collection of hardware he couldn't or wouldn't sell. There were an appalling number of blocks with plastic ball bearings that had an affinity for flattening out in use, lightweight racing blocks fitted with stainless steel perforated strapping so *light* they would tear under the slightest strain, "quick-release" snap-shackles that required two hands to operate and

snap shackles that exploded on the first yank of the release line. We found sheet leads and spinnaker eye cars that were plated right out of the mold without being polished first, so they would grind and wear on the track. Considering that all these items had first been offered as new gear and at full price, it makes you wonder again about the phrase "marine quality."

One thing to watch for when you're looking at sail track and genoa track—make sure the holes are drilled on regular centers. Some of them aren't, making it impossible to replace the track without plugging dozens of holes and drilling new ones.

Whether of stainless steel or bronze, a forged piece of hardware is always better than a cast one. We had several bronze shackles on *At Last* that broke under a twisting strain. We replaced them with Schaefer forged stainless steel shackles. Most of the hardware we use now is Schaefer. The shackles and blocks all have held up under sometimes tremendous strains, and the genoa and spinnaker cars run smoothly on their tracks. Vetus also makes an excellent line of marine hardware.

Paints and varnishes have given us our share of headaches, too. We've had varnish so thick and gooey you couldn't brush it out and varnish so thin it was like trying to paint with water. We like to use satin (matte finish) varnish inside the boat. One brand I tried contained, not powdered pumice, but a black, grainy substance that never really stirred into the varnish and left a dark-blue stain in the grain of the wood and anywhere the varnish overlapped. Two weeks passed before it was hard enough to sand off.

At Last had 63 wood-shelled blocks, all of them finished bright. A lot of work went into making them, so naturally we wanted the very best varnish. The first coat took a week to dry, the second coat alligatored, the third coat went flat. We kept thinking it was *our* fault—too much humidity, varnishing too late in the day, not getting the brushes clean enough—*something!* Those 63 little wooden blocks required days of tedious sanding between coats. I was on the verge of painting them dado brown when Bruce called the paint company. "Oh, my goodness!" said the company rep when Bruce read him the batch number off the can. "That was a bad batch. I thought we had recalled all of it." No, fella, you missed one! To their credit, they did offer to send a man out to refinish all the blocks for us. Once again, my faith in mankind was restored. They were so kind that I kept buying their varnish, but every other can seemed to be a bad batch, so I finally gave up.

After years of trial and error, we have settled on a few brands that we trust, like Z-Spar's white undercoater, and I refuse to try anything else—no matter how good someone assures me their product is. I have learned one thing about varnish, though: once the can is opened and air gets to it, the varnish will go bad in a short period of time, so now I only buy it in pints. The best interior varnish we've found is called Last 'n Last Satin Varnish. It's sold in lumber yards and general hardware stores at half the price of marine varnish. And it really does "last 'n last."

Marine electronics are sophisticated and expensive—marvelous when they're working and a royal pain in the neck when they're not. Here again, you get what you pay for. After we bought At Last and paid for the trip across the country to take possession of her, we were quite low on money. Still, we wanted her to have at least a depth sounder and distance log. We bought an inexpensive but well-known "package" with depth sounder, distance log, wind direction indicator and combination anemometer/hull speed indicator. After several thousand miles the log showed 32, and the depth sounder packed up—as soon as it was off warranty, naturally. The mounting bracket for the wind vane was so ridiculous the vane would fall off in the slightest breeze. We always knew when it was blowing over seven knots because at that speed the wind vane was slapping against the mast.

DO YOUR HOMEWORK

When you start shopping for electronics, you're getting ready to spend a great deal of money, so how do you know if you're getting your money's worth? Unless you're an electronics engineer, *you really don't know*. But if you

want, say, an RDF, talk with everyone you can find who has one and ask them what kind they have, how much trouble they've had with it and how hard or easy it's been to get it serviced. Then read everything you can get your hands on about RDFs, so you know enough to ask intelligent questions when you start shopping. We know of one manufacturer that makes an RDF with no null, whatsoever.

Our Aqua-Guide Columbian Hydrosonics RDF has given us three years (to date) of absolutely trouble-free service. Once, it got caught under one of At Last's deck leaks. We turned it on its side and at least a pint of water poured out through the vents. That was several years ago and it's still going strong.

We know several people who have built Heathkit RDFs and VHF radios, and they all swear by them.

Sabrina came equipped from the factory with Datamarine Instruments, and they have performed admirably. We did have one problem with the depth sounder—in the shallow waters along the ICW, it was flashing 2 feet much too often. We solved the problem by reading the manual and turning a screw on the back of the instrument one-eighth of a turn. If all else fails, read the instructions. Both Brookes & Gatehouse and Combi Systems are considered by many knowledgeable sailors as being the top of the line in marine instrumentation.

Our ship's chronometer has always been a Timex quartz-crystal watch. At its worst, it loses .03 seconds per day. Bruce tells me he navigated for years both in the Navy and when he was delivering boats up and down the East Coast using a waterproof wind-up Timex.

Whenever we have a problem with any item

of gear, we try to return it to the manufacturer for repair if that is at all possible. It makes them aware of a problem with their product and they should know better than anyone else how to fix it.

I love the sound of my ship's clock's chimes. I listened one day as it struck 8 bells. Strange, I thought it was only about 2 o'clock. It didn't stop at 8 bells, it kept going—10 bells, 12 bells, 14, 16, 18, 20 bells—a clock gone mad! I couldn't bear the thought of parting with it long enough to send it back to the maker and feared damage to it in the hands of the post office.

So I took it, instead, to a local clock shop where they assured me they understood the inner workings of a ship's clock. After one month the clock was ready. But all they'd done was clean it (I didn't know it was dirty) and it still chimed erratically.

I took it back. "It's the bells," I explained patiently. Three months went by that time. I took it home and wound it up. At 8 o'clock—8 bells; *fine*, it works. At 9 o'clock—9 bells. What's this? At 10 o'clock—10 bells! Back to the clock shop.

"This is not a grandfather's clock," I explained patiently.

Three *more* months before its return, accompanied by a note saying that it couldn't be fixed. Only the manufacturer knew the deep, dark secret of the bells. I should have sent it there in the first place.

We all can tell stories about bad experiences with marine equipment, but what can we do about it? How can we keep from getting ripped off? I have already mentioned shopping with a magnet if you're looking at anything metal, talking with other sailors about their gear and learning all you can through reading and studying before you buy.

SPEAK UP

But once you get stung by poor engineering or faulty construction, don't just grumble to the guy in the next slip. Complain to the manufacturer, the dealer, the store where you bought it. When you write to a company, write to the president. He may pass it along to the repair department. But your chances of a quick response are better if you start with the person at the top. And send the offending gear back if it's possible, so they can see for themselves what went wrong.

Our Tillermaster autopilot developed a small problem, so I took it to the Tillermaster booth at the boat show. The representative fixed the problem in about five minutes and it's working perfectly once again. Tillermaster is one company that stands behind its products, as do the PYHI people. If one of its portlights breaks, they'll replace it, period.

When one of our "unbreakable" dishes broke, I wrapped it up and sent it back to the company. They promptly sent me two new pieces. Unfortunately, they mailed them in a padded envelope, so the new bowls arrived smashed into a million pieces. But at least they tried.

I think most manufacturers *are* willing to try, if you give them a chance. They can't know there's a problem unless someone tells them and that someone is you and me—the buying public. I think we wield more power than most of us realize. But we can't be silent about our complaints. They're not mind-readers. Write a letter, make a phone call, pound on someone's desk—*anything*—but SPEAK UP!

I might add that while I haven't mentioned by name any products we've experienced trouble with, I have mentioned the names of ones we've found lived up to our expectations. This is because such companies are a rarity and deserve to be mentioned.

25

Awaiting Delivery

"Coping with D day jitters"

So you've ordered a new boat! Now comes that dreadful period when you X out each day on the calendar feeling as if D Day (Delivery Day) is light-years away. Rest assured, there will be at least *one* delay at the plant to push it *even* farther down the road.

Bruce and I went through it for a third time with *Saga*. The waiting was as painful as ever. But the waiting was balanced off by the pleasures of shopping for gear and making endless pages of notes. Meanwhile, the apartment took on the appearance of a combination marine hardware store and carpenter shop.

There is one thing that has always made me wonder about the sanity of boat buyers. What is the strange compulsion that makes so many people (including us) buy boats from companies or brokers thousands of miles from home? There we were in California, surrounded by literally thousands of boats, both old and new, yet we bought a schooner in Massachusetts. Then when we were in New York, the new boat was coming from —where else?—California.

If your boat is coming a long distance by truck, the first items on your shopping list should be fiberglass cleaner, boat wax, teak cleaner, lots of rags and a bucket. The boat will arrive stained by truck exhaust fumes, road dirt and grime—and possibly nicked and scratched as well. It's going to take some elbow grease to make your new boat look like it's new, so it's best not to plan on launching immediately but to allow yourself several days of yard time. While you're scrubbing the boat, don't neglect any line or rigging that's been exposed or all the grimy dirt will rub off on your new white sails.

Next on the list comes bottom paint, brushes and wet/dry sandpaper. Even if she got bottom paint at the plant, you won't know how long the paint has been on, so it may have lost some of its toxic effectiveness. The workers on the assembly line aren't going to be as concerned as you are about how smooth the bottom is, so you'll probably do some sanding before the final coat goes on. If you didn't specify the bottom paint to be used, write the builder for the type and brand name of the paint he's using, so you'll be sure to apply paint that's compatible.

Make sure to get, from the builder, a pint of gel coat of each of the colors used on the boat. This way you'll have a touch-up kit—*in case.* This is a particularly important thing to order if your boat is anything other than basic white.

Let's move up to the mast and boom. Are they arriving with all the hardware you want installed, or will you be adding more items? We added the following to a "sailaway" boat: flag halyard, blocks and cleats, spinnaker block, spinnaker track, storm trysail track, jiffy reefing gear, tri-color masthead light and mast bow light, mast winches and a boom vang bail. We also made an angle template for the spreaders so they could be pre-set on the ground.

All hardware or hardware "systems" (i.e. flag halyard block, cleat, pre-cut halyard with clips and all necessary fastenings) should be placed in clear plastic bags and labeled. When the boat finally arrives, you simply have to grab the appropriate bag and begin installing the hardware. This requires some careful planning beforehand, but it beats running back to the hardware store several times because you didn't buy enough of the right size screws. Assuming the mast is aluminum, you'll want to buy the appropriate tap for each size of machine screw.

Halyards and sheets can be made up in advance. Take careful measurements from the sail plan and then allow a few feet extra. After they are cut and the ends are whipped, coil and label them with a piece of masking tape wrapped around a bight. Anchor rode and dock lines can be made up as well, and lines spliced into the fenders. You'll be surprised how many evenings can go into just splicing and whipping! If you have any extra line lying about or old and tired line from your last boat, why not whip up some rope ladder mats or thump mats for your new baby? If you don't know how, this is a great time to get a *good* knot

book and teach yourself to tie a double Turk's Head and how to do fancy macramé work.

There are bound to be numerous items of deck hardware that you'll want to install yourself. We contacted the builder to determine the specific thickness and type of construction used in the deck and cabin top so we could predetermine the size and type of fastenings to buy. Any deck fittings that are going to work under strain will require backing blocks. These can be fashioned in advance and added to the appropriate hardware bag. As with the spar hardware, it seems easier to remember everything in terms of *complete systems* rather than individual pieces of gear.

Look over the deck gear checklist to see how much gear you'll want to add. A satisfying project for an evening is to letter the life ring with the new boat's name and hailing port. Some of the items, such as the brackets for the horn and binoculars, could be made instead of purchased.

If you're buying a "sailaway" boat, you're probably only getting the basic working sails. Generally, you'll get these sails at a good price, since the builder gets a hefty discount for buying large quantities. But be forewarned, it's unlikely that these sails will be top quality—"adequate" would be a better term. Discuss it with your local sailmaker and make arrangements for him to look over the new sails when they arrive. He may suggest adding additional stitching or extra reinforcing patches or making some minor adjustments if they don't set properly. Take him a copy of your sail plan if you're going to order additional sails.

You may pay more by going to your local sailmaker rather than buying through the builder, but you'll be better off in the long run. You will get a higher quality sail and you can beat him over the head if the sail doesn't fit correctly—something that's tough to do long distance, and even tougher if you have to work through a middleman, the dealer.

Sails coming through the builder may have wood battens. If you want fiberglass battens, you can order them in advance. If you plan to race the boat, remember that the rules require the number to be sewn onto the sails.

While talking with your sailmaker, you also

can get quotes for sail covers and cockpit cushions if these are not included with the boat, although they can't actually be made until the boat arrives.

Two items that always seem to be missing from a new stock boat are sail stops (gaskets) and the luff groove stop. We bought several yards of 1½-inch nylon webbing for sail stops so we'd be ready to measure and cut them once the boat was rigged. The luff groove stop was a small $4 item. Even if by some miracle one should come with the boat, it's nice to have a spare.

Make a list of all safety equipment you'll want. Coast Guard requirements are minimal, so you'll want a lot more gear if you plan to sail offshore. If you're going to race the boat, get a copy of the safety requirements *now,* to make sure your boat will meet all of them. Some items should be double-checked while the boat is being built. For example, life line stanchion heights are carefully defined under IOR, and that's not the sort of thing that could be easily changed after you take delivery. Even if you don't plan to race, the safety regulations published by the racing associations make an excellent checklist for a well-laid-out cruising boat.

Assembling all your navigation equipment is a good project to keep you busy while you're anxiously waiting for D Day. I've included a list of navigation gear in the Appendix. You may not need or even want everything on the list but it should help you to prepare a list of your own.

There are some items that you *know* you'll need but can't calculate exactly. With this in mind, we purchased 30 feet of shock cord, 15 feet of Velcro and two dozen brass hooks. We knew that sooner or later it would all be used.

Fitting out a new boat below decks will depend a great deal on how you plan to use her. If it's permanent living aboard, then you're moving body and soul. Only you can decide what to take along and what to leave behind. If the boat will be used frequently, we think it's best to equip her *completely.* Bruce's brother and sister-in-law used to sail their boat every weekend. Every Friday night they pulled up to the dock with their van loaded to the hilt and made a dozen trips up and down the ramp to

unload pillows, blankets, pots and pans, groceries, foul weather gear, towels, ice, sun tan lotion, etc., etc. Sunday night brought a repeat performance in reverse.

We always thought that routine took a lot of the fun out of a weekend cruise. If the boat is well ventilated (and it certainly should be) and is used often, there should be no problem with mildew on sleeping bags or clothes left aboard.

So let's go below and continue with our "get-ready" projects. We made pillow covers for standard-size pillows out of a brightly colored cotton duck and roped the edges so they could double as "throw pillows" on the settee when not in use for sleeping. Our clock and barometer were ready and waiting, with their fastenings taped to the backs and a brass hook to hang the key on. We were ready to add two kerosene lamps with smoke bells, since the boat came equipped with electric lights only. Everything brass had been polished and sprayed with two coats of a clear acrylic spray to keep them shiny. (Refer to the checklist for other equipment you might need.)

It's an excellent idea to get a 3-ring looseleaf notebook to hold all your maintenance and instruction manuals for the equipment installed on your boat and to keep a separate record of serial numbers and parts numbers. When a piece of gear breaks down, you'll know right where to look to learn how to fix it or where to order new parts.

You can do some detective work now, too. Call around and find a local painter to put the name and hailing port on the boat, unless you plan to do it yourself. If you're getting a propane stove, it will arrive with an empty tank. Find out the nearest place to get it filled. I can almost guarantee it won't be anywhere near the marina! If you need kerosene for stove or lights, start early to find out who carries it locally. We've found that it's getting scarce in many areas. Try to find a dealer who sells kerosene in bulk. Then take your own container —it's much cheaper that way. Line up your sources for hardware, sails, electronic equipment and repair, and a parts and repair facility for your engine.

Will the boat swing on her own ground tackle, or will you have a mooring or dockage in a marina? Make arrangements well in advance to be sure your mooring is in place *on time* or that dock space will not be available when you need it. Will you need boarding steps at the dock and is there locker space available or room for you to place a dock box? Inspect the cleating facilities on the dock and check how the other boats are tied. You may find you're going to need fender boards. Electrical outlets can vary, so you might have to purchase a special adapter or plug. Assuming you have access to an electrical source, consider investing in a battery charger.

The final items on the list are the least fun, but they're important and we might as well get as much as possible out of the way in advance. We're referring, of course, to *paperwork*. Are you going to insure your boat? If so, take the time to shop around for the best coverage and rates.

If you're simply going to register the boat, there's little to do until the boat arrives and you have the bill of sale in hand, although you should know what your sales tax will be and how much time you'll have to pay it.

To document a pleasure boat, you will need a Master Carpenter's Certificate from the builder, as well as dimensions required for measurement. Contact your local Coast Guard office to get all the steps necessary for documentation.

We don't promise these jobs will alleviate all the pre-D Day jitters, but keeping busy will help. And once the boat arrives you'll have her commissioned and sailing a lot quicker than you might have thought.

Making the Commitment

26

"I'd love to, but. . . ."

MORE AND MORE people each year are discovering the intrinsic values of living aboard: the slower pace; more time to call their own; the peacefulness of living close to nature. It's a way of life that is both simple and healthy. And, in this era of runaway inflation, the cost of living aboard can be almost ridiculously low. Yet, for every person who makes the transition, hundreds never get past the dreaming stage.

TESTING THE WATER

I can't begin to count the number of people who have told Bruce and me they would give anything to live the way we do, to be free and independent, to travel and go where they wished, to live aboard a boat and be answerable to no one. My response is always, "Well, why don't you?" Then the excuses start: "the job, the mortgage, the cars, the spouse, the children, the company retirement fund." I call them excuses instead of reasons, because I think that's what they are. Those who really want something badly enough will figure out a way to get it. We did and so can you.

A reason might be fear: fear of the un-

known, fear of committing yourself to a new lifestyle and finding out you don't like it and fear of losing that regular monthly income—although that doesn't have to be the case.

Another reason might be guilt. Most of us are instilled from birth with that good old work ethic that says we all must labor from nine to five, own a house, cut the lawn, buy a new car every three years and send the kiddies to college. So we feel guilty when we think about opting for a vagabond life and letting Junior get a job to put himself through school. This deep-rooted guilt can be the biggest stumbling block to making the break.

Well, how hard is it, really, to achieve the live-aboard way of life? Is it as carefree a life as many suppose? How much sacrifice is necessary to achieve it? Let's take a look at the obstacles, one by one, and see just how big they really are.

THE JOB

Some might say Bruce and I are "lucky" because we are able to earn a living while aboard, wherever we happen to be. Bruce writes and illustrates. I write. And we both keep our fingers in the design business. But that didn't happen through blind luck. Both of us spent years working at salaried jobs. Then we had our own design offices and worked 12- and 14-hour days. When we chucked it all we were not sure we could support ourselves by writing and illustrating. We are managing, but not through luck—through hard work.

Not everyone can write or draw, but there are many other ways to make a living afloat! It just takes a bit of ingenuity. For example, a guy in California makes and sells canvas hats. A psychiatrist takes patients on sailing sabbaticals, finding gentle ocean swells better therapy than the traditional couch. We know one couple who have a small workshop on their boat—he's a rigger and she does painting and varnishing work.

Bruce knows a sailing bricklayer who checks into the local union hall in various ports and almost invariably finds work. If there's no work in one town, he sails on to the next. We've met several artists and photographers who sell their handiwork along the way. Another fellow is an electronics expert who carries a large inventory of parts so he can repair gear on other cruising boats.

Most large towns and cities have employment agencies, such as Manpower and Kelly Girl, that offer temporary jobs for secretaries, typists, draftsmen—all sorts of skilled and semi-skilled workers.

Boatyards are obvious places to look for occasional work and delivering yachts for other people can provide income. Some can find work crewing on local fishing or charter boats, as deck hands, cooks, baiters, or whatever.

I could go on and on listing ways of supporting yourself. But the point is that you *can* find work if you want it and if you're willing to try just about anything. If you're used to sitting behind a desk all day giving orders and feel that scraping boat bottoms or slinging hash on a fishing boat is beneath you, well, maybe you secretly don't want to pay the price to escape that desk, after all.

One curious thing we've noticed is that people with low-paying jobs find cutting loose much easier than those in the higher income brackets. Perhaps they have less to lose, and maybe they haven't gotten enmeshed so deeply in keeping up with the Joneses.

THE SPOUSE

Getting one's partner to take the plunge can be a bit ticklish, to say the least. If one wants to, and the other doesn't (most often it seems the man is gung-ho and the woman reticent), the spouse can be a big, perhaps insurmountable, obstacle.

Advice here is problematic. Much depends on the individual relationship—how well the couple gets along, how well each understands the other and how much each partner is willing to sacrifice. It may be possible to compromise and try living aboard for a year with an agreement to then re-evaluate the experiment at a specific date.

The advantages of a trial live-aboard period are that you can *rent* the house instead of selling it. You can put your belongings in storage and possibly even take a leave of absence from your job instead of quitting. Another alternative is to stay at your job while you move aboard and get used to the day-to-day routines of life afloat. Living on a boat doesn't require casting off for a world cruise! Many people never actually go anywhere. They find they're content simply being on the water.

I can guarantee a year of living aboard will change your outlook. Your sense of values will change drastically, often taking twists you never expected. I know one couple who quit high-paying jobs in advertising, sold their huge home, furniture, cars—virtually everything—bought a larger boat than the one they had owned and took off. The sell-out gave them enough cash to live comfortably for two years.

After about six months, they were constantly at each other's throat—24 hours a day was more togetherness than they could handle. And life in a pitching boat on a rolling sea was not as much fun as they had envisioned. The rewards did not compensate them for what they had given up. She quit first and flew back to California. He got a crew to help take the boat back and then promptly sold it.

This story shouldn't discourage anyone. I don't consider their adventure a failure. In the long run, it was a smashing success. First, they were not happy with their old lifestyle and had the courage to try something new. Second, they learned a great deal about themselves and about each other. If you guessed they got a divorce, you'd be wrong. They're still together, living in a tiny mobile home near the water. They own a small sailboat and take short weekend cruises.

The most interesting point is how their values changed. Neither of them could bear the thought of going back to their high-pressure, fast-paced jobs. She does free-lance writing now; he drives a taxi and loves it. They're happy with their work, their way of life and with each other. If they hadn't made that first break, they probably would still be on the treadmill of success, hating every minute of it. They have no regrets and say they gained far more than they lost.

Only you can deal with an unwilling spouse, but if she (or he) realizes just how serious you really are, it's possible she (or he) might be willing to give it a try. Get your feelings out in the open and talk about it. But both must agree to the move. There's no room on a small boat for a martyr.

Living together in the relative confinement of a boat requires a greater degree of tolerance, patience and consideration of one another's feelings than on shore. Little irritations can become magnified all out of proportion unless both are able to communicate freely. If one feels coerced into living on a boat and would

truly rather live in a house, for whatever reason, the experience can only end in failure.

CHILDREN

We have met a lot of people living aboard with happy, well-adjusted children. I have read many articles written by cruising parents about the benefits of the live-aboard life to their offspring. I can't believe having children should keep anyone shorebound. It may take a somewhat larger boat (but then you have a built-in crew!) and a great deal more planning, but it certainly can be done. And I'm sure it would bring all members closer together as a family unit.

Youngsters think living aboard is a great adventure. They are tan and healthy, capable of keeping themselves entertained and for the most part seem better behaved and happier than the unruly kids who hang around street corners on shore.

The individual attention live-aboard children, particularly those who are cruising, get from their parents-turned-schoolteachers seems to enhance their formal education, which can be obtained through various accredited correspondence schools. In addition, the lessons learned about getting along with people from different cultures, the challenges of an ever-changing environment and the shared responsibilities of working on the boat, gives them a real education about how to get along in life—one they could never receive in the average classroom ashore.

I've heard people say children need the security of a permanent home, of putting down roots and growing up in familiar surroundings. But it seems to me it's not *places* and *things* that make us feel secure—it's the love and understanding we get from other people! If you come home at night from a job you despise, and slump down in your easy chair feeling grumpy and tired, how much attention and love can you give your children? You might be buying them material possessions, but perhaps they'd rather just have more of *you*. And a relaxed and happy you, at that. Live-aboard families are close-knit units. I've yet to meet a live-aboard child who feels either insecure or deprived because he lives on a boat!

POSSESSIONS

Our worldly goods—the physical measure of our success—who needs all that stuff anyway? Giving up many of my possessions was undoubtedly the hardest part of moving aboard a boat. I don't regret it now and I can't honestly say that I miss those things that much.

I must confess, however, that I didn't actually get rid of *all* of it. (Bruce's brother's attic will attest to that.) I kept all my books (they weigh enough to sink anything less than a 60-footer) and my lovely blue-and-white china and a few other treasures I couldn't bear to part with. Primarily, I kept items with sentimental value, things I could never replace. I can always buy another sofa or a new television set. Now, not only do we no longer miss those things we thought we couldn't live without, but we can't even *remember* half the stuff we used to own!

GUILT

This is the big obstacle to overcome. There is always someone around more than willing to tell you how to live your life, what you "ought" to do—a parent, the government, Dr. Spock or your meddling great-aunt Millie. But who are they to tell you what to do? Only you know what's best. You don't need anyone's approval to change your lifestyle. Your real friends will support you. Who needs the rest? Once you make the move, you'll start meeting more and more people who share your views.

We recently visited two friends from New York who are now living aboard their boat in Florida. Ed had suffered two heart attacks before he decided there must be more to life than 40 hours a week at a job he detested. He and June sailed from New York with a little money in a boat that wasn't fully paid for, with no job prospects and no firm plans about where they would stop. They were looking forward to new adventures (including their first night offshore) and a new and better way of life.

We met them in Florida and found them both happier and healthier than they ever had been. They had had a grand adventure—we spent hours swapping sea stories and waterway tales. They had located a marina that welcomed live-aboards and had found jobs long before they were anywhere near starvation—jobs they like, by the way.

They only have one regret—that they didn't do it sooner. Here's a couple who finally stopped feeling guilty because a "normal" life made them miserable. Their reward is a relaxing and enjoyable new life.

FEAR

Fear of the unknown is probably the biggest fear, even if most of us don't easily admit it. It's human nature to hug the familiar. The longer we stay in one place, hold the same job, see the same faces week after week, the harder it is to break free. We're all creatures of habit, and habits are hard to break—even the ones that make us unhappy!

It's easy to fall into safe, but dull, routines. The years slip away before we know it. So, it's not so easy to force a change. That takes courage, since the world becomes suddenly different, unfamiliar and we have to cope with new problems and new responsibilities.

The *first step is the hardest*. We've found that once people move aboard, especially those who cruise away from old familiar surroundings, they usually keep going, seeking new places and new experiences, becoming more and more adventurous. Each new place to drop the anchor brings a whole new world to explore— new sights and smells, different people with their own lifestyles, new foods to eat and new places to shop. Living aboard becomes a constant and fulfilling growth experience.

Actually, live-aboards carry their familiar surroundings and security around like turtles. We sleep in the same bed every night and look out the same windows during the day. The boat always makes the same familiar and comforting sounds. Unlike the traveler living out of a suitcase who soon yearns for something, anything, familiar, our "culture shock" is softened by returning each evening from a day of exploring to our cozy and friendly little haven. We've discovered that's all the security we really need.

Bruce and I have spent each of the past seven Christmases in a different place. Each holiday has been a delightful new experience, but it always felt like a "traditional" Christmas once we pulled out our familiar decorations and started making plans for our traditional Christmas feast.

We've found, too, that when we stay in one place for awhile, it's hard to leave new friends. But we've learned that sooner or later we run into them again—and what joyous reunions they are! All the live-aboards we've met approach life a little differently. Some are cruising around the world, some are just putt-putting up and down the inland waterways, others are living aboard in marinas while they work ashore. But all seem to share a few basic philosophies.

All tried living ashore and found it dull, expensive and unfulfilling. All were looking for a life, not free from responsibility, but from artificial pressures. All felt there must be a better way and all believe they've found it. Many who

live aboard say, "What! Move ashore? Then I'd have to go back to work!"

Yet most live-aboards are very hard-working people. The difference is, they *like* what they're doing, so it doesn't seem like work. We've found it doesn't take a great deal of money to live comfortably, as long as you don't get caught in the trap of buying things merely for the sake of acquiring them.

Without exception, we all find inner peace and a continuous joy through our constant association with nature. We see eagles soaring above the boat, great blue herons on shore, pelicans diving into a school of baitfish, a deer swimming beside the boat, porpoises frolicking in the bow wave—all this is an ever-changing panorama of natural beauty. Each day, it seems, we see something we had only read about previously. Our log book reads like a record of firsts: our first sea turtle sighting, our first whale, our first coconut palm, our first reef seen through crystal-clear water, our first sighting of the Statue of Liberty.

The weather undoubtedly is one of our major interests, always a prime topic of conversation. It certainly has a greater impact on our lives than it ever did on shore. We never tire of watching cloud formations march across the sky, or of watching the constantly changing waters around us. And sunsets are always spectacular! Watching a line-squall forming on an unobstructed horizon from the deck of a boat is an awe-inspiring sight.

CULTURE

Boat living to many people implies a simplicity that is close to "primitive." This is felt especially of city dwellers: "I'd love to, but there's so much to *do* in the city—museums, art shows, symphonies, ballet, theater." They imagine living aboard as being at anchor in a secluded tropical cove, trapped without the New York Times and without ice cubes for evening cocktails. Nothing could be further from the truth. It *can* be that way, but doesn't *have* to be—and it certainly isn't that way for us.

When we stay in one place for awhile, it's invariably in a port town large enough to offer the kind of shoreside amenities that interest us. Even the smallest villages generally have some kind of cultural attraction, it's just a matter of ferreting them out. One of the first things we look for when we arrive in a new port is a museum. More often than not we find one and it's usually chock full of the history and folklore of the surrounding area, giving us a fascinating insight into the countryside and its people.

The advantage to traveling in your boat/ home are twofold. First, if you don't like where you are, you can leave. It allows you to enjoy the hustle and bustle of the city until it palls, then move on to a more secluded place. We found that sometimes just leaving a marina and anchoring a few hundred yards away brings us the peace and quiet we need. It's the kind of mobility we never could achieve living on shore.

Second, traveling by boat frequently enables you to visit a resort area unaffordable by land or air. During major sporting events, hotels and motels are jam-packed and their rates sky-rocket, yet you can slip into a marina at a fraction of the cost. And you don't have to eat every meal out. Many attractions, such as maritime museums, aquatic parks and historical monuments maintain free guest docks. If people are culturally deprived because they live on a boat, it's because they choose to be and not because that's an unavoidable part of the lifestyle.

AGE

Age is no obstacle to living aboard. For the most part, the younger live-aboards seem to prefer small sailboats, while older people occupy motorsailers or powerboats. If you're 35 to 40 now and planning to sail off when you retire, ask yourself this: are you going to be able to physically handle living on a sailboat or is it just going to be too much hard work?

If you live three blocks from a grocery store, do you walk or drive for a quart of milk? We think nothing of walking three *miles* or more to buy groceries.

After years of sitting behind a desk, will you have the stamina to sail and cruise as a way of life? Between sailing, rowing, walking and all the physical exercise we get caring for our boat, we're both lean and strong. But we were in good health when we started, not having waited until the pressure of "achieving success" gave us ulcers or high blood pressure. Think of this carefully when you choose a boat.

We live in a cleaner, healthier environment than most city folk. Sailing through the murky waters of the East River in New York City, past hundreds of joggers huffing along the riverbank breathing polluted air, we looked back at the pallor of smog hanging over the city and reflected on our good fortune. The air we breathe is cleaner and fresher—and we certainly get more of it than most people.

There's another point to consider if you're waiting for retirement. After all those years of living in a spacious house or apartment, will you be able to adjust to the smaller quarters of a boat? Or will you want a boat so big that it's difficult and expensive to operate and maintain? A strong case can often be made for small boats. Bruce and I went from a large apartment to a 36-foot schooner to a 20-foot sloop. The transitions were not terribly difficult. But after a year on a 20-footer we found ourselves ready for something larger.

Several couples we know have graduated from sailboat to motorsailer to powerboat. As they grew older the rigors of sailing became more work than pleasure and the joys of sailing no longer outweighed the inconveniences and cramped quarters of a sailboat. Sacrifices are part of the adventure the young are more willing and able to accept.

We did meet a couple in Florida in their 70's who fulfilled their dream of living on a sailboat. They were delightful people, thoroughly enjoying their new lifestyle. I found it interesting that they rarely sailed the boat. Virtually all their traveling was done under power! It's true that Eric and Susan Hiscock, for example, are still cruising under sail. But they have a *lifetime* of sailing behind them, not a life of sitting behind a desk. The Hiscocks are hardly your typical, everyday couple! A powerboat or a houseboat can be an excellent retirement home.

SEARCHING FOR PARADISE

Considering how many more people are living aboard and cruising today than even 10 years ago, I can't help but wonder what it will be like in another 10 or 20 years. Anchorages are getting crowded. Marinas have waiting lists and many are placing greater restrictions on live-aboards—if they allow them at all. We have to go farther and farther away to find seclusion. In the mid-1960s Bruce lived aboard a schooner in Ft. Lauderdale, Florida. He was

moored in a lovely little cove right in the heart of the city, surrounded by the grassy banks of a wooded park; his boat was the only one anchored there. Imagine his shock when we returned there a few years ago in *Sabrina*. Huge high-rise buildings overlooked the water and the now cement-walled park. The "anchorage" was filled with boats swinging on permanent moorings.

We squeezed into a small corner near shore and set out bow and stern anchors for the night. The next morning a police boat informed us we would have to leave: Ft. Lauderdale does not allow boats to anchor anywhere within its city limits. We went further south and did find a beautiful, protected cove where we could anchor and work for awhile. Each weekend, however, we were surrounded by more than a dozen other boats.

Yes, paradise *is* getting crowded. To anyone thinking about moving aboard a boat, and especially to anyone who wants to go cruising, I would have to say, "Do it now, and quickly, before paradise disappears altogether!"

THIRTEEN WHO DID

ALL HOURS

Betsy Greenacre, owner and captain of the 42-foot trawler *All Hours,* is not your typical grandmother. After her husband Johnny died in 1977, friends and relatives assumed Betsy would sell the family boat—a 34-foot Marine Trader. Instead, she put the 11-room house in Connecticut up for sale, moved aboard the boat and headed south on the Intracoastal Waterway.

When Betsy first got to Florida, she did look at houses and condominiums, but always went back to the boat.

"I finally realized," she says, " that what I really wanted was to keep living aboard; perhaps build a larger boat so my children and grandchildren would have room to visit and cruise with me."

Her friends throught she was crazy and her attorney was convinced that someone was surely taking advantage of her. But she pursued the dream (with 100 percent moral support from her children) and the impeccable *All Hours,* designed by Charles Wittholz and built by John Johnsen of Palm Bay, Florida, is the result.

Betsy says she's often asked if a 42-foot boat isn't an awful lot of work for her.

"If my boat gets dirty," she laughs, "I just turn the hose on it. You can't do that to the kitchen floor!" She keeps *All Hours* in mint condition and insists, "there's nothing you can't do on a boat if you make up your mind that you *want* to do it."

Many of Betsy's old friends still don't understand what she's doing.

"I could have stayed in Connecticut and kept the house, wrapped it around me like a security blanket. But you can't live in the past that way, it's just not healthy! I needed to move ahead, to try something different. This is a new phase in my life." It's a new phase, and one that obviously agrees with her. Betsy looks trim and tan, alive with an enthusiasm for a lifestyle that keeps her young.

ENDYMION II

Gainor Roberts and George Cranston were hardworking, successful people. Gainor is an artist, she had built a beautiful studio behind their home in the hills outside Mystic, Connecticut. George devoted most of his time to managing a restaurant in Mystic.

"I loved my work," says Gainor, "and we were doing okay. But we lacked a sense of achievement. We weren't *going* anywhere. I felt like we were stagnating. The biggest thing in our lives was getting away for little cruises on our Samurai sloop.

"We kept reading about other couples living aboard full time, going cruising. Why couldn't *we* do that, we kept asking ourselves. It was kind of scary; we had so much *stuff*, we were so entrenched in the house in Mystic!"

They took the plunge, ordering a new Camper & Nicholson 31, *Endymion II*. Then began a trying year of divesting themselves of the house, the cars, the tons of possessions.

Endymion II has been their only home now for three years. Any regrets? "Not one!" they said. "It's the best move we ever made," says George. "We just wonder why we waited so long."

George and Gainor follow the sun, spending winters in southern waters and returning north in the summer to visit family and friends. Gainor still paints—her only concession to the boat is to use smaller canvases—and she's found her paintings are marketable in any port of call.

DASEIN

Chuck and Laurie Paul bought *Dasein,* a 35-foot Lion sloop built in 1954, for two reasons: as an investment and because they wanted a project they could work on together. *Dasein*'s sizeable mortgage meant they could only afford her by living aboard.

The first two years were spent dockside. They completely rebuilt the interior while working at full-time jobs and going to school. Occasionally, they even found time to go for a sail.

"Our lives were moving at a feverish pace," says Laurie, "and yet I wasn't sure *why* we were doing any of it or what we were trying to accomplish. I started thinking we could live cheaper, and with less stress if we went cruising."

They then learned Laurie was pregnant. Chuck confesses he had some misgivings. He was sure that baby meant "settling down in a house with a white picket fence." Laurie convinced him otherwise. Daughter Michal was less than a month old when the family untied the dock lines and headed south. A year later, Michal is as happy and healthy as any baby on shore.

They still stop frequently to find employment. Chuck is working for a boatyard in southern Florida. They're slowly working their way down into the Caribbean and hope to find work there. Laurie believes that as a family they are closer to one another than ever before.

"Our lives aren't hectic anymore. We have time now, for each other and for our daughter. This is a fantastic environment for bringing up a child. We started out thinking we would cruise for a year. Now we say we're cruising for two years to forever."

Swan

Walter Swanson has been living aboard his boats for more than 20 years, including a 47-foot ketch that he used for chartering in the Caribbean. Now he is semiretired from his building supply business in Rhode Island.

When he married Marjorie a few years ago, she agreed that living aboard would be fun—but more fun on a powerboat than on a sailboat.

They bought the *Swan*, a lovely 57-foot Trumpy, built in 1937. *Swan*'s age dictates that she needs constant care and attention and Walter and Marjorie agree that neither of them are "mechanical types." Unlike most live-aboards, they hire professionals to do much of the maintenance. Still, the *Swan* gives them all the comforts of home, with enough living space below to rival most apartments on shore.

Marjorie loves it all, particularly the easy pace of cruising in protected waters. Walter says he's glad now that Marjorie wanted a powerboat, since it's introduced him to a new and different (and totally enjoyable) way of life.

HERON

Dick and Helen Pentoney have been living aboard *Heron,* their 35-foot Fantasia motor-sailer, for the past six years.

Dick had a successful career as a vice president of a New York college. But he chose an early retirement at age 56 despite the reduced income so he would have more time to cruise. He finds sailing, "a unique combination of a physical and intellectual challenge."

They both love to travel, but slowly, with time to savor each new place and each new experience. They believe that's inherent with cruising under sail. After hectic lives ashore, they refuse to set schedules or deadlines.

"If we don't get to Europe this year, we'll go next year," Dick told me. They *did* make it this year, however, and are now in England with daughter Valarie as crew.

Helen admits she had a few reservations at first. But she and Dick spent many long hours talking and planning, making sure they were in total agreement about the move. Then she sold a three-story, five-bedroom home, auctioned off the furnishings, packed and moved aboard *Heron:* all in one weekend! Now she's as enthusiastic as Dick about their lives.

"I can't imagine going back to shore. I miss a few of my close friends, but we write long letters. Other than that, I wouldn't give up this cruising life for anything!"

SWEETIE FACE II

Twenty years ago, Dave and Dottie Etzel were messing around the Chesapeake in their small runabout. They were lucky enough to meet the late Jim Emmett (a veteran waterway traveler even then) and determined that some day they would follow in his wake.

Fifteen years passed before "some day" arrived. After selling their house to their daughter and son-in-law, they moved onto their 36-foot Marine Trader, *Sweetie Face,* living dockside in Baltimore, Maryland, where Dave worked as a buyer for a department store.

They returned to land briefly when Dave's job sent him to Albuquerque, New Mexico. "We were like two fish out of water," said Dottie. "*Sweetie Face* was sold in New Jersey and I made a special trip back there to pick up the dinghy so we could at least have *some* kind of boat!"

The lure of the water was too great. Dave quit his job, they sold everything (again!) and bought a 40-foot Marine Trader, *Sweetie Face II.*

They travel up and down the waterway and across to the Bahamas, stopping to work whenever the cruising kitty runs low. Like a lot of other live-aboards, they've found that work is available as long as they're flexible and willing to tackle something new. This past summer, Dave captained a sightseeing boat in Baltimore Harbor and Dottie crewed for him on weekends—a far cry from the high-pressure lifestyle that preceded their present adventure.

Appendix

DECK GEAR CHECK LIST

- Anchor(s)
- Anchor light
- Anchor rode and chain
- Binoculars rack
- Barbeque
- Boat hook
- Bug candles
- Canvas covers for hatches, tiller or wheel
- Chafing gear for anchor and dock lines

- Hatch and port screens
- Owner's private signal
- Sail covers
- Sail stops
- Telltales
- Turnbuckle covers
- U.S. or yacht ensign
- Ventilators with screens
- Winch covers
- Winch handle holders
- Yacht club burgee

- Cockpit awning
- Cockpit cushions
- Code flags
- Compass brackets
- Dock lines
- Dodger
- Drink holders
- Fenders
- Flagpole socket
- Flashlight and spare batteries
- Hatch locks

NAVIGATION EQUIPMENT CHECK LIST

- Binoculars and rack
- Bowditch (or other)
- Charts
- Chronometer
- Coast pilots
- Compass
- Cruising guides

- Dividers
- Hand-bearing compass
- Light list
- Log book
- Nautical almanac
- Parallel rules
- Pencils

- Sextant
- Sight reduction tables
- Star finder
- Tide and current tables
- Time/speed/distance calculator
- Three-arm protractor

ELECTRONICS CHECK LIST

- Apparent wind indicator
- Autopilot
- Calculator
- Depth sounder
- Distance log

- Emergency Position Indicating Radio Beacon (EPIRB)
- Knotmeter
- Loran C
- Radar or hand-held radar

- Radio (VHF, CB, shortwave receiver and broadcast, single sideband)
- Radio direction finder
- SatNav (Omega, Transit)
- Weather facsimile recorder

Bo'sun's Locker Check List

- [ ] Bo'sun's chair
- [ ] Bucket
- [ ] Chamois for brightwork
- [ ] Cleaners, wax, polish
- [ ] Clothespins
- [ ] Deck mop and brush
- [ ] Ditty bag for sail repair
- [ ] Drop light
- [ ] Extension cord
- [ ] Extra paint, varnish
- [ ] Oil soak-up rags
- [ ] Paint brushes
- [ ] Paint thinner
- [ ] Rags
- [ ] Spare line
- [ ] Sponges
- [ ] Tool box (see next list)
- [ ] Water hose
- [ ] Wisk broom set

Basic Tools Check List

- [ ] Crescent wrench
- [ ] Electrician's tape
- [ ] Extra electrical wire
- [ ] Hacksaw
- [ ] Hammer
- [ ] Hand drill and bits
- [ ] Hex key set
- [ ] Pliers
- [ ] Screwdrivers, several sizes— Phillips and single-slot
- [ ] Spare fuses
- [ ] Spare hardware, fittings, fastenings
- [ ] Special tools required for engine
- [ ] Stainless seizing wire
- [ ] Vice grip pliers
- [ ] Wire cutters

Safety Equipment Check List

- [ ] Bell and/or whistle
- [ ] Dye markers
- [ ] Emergency food and water rations
- [ ] Emergency ship's compass
- [ ] Emergency tiller
- [ ] Emergency Position Indicating Radio Beacon (EPIRB)
- [ ] Flare gun set
- [ ] Fog horn
- [ ] Fuel shut-off hand valve
- [ ] Fire extinguishers
- [ ] Hand flares
- [ ] Hand-held compass for life raft
- [ ] Hand pump for life raft
- [ ] Heaving line
- [ ] Life lines, pulpits and stanchions
- [ ] Life jackets with whistles
- [ ] Life rings
- [ ] LP fuel shut-off solenoid valve
- [ ] Man-overboard pole
- [ ] Man-overboard light
- [ ] Manual bilge pump
- [ ] Orange smoke day signals
- [ ] Parachute star flares
- [ ] Radar reflector
- [ ] Safety harnesses
- [ ] Sea anchor
- [ ] Sea anchors for life rings, life raft
- [ ] Self-inflating life raft
- [ ] Spare battery-powered running lights
- [ ] Storm jib
- [ ] Storm trysail
- [ ] Waterproof flashlight

Galley Check List

- [ ] Asbestos burner pads
- [ ] Baking pans
- [ ] Bottle opener
- [ ] Can opener
- [ ] Cheese grater
- [ ] Cleaning products
- [ ] Colander
- [ ] Cookbook
- [ ] Corkscrew
- [ ] Dishes
- [ ] Dish towels
- [ ] Foil
- [ ] Folding toaster
- [ ] Icepick
- [ ] Insulated mugs and cups (with hooks)
- [ ] Knife sharpener
- [ ] Knife set
- [ ] Measuring set
- [ ] Mixing bowls
- [ ] Oven mitt
- [ ] Oven thermometer
- [ ] Paper towels
- [ ] Paper towel rack
- [ ] Plastic glasses
- [ ] Plastic storage bags
- [ ] Plastic storage containers
- [ ] Pot holder
- [ ] Pressure cooker
- [ ] Priming bottle (alcohol)
- [ ] Salt and pepper shakers
- [ ] Sauce pan with lid
- [ ] Silverware

- [ ] Skillet with lid
- [ ] Slotted spoon
- [ ] Spatula
- [ ] Spice rack and spices
- [ ] Sponges
- [ ] Spoon (large)
- [ ] Tea kettle
- [ ] Timer
- [ ] Thermos jug
- [ ] Tongs
- [ ] Trash bags
- [ ] Vegetable peeler
- [ ] Waxed paper

GALLEY STORES CHECK LIST

These are basic items that can be kept in airtight containers:

- [ ] Bouillon cubes
- [ ] Coffee
- [ ] Dried, minced onion and garlic
- [ ] Dry soup mixes
- [ ] Hot chocolate mix
- [ ] Matches, waterproof
- [ ] Powdered milk
- [ ] Powdered non-dairy creamer
- [ ] Powdered soft drink mixes
- [ ] Salt
- [ ] Spices
- [ ] Sugar
- [ ] Tea
- [ ] All kinds of canned goods, bottled soft drinks, beer, etc.

MAIN SALOON CHECK LIST

- [ ] Ashtrays
- [ ] Barometer
- [ ] Book racks
- [ ] Cassette tapes and tape rack
- [ ] Clock
- [ ] Curtains
- [ ] Cushions
- [ ] Lamps (with spare bulbs and/ or wicks and kerosene)
- [ ] Magazine rack
- [ ] Pillows

STATEROOM CHECK LIST

- [ ] Alarm clock
- [ ] Blankets
- [ ] Bunk covers
- [ ] Curtains
- [ ] Lamps (particularly suitable reading lamp)
- [ ] Packets of moisture-absorbent material (for clothes drawers, lockers)
- [ ] Pillows
- [ ] Pillow cases
- [ ] Plastic clothes hanger
- [ ] Plastic storage bags
- [ ] Sleeping bags or sheets

HEAD COMPARTMENT CHECK LIST

- [ ] Brush and comb
- [ ] Chemicals for head
- [ ] Cleaning products
- [ ] Curtains
- [ ] Drugs (prescription and over-the-counter)
- [ ] First aid book
- [ ] First aid kit
- [ ] Kleenex
- [ ] Medicine cabinet
- [ ] Mirror
- [ ] Packets of moisture-absorbent material
- [ ] Plastic cup or paper cup dispenser
- [ ] Shower
- [ ] Shower curtain
- [ ] Soap and soap dish
- [ ] Sponges
- [ ] Toilet paper
- [ ] Toilet paper holder
- [ ] Toothbrushes
- [ ] Toothbrush holder
- [ ] Toothpaste
- [ ] Towels
- [ ] Towel rack

PERSONAL GEAR CHECK LIST

- [ ] Camera equipment and film
- [ ] Deck shoes
- [ ] Foul weather gear (including boots)
- [ ] Hat
- [ ] Sweaters
- [ ] Jackets
- [ ] Prescription eyeglasses
- [ ] Sunglasses
- [ ] Suntan lotion and/or sunscreen

Index